THE GEORGE GUND FOUNDATION
IMPRINT IN AFRICAN AMERICAN STUDIES

The George Gund Foundation has endowed
this imprint to advance understanding of
the history, culture, and current issues
of African Americans.

The publisher and the University of California Press Foundation gratefully acknowledge the generous support of the George Gund Foundation Imprint in African American Studies.

King and the Other America

King and the Other America

THE POOR PEOPLE'S CAMPAIGN AND THE QUEST FOR ECONOMIC EQUALITY

Sylvie Laurent

Foreword by William Julius Wilson

UNIVERSITY OF CALIFORNIA PRESS

University of California Press, one of the most distinguished university presses in the United States, enriches lives around the world by advancing scholarship in the humanities, social sciences, and natural sciences. Its activities are supported by the UC Press Foundation and by philanthropic contributions from individuals and institutions. For more information, visit www.ucpress.edu.

University of California Press
Oakland, California

Library of Congress Cataloging-in-Publication Data

Names: Laurent, Sylvie, author. | Wilson, William J., 1935– writer of supplementary textual content.
Title: King and the other America : the Poor People's Campaign and the quest for economic equality / Sylvie Laurent ; foreword by William Julius Wilson.
Description: Oakland, California : University of California Press, [2018] | Includes bibliographical references and index. | Identifiers: LCCN 2018015301 (print) | LCCN 2018018593 (ebook) | ISBN 9780520963436 (epub and ePDF) | ISBN 9780520288560 (cloth : alk. paper) | ISBN 9780520288577 (pbk. : alk. paper)
Subjects: LCSH: Equality—United States. | Poor—United States. | Poor People's Campaign. | King, Martin Luther, Jr., 1929–1968—Influence.
Classification: LCC HN90.S6 (ebook) | LCC HN90.s6 L35 2018 (print) | DDC 305.5/690973—dc23
LC record available at https://lccn.loc.gov/2018015301

Manufactured in the United States of America

26   25   24   23   22   21   20   19   18
10   9   8   7   6   5   4   3   2   1

In a sense, you could say we are engaged in a class struggle, yes. It will be a long and difficult struggle, for our program calls for a redistribution of economic power. Yet this isn't a purely materialistic or class concern. I feel that this movement in behalf of the poor is the most moral thing—it is saying that every man is an heir to a legacy of dignity and worth.

Martin Luther King, Jr. (March 1968)

I was about 11 years old; my family lived in one of the suburbs outside Washington DC. My father took my sister and me to Tent City one Sunday after church. Friends and family told him he was crazy, irresponsible to take two young girls "down there." Nope, my father said, I want my children to see and understand what is really going on in this country. My experience of walking around the fringes of Tent City on the Mall that sunny afternoon was one of the most formative experiences of my early life. My first visual impression of Tent City from a distance is embedded forever in my mind.

Irene Jarosewich (November 2012)

Contents

Foreword

Sylvie Laurent's *King and the Other America* will change the way we think about Martin Luther King Jr.'s valiant efforts to combat inequality. Works on MLK and his legacy have focused mainly on his efforts to ensure that individuals seeking desired goals and opportunities be judged solely on the basis of individual merit and therefore ought not be discriminated against on the basis of race or ethnicity. However, as Laurent so clearly points out, in the second half of the 1960s King and several other prominent black spokespersons, such as Bayard Rustin and Kenneth B. Clark, began to realize that programs based solely on the principle of individual opportunity were inadequate to address the complex problems of racial inequality in America.

These insightful observers made it clear that from 1955 to 1965 the civil rights movement's chief objectives were to integrate public accommodations and eliminate black disfranchisement. These were basic issues of constitutional rights and human dignity that primarily affected African Americans and other people of color, and therefore could be defined and addressed simply as problems of civil rights. However, King and other perceptive observers noted that despite the spectacular civil rights victories during the first half of the 1960s, a more fundamental and complex set of problems had yet to be confronted—problems of jobs, education, and housing that not only affected African Americans and other people of color, but whites as well. "To the segregation by race," Bayard Rustin observed, "was now added segregation by class, and all the problems created by segregation and poverty—inadequate schooling, substandard and overcrowded housing, lack of access to jobs and job training, narcotics and crime—were greatly aggravated."[1] Martin Luther King Jr. stated the problem more succinctly shortly before his death in 1968, "What good is it to be allowed to eat in a restaurant if you can't afford a hamburger?"[2]

This particular emphasis on the problems of inequality relates to what the political philosopher James Fishkin calls "the principle of equality of life chances."[3] According to this principle, if we can predict with a high degree of accuracy where individuals end up in the competition for desired positions in society merely by knowing their family background, race, or gender, then the conditions that affect or determine their motivations and talents are grossly unequal. Proponents of equality of life chances recognize not only that those from higher social strata have more-than-equal opportunities or greater life chances, but that "they also have greater than equal influence on the political process and greater than equal consideration from the health care and legal systems."[4]

The major factor distinguishing the principle of equality of life chances from the principle of equality of individual opportunity is that the problems of the more disadvantaged individuals—class background, low income, inadequate housing, poor education, a broken home, and cultural or linguistic differences—may not be clearly related to prior discrimination. Nonetheless, children reared in homes impacted by these disadvantages may be denied an equal chance in life because their circumstances effectively impede the development of their talents and aspirations.[5]

Sylvie Laurent's *King and the Other America* brilliantly captures the evolution and crystallization of King's philosophy, from an emphasis on the equality of individual opportunity to a focus on the equality of life chances, and how this shift in philosophy was embodied in his 1968 Poor People's Campaign. As Laurent points out, although King expressed concerns about economic injustice even before he set in motion the Montgomery bus boycott in 1956, his forceful articulation of these concerns accompanied the introduction and unfolding of his Poor People's

Campaign. This last crusade for justice, in harmony with his simultaneous support of the Memphis sanitation workers, focused on the misery and injustice of the poor and of the working classes of all races and ethnicities. However, the progressive populist demands of an interracial Poor People's Campaign were at first overshadowed by his death and then faded swiftly from political memory.

In dismissing the Poor People's Campaign as a debacle, historians and civil rights activists have failed to capture the import of King's reframing of the civil rights movement in economic and redistributive terms. Sylvie Laurent effectively brings to center stage the significance of the Poor People's Campaign and the culmination of King's views on equality. This thought-provoking book also details the intellectual roots of King's highly egalitarian, social democratic vision of society, including the inspiration King drew from activist social movements fighting poverty, racial injustice, and wealth disparities, as well as their calls for fundamental redistributive policies. Moreover, King's Poor People's Campaign and his developing social democratic vision of society are insightfully revisited through the lens of contemporary social science scholarship, which examine various aspects of social and economic inequality.

In the age of Donald Trump, the publication of Sylvie Laurent's *King and the Other America* is very timely. Thoughtful readers will quickly realize that King's evolving arguments in the formulation of his Poor People's Campaign, arguments on how the problems of ordinary Americans can be addressed in an era of rising inequality and that are consistent with Fishkin's principle of equality of life chances, are just as relevant in today's political climate. King advanced an inclusive populist message on the eve on his Poor People's Campaign, a message that makes us more aware of the concerns that ordinary Americans of all racial and ethnic groups share today—including concerns about declining real wages, job security and unemployment, escalating medical and housing costs, the availability of affordable childcare programs, and pensions or retirement security.

King was clearly cognizant of the need for the careful framing of issues to address the problems of ordinary Americans, a framing designed to enhance the possibility of a new alignment in support of major social rights initiatives, such as universal health care or child care subsidies for working parents. When I read Sylvie Laurent's discussion of the inclusive rhetoric King used in organizing a multiracial coalition to combat poverty, I thought how great it would be to have a similar charismatic leader to highlight and articulate a similar public rhetoric in the age of Trump. I am speaking specifically of a rhetoric that focuses on and addresses the problems of all racial and ethnic groups, and that could be used to effectively mobilize these groups through coalition politics. As Martin Luther King Jr. was fully aware, although such groups are often seen as adversaries, they are potential allies in a reform political coalition due to their suffering from a common problem: economic distress caused by forces outside of their control.

By bringing the Poor People's Campaign, and King's inclusive vision that supported it, to center stage in the public arena, Sylvie Laurent's *King and the Other America* not only provides a significant correction of an important event in our nation's history, it also offers a very useful reference for how we can address today's growing inequality.

William Julius Wilson
Harvard University

Introduction

On June 24, 1968, the makeshift housing that Martin Luther King Jr. had dreamt of, built on the Mall in Washington, DC, and known as Resurrection City, was wiped out. Police tear gas filled the air. Hundreds of people were arrested. Bulldozers smashed the plywood shacks. A sign on one of them read, "No more Hunger."

The erasure of the activists' encampment is a dramatic metaphor for what is left in our collective memory of the concern for economic justice as a civil right during the black liberation movement. The "insurgent democracy" King had fought for and his Poor People's Campaign's dramatization of the dispossessed were lost in the smoke of the burning cities of the late 1960s. As racial resentment simmered, the campaigning Republican presidential candidate Richard Nixon allegedly uttered, after a visit to the shantytown, "those people out there are electing Richard Nixon."[1]

The "voice of the poor" was silenced and "the voice of the unheard"—the way King named the uprisings—was suddenly strident and subjected to political maneuvering. The egalitarian economic demands of an interracial Poor People's Campaign (PPC), overshadowed by King's death, quickly faded from popular political memory. Most historical interpretations of his last crusade have tended to emphasize its utopian and delusional features, its doomed fate, only minimally exploring its underpinnings so as to insulate King's reputation from disgrace for this final campaign.[2]

Here is what King had pictured. Masses of the "truly disadvantaged," precisely because of their multiracial makeup, would gather in Washington to exert pressure on the White House and Congress, forcing the reform of an unjust system and the relocation of power toward those disenfranchised either by race or class. The campaign would, as King envisioned it, challenge a flawed liberal democracy which had thrived on a racially divided working class as well as those unemployed or underemployed. Following social democratic principles, he expected to substantiate democracy by extending it from the political sphere into the economic and cultural realms. King's last campaign, consistent with his simultaneous involvement with striking sanitation workers in the city of Memphis, was an embrace of the poor and the working classes of all races and ethnicities afflicted by injustice, exploitation, misery, and disenfranchisement.[3] He was indignant at the dramatic wealth inequality that plagued an oblivious nation and exacerbated racial disparities. Underneath the veneer of American prosperity, such a view of real income discrepancies was hardly farfetched. Although still marginal, a U.S. household belonging to the top one percent in the early 1960s possessed 125 times the wealth of an average family.[4] The poverty rate was 19 percent.[5]

If today Americans are fully aware that the United States exhibits impressive disparities of wealth between rich and poor, this recognition was not the case in the 1950s and 1960s.[6] In those early postwar decades of sustained economic growth, American families enjoyed the shared prosperity of an egalitarian society in which income, savings, and wealth were not so starkly concentrated in the hands of a few top wage earners. Yet, precisely because everyone seemed to benefit from a fair distribution of wealth, King and others worried about the invisibility of those left behind.

King perceptively called for strong federal policies and national recognition of the extent to which the nation had become divided, not only along the lines of race but also the lines of wealth. The PPC claimed that the unequal access to opportunity and wealth that Americans of color experienced more than anyone else not only offended sacred American values but corroded the social fabric of the nation. A peaceful "army of the poor" would try to send the message previously clearly articulated by Ralph Ellison: "first, something happens to us and then, just wait, it happens to every other group in America."[7] Ellison referred to black Americans and King would not disagree with such a statement. But he expanded the framework of "us" to all the disinherited, the forgotten, the exploited. The poor who would be brought together in Washington by King's campaign were indisputably the "miner's canaries" of the American people.[8]

By denouncing "the tenacious poverty which so paradoxically exists in the midst of plenty," King was prescient: the growing divide between the haves and have-nots, between a handful of the extremely wealthy and a growing impoverished population, put the very idea of democracy at risk.[9] His analysis of the destructive effects of a growing concentration of wealth and power was sound but provocative. He pointed out the limits of a liberal, capitalist democracy in the absence of substantive justice and economic security for all. On December 4, 1967, the leader unraveled his new undertaking in a long and strongly argued statement, in which the purpose of the PPC as well as its motive and revolutionary significance are clearly explained:

> The SCLC [Southern Christian Leadership Conference] will lead waves of the nation's poor and disinherited to Washington DC next spring to demand redress of their grievances by the United States government and to secure at least jobs or income for all. . . . Affluent Americans are locked into suburbs of physical comfort and mental insecurity; poor Americans are locked inside ghettos of material privation and spiritual debilitation; and all of us can almost feel the presence of a kind of social insanity which could lead to national ruin . . . a nation gorged on money while millions of its citizens are denied a good education, adequate health services, decent housing, meaningful employment, and even respect and they are told to be responsible. The true responsibility for the existence of these deplorable conditions lies ultimately with the larger society, and much of the immediate responsibility for removing the injustices can be laid directly at the door of the federal government.[10]

King did not live to see his ultimate crusade materialize. The Poor People's Campaign and the initiatives associated with it turned out to be a living memorial for the leader who was assassinated just weeks before its starting date. For more than a month though, thousands of poor people of all races poured into the capital, by foot, train, or from mule wagons, camping out on the Mall in a shantytown they named Resurrection City. They occupied the space for six weeks and attempted to get the powers that be to take notice. Ralph Abernathy, Andrew Young, Hosea Williams, James Bevel, Walter Fauntroy, Joseph Lowery, and Jesse Jackson strived to carry on their missing leader's grand scheme. Although physically absent, King and his vision were omnipresent as his co-visionaries spawned and sustained the forty-five-day march and the six- week encampment in Washington. Although not as confrontational as initially planned, the protesters took disruptive actions, hoping to seize the momentum of President Lyndon B. Johnson's War on Poverty in order to break into the national consciousness. The main rally of the campaign, held on Solidarity Day (June 19, 1968), managed to draw fifty thousand people to Washington, with demands to combat runaway inequality and, in the words used by Coretta King Scott that day, "the violence of poverty."

Following King's beliefs, the Southern Christian Leadership Conference (SCLC) hoped, through a sensational march and occupation of the Washington Mall, that a "second phase" of the civil rights movement would bring about *real* equality, giving full substance to the legal accomplishments of 1964 and 1965. Civil rights meant little, they argued, without the substance of economic power behind them. King had been also hopeful that, in the post-Watts context, a nonviolent march and protest would deflect national attention away from the urban uprising of disenchanted blacks which had erupted just months before in Detroit and Newark. A younger generation of blacks was growing increasingly vocal in their discontent with civil rights legislation—albeit hard-won—which had failed to bring about their own full-scale incorporation into the promise of social justice. Scores of young activists, acting in a more radical tradition of black protest, now demanded self-determination and a real liberation. King hoped to contain their frustration and despair. He too was disquieted by the flawed and lopsided nature of racial progress in the post-civil-rights-legislation years. Chief among the campaign's demand was to wipe out the ghettoes, symbols of an ongoing exploitation. Organizing a "revolution" against an intrinsically unjust system was also on his horizon.

Yet, as he explained at length in his late writings, King could not and would not endorse former comrade Stokely Carmichael's rallying cry nor the politics of the thriving Black Power movement. Among King's motives was his strongly held belief that bridging the racial gap and building inter-racial coalitions were still essential components of the struggle. To some extent though, he shared Carmichael's concern with unfair and sustained asymmetries of power, stating that "there is nothing essentially wrong with power. The problem is that in America power is unequally distrib-uted."[11] King was also cognizant of the definition of American inequality along arbitrarily assigned lines of race and class. With regard to economic disparities, race was indeed a tremendous determining factor: in 1963, whites held seven times more wealth than African Americans (as much in 2013 as in the aftermath of the Great Depression).[12] But the plague of inequality of wealth and power crossed racial lines and King expected to tackle it as such. Disputing the nationalistic rhetoric of the Black Power movement, he claimed:

> One unfortunate thing about [the slogan] Black Power is that it gives prior-ity to race precisely at a time when the impact of automation and other forces have made the economic question fundamental for blacks and whites alike. In this context, a slogan of "Power for Poor People" would be much more appropriate.[13]

Still, unlike social democratic leaders to whom he was close, such as A. Philip Randolph, King refused to publicly condemn Black Power activ-ists or to fuel the divide between integrationists and nationalists. The Poor People's Campaign was envisioned as an inclusive, class-based project that, to him, would transform the black liberation movement into the van-guard of a universal revolution on behalf of the dispossessed. Like most radicals of the struggle, he thought the abolition of racism would remain illusory unless a profound transformation of the economic structures occurred. By no mean a wholesale repudiation of black radicalism, the campaign sought to combine the nonviolent struggle for racial justice with the fight for universal economic equality, asserting their bound fates. He echoed reformist liberal social scientists and the Kerner Commission (appointed by Johnson in 1967 to investigate the uprisings),[14] which advo-cated for quickly proceeding "beyond civil rights" toward economic equality to quell social unrest.[15] But King envisioned the campaign as uncompromising and disobedient. Welfare rights activists' presence, instrumental to the campaign, embodied his desire to reconcile various forms of black protest on behalf of an overarching cause. King had invited Carmichael and many Black Panther chapters to join the campers and refused to ostracize them. Still, he felt the urge to reach beyond racial civil rights, "for our program calls for a redistribution of economic power" he asserted.[16] King was concerned about the plight of the "other America."

Mark Twain talked about two Americas divided by race. One America was committed to real equality while the other America was subjugated and oppressed.[17] In 1962, Michael Harrington described the "other America" as invisible and subjugated. His eponymous book, *The Other America: Poverty in the United States,* sent shock waves through political circles, which "redis-covered" that poverty in the midst of plenty was real *and* multiracial. Appropriating Harrington's metaphor and purpose, King in his late writings deplored an American economic "dualism," a "schizophrenia" which offered "the milk of prosperity and the honey of opportunity" to the affluent while it condemned an "other America" to misery. While most were black, King claimed this "other America" also included Mexican Americans, Puerto Ricans, Native Americans. and "millions" who were "Appalachian whites." This "other America," burdened by economic oppression, was still unfree.[18]

To King, race and class were not mutually exclusive imperatives, and he was fully aware of the racialized construction of class in the United States. According to him, race should not be subsumed under class, or simply function as an addition to the real burden of class. As many before him, his analysis of race and class was dialectical and their relation was evolv-ing and reciprocal. A social fiction but an historical reality, the ideology of "race" (and racism as a social practice) has ensured the unfair distribution of wealth and power. The campaign's radical egalitarianism formulated a class framework in which exploitative socioeconomic relations were instrumental to the racial subordination of black Americans. Charles Mills calls "black racial liberalism" an attempt "to combine the racial jus-tice political project with a larger social justice project," highlighting the staggeringly unequal distribution of wealth and income of the country.[19]

Generations of activists before King had analyzed racial inequality in socioeconomic terms, denouncing systemic material deprivation, the scarcity of jobs available to blacks, poor medical care, and lack of decent housing. The economic program of civil rights organizations and their commitment to alleviating black poverty, from the National Urban League to the Student Nonviolent Coordinating Committee, was substantial. They pursued a "dual agenda" (legal equality *and* economic justice) that only if fully achieved would stand for "civil rights."[20] Their lobbying effort seemed to be successful when President Johnson publicly contended in 1965 that the country should aim for "not just equality as a right and a theory but as a fact and as a result," connecting his War on Poverty to racial progress.[21] But a national dedication to eradicating poverty and achieving substantive racial equality was nowhere in sight when King planned the Poor People's Campaign.

King knew all too well the violence of race-based socioeconomic inequalities. In 1966, he moved into a tenement on Chicago's West Side to "help eradicate a vicious system which seeks to further colonize thousands of Negroes within a slum environment."[22] That same year, he broke down while visiting the black sharecropping community in Marks, Mississippi, whose children were starving. Haunted by them, he would make sure the campaign's march would depart from the town of Marks.[23] And although he made the case for greater economic benefits for all in a more egalitarian system, King never relegated his quest for racial equality nor succumbed to a reductionist position. While asking for universal public policies, he also explicitly requested preferential compensation for blacks, modeled on the GI Bill, a previous "preferential treatment" policy; his proposal, he stressed, would not only be far less costly than the veterans' program but would "certainly be less expensive than any computation based on two centuries of unpaid wages and accumulated interest."[24] Influenced by W. E. B. Du Bois and also by welfare rights activists, King recognized the preponderance of class and economic position in his analysis of race.

But, in order to successfully put poverty on the national agenda, in a context of racial fatigue, budget cuts by the embattled Johnson administration, and widely shared misrepresentation of black destitution as an entrenched "pathology," disentangling poverty from blackness was a prerequisite.[25] Besides, "the poor" King wished to mobilize in 1967 were not a proxy for blacks. The have-nots of the nation were of all stripes and colors, poverty-afflicted Appalachians as well as Latinos and Native Americans, and to King, only an interracial coalition of the poor could gain political leverage. The strategy was to make poverty conspicuous but also to coercively "expose Congress" and its lack of answers.[26] Although not a Marxist upheaval against capitalism, nor a call for the overthrow of the existing institutions or the establishment of a people's government, the Poor People's Campaign hinged on the revolutionary potential of a unified, multiracial. and multiethnic coalition of the poor. "The only real revolutionary, people say, is a man [or woman] who has nothing to lose. There are millions of poor people in this country who have very little, or even nothing, to lose," King argued.[27] Without brushing racism aside, King intended to expand the scope of the civil rights revolution, progressing through and beyond race toward a just and fair society for all. In a 1965 interview with Alex Haley, King explained his belief in the power of a transracial coalition:

> The unemployed, poverty-stricken white man must be made to realize that he is in the very same boat with the Negro. Together, they could exert massive pressure on the Government to get jobs for all. Together, they could form a grand alliance. Together, they could merge all people for the good of all.[28]

History did not oblige. The SCLC and its allies had hardly finalized the campaign when King was shot. Although the campaign was carried on posthumously, its fate was sealed. The army of the poor was seen as yet another source of public disorder by mainstream media and former allies, and King's hope that Resurrection City and its nonviolent inhabitants would provide a counter-narrative to burning cities proved illusory. Many pundits expressed their utter contempt for what one portrayed as a "revival meeting within a carnival within an army camp."[29] As with many other projects carried out after 1965, the widely accepted narrative points to the ineffectiveness of King's late nonviolent strategies as a means of confronting social and economic problems and to the lack of tangible policy accomplishments, be they in Chicago or Resurrection City. Although the tradition of dissent in America comprises as many unfinished tasks as it boasts enshrined accomplishments, the civil rights movement's unfulfilled agenda, particularly in the post-1965 era, is read in retrospect as evidence of its irrelevance. Most historians and civil rights leaders have dismissed the PPC as an unfortunate mistake, calling it "a Little Big Horn," a "Waterloo," an utter "debacle."[30] This book argues that, in reality, the question of whether the Poor People's Campaign was a "failure" has to be reframed.

Unsurprisingly, the crusaders against poverty made little headway. Public support for civil rights had already begun to falter but without King, the SCLC was unable to cultivate sympathy. Among the youngest campers, a general distrust toward journalists turned to bitterness, antagonizing the press, who questioned the relevance of the slain pastor's last crusade. Bringing populist discontent to the doors of those who presided over and sustained the glaring contrast between poverty and wealth, demanding redistribution but also condemning the ongoing war in Vietnam, the campers' enterprise was undermined by the FBI, who framed it as a subversive communist-inspired uprising.[31] The poor's insurgency and their "American Commune"[32] were all the more intolerable in the context of activism by white leftist radical groups such as Students for a Democratic Society (SDS).[33] Many civil rights opportunities to build broad cross-racial grassroots movements tying together economic justice and racial equality had already been crushed by malignant FBI activities, and the defamation of the PPC stood as an indisputable example of such political malice.[34] From the moment he began voicing his rebuke of the Vietnam War, King had been vilified as an anti-American member of an international criminal conspiracy.[35] Accordingly, the FBI made sure that misrepresentation of the campaign dominated public opinion and prevailed among law makers. Intimidation, defamation, and repression were used to brand Resurrection City as a subversive nest and a threat to national security, and to sever the coalition. The sabotage proved effective. From the beginning of the campaign, which they labeled POCAM, intelligence services spread false rumors about the criminality and depravity of PPC participants and provided the government with misleading and mendacious reports on Resurrection City.[36] For most officials, the encampment was nothing but a place of lawlessness.

Furthermore, despite their shared belief that the symbolic struggles for black civil rights and American democratization could not be separated from material struggles over unequal distribution, most of King's partners were unsettled by the project. From James Farmer to Bayard Rustin and Marian Logan, the campaign was viewed as unfortunate. They judged the PPC, like King's indictment of the war in Vietnam, as ill timed and off topic for a "civil rights" leader. The main assumption then, for his associates as well as in the mainstream press, was that King's late positions undermined black moderates by discrediting the civil right movements' activities. Indeed, in July 1968, *Time* magazine claimed that "the shanty-town capital and symbol of the Poor People's Campaign had long since become an ugly, anarchic embarrassment to their cause."[37] Moreover, mainstream media silenced the multiracial makeup of the campaign, ignoring its unprecedented militancy.[38] To them, it was yet another civil rights march.

The widely accepted narrative was, and still is to some degree, that the PPC diverted the fervor for further civil rights to less fruitful channels and would have failed where the 1963 movement had succeeded—specifically by dismantling the liberal coalition of churches and synagogues, government bureaucracies, labor unions, universities and foundations, and parts of the media that had supported the pre-1965 progress toward greater equality. Today, despite countless studies rebuking it, this line of argument still accompanies the assertion that the fecund postwar liberal consensus fell victim to urban riots, Black Nationalism, and the New Left.[39] The civil rights struggles of late 1960s and early 1970s have therefore been long marginalized from the grand narrative of the movement, if not presented as its downhill path,[40]

This mainstream rendering overlooks the contingency that allowed for the civil rights insurgency to achieve major progress and ignores the fact that during every step along the way from 1954 to 1964, the black liberation struggle in the United States had consistently been dubbed "illusory," "ill timed," "impractical," and doomed to fail. Likewise, since the 1930s, black radicalism was commonly deemed inconsistent with the American "universalist" tradition and accused of having failed blacks.[41] Not only are these views inaccurate (to the extent that scholars agree on how to measure *failure* or *success* with regard to social movements),[42] as well as dismissive of local activists and more radical struggles such as that of the Black Power movement, but they also curtail King's thought and legacy.[43]

Although the Poor People's Campaign did not usher in the redistributive policies that it had demanded, placing exclusive blame on the campaign itself rather than the chaotic events of the year 1968 would be to dangerously simplify history. The racial backlash which King continually condemned was in the making for many years and reached its boiling point in the months preceding Nixon's election. African Americans' ongoing demands for full equality, including in the North, did alienate former allies among affluent white liberals and the white suburban working class. King's reframing of a populist and progressive constituency based on a diverse grassroots movement was clairvoyant, although premature. His outreach to many groups, including urban black youth, Latino farmers, welfare mothers, Native Americans, black and Latino nationalists, and white Appalachians is worth considering because it foretold further progressive tactics.[44] Along with the union-affiliated white-collar workers, southern black sharecroppers, and gang members from inner cities who congregated in Resurrection City, the inclusion of these diverse social groups suggested a new, larger coalition of the American disenfranchised. A diverse "socially conscious" movement, King reasoned, would regenerate the American social contract, giving voice and rights to those who had been excluded from democratic participation.[45] Its unprecedented protest for social justice envisioned universal rights that would benefit the nation as a whole. Labor unions were expected to be strong proponents of the campaign and, if the American Federation of Labor and the Congress of Industrial Organizations (AFL-CIO) rejected it because of its antiwar rhetoric, King believed the United Auto Workers and many small unions would enthusiastically support it.

Despite the documented internal squabbling, lack of money, and poor infrastructural organization which crippled the campaigners' ability to mobilize, some scholars have begun to take note of the obscured campaign.[46] Admittedly, they have documented how most participants grew discouraged as the campaign failed to gain political leverage, a defeat rendered almost irremediable after the assassination of Bobby Kennedy, who, while running for the Democratic presidential nomination, had expressed sympathy with the PPC. But for all its limitations, most participants recognized afterwards that the Poor People's Campaign was nowhere near worthless.[47] The strategy, although chaotically conducted, was framed not only by its policy impact but also by its ability to dramatize for the public the urgent need to remedy wealth inequalities and to offer an alternative. Furthermore, the campaign's demands, the most salient of which was an "Economic Bill of Rights for the Disadvantaged" and a robust antipoverty blueprint, delved into ambitious policy proposals, such as a ten-year, $20 billion-per-year federal plan to eradicate slums, unemployment, subpar education, and entrenched poverty through a guaranteed annual income. The latter proposal had already been forcefully advocated by King in 1967, in his last book, *Where Do We Go from Here" Chaos or Community?*, and in "The Other America," a speech he gave at Stanford University on April 14, 1967.[48]

However familiar to a progressive-minded audience, these demands for universal economic rights challenged the collective acceptance of pervasive racial and increasingly stark class inequalities. Moving away from the common economic wisdom of the era—the virtues of individualism, the belief that economic growth "lifts all boats," the efficiency of corporate liberalism—the campaign was an act of dissent and a claim for a real social democracy. King wanted to converge economics, race, and social and political equality.

Not only was the call for the enshrinement of economic security in the Constitution not unheard of in American history, but it could have successfully capitalized on the political momentum. The urban uprising and King's death influenced public opinion; according to a poll conducted by Lou Harris and published in the November 20, 1967, issue of the *New York Times*, a majority of Americans supported the idea of a "decisive Federal action to raze slums, establish work programs to provide jobs for the unemployed, create a Federal rat extermination program and provide summer camps for poor children." What's more, almost 60 percent endorsed "a Federal program to tear down ghettoes in American cities" and to "provide jobs for the unemployed of the ghettos."[49] But the campaign unleashed more hostility than support, and a biased depiction prevailed. Its radical thrust has been buried under the falsifying celebration of King "the healer," the dreamer of 1963, fervently committed to racial reconciliation.[50] Another way to dismiss his call has thus been to cast it as the symptom of a "radicalized" King, blinded by resentment. A post-1967 lonesome King, the mainstream narrative goes, had grown disgruntled with the slow pace of reform, the war in Vietnam, and his own inability to contain black violence. Turning away from the formal conquest of citizenship rights, he is said to have resorted to subversive methods and demands formerly alien to him, abandoning the American creed in favor of an extremism close to that of political radicals. Precisely because King has been misremembered by a bowdlerized narrative as unconditionally devoted to the reformist, integrationist, middle-class oriented liberal paradigm until 1966, his reframing of the civil rights revolution on economic and redistributive terms appeared as a derailment, a departure from his longstanding middle-of-the road approach.[51] To challenge such distorting views, this book argues that the Poor People's Campaign and King's democratic-socialist statements have been inaccurately trivialized. His last project was neither a gesture aimed at revamping his declining aura, as mainstream commentators pretended, nor the reflection of his deep change of mind.

King's black radical critique of the liberal paradigm and his indictment of America's systemic flaws with regard to economic injustices and imperialism did not develop after 1965 although his views were perhaps more trenchant than two decades before. For years, King had indeed hammered the issues of poverty and misdistribution of wealth; economic justice was, to him, a prerequisite for racial equality. As Thomas Jackson brilliantly demonstrates, King's concerns about the inconsistencies of the American system and his critical theoretical framework had developed very early on.[52] In June 1956, months before the Montgomery boycott was even set in motion, he stressed the perils of economic injustice as being as harmful to inclusion as was racial prejudice, asserting, "I never intend to adjust myself to the tragic inequalities of an economic system which takes the necessities from the masses to give luxuries to the classes."[53] In 1968, when a journalist, pointing to the transracial nature of the PPC, told him that he was not "within civil rights" anymore, the preacher replied, "but you can say I am in human rights."[54] To accurately historicize such a comment, one should bear in mind that King's concern for universal human rights had been present consistently throughout his life.[55]

Of course, his thoughts continued to evolve, and to teleologically essentialize King's thinking on class and its relationship to race would be dismissive of major evolutions in his worldview. But I concur with Robert Birt's statement that "the themes of economic justice versus exploitation and indeed the need for a global struggle against poverty and imperialism, are to be found even in the pre-movement expression of his thinking."[56] The simplistic "radicalization" thesis should therefore be dismissed if it suggests a sudden shift toward new extreme beliefs, the disavowal of integration, or a sudden embrace of socialism as a new framework. His understanding of a truly liberal democracy as a site of power and revenue reallocation had remained constant, and it crystallized when the context made such a stance urgent. His evolution should therefore not be misunderstood as an unfortunate intellectual perdition that estranged him from his lifelong commitment to the liberal tradition. But it had to be a refurbished one.

The principles of redistribution and solidarity that he fleshed out during the Poor People's Campaign entailed drastic structural reform of liberal democracy but not its utter repudiation. As had many activists before him, King grew distressed with the limits of a liberal ideology wherein blacks were almost the only ones to remain dedicated to the redistribution of wealth and resources.[57] Although it would certainly take King some time to distance himself from reform-minded liberalism and to articulate his *aggiornamento*, his evolution is neither an embittered deviance nor an abnormal evolution in black political thought. Skepticism about the limits of U.S. liberal democracy and subsequent disenchantment is itself a black tradition.[58] The rich legacy of radical visions of an egalitarian democracy and its influence on the freedom movement has been unearthed by "long civil rights movement" scholarship, and my book has benefited tremendously from it. Taking this tradition into account, we should not question whether King became "radicalized" but rather whether he was a "black radical," cogently defined by Minkah Makalani as "those who considered restructuring the dominant political economy a central feature of ending racial oppression and considered some form of socialist economic organization essential to racial liberation and national self-determination for colonial Africa and Asia."[59]

Considering such insights, a nagging question has hampered a deep and fair examination of King's thought and last campaign: to what extent was he influenced by Marxist ideology? Was he placing class above race, anti-imperialism above patriotism, expecting the American proletariat to join left-wing activism and embrace its use of coercive means?

The anticommunist hysteria that characterized a major part of the American twentieth century, and which King himself deplored and suffered from throughout his life, has cast a shadow of suspicion on King's commitment to restructuring the American economic framework in a radically egalitarian yet democratic fashion.[60] That he privately called himself a "socialist," a statement vilified by his opponents, who used it to discredit his endeavor, is critical to comprehending King's explicit rejection of the basic underpinnings of the capitalistic economic system.[61] His brand of socialism is more accurately described as "democratic socialism" or social democracy, oftentimes associated with northern European countries.[62] But the Poor People's Campaign, envisioned as a mass movement seeking a massive redistribution of wealth and power, was the fruit of a companionship with socialist leaders and ideas which, far from being alien to American culture, shaped its intellectual and social history.

This book argues that a close examination of King's political thought entails a dismissal entirely of the assumption that King was a procommunist Marxist—although the definition of "Marxist" is still up for debate as even the German philosopher himself denied being one. King remained a democrat and a Christian to the core, committed to the individual's natural rights, at odds with basic Marxist premises. He never entertained the overthrow of American democracy or the replacement of it by a regime in which the State would own the means of production (before it too vanished). However, he was certainly "Marxian" in most of his systemic analysis, which was predicated on the conviction that deep historical structures had shaped American history and both· the black and the poor experience.[63] King also thought that uniting the oppressed regardless of their racial and ethnic identities was imperative. This Marxian assumption was constantly mobilized by King to analyze race and oppression in America, and the Poor People's Campaign resulted from such creed.[64]

Rather than a sideshow or a deviation, the Poor People's Campaign is brought to center stage in these pages and cast as the culmination of King's lifelong thinking on the nature of justice. I explore its significance, considering a particular subset of issues regarding how King's thoughts on equality were the product of his own maturation on substantive justice and liberal democracy, and of an intellectual environment that had preceded and has outlived him.

King's highly egalitarian, social democratic vision of society was neither new nor marginal. The first part of this book, "The Long March," examines the intellectual roots of King's radical egalitarianism, showcasing the many influences that propelled him toward it. Indeed, in formulating the redistributive demands of the Poor People's Campaign, King drew inspiration from figures and social movements oftentimes belittled although their views on the entwinement of race and class and their deep concern for the unequal distribution of wealth in the United States shaped the contours of King's coalition of the poor.

The first four chapters trace the history of race and class dialectics as debated by Black America very early on, showing how it foreshadowed the 1968 campaign. The three chapters in the second part of the book, "The Campaign," chronicle the project from its remote inception, how it was carried out despite King's death, and investigate how its interracial encampment of the poor was spearheaded by the National Welfare Rights Organization, welcomed Black Power advocates, and reconciled cultural nationalists' demands from the Chicano and Native American movements with a class-based indictment of economic exploitation and unbridled capitalism. The third part, "The Vision," seeks to speculate about the many political ideas, scholarship, and theories on social justice that vindicated the relevance of the campaign. Major academic works have echoed the campaign's groundbreaking insights, namely its concern for the dynamics of structural inequality and a demand for a social citizenship embedded in an Economic Bill of Rights that redefined the scope of justice.

By way of conclusion, I assess the radical political and intellectual potentialities of the Poor People's Campaign in light of today's major concern about inequality. I suggest that its insightful castigation of unfair distribution of resources helps us to understand how missed opportunities shape our present and still inspire us to keep fighting for economic justice and substantive equality. Reclaiming King, as some have demanded, is a good way to celebrate the fiftieth anniversary of his death.[65]

Ironically so, the anniversary is celebrated under the presidency of Donald Trump, whose election engendered the current debates about white working-class politics in America. The resurgence of concern for the intricacies of race and class following the election of 2016 and the controversial rhetoric of identity politics illustrates how the idea of universal emancipation remains constrained by race. Assigning, as Nell Irvin Painter notes, "class only to Trump voters and identity only to people who are not white," we forget that it has always been so misconstrued.[66] King's Poor People's Campaign was an attempt to overcome this "reluctance to see people of color as people with class status" but also to challenge the color line that has separated the poor. This book hopes to resurface King's thoughts on race and class, and his perceptive concern over wealth inequality, and to foreground the Poor People's Campaign's inspiring suggestions at a time of great anxiety over these issues.

PART I   The Long March

King was neither the first one to draw attention to the linkages between racism and class exploitation nor the first to suggest that class-based, cross-racial alliances were the privileged means through which substantive equality should be achieved. Long before him, radical black thought sought to reveal the racial dimensions and grounds through which class relations and ideology were formed, underscoring how racial and economic oppression were mutually constitutive. Since Emancipation and its major demand for land redistribution, many black intellectuals and activists have provided insights into the political economy of racial exploitation.[1] The Poor People's Campaign is a link in a long chain of black progressives' deeds.

1 The Patriarchs

King's radical democratic visions were rooted in his own existence but also in a long yet underestimated black tradition of dissent and communistic appeals transmitted across generations. The continuous development of an organized "protest community," an indictment of the nation-state's claim for true liberal democracy, has been disparaged as "un-American"—outside of the realm of American citizenry.[1] The key dialectic of race and class had therefore to be articulated within a prejudiced framework of race and nation, yielding the notion of black disloyalty and lack of patriotism.[2] From Frederick Douglass's 1852 oration interrogating "What to the Slave is the Fourth of July?" to King's harsh criticism of American capitalism and militarism, black dissent has brought suspicion of blacks as unreliable citizens. The incorporation of currents of democratic socialism into the black liberation struggle in the United States have thereby long been obscured but coming to terms with it enriches and complicates our understanding of the black liberation movement's ideas of justice as well as King's. A "fusion of critical analysis and vision," this tradition of black "democratic indignation" has called upon America to translate its egalitarian principles into substantive justice.[3]

King's radical ruminations were infused with a history of quarrels and debates on the centrality of class in American racial oppression. The time and place of his coming of age also promptly led King to understand the relation between economic status and race. Born in 1929, he witnessed at a very young age the economic oppression endured by the black worker and the ravages of structural racism during the New Deal. No African American born and raised in Georgia could ignore poverty, even less so in a household. deeply committed to justice. The young King heard about poverty and exploitation at his father's table as well as in the streets of Atlanta where he fathomed that "the inseparable twin of racism" was "economic injustice."[4]

King's later insistence on economic justice did not come out of a vacuum; he also carried with him traditions and heritage that he might not even have been aware of. Memory of social movement operates in subtle ways. Looking back at, in the words of Toni Morrison, the "milieu of buried stimuli" which bred King may illuminate his gravitation toward democratic socialism. Stories were passed on by sharecroppers who had migrated to large cities and then from militants to younger generations; their narratives were as instrumental to the dissenting spirit of the King family as was their immediate environment. Assuredly, the black radical tradition was primarily passed on to King by the Church. Yet, what Keith Miller called "a system of knowledge and persuasion created by generations of black folk preachers, including his father and grandfather" was as much made of oral recollection of histories of oppression as it was by theological knowledge.[5] King's father, his neighbors, community, acquaintances, and professors undoubtedly shared with him the plight of the sharecropper and the structural conflation of race and poverty in the Southern economy. They indirectly awakened in him the desire to explore the ways through which class and race intersected in American society. Such recollection shaped a collective as well as personal memory. Later on, mentoring by Benjamin Mays—son of a tenant farmer—and Howard Thurman—grandson of a slave—who both went to India in the 1930s and 1940s and witnessed the caste system, expanded the scope of King's intellectual formation. To some extent, the confluence of the streams of civil rights and socialism, black liberation struggle and pacifism ineluctably flowed toward him. They all trickled down to him through many channels, as much within his familial environment and narratives as through his formal education. A process of permanent rethinking and reworking of the past forged King's intellectual sensibilities and connected him to a tradition of black radicalism that, although not reified, was both religious and secular, and formed a coherent political vision, particularly in the South.

To recast King's thought in the long history of a dissenting black counter-voice, lodging the roots of his social critique in a collection of seminal voices of resistance, spares us the "great man theory," already challenged by King's scholars, most notably by Clayborne Carson. If the significance of grassroots civil rights activism and 1930s labor and radical activism has been reappraised in long civil rights historiography, the preceding black radical thought is still underexplored. More "torchbearer than trailblazer," King, consciously or not, framed his dissent on theirs.[6] Interestingly, he particularly echoed Frederick Douglass, who ushered in a tradition of black radical thought dedicated to the idea of substantive justice.

FREDERICK DOUGLASS

Although they lived in very different spaces and times, King and Douglass's resemblances have been explored with regard to their position of public authority and rhetorical mastery of the black jeremiad.[7] But it bears reflecting on the similarities of their calls for redistributive justice as part of the achievement of racial equality as well as a precondition to the real democratization of the United States. Their resemblances in content stems from a similar view on the means through which justice could be achieved. Their radicalism originates in a belief that only through struggle may justice be achieved. Adamant that "moderation" and "patience" were code words for maintaining the status quo, they called for a true uprising, moral and/or physical, of the oppressed. Frederick Douglass clearly expressed his rebuttal of political moderation:

> Those who profess to favor freedom and yet deprecate agitation are men who want crops without plowing up the ground; they want rain without thunder and lightning. They want the ocean without the awful roar of its many waters. This struggle may be a moral one, or it may be a physical one, and it may be both moral and physical, but it must be a struggle. Power concedes nothing without a demand. It never did and it never will.[8]

Directly echoing Douglass, King wrote in his 1963 "Letter from Birmingham Jail" that "freedom is never voluntarily given by the oppressor; it must be demanded by the oppressed." Only a sustained radical reconstruction of democracy, challenging the economic power structure and enforced by the federal government, could usher in justice, King believed.

Black radicals' concern for the unfairness of wealth distribution inherent to capitalism harks back to the foundation of American agrarian capitalism. In other words, racial and economic oppression have been intertwined since the early days of slavery. Their historical interplay resulted in a distorted African American class structure (overwhelmingly constituted of laborers) and hindered the development of a "class consciousness" among workers). In the wake of Reconstruction, freedmen, forced to remain sharecroppers by design, formed the bulk of a laboring class vital to the Southern political economy. Precisely because they were overwhelmingly laborers, Douglass argued, blacks had to organize to be emancipated from the domination of market forces. If not strictly a "class," African Americans, particularly in the South, have come to perceive themselves as "workers." As U.S. economic inequality rose substantially in the Reconstruction era, the "class question" and the critique of the skewed principle of property rights became intertwined with black liberation. Deprived of their means of production—land—emancipated blacks and propertyless whites were dependent on a market which demanded the lowest cost possible and coerced them into selling off their "labor power" for wages.[9] Douglass was the voice for millions of freedmen who regarded wealth redistribution and land ownership as essential to their citizenship. In 1869, he concocted a land reform proposal that called for the federal government to thwart concentration of wealth in the hands of the Southern ruling class by purchasing and redistributing land. He challenged the principle of "property of soil," instead bringing forth the "property of man,"[10] and he rejected land monopolies.[11]

In his essay "The Labor Question," Douglass dared to ask, "what manner of holding property in the soil is best, which best secures the happiness of the whole human family?"

The non-producers now receive the larger share of what those who labor produce.... The question, whether civilization is designed primarily for

Man or for Property can have but one direct answer. . . . The happiness of Man must be the primal condition on which any form of society can find a title to existence.[12]

It is hard not to hear King's plea for a "person-oriented society" instead of one that is "thing-oriented," as he also added that "when machines and computers, profit motives and property rights are considered more important than people, the giant triplets of racism, materialism, and militarism are incapable of being conquered."[13]

Reconstruction renewed expectations and many claimed that an effective redistribution of wealth was central to fulfill the promises of equality. In January 1865, Union Army general William Tecumseh Sherman issued Special Field Order N°15, geared toward confiscating 400,000 acres of Confederate territory to redistribute to blacks, insuring a "social Reconstruction." Radical Republican congressman Thaddeus Stevens unsuccessfully defended a bill to expand the initiative throughout the South. By claiming substantive egalitarian land redistribution, Republicans in the mold of Stevens called for the restoration of slaves' property rights. Douglass, in contrast to Stevens (and Sherman), did not espouse confiscation.[14] Neither did he call for the abolition of property. Yet, by supporting the core Lockean principle of property rights for former slaves and by claiming the right to a decent job and a decent wage, he was more than a "liberal democrat."[15] Douglass and the advocates of a radical democracy not only challenged the institutional arrangements that sustained the economic and political power of the former planters' class but also the de facto racial inequities of the sharecropping economy.

Although Douglass seemed to be dismissive of the socialist, Fourier-inspired alternative to liberal democracy, he voiced his concern with the unfairness of the wage system. In 1869, he prompted abolitionists to "defend the black man's equal rights to work as well as his equal right to vote"[16] and to guarantee black workers "employments by which they can obtain something like a respectable living."[17] Certainly a reformer, an integrationist, and a liberal democrat, Douglass was also a radical egalitarian.

That the government would hold a double-standard policy at the expense of the poor was also a common concern. Douglass blamed the federal government for granting "millions upon millions of acres of public land to soulless railroad corporations to get rich."[18] The unfulfilled promise of land redistribution for freedman, now known as General Sherman's plan to supply them with "40 acres and a mule," is the backdrop of his critique. More straightforward, King, in 1968, would point out the 1862 Homestead Act, which gave away 270 million acres of western land to white settlers coming from Europe. Upon launching the Poor People's Campaign, King substantiated Douglass's indictment, explicitly pointing out the racial ground of such bias:

> At the very same time that America refused to give the Negro any land, through an act of Congress, our government was giving away millions of acres of land in the West and the mid-West, which meant that it was willing to undergird its White peasants from Europe with an economic floor.[19]

Absent significant wealth redistribution able to fulfill the first and second Reconstruction promises, most radicals shifted to a narrowly defined legal conception of racial equality, contrasting with both Douglass and King, who challenged the definition of citizenship as a merely property-based civic membership and identified the labor market, enforced by the State, as a site of oppression. They shared the belief that a wealth- and profit-driven society was doomed to alienate and dispossess black and white workers alike. Predating King, Frederick Douglass, remotely familiar with Marxian theory, was resolutely opposed to the perpetuation of an exploitative economic system that degraded the worker, regardless of his color.[20] They both belong to a "black radical tradition" which—as Manning Marable contends—overcame the dichotomy between nationalists and integrationists and connected institutional racism to class inequality, making integration conditional upon structural reforms and economic justice.[21] Achieving these revolutionary tasks entailed their crossing the color line.

Contrasting with nationalists, both King and Douglass indeed favored interracial coalitions. Before the industrial revolution had even swept throughout the South, Douglass promoted interracial labor unionism as a path toward equality. During the 1840s and 1850s, Northern abolitionists called for working-class trade unionism and utopian socialism, and Douglass entertained the idea of a black avant-garde prompting the workers of all races to join in a common fight for economic justice. He pointed out that, as "the colored people of the South are the laboring people of the South," they might trigger a large poor people's movement for justice. He consequently called for an alliance with white labor: "it is a great mistake for any class of laborers to isolate itself . . . the labor unions of the country should not throw away this colored element of strength."[22]

In a February 1866 conversation with President Andrew Johnson, Douglass argued: "Let the negro once understand that he has an organic right to vote, and he will raise up a party in the Southern States among the poor, who will rally with him. There is this conflict that you speak of between the wealthy slaveholder and the poor man."[23] In a pre-Duboisian fashion, he elucidated how the racial divide among the poor was fabricated during slavery: "both are plundered and by the same plunderers. The slave is robbed by his master, of all his earnings above what is required for his physical necessities; and the white man is robbed by the slave system, because he is flung into competition with a class of laborers who work without wages."[24]

This vision of a laboring class being structurally exploited beyond the color line, gravitating toward the notion of "class," was deeply felt by King himself. In a speech in 1964 at the NAACP Legal Defense Fund, King echoed the former slave:

> Historically, large segments of the white population were the derivative victims of slavery. As long as labor was cheapened by the involuntary servitude of the black man, the freedom of white labor, particularly in the South, was little more than a myth. It was free only to bargain from the depressed base imposed by slavery upon the whole labor market . . . to this date the poor in white skins also suffer deprivation and the humiliation of poverty, if not color. They are chained by the weight of discrimination though its badge of degradation does not mark them.[25]

King's reading of the economic underpinnings of slavery reflects his cogent understanding of the historical circumstances in which racialized class identities emerged and developed in the United States. The coalescence of racial subordination and economic exploitation made the political economy of the black American, although not the only one to suffer from economic disenfranchisement, rather peculiar.

To King, it wasn't simply that racism and slavery kept white workers down, but that the elimination of slavery and racism were *preconditions* for the emancipation of all workers. In other words, dismantling structural racism was requisite for any serious transformational class politics. Albeit not concepts of the same order, as "class" would mostly refer to objective material circumstances where "race" is an ideology, racism and "racecraft"[26] were the products of a system of production and social relations in which the labor of exploited slaves conflates class with skin pigmentation.[27] Besides, "class," far from stemming only from a worker's income or his relationship to modes of production, is also an ideological construct that makes sense of the existing distributions of power and wealth. The planters' class forcefully shaped class consciousness in racial terms.

Strikingly enough, the Second Reconstruction succumbed to forces broadly similar to those undermining the first one when the economic interests of Northern whites and African Americans diverged after a brief but eventful political unity. In Jim Crow states such as Mississippi, freedmen elected to office were determined to unite with poor whites to form progressive coalitions, or "fusion tickets."[28] A century after Reconstruction, sharecroppers from Marks, Mississippi, launched King's interracial anti-poverty campaign. Both times, the full realization of black citizenship entailed an expansive conception of racial equality as well as social justice. Social Reconstruction failed because the antebellum's hierarchical distribution of land remained untouched. Both times, redistribution of wealth as a core requirement for equality has been the breaking point for progressive coalitions. The racial democratization of the South could have destabilized the political economy of sharecropping and the unequal distribution of economic privileges and political power. Both times, racial counter-revolutions halted progress.

But the black radical egalitarianism of the nineteenth century ushered in a vast array of social movements, from populists to socialists, who reinvented an American progressivism to address the "race question." A critique of capitalism that predated Marxism but developed alongside it pointed to the duplicity of a system harmful to both black and white workers. More and more intellectuals came to see blacks as the chief agents for a revolutionary change which would benefit an interracial proletariat. Free labor was the core argument of a growing interracial radical labor critique of capitalism. Douglass accurately anticipated that some poor whites, emulating blacks and willing to substantiate the notion of "rights" to encompass economic security, would attempt to democratize the entire nation.[29] The Knights of Labor, created in 1869, organized black and white unskilled workers to secure their social and economic independence.[30] Their demands for an egalitarian economy of national-ized public utilities and for racial equality pursued the unfulfilled prom-ises of Reconstruction.

Toward the end of the nineteenth century, the racialized dimension of the American working class was also discussed at length by those who pioneered the socialist-communist framework and hoped to adapt it to the United States. The assimilation of the "black question" to that of labor and its articulation through a proletarian framework had indeed been a bruising point of contention for blacks long before Peter H. Clark publicly claimed he was a "socialist"—in 1877. the first African American to do so.[31] Clark, an abolitionist who had met and worked for Douglass, joined the Workingmen's Party of the United States in 1876. Drawn to socialism and labor activism, he parted ways with his former mentor when he favored a strong anticapitalistic posture over a true commitment to racial equality and integration. It is telling that 1877 saw the withdrawal of the Union Army from the Reconstruction South, leaving the freedmen subjected to systematic repression from Jim Crow and trapped in a new system of eco-nomic exploitation, and the appearance of the first self-proclaimed black socialist. Northern workers and unions were simultaneously put back. That Clark was an abolitionist before becoming a socialist illuminates the continuities and interplays between social movements for justice. Because they attacked the legitimacy of private property, doctrines of socialism and communism echoed radical abolitionism. Abolitionists and radical Republicans were disparagingly labeled "socialists, communists, red Jacobins" by white supremacists.[32] No one more clearly than W. E. B. Du Bois perceived that the "struggles for black rights and recognition . . . could not be separated from material struggles over distribution."[33]

In the footsteps of Douglass, Du Bois was the key figure of a new post-Reconstruction black radicalism whose opposition to institutional racism and class oppression dovetailed with American socialists' platforms. To the extent that he fully endorsed socialism's ambivalent messages as they related to racial equality, Du Bois's radicalism combined a reflection on citizenship, class oppression, and self-determination that amounted to a "revolutionary integrationism."[34]

W. E. B. DU BOIS

Forebear and figurehead, W. E. B. Du Bois paved the way for a black struggle articulating the black radical tradition with historical and dialectical materialism. The latter, a form of secularized millennialism, stood as the defining component of nineteenth century socialism. Rooted in Atlanta from 1897 to 1910 and again from 1934 to 1944 (where he founded the Atlanta University journal *Phylon*. written by and for African Americans), Du Bois the university professor, mentor, and social activist developed a reflection undoubtedly familiar to King. An exploration of Du Bois's evolving writings on labor and therefore on the intertwined concepts of race and class illuminates how King grasped this critical issue.

Interestingly enough, King's call for radical democracy was belittled as an idiosyncrasy of its old age, echoing the arguments brought up about Du Bois's socialism. Equally, their leaning toward a radically egalitarian social democracy was construed as an alien import, coming from a hostile Soviet Russia. Socialism and Marxism were naturalized (in the sense of essentialized) and de-naturalized (deemed foreign).

Du Bois had expressed socialistic views before the Bolshevik revolution and the Third International and King before the Vietnam War. In both cases, their egalitarian, socialist-infused calls for a radical democracy were deeply grounded and originated primarily from a black American tradition which cohered at times with the Marxist framework. In both cases, their anticapitalistic feelings developed while they were in their youth. Du Bois wrote in a 1904 private letter that, although he eschewed the word "socialist." he fully embraced European social democracy's commitments to ending wealth inequalities.[35] That same year, he invited socialist activist Mary White Ovington to his annual Atlanta Conference of Negro Problems. She would soon become a close friend and an instrumental co-organizer with Du Bois in the NAACP, shedding light on its socialist underpinning. Ovington officially joined the Socialist Party in 1905. six years before Du Bois did. Recent scholarship compellingly demonstrates that his 1911 novel, *The Quest of the Silver Fleece*, was reflective of his early socialistic convictions, offering a searing critique of U.S. capitalism as well as a charge of its manipulative ability to pit white workers against blacks.[36]

Du Bois only came to closely read Karl Marx in 1933, long after he began publicly praising the Industrial Workers of the World, the socialist union that organized black and white workers. Foretelling the African Trinidadian Marxist C. L. R. James's 1938 study *The Black Jacobins: Toussaint L'Ouverture and the San Domingo Revolution* and Cedric Robinson's 1983 seminal book *Black Marxism*, Du Bois's 1935 *Black Reconstruction* traced the roots of black radicalism back to the slave revolts. making clear that the communal and socialistic features of black Americans predated western Marxism and had a genealogy of its own: the "history of the American Negro is the history of this strife, this longing to attain self-conscious manhood, to merge his double-self into a better and truer self."[37]

Correspondingly, King inherited his communalistic notion of "collective deliverance" from the black church and slave resistance.[38] His brand of "socialism" (the defense of equality through collective action and the call for the reform of private property) and of a "Marxian" framework (the materialistic conception of history and the notion of class struggle) were also rooted in a black radical past in which the black worker and his rebellions shaped the black political tradition. If black intellectuals and activists appropriated European political theories and tradition, they customized and constantly reinterpreted it. Du Bois epitomized the process.

Both his articles in *The Crisis*, which he founded in 1910 and edited until 1934, and his repeated qualified endorsements of socialist candidates revealed how Du Bois fretted over committing himself and his readership to Marxist institutions. But his views on the appropriate relationship between black Americans and either the Socialist Party or the Communist Party, predicated on his personal political disappointments, are less illuminating than the core principles he held as the defining features of *his* socialism. Three key analyses form the Duboisian socialist framework: his historical examination of the interplay between race and class during slavery and Reconstruction, his belief in an interracial coalition to obtain justice and his indictment of profit-driven wealth inequalities. King would echo Du Bois in each one of these assumptions.

Du Bois's embrace of socialism as intellectual framework shines through in his monumental 1935 *Black Reconstruction in America: An Essay Toward a History of the Part Which Black Folk Played in the Attempt to Reconstruct Democracy in America, 1860–1880*. His class-based analysis of the post–Civil War years smacked of Marxian theory but also paralleled and deepened Douglass's insights. Du Bois theorized about the historical role of the "black worker," the title of his first chapter and the core notion of his analysis. Like Douglass and preceding King, Du Bois cast the black laborer as the utmost revolutionary agent, asserting: "It was thus the black worker, as founding stone of a new economic system in the nineteenth century for the modern world, who brought civil war in America. He was its underlying cause, in spite of every effort to base the strife upon union and national power."[39] After the war, the freedmen identified themselves with workers, the most exploited of them, forming in 1869 the National Colored Labor Union of which Douglass would become president. Accordingly, Du Bois portrayed black Americans as "an exploited class of cheap laborers"[40] who "belong distinctly to the working proletariat."[41] Appropriating the concept of the "proletariat," a class designed to launch the revolution, Du Bois stressed the decisive role of the "General Strike," the mass exodus of slaves from southern plantations during the Civil War, which he characterized as "one of the most extraordinary experiments of Marxism that the world, before the Russian revolution, had seen."[42]

Like Douglass, Du Bois also laid out the common interests of white and black laborers while deploring the entrenched racism that, particularly through unions, kept them apart. Recent and compelling scholarship has demonstrated how interracial coalitions in the South and Midwest did attempt to challenge Jim Crow. Class consciousness, although unarticulated as such, bounded workers beyond the color line.[43] From the Knights of Labor to populist movements, attempts to bring about economic equality through interracial coalitions challenged segregation and concentration of wealth throughout the land. During the 1880 and 1890s, for over two full decades, insurgencies, strikes, and mass political action engaged workers and farmers who strived to build broad class unity over a wide sector of the laboring population. Under the leadership of the Colored Farmers Alliance, the Farmers Alliance, and the People's

Party, disenfranchised and coerced poor whites opposed the rigid system of white supremacy that would eventually prevail in the late 1890s. Once crushed, these militant interracial struggles had long-lasting consequences on class- and race-based social relations in the entire country.[44] Although the "boundaries of the movements were both inclusive and exclusive in equal measure"[45] and although white racial solidarity often trumped efforts at solidarity across racial lines, micro episodes of workers' cross-racial solidarity in the South as well as in the North did constitute a threat to the emerging capitalist order.[46] In his biography of John Brown, Du Bois praised the white abolitionist not only for his act of interracial comradeship and solidarity but also for his rejection of an individualistic capitalism. Brown, according to Du Bois, "thought that society ought to be organized on a less selfish basis; for while material interests gained something by the deification of pure selfishness, men and women lost much by it. . . . He condemned the sale of land as a chattel."[47]

Du Bois began writing his seminal work during the Great Depression, which had worsened dramatically the plight of black Americans, laying bare the vulnerability of black workers and vindicating Du Bois's insight that capitalistic modernity was "based on the recognition and preservation of so-called racial distinctions."[48] In this regard, the Depression era was reminiscent of Reconstruction, exposing the unfinished quest for racial justice as both eras were equally limited in their definitions of democracy and citizenship for African Americans. But the Depression, coming on the heels of the First World War, also prompted Du Bois to question the sustainability of capitalism. In *Black Reconstruction,* he charted the decades following the Civil War in a dim light as, for him, "greed and jealousy became so fierce that they fought for trade and markets and materials and slaves all over the world until at last in 1914 the world flamed in war." The bloodshed, he added, would result in "grotesque Profits and Poverty, Plenty and Starvation, Empire and Democracy, staring at each other across World Depression."[49] The intrinsic values promoted by capitalism were to blame and, echoing Douglass, Du Bois lambasted the sanctity of private property in the United States. In a 1933 issue of *The Crisis,* he lauded President Franklin D. Roosevelt's "re-examination of the whole concept of Property" and pointed to the structural dysfunction of his country in which "there is something radically wrong with an industrial system that turns out simultaneously paupers and millionaires and sets a world starving because it has too much food."[50] In a 1948 article for the *Chicago Defender*, Du Bois defined socialism as "the attempt to regulate the activities of men for the good of the mass of people, instead of letting government or industry be run for the benefit of certain individuals." America's unfettered capitalism, he charged, "produces primarily for the profit of owners and not for use of the mass of people."[51] During his entire life, he called out a society oriented principally toward capital accumulation, competition, and wealth for the few.[52]

Despite his intellectual maturation and his admission that race was an independent category deserving its own analysis, Du Bois explicitly connected race with class and white supremacy with capitalism. Interracial struggles were necessary to truly rebuilding an egalitarian U.S. democracy. A real democracy had to be social and could only be substantive if workers were to unite to restructure the entire society: "The rebuilding, whether it comes now or a century later, will and must go back to the basic principles of Reconstruction in the United States during 1867–1876— Land, Light and Leading for slaves black, brown, yellow and white, under a dictatorship of the proletariat."[53]

His critique of the capitalist order was grounded in his reflection on race formation. If Du Bois had a race-based framework of inequalities and oppression, notoriously elevating the "color line" as the utmost world problem of the twentieth century, he would defend a Marxian philosophy which located racial exploitation "in political economy and class conflicts."[54] Pointing to the historical necessity of race for the marketplace, he contended that, notably during the King Cotton era, the "income bearing value of race prejudice was the cause and not the result of theories of race inferiority," locating racial ideology in the broader frame of wealth. Race was valuable because it was lucrative. It allowed for the accumulation of capital based on forced labor—blacks as *commodities*—but also, as Michael O'Malley suggests, as the sine qua non condition to the installment of a free-market-based industrial capitalism during Reconstruction, whose uncertainty was conjured by blacks as a reassuring *currency*.[55] Du Bois saw the subjection of blacks as most fundamentally an artifact of capitalist labor dynamics, a relation that originated in slavery. King too would remind his audience that antebellum slavery was the cornerstone of an American market-based economy which deliberately conflated race and class.[56] In 1965, King publicly embraced this Duboisian Marxist-inspired analysis of the construction of race by capital-holders. At the end of the Selma march, he unraveled "the economic foundation of the modern world" in a speech which deserves to be quoted at length:

> Toward the end of the Reconstruction era, something very significant happened. (*Listen to him*) That is what was known as the Populist Movement. (*Speak, sir*) The leaders of this movement began awakening the poor white masses and the former Negro slaves to the fact that they were being fleeced by the emerging Bourbon interests. Not only that, but they began uniting the Negro and white masses (*Yeah*) into a voting bloc that threatened to drive the Bourbon interests from the command posts of political power in the South. To meet this threat, the southern aristocracy began immediately to engineer this development of a segregated society. (*Right*)
>
> I want you to follow me through here because this is very important to see the roots of racism and the denial of the right to vote. Through their control of mass media, they revised the doctrine of white supremacy. They saturated the thinking of the poor white masses with it, (*Yes*) thus clouding their minds to the real issue involved in the Populist Movement. They then directed the placement on the books of the South of laws that made it a crime for Negroes and whites to come together as equals at any level. (*Yes, sir*) And that did it. That crippled and eventually destroyed the Populist Movement of the nineteenth century.
>
> If it may be said of the slavery era that the white man took the world and gave the Negro Jesus, then it may be said of the Reconstruction era that the southern aristocracy took the world and gave the poor white man Jim Crow. (*Yes, sir*) He gave him Jim Crow. (*Uh huh*) And when his wrinkled stomach cried out for the food that his empty pockets could not provide, (*Yes, sir*) he ate Jim Crow, a psychological bird that told him that no matter how bad off he was, at least he was a white man, better than the black man. (*Right sir*) And he ate Jim Crow. (*Uh huh*) And when his undernourished children cried out for the necessities that his low wages could not provide, he showed them the Jim Crow signs on the buses and in the stores, on the streets and in the public buildings. (*Yes, sir*) And his children, too, learned to feed upon Jim Crow, (*Speak*) their last outpost of psychological oblivion. (*Yes, sir*)[57]

The ruling class fed the poor white man with Jim Crow, King said boldly, reiterating Du Bois's radical interpretation of the invention of race.

In line with Marx's reading of the American situation with regard to labor and race, Du Bois had indeed argued that, as racism was an integral part of capitalism, the ruling class forcefully blunted class consciousness among workers, sabotaging Reconstruction's promises and enforcing racial hierarchy. He cogently argued that the "resulting color caste founded and retained by capitalism was adopted, forwarded and approved by white labor, and resulted in subordination of colored labor to white profits the world over."[58] In 1948, the Trinidadian-born sociologist Oliver Cromwell Cox developed a similar framework in his seminal work *Caste, Class and Race*, which demonstrated how racial subjection has been a crucial element of capitalist labor discipline. But whereas Cox, in a strict orthodoxy, would propose that "racial exploitation is merely one aspect of the problem of the proletarianization of labor, regardless of the color of the laborer," Du Bois never submitted race to class.[59] As Nikhil Pal Singh notes, if "Du Bois retained a commitment to race as the dialectical challenge to modern racism, just as Marxists retained class as the dialectical challenge to modern capitalism," he pondered that the universals of human freedom and equality he cherished "had been elaborated within and not against the European and American racialization of the world."[60]

In 1921, Du Bois questioned the relevance of a strictly class-based analysis to grasp American oppression, pondering that if "theoretically we are part of the world proletariat in the sense that we are mainly an exploited class of cheap laborers," he mitigated that assertion by adding that "practically we are not a part of the white proletariat to any great extent. We are the victims of their physical oppression, social ostracism, economic exclusion and personal hatred."[61] Though he joined the Socialist Party in 1911 and the Communist Party in 1961 (at the late age of 93), he always remained critical, bringing a "black point of view" to socialism.[62] His main qualification lay in the socialist scheme's inability to dislodge racial prejudice. To him, the concern of any socialist movement over the "excluded class"—blacks—was the litmus test of a true social democracy.[63] Two years before the publication of *Black Reconstruction*, he pointed to the inconsistencies and unsuitability of the Marxist paradigm to address American racial capitalism:

> How now does the philosophy of Karl Marx apply today to colored labor? First of all colored labor has no common ground with white labor in order

to raise the status of whites. No revolt of a white proletariat could be started if its object was to make black workers their economic, political and social equals. It is for this reason that American socialism for fifty years has been dumb on the Negro problem, and the communists cannot even get a respectful hearing in America unless they begin by expelling Negroes.

... [Marxism] must be modified in the United States of America and especially so far as the Negro group is concerned. The Negro is exploited to a degree that means poverty, crime, delinquency and indigence. And that exploitation comes not from a black capitalistic class but from the white capitalist and equally from the white proletariat.[64]

Du Bois struggled over the relevance of Marxism to black liberation until the end of his life. When in Atlanta, he shared his complex analysis with the students who attended his "Marxism and the Negro" seminar. Although he eventually joined the Communist Party, his belief on the crippling effect of an economic system skewed to the wealthy and dedicated to profit intellectually anchored him in a European social democratic tradition. Not only would he suggest that "the average man must give up the idea that the chief end of an American is to be a millionaire," but he also praised European welfare states, some of which he visited. He recalled being "astonished and encouraged" by what he saw socialism doing, particularly "the results of socialized medicine in England and progress in housing, health and worker's pensions in Sweden, Holland, Belgium and France" and their democratic control of the wealth they create in common. He urged the most oppressed citizens in the United States to draw from them. African Americans, because their experience has been interwoven into the tapestry of rebellions and dissent, and because they embody the social contradictions of bourgeois society, should lead the struggle for economic justice: "It is for American negroes in increasing numbers and more and more widely to insist upon the legal rights which are already theirs and then to add to that increasingly a socialistic form of government an insistence upon the welfare state which denies the further carrying out of industry for the profit of those corporations which monopolize wealth and power."[65]

Du Bois's charge against wealth inequality and cupidity surpassed economics reasoning to address morals and ethics. Predating King, Du Bois deplored the sickened values of American society. Even long before he joined the Socialist Party, Du Bois hammered his contemporaries for their materialism, deploring in 1904 that "the Gospel of money has risen triumphant in Church, State and University," a social deviance which "blinds us."[66] Three generations had elapsed since he first castigated the object-oriented leanings of society; in 1933 he kept admonishing Americans for their delusions: "We must rid ourselves of the persistent idea that the advance of mankind consists of the scaling off of layers who become incorporated with the world's upper and ruling classes, leaving always dead and inert below the ignorant and unenlightened mass of men," he lectured.[67]

His views on the role of what he called the "Talented Tenth" evolved accordingly, as he would come to doubt that a revolutionary elite of intellectuals could organize and launch the expected egalitarian racial upheaval. He initially had promoted his concept of the "Talented Tenth" in 1903, in the context of a dispute with Booker T. Washington, who advocated technical training and accommodation with whites as a means to empower blacks. Repudiating Washington's strategy, Du Bois held that racial progress was incidental to and derived from a militant black intelligentsia, an aristocracy endowed with a unique ability and responsibility to uplift and catapult black people from marginalization. Whether Du Bois remained committed to the elitist idea that "exceptional men" should lead blacks' emancipation is debated. He surely wrestled with the contradictory views that either the black proletariat or the Talented Tenth were the messianic forces able to propel justice. He hoped that, whether because of their working class origin or because of their immersion into the world of the dispossessed (as narrated in his 1928 novel, *Dark Princess*), the black elite would confront wealth inequities. Furthermore, he originally rejected applying class-struggle dynamics within the black world, pointing out that it does "not have the economic or political power, the ownership of machines and materials, the power to direct the processes of industry, the monopoly of capital and credit."[68] Accordingly, he defined the "more educated and prosperous class" of blacks as nonoppressive, with only a "small connection with the exploiters of wage and labor."[69] Rejecting the communists' critique of the black "petty bourgeoisie," he argued that black Americans were immune to class distinction and instead that the elite and the masses joined in solidarity to overcome oppression. "There is probably no group of 12 million persons in the modern world," he claimed in 1931, "which exhibits smaller contrasts in personal income than the American Negro group."[70]

Yet he gradually tipped into a disheartened view of intraracial class conflict, eventually excoriating the individualism and greed of the black bourgeoisie. In his 1940 memoir, *Dusk of Dawn*, he reconsidered the ability of any privileged class to transcend its power and to lead masses—and he bemoaned black elitism. He grew dispirited with a black middle-class loath to renounce its economic privilege and to serve the working class. In a 1933 address, Du Bois shunned those black professionals who held in contempt the "ignorant and unenlightened mass of men."[71] His indictment climaxed in 1948 when he reconfigured the concept of the "Talented Tenth." Only those who "realize the economic revolution now sweeping the world, and do not think that private profit is the measure of public welfare" are worthy of the label. "My Talented Tenth must be more than talented, and work not simply as individuals. Its passport to leadership was not learning, but expert knowledge of modern economics as it affected American blacks; and in addition to this and fundamental, would be its willingness to sacrifice and plan for such economic revolution in industry and just distribution of wealth, as would make the rise of our group possible."[72] By 1960, he had evolved into deploring that "a class structure began to arise within the Negro group which produced haves and have-nots and tended to encourage more successful negroes to join the forces of monopoly and exploitation and help victimize their own classes and any other lower classes that were possible."[73] Although a pure product of the black middle class in Atlanta, King expressed similar concern for the scorn with which some members of the black bourgeoisie endorsed the gospel of wealth while displaying scorn for the black urban poor.[74] Longing to belong to the American mainstream, this black elite was blind to the social perils entailed by an inclusion in a deeply "sick society," contaminated by the interplay of racism, imperialism, and capitalism.

The corrosive impact of this nefarious triangle on equality and justice were identified and protested by Du Bois. The substance of his critique of U.S. liberal democracy rested upon its very unequal and unfair fallout and upon the imperialistic impetus of laissez-faire capitalism. It is the irony of Du Bois's position in the 1930s that he was "simultaneously too egalitarian on class issues for the NAACP, whereas he was simultaneously too egalitarian on race for the Communist party."[75] Herbert Aptheker is right to suggest that, as with most African American leftists of his time, Du Bois "advocated his own brand of socialism, independent of any ideology or sponsorship."[76] Throughout his life, he remained steadfastly committed to an egalitarian definition of democracy. Fitting the definition of social democracy with its emphasis on economic security, universal rights, and strong redistributive government, Du Bois's views foreshadowed King's late pleas.[77] Although never close, they often echoed each other.

In an April 1960 piece entitled "Socialism and the American Negro," Du Bois once again called for "the stopping of a government of wealth for wealth" and "an industry carefully organized for the good of the masses of people and not for the manufacture of millionaires," concluding that capitalism was only able to bring war.[78] A handful of years later, in sync with these words, King wondered: "One day we must ask the question, 'Why are there forty million poor people in America?' When you ask that question, you begin to question the capitalistic economy."[79] Likewise, Du Bois prophesized that "unless we suffer a spiritual revolution by which men are going to envisage small incomes and limited resources and endless work for the larger goals of life, unless we have this, nothing can save civilization either for White people or Black."[80] King fully espoused this statement, as auguring for a "true revolution of values" which "will soon look uneasily on the glaring contrast of poverty and wealth."[81]

2 The Prophets of Justice

If Du Bois puzzled over the question of party affiliation, he typified many black radicals who, because of their anti-imperialism and searing indictment of an economic exploitation based on race, were drawn to either the socialist or the communist parties. The civil rights movement, whose official origin could be dated to the 1884 call for the National Afro-American League (founded in 1890), unfolded in a post-Reconstruction era filled with radical demands for economic justice.[1] The labor movement, Progressivism, the Social Gospel movement, and Socialism sprang from them. The radicalism of Southern African American leftists since then was transmitted to King through his readings and encounters, but also through the memories of labor and communist militancy in Atlanta during the 1930s.

Segregated in the most menial jobs, black workers were eager to hear a political message combining race and class consciousness in a coherent form of radicalism. Against all odds, black workers engaged in radical activities to challenge their exploitation in the workplace, hardly ever considering the "race question" apart from the "labor question."[2] By the end of the nineteenth century, tens of thousands of black workers were union members, both in the North and the South. The movement expanded as millions of unskilled black Southerners migrated (either to southern cities or above the Mason-Dixon line) between the wars. The rise of an industrial unionism in the 1930s elaborated a social citizenship and the revival of a radical tradition which had remained unbroken since the freedmen were denied land tenure and driven primarily into the working class.

Concerns over economic justice and racial equality, blending a class-based analysis with a subtle view of black liberation, were widely shared in the North but not exclusively. Born and developed in the northern states, the radical left was, although minor, a significant presence in the South. Communists, Socialists, and unions challenged white supremacy and labor exploitation in ways that appealed to the Southern black "culture of opposition."[3] Because Southern blacks were mainly exploited workers whose cheap work was central to the New South, economic justice took center stage in their demands. The NAACP branches established in the South therefore took an undeniable working-class and labor activism flavor.[4] The political agenda of black workers claimed a dimension of citizenship involving economic rights and the reallocation of resources. Their perception that alternatives to the existing distribution of power and property were imperative to racial equality fed their socialistic leaning.

THE NEGRO AND SOCIALISM

Founded in 1901. the American Socialist Party was split over the issue of race. If some sections in the right wing and prominent members like Victor Berger (in 1902, the first Socialist to be elected to Congress) endorsed segregation, key figures did speak out for racial justice.[5] Some of them actively cooperated with Du Bois's Niagara movement to promote racial justice, and Socialist activists like Mary White Ovington were instrumental in the foundation of the National Association for the Advancement of Colored People (NAACP) in 1909. Socialist leaders such as Eugene Debs and Big Bill Haywood along with Daniel De Leon (of the Socialist Labor Party), created the Industrial Workers of the World in 1905 to explicitly challenge the American Federation of Labor's blatant racist practices. Debs, who ran four consecutive presidential campaigns from 1904 on, put the issue of the entanglement of race and class at the forefront. The meaning of his notorious statement that socialism had "nothing special to offer to the Negro" has been scrutinized and debated.[6] Whether he meant that, by nature, class trumped race in the Socialist framework, is still not settled. Furthermore, his equivocal call to being "committed to colorblind justice" was evocative of the ongoing tensions on the race issue within the party, which was closely tied to prejudiced organized labor. Ambivalent and at time inconsistent on the race question, Debs nevertheless worked to solve the problem organized labor presented to blacks by promoting absolute racial equality. He indubitably advocated economic freedom along with political equality but, mostly, he fought for a profound reform of his party's own racial prejudices: "I say that the Socialist Party would be false to its historic mission, violate the fundamental principles of Socialism, deny its philosophy and repudiate its own teachings if, on account of race considerations, it sought to exclude any human being from political equality and economic freedom."[7] Probably influenced by Du Bois's works, Debs elaborated an evolving dialectic on the role of black workers relating class exploitation to racial oppression. which added fuel to the Socialist Party's attractiveness among African Americans, notably Du Bois, who voted for Debs in 1904 and joined the party in 1911.[8]

Hubert Harrison, a West Indian immigrant who came to New York in 1906, joined the Socialist Party in 1909. About to become the most promising Socialist intellectual in New York, Harrison founded the Colored Socialist Club and co-edited the Socialist Party's newspaper *The Masses* in 1911. That year, A. Philip Randolph Joined the party. North Carolina native Chandler Owen, who was also rooted in organized labor, joined Randolph in founding *The Messenger* from a black unionist monthly, which turned out to be "the only radical Negro magazine" in 1917. Along with another West Indian immigrant, Frank R. Crosswaith, they championed the formation of interracial alliances between black and white workers and labored to strengthen the cooperation between the party and antiracist activists, notably the NAACP. Publications like *The Messenger* or the *New York Call* sought to reconcile black workers with a classist analysis of oppression, urging them to join the colorblind Industrial Workers of the World, while helping the Socialist Party to grasp the full extent of racial oppression. In 1909, Harrison, who was the leading black Socialist spokesman until 1914, published a commentary that echoed Du Bois's analysis:

> In short, the exploitation of the Negro worker is keener than that of any group of white workers in America. Now, the mission of the Socialist Party is to free the working class from exploitation, and since the Negro is the most ruthlessly exploited working-class group in America, the duty of the party to champion his cause is as clear as day. This is the crucial test of socialism's sincerity. . . .[9]

Yet, when Harrison launched the Colored Socialist Club, Du Bois lambasted such racial separation. Most black Socialists, concentrated in the Harlem unit (A. Philip Randolph, Chandler Owen, Richard B. Moore, Otto Huiswood, Cyril Briggs, William Bridges, W. A. Domingo, and Lovett Fort-Whiteman) pleaded for interracial solidarity within the party. Following Debs's hope that a unified working class would overthrow capitalistic exploitation and hence racial prejudice, Randolph assumed that racial prejudice was "an incident of the larger world problem of class conflict."[10] The goal was to build an interracial industrial democracy, sustained by a worker's culture of solidarity. Randolph suggested that blacks give up on the AFL (American Federation of Labor) and instead join the Wooblies (Industrial Workers of the World).

Most of the black Socialists would grow dispirited by the reductionist approach to race harbored by the Party's leadership. Du Bois and Harrison left in 1912. Socialists Cyril Briggs and Fort-Whiteman migrated to the Communist Party in 1920, longing for a radical egalitarianism explicitly focused on the needs of the most despised and "most thoroughly exploited of the American proletariat."[11] Despite its best effort to contain black activists' flood, with leaflets titled "Why Negroes Should Be Socialists"[12] and regular editorials in *The Messenger,* the Socialist Party succumbed to what was seen as their penchant to—to put it in Harrison's words—"put [the white] race first, before class."[13]

In 1919, the American Communist Party (CPUSA) sprang from a split of the Socialist Party. It adapted Marxist-Leninist principles to the American setting, in ways that would cater to blacks. Both Vladimir I. Lenin and Leon Trotsky addressed the confluence of race and class in the United States.[14] The CPUSA initially disregarded the racial nature of blacks' oppression but evolved toward an imperialistic framework in which Southern blacks would become yet another colonized nation of color. In 1928, at the Sixth Congress of the Comitern held in Moscow, a Negro Commission, a subcommittee of the Colonial Commission, debated on whether American blacks were entitled to nationhood. Harry Haywood, a black Communist, replied for the affirmative and defended the right to self-determination. which he saw as the proper way to circumvent the class versus race pitfall in which the Socialist Party was engulfed:

> What was clear to me was that our thesis of self-determination had correctly elevated the fight for Black rights to a revolutionary position, whereas the (other) theories attempted to downgrade the movement, seeing it as a minor aspect of the class struggle. Our thesis put the question in the proper perspective: that is, as a struggle attacking the very foundation of American imperialism, an integral part of the struggle of the American working class as a whole.[15]

To Haywood, African Americans' liberation in the Black Belt was a national revolutionary movement, synecdochical of a worldwide proletarian upsurge.[16] The Black Belt secession was an extension of democratic self-determination, which at the micro-level, would extend democracy in the workplace. providing workers with social control over what they produced and the social surplus created. Claude Lightfoot, a black Communist leader from Arkansas based in Chicago, defined the process of black liberation as the first step toward the overthrow of the entire economic system, reasoning that "since capitalism is the source of the inferior status of black people, it would follow that only with the elimination of the system can Negroes gain equality."[17] As opposed to Garveyism, Southern blacks' secession was spared from the accusation of standing for petty bourgeois nationalism at odds with working-class internationalism.

The inroads made by Communism into the black liberation struggle and the ability of the Bolshevik revolution to speak to black Americans' yearning for justice in the context of a racialized economic exploitation should not be overlooked. It was for instance illustrated by Harlem publications like *The Crusader*, a monthly newspaper affiliated with the African Blood Brotherhood (ABB). The black liberation group and its journal were founded in the wake of the Russian revolution by West Indian journalist Cyril Briggs. Willing to create a black Socialist commonwealth, Briggs substantiated the interface between class consciousness, socialism, racial pride, and anti-imperialism. *The Crusader,* published from 1919 to 1922, embodied the intellectual attempts to reconcile Communism and black liberation by offering a subtle analysis of the race and class dialectic. If the newspaper praised the Bolshevik revolution as the utmost template for emancipation, race relations and class solidarity in the United States were the core issue addressed. Briggs challenged the notion that interracial strategy was specious and self-deceptive, calling for pragmatism. Acknowledging that whites were still "potential enemies," he nonetheless defended unity across the color line:

> The Negro masses must get out of their minds the stupid idea that it is necessary for two groups to love each other before they can enter into an alliance against their common enemy. Not love or hatred, but identity of interest at the moment dictates the tactics of practical people.[18]

Predating the mindset of Socialist civil right activist and organizer Bayard Rustin, Briggs sought to build a large interracial coalition, pushing for an economic-justice agenda and the desegregation of labor. To African American leftist intellectuals and activists, blacks would not attain or secure full citizenship rights absent economic power. But Briggs, no more than Du Bois, never surrendered on the centrality of race. During its four years of publication, the newspaper defended racial pride along with interracial solidarity. Briggs, upon joining the Communist Party, as did most of the ABB, voiced his radical position on the role of the black revolutionary: "Let it be understood then that I am a Negro—Negro first last and all the time. Negro by birth, choice and by the treatment which denies to Negroes the right of being American citizens."[19] For many African American Socialists, far from collapsing their racial identities into a classist framework, endorsing Marxism was consistent with black liberation and nationalism. Fort-Whiteman, the first African American to study in Moscow, proposed an American Negro Labor Congress (ANLC) to achieve "working-class hegemony" in the community.[20] The Communist Party, endorsing Haywood's position, officially supported African Americans' self-determination in the South, viewing them as an internal colony seeking its independence. But as far as the party's leadership was concerned,

the "Negro nation" paradigm—despite a commitment to equality—
remained contentious.

A year before the Sixth Congress Leon Trotsky was expelled from the
Party. He had developed a more nuanced approach to the "Negro ques-
tion" in America and by the early 1930s, his supporters gained currency in
the United States. Impressed by Garveyism's outreach to the northern
black working class, Trotsky pondered over African Americans' profound
nationalist impulse.[21] Viewing them as the most dynamic element of the
American working class, he leaned toward the self-determination line.
But within the Communist League of America (CLA), supporters of
Trotsky's dissent denied this assumption and reformulated the black
American experience, pointing to its quest for an inclusive citizenship in
the U.S. nation-state. African Trinidadian historian C. L. R. James, close to
Trotsky, opposed the Black Belt thesis on the ground that black Americans
were first and foremost, *Americans:*

> The Negroes are for the most part proletarian or semi-proletarian and
> therefore the struggle of the Negroes is fundamentally a class question. The
> Negroes do not constitute a nation, but, owing to their special situation,
> their segregation; economic, social, and political oppression; the difference
> in color which singles them out so easily from the rest of the community;
> their problems become the problem of a national minority.[22]

The Socialist Worker's Party (SWP; a merger of the CLA with A. J.
Muste's American Workers Party in 1934) eventually defended a less clear-
cut agenda: at its first convention, held in 1939, it adopted two contradictory resolutions on the black question. "The SWP and Negro Work,"
defined blacks as "the vanguard of the proletarian revolution" whereas the
second resolution, "The Right of Self-Determination and the Negro in the
United States and North America," was geared toward the defense of a
"Negro State." But, like the CPUSA, the SWP (which attracted far fewer
black workers than did the CPUSA) sought to challenge black nationalism
by asserting that national, race, and class consciousness were dialectically
interlinked. In any case, leftist parties' call for an interracial proletarian
regime gained traction among northern blacks, disenchanted by other
progressive movements and willing to reconcile racial pride with the fight
against exploitation. Whether Trotskyites or not, communists' strong

mobilization for racial justice and unionization blended demands for human rights in the Jim Crow South as well as economic justice for black workers. The only political institution promoting and practicing racial equality, the Communist Party attracted a significant number of African Americans. Furthermore, from an ideological standpoint, blacks were generally more favorably disposed toward a party championing peace and anticolonialism abroad and economic justice at home than was the rest of the population. Even if they doubted the advent of a proletarian revolution and the overthrow of a capitalist government, the scope of blacks' "radical imagination" was worldwide.[23] For most black leftist radicals, anti-imperialism, freedom, and economic rights were closely tied.

BLACK DISSENTERS AND THE POLITICAL ECONOMY OF RACE

Far from being manipulated by Moscow, black workers exerted their agency and used the Communist Party to call attention to racialized economic and social inequalities. In 1925, the American National Negro Congress (ANLC) was established as the main black communist organization. The Congress championed a "New Negro," defiant and militant. In the pages of *The Liberator*, the ANLC's official publication launched in 1929, the communist-led revolution was presented as the natural inheritor of the black protest and slaves' resistance tradition. *The Liberator*, named after Garrison's abolitionist newspaper, defended interracial solidarity but articulated class consciousness in ways that never belittled racial specificity. Black agency shined through the newspaper's editorials and challenged the notion that African American workers were "used" by the CP, inactive instruments of a leftist agenda. Instead, the black worker was portrayed as the pivotal agent of the expected anticapitalist and anticolonial upheaval. Eschewing separation as well as assimilation, the journal was a black working-class radical voice castigating accommodation but disavowing black separatism. Unflinching against the white ruling class, its editorials called for the formation of a proletarian vanguard composed of class-conscious blacks along with antiracist white workers.[24] Notably, the newspaper circulated throughout the South amongst radicals. Hosea Hudson, a prominent Communist and union organizer in Alabama and Georgia, pointed out in his memoir that, as many southern black workers were illiterate, a copy of the *Liberator* would often be read aloud.[25]

African Americans' gravitation toward the Marxist left in the first part of the twentieth century is not to be overstated but neither to be ignored. Certainly, only hundreds of dues-paying blacks were members of the Communist Party, but approximately 20,000 people were directly involved in communist-led or sponsored organizations such as the International Labor Defense, the Sharecroppers Union, the International Workers Order, the League of Young Southerners, and the Southern Negro Youth Congress.[26] Many intellectuals supported left-wing movements until the 1920s and 1930s not only because they doubted the ability of liberal capitalism to free blacks but also because they had grown convinced that only international support and solidarity could to break the back of Jim Crow. Du Bois reasoned that Pan-Africanism, internationalism, and the couching of black liberation in terms of human rights were the paths to freedom and equality. Du Bois was accordingly the torchbearer and figurehead of the Pan-African Congresses, whose first edition was held in Paris in 1919, modeling itself on the Versailles Conference that ended the First World War. The Congress presented resolutions to the new League of Nations, requesting deep changes in European black colonies and throughout the Americas. Du Bois also represented the NAACP at the first conference of the League of Nations in 1921 in the hope that the loyalty of peoples of color during the war would result in their gaining full citizenship. African Americans' hope for freedom and equality after the First World War turned out to be an unfulfilled promise, throwing the more militant among them into the arms of more radical organizations.

The economic Depression and Franklin D. Roosevelt's election provided the context for the re-emergence of class-based demands on the part of black workers, hit harder than any other group in American society, by virtue of a discriminatory labor market. If a quarter of the general American workforce was unemployed at the peak of the economic downturn, on average more than half of black workers lost their jobs. They were the "last to be hired and the first fired," a discriminatory pattern captured in Martin Luther King's hometown by the popular saying: "No Jobs for

[Blacks] Until Every White Man Has a Job."[27] In the South, where the majority of African Americans farmed, the dramatic drop of agricultural prices added to their deprivation. Besides, as Jim Crowism tightened its grip on their daily lives, blacks also faced tremendous hardship when seeking governmental relief and protection.

For many black intellectuals, the New Deal era bolstered their strong radical critique of American liberalism's neglect of democratic concerns. Simultaneously, blacks' plight and strength as workers committed to interracial solidarity placed them at the center of labor organizing strategies. They nudged the government leftward and supported a Democratic president who promised economic security for all. Roosevelt doubtlessly transformed the nature of American liberalism to the extent that the role of the federal government was revisited as well as the substance and scope of American citizenship. Linking the latter to social rights was a revolutionary ambition and although it went unfulfilled, the aspiration was unprecedented since the days of Reconstruction.[28] If most black institutions also praised the president for appointing African Americans to government jobs and starting a dialogue with the black community, many black intellectuals, however, like Du Bois and Ralph Bunche, called on Roosevelt's administration to solve the glaring tension between its egalitarian commitments and the welfare social policies actually being implemented. The bulk of New Deal legislation aided the middle classes, they argued, not the working poor, let alone the black poor.

Even civil rights leaders who wholeheartedly aligned themselves with New Deal policies pushed for a more expansive view of justice and equality. Lester Granger of the National Urban League, Walter White of the NAACP, John P. Davis of the National Negro Congress, and A. Philip Randolph of the Brotherhood of Sleeping Car Porters (BSCP) praised the New Deal's relief programs, notably Roosevelt's Works Project Administration (WPA), but bemoaned the fact that while the unemployed were provided much needed jobs, black Americans did not share in the fruits of those jobs on an equal basis with whites. They too, in the footsteps of black leftists, came to acknowledge that African Americans were inherently working class, granting that racial equality could only be achieved through a combination of antiracist policies and a robust wealth redistribution. Despite their new consideration of the workers' condition, these liberal institutions were seen as insufficiently militant. In 1934, socialist Abram Harris urged mainstream civil rights leaders to set aside their core agenda to demand radical economic reform, confronting the NAACP:

> Instead of continuing to oppose racial discrimination on the job and in pay and various manifestations of anti-Negro feeling among white workers, the Association would attempt to get Negroes to view their special grievances as a natural part of the larger issues of American labor as a whole.[29]

Still struggling in the late 1930s against the ravages of the Great Depression, many blacks hoped that a radical revision of the New Deal would bring substantive economic and racial justice to the country, particularly in the Jim Crow South. The Popular Front that emerged in 1935 saw American Communists joining New Dealers and trade unionists to build a multiracial cultural and political movement. The Southern Conference for Human Welfare (SCHW) too, launched in 1938, intended to spur New Dealers into adopting stronger redistributive policies. An off-spring of the Popular Front and comprised of liberals and radicals, the SCHW was an interracial organization promoting economic justice and racial equality. Dedicated to enacting fully the New Deal's reforms, the SCHW attracted many southern blacks. They accounted for one-quarter of the organization's twelve hundred delegates and actively participated (to the extent that the SCHW had leverage) in the economic and social reconstruction of the South.[30] Dismissed *de facto* by the FBI as a subversive "communist" organization, a label the SCHW tried to straddle, it was indeed hospitable to leftist radicals.

Sponsored but not controlled by the Communist Party, the Popular Front attracted black artists and activists such as Langston Hughes and Richard Wright. In 1934, international performer Paul Robeson went to Moscow and began to lean toward left-wing radical ideas. In 1939, during a CBS radio program, he sang the "Ballad for Americans," which captured the progressive mindset of the time and celebrated solidarity and equality among workers of all races.[31] A personal friend to Robeson, Howard University political scientist Ralph Bunche met with black expatriate radicals and attended socialist rallies addressed by Norman Thomas. Lambasting New Deal policies for their inadequacies in addressing the plight of black workers, he published his first book in 1936, *A World View of Race,* hailed by Du Bois, in which he averred, "if we can remedy the fundamental economic dilemmas of our social structure . . . the race problem will take care of itself."[32] To him, radical revolutionaries seemed well fitted to address the conflation of race and class.

Organizations in the cultural orbit of the CPUSA like the League of Struggle for Negro Rights, the American Negro Labor Congress, the United Front Scottsboro Committee and the National Unemployed Councils were central to the civil rights movement of the 1930s and 1940s. In northern cities like Chicago, which greeted hundreds of thousands of blacks who had migrated from the rural South, an interracial coalition and a Negro People's Front exemplified how African Americans appropriated, accommodated, and vigorously deployed communism in ways that spoke first and foremost to the objective conditions of the black urban working-class.[33]

Chicago, however, was also home to another black civil rights organization, the National Urban League, which defended, along with the NAACP, a more liberal definition of racial progress: economic racial uplift. Arguably, it entailed a middle-class approach to emancipation and, according to Touré Reed, a form of respectability politics predicated upon "the elimination of black undesirables and the simultaneous elevation of the so-called Negro better classes."[34] This strategy exposed class tensions among African Americans and the degree to which economic inequality and the moral authority of the black elite somewhat hindered a radical embrace of socialism. Besides, although the revolutionary left offered African Americans a vehicle to address their grievances, most civil rights activists of the period abstained from reference to socialism and communism as they dreaded the anti-American stigma attached to these labels and doubted an ideology alien to them. Moreover, most black Americans yearned to obtain full inclusion and expected their share of property rather than to abolish capitalism. Even those who had come to understand class conflict as fundamental to black subordination distrusted labor organization and leftist institutions. They also saw a Communist Party rife with contradictions with regard to imperialism, which culminated with the unexpected German-Soviet nonaggression pact in 1939. Unexpectedly, the Communist leadership accommodated the utmost racist regime of Hitler's Germany. The withdrawal of the pact two years later eventually resulted in Russia's participation in the allies' war effort against Nazism and, despite the subsequent CPUSA's embrace of the segregationist Democratic Party, it would retain most of its antiracist credit in the United States.

Adding to the perplexities caused by mounting perils in Europe and Russia's position, the nagging question in black American leftists' ranks remained the domestic issue of the conflicting entanglement of class and race consciousness. More than most, the prevalence of an entrenched white racism amongst white workers discredited radical leftist parties as delusional.[35] Blacks' lived experience of "race," chiefly in the South, complicated the theoretical Marxist framework, as joining unions was fraught with perils and difficulties. The ability of white workers to overcome their prejudice for the sake of building an interracial revolutionary coalition demanded way too big a leap of faith on the part of most black workers.

Claude McKay, one of the many Caribbean immigrants in New York gravitating toward communism, who joined Briggs to establish a revolutionary working-class organization in Harlem, quarreled with Du Bois over the main source of African Americans' subjection. Capitalism being contingent on black oppression, could black workers win white workers to the centrality of racism in their proletarian experience? Should black workers sacrifice their racial demands to those of the working class as a whole? McKay contended that capitalism and class oppression prevailed over racism, to which Du Bois answered wondering whether it was up to blacks to "assume on the part of unlettered and suppressed masses of white workers, a clearness of thought, a sense of human brotherhood, that is sadly lacking in the most educated classes."[36] While connecting white supremacy with capitalism, Du Bois reflected the views of many of his contemporaries when doubting leftist parties' ability to be more than relevant bully pulpits for addressing racism and colonialism. A former friend of his, Howard University economics professor Abram Harris, who published *The Black Worker* in 1931, contended for his part that class, not race, was the main source of racial exploitation and admonished Du Bois for his distrust of white workers and his racialist philosophy.[37]

A. Philip Randolph, a committed Socialist until 1940, faced similar dilemmas, vacillating throughout his life between organizing black workers interracially within the AFL or autonomously. In 1925, he became the general organizer and ultimately president of the Brotherhood of Sleeping Car Porters, made up mostly of black workers. He labored relentlessly to associate it with the AFL, despite or because of its structural racism and regardless of the creation of the racially egalitarian Congress of Industrial Organizations (CIO) in 1935.[38] His growing animosity to the Communist Party and his faith in his ability to challenge the AFL's pattern of prejudice sustained his choice. However, when the National Negro Congress (NNC), was created in 1935 to unite black and white workers and to pressure New Deal administrators for labor and civil rights, Randolph consented to become its president notwithstanding its communist origin. Ralph Bunche and also Ella Baker, who would play a key role organizing southerners during the 1950s and 1960s, were also active members in the newly formed organization. Randolph, willing to enmesh black liberation with labor rights, also soldiered to ally the new organization with the CIO.[39] The opening session of the NNC gathered an impressive crowd of 5,000 progressives of all striped from New Dealers to Garveyists, Communists to Republicans.[40]

If he would leave the NNC in 1940 after a communist upheaval within its ranks, Randolph never gave up his idea that there would be no racial equality without socialism and that the latter entailed bridging over racial lines. To him, organized labor was the best vehicle to address African Americans strivings. Yet, he came to grasp the peculiarity of the black experience in America. The formation of the March on Washington Movement (MOWM), which he created in 1941 to persuade President Roosevelt to desegregate the military, was, like the BSPC, a *black* working-class movement, only open to African Americans. In both instances, in line with Briggs and *The Crusader*, racial pride was a prerequisite for an effective cross-racial alliance. As Cornelius Bynum notes, Randolph's recognition of the interrelatedness of "civil, social and economic rights in securing genuine social justice harkened back to Du Bois."[41] Like him, Randolph remained convinced that capitalism fomented racial violence to divide and conquer along class lines and yet, that an interracial alliance should never entail curtailing blacks' racial pride.

Such an equation was of utmost relevance in the South where the Communist Party had organized four hundred textile-industry black workers along with whites during the 1929 Gastonia strike. To many southern blacks, Communist involvement in Gastonia showed that their comprehension of exploitation did not entail subsuming race under class but rather that the party "committed itself to racial equality in the service of class struggle."[42] Moreover, as most southern blacks were agricultural workers, left-wing organizations including the Alabama Sharecroppers Union (communist-led) and the Southern Tenant Farmers Union (socialist-led and mostly active in Arkansas, Texas, Missouri, Tennessee, Oklahoma, and Missouri) adapted their tactics and organizing methods to their particular grievances.

During the 1930s, communist organizers campaigned throughout the South to promote labor reform and interracial cooperation and attempted to organize black workers according to these principles. In 1932, Socialist and Christian activist Myles Horton, who had visited Denmark, Europe's poster child for Social Democracy, founded Tennessee's Highlander Folk School in 1932.[43] Championing labor organizing, free education, and racial integration, the school blended Social Gospel theology and leftist politics and trained generations of activists. Rosa Parks and Martin Luther King Jr. would stand as the school's most prominent seminar's attendees in the 1950s. Wrongly portrayed as "hot-bed of communism" by the FBI, the school was undoubtedly subversive in the South. It enmeshed radical labor with opposition to Jim Crow, infusing workers' struggle with racial egalitarianism and, after the Second World War, civil rights organizing with a proletarian framework.[44] Overcoming racial prejudice to unite workers remained indeed an ambitious task, humorously captured by George Schuyler's 1931 satire *Black No More* : "The mill hands kept so busy talking about Negro blood that no one thought about discussing wages and hours of labor."[45]

The Southern Negro Youth Congress (SNYC), an offshoot of the National Negro Congress, was founded in 1937. Based in Richmond, Virginia, the SNYC gathered communists and noncommunist leftists and planned on campaigning throughout the South for voting rights and desegregation as well as for jobs and labor rights. Among the key founders was Richmond native James E. Jackson. whose university research on black poverty in the South had been supervised by Ralph Bunche at Howard. His wife-to-be, Esther Cooper, who would be elected executive secretary of the SNYC in 1942, fostered a Marxist critique of gender inequality.[46] Esther and Jim Jackson, friends to Du Bois, viewed black liberation as contingent on "a broad multiracial coalition of the oppressed and exploited to put an end to the rule of the monopoly successors of the slave power."[47] Interestingly, both Robeson and Du Bois attended the inaugural convention of this revolutionary movement. The SNYC, according to Julian Bond, was the Students Nonviolent Coordinating Committee's most inspiring forerunner, giving the next generation of black activists a strong sense of the degree to which "race was immensely complicated by greed, that prejudice and poverty were necessarily linked and that it would tale organized massaction to carry the day for freedom."[48] The opening convention of the Congress in 1937 assembled 534 delegates representing 250,000 young people in 23 states willing to organizing "wave upon wave of Southern Negro Americans, united in fraternity with the awakening white South, leading a crusade of freedom for rightful place in the rebirth of the South."[49] Dedicated to representing the southern working class and to addressing the economic strivings of the black southern worker, the inexperienced delegates were assisted by adults.

Mordecai Johnson, president of Howard University, was one of them and the keynoter at the Congress. A black Christian Socialist, the Baptist preacher who would mentor and deeply influence King, contended before the young radicals assembled: "The greatest damage to Democracy in America is not Communism or Socialism, but the political situation in which most men are no longer free to express themselves."[50] He illustrated how, as Robin Kelley notes, a radical interpretation of Christianity "was a major factor in drawing blacks into the Communist Party and its mass organization."[51] Interestingly enough, also present among the adults was Angelo Herndon, a Young Communist League member who would change the face of radicalism in King's hometown.

3 The City and the Church

The surroundings of King's upbringing were indeed closely interwoven with people and groups mobilizing to restructure the relations of political and economic power in Dixie. The most telling example was Benjamin Mays whom King, his student at Morehouse College when King was fifteen years old, would call his "spiritual mentor." Son of a tenant farmer in rural South Carolina, Mays had roots in Atlanta long before he became Morehouse College's sixth president in 1940. He served as pastor of Shiloh Baptist Church from 1921 to 1923 and was then recruited by Morehouse president John Hope as a mathematics teacher and debate coach. In 1926, while Mays was a faculty member, Martin Luther King Sr. started his ministerial degree at Morehouse. Mays, an influential figure and a role model for many young black Atlantans, had long appreciated Marxists' increased attention to organizing African American workers and to theorizing about the path to black liberation. Though he bemoaned communist atheism, May publicly praised Eugene Debs, whom he credits for his personal dedication to justice:

> I'm deeply impressed with the words of Eugene Debs writing while a prisoner in a federal prison in Atlanta. These are the words, "As long as there is a lower class, I'm in it. As long as there is a man in jail, I'm not free." Eugene Debs inspired me greatly. To me, Eugene Debs has shaped my sensitivity for

the poor, the diseased and those who have given their lives for those sick and poor, the great and the small, the high and the low.[1]

Another Morehouse professor at that time, sociologist E. Franklin Frazier, was supportive of socialist ideas (he was an avid reader of *The Messenger* when he was in New York). Frazier praised social democracies' public policies, which he had witnessed firsthand during his stay in Denmark in 1921–1922 as a fellow of the American Scandinavian Foundation. Influenced by Marxian theory, he engaged in life-long social science scholarship to come to terms with the entanglements of race and class. Appointed at Morehouse in 1923 and also serving as director of the Atlanta School of Social Work at Atlanta University from 1926 to 1927, he developed a keen interest in class distinctions, which would culminate with his seminal 1957 book *Black Bourgeoisie*. Mays, Du Bois, Frazier, and many other black socialists were spiritual and intellectual figureheads who shaped Atlanta's intelligentsia, instilling a new understanding of capitalist exploitation as it related to race.

RED ATLANTA

Atlanta was home to a strong dissenting tradition within black communities in which labor, race, civil rights, class, and gender issues were consistently intertwined. The 1906 riot, which decimated many black districts and inspired Du Bois's "litany," was a touchstone of Atlanta's black community's collective history and identity in which class and racial tensions coalesced.[2] About Georgia, Du Bois wrote that "the Negro problems have seemed to be centered in this State," and while community protest in the Black Belt was nothing short of dynamic, the state capital held a unique position.[3] Home to the South's largest population of college-educated African Americans, Atlanta was a cradle of black resistance. The distinctive collective historical consciousness of black Atlanta was also filled with interracial labor organizing and proletarian protest against racial economic exploitation. Not only was Atlanta "exceptional because of its keen orientation toward a world capitalist system" but more than anywhere else in the New South, its identity and history were rooted in race.[4]

The 1881 Washerwomen's Strike in Atlanta, one of most successful direct action protests carried out by working class African Americans in the late nineteenth century, exemplifies a tradition of protest linking class, race, and gender. More than three thousand laundresses, supported by black Atlanta's churches and main institutions, established an interracial labor organization and mobilized for better wages and the recognition of household domestic workers.[5] African American women were the most engaged in organized agitation in many areas.[6] Although the Communist Party picked Birmingham, Alabama, to reach out to southern workers, its influence percolated throughout Dixie and reached Atlanta. As the Great Depression swept the South, resulting in the flare-up of racism as workers competed for scarce resources, a labor-based civil rights movement dovetailed with the Communist Party's sharp criticism of the economic and social order.[7]

The effects of the Great Depression were so severe in the city of Atlanta that it almost drove the local government to bankruptcy. If black agricultural workers faced major economic hardships, hundreds of thousands lost their jobs in the city of Atlanta itself: only 48 percent of the city's workforce was gainfully employed in 1930. In 1933, sixty thousand Atlantans were on the welfare rolls. Though still a child, Martin Luther King was struck by the violence poverty wrecked on his region. As more and more analysts described the depression as an implacable result of capitalism's internal contradictions, King situated the origin of his economic critique in the traumatizing spectacle of misery during the Depression:

> I was born in the late twenties on the verge of the Great Depression, which was to spread its disastrous arms into every corner of this nation for over a decade. I was much too young to remember the beginning of this depression, but I do recall, when I was about five years of age, how I questioned my parents about the numerous people standing in breadlines. I can see the effects of this early childhood experience on my present anticapitalistic feelings.[8]

In rural areas, Georgian sharecroppers were plunged into extreme poverty, which added to and worsened preexisting economic exploitation and disenfranchisement. Until Roosevelt's election, almost no black Atlantans had been allowed to participate to public life, whatever his social standing. Thousands of black Georgian sharecroppers were thrown off the land by the discriminatory practices in the 1930s. This situation bolstered leftist organizing, further deepening the intraracial tensions between workers but also between black workers and the black middle class.

Since Booker T. Washington's accommodationist 1895 Atlanta Compromise, in which he advised southern blacks to favor racial "uplift" and economic independence over demands for political and social rights, intraracial class polarization had been salient in the city. Washington rose to fame with this conciliatory call not only to tone down racial grievances but also to ally with capitalists rather than join labor unions. He therefore alienated many black workers despite his claim to give "purpose and dignity to the black working-class."[9] Notwithstanding a strong network of racial solidarity and bonds of community, the black middle class in the South experienced racial inequality differently compared to poor and working-class African Americans. At times, they expressed their contempt for the dispossessed in ways that ignited intraracial class tensions.[10] Interestingly enough, the elitist term "Talented Tenth" was used for the first time in Atlanta in 1896 by Henry T. Morehouse, the white founder of the eponymous school King and scores of young African American men would attend. Atlanta was hence home to the most significant signifier of intraracial class differences.

Lingering class-based conflicts among black Atlantans during the 1930s would have particularly far-reaching consequences, setting "the stage for the widening gulf between those African-Americans who have been able to take advantage of positive recognition from the state since the New Deal and those consigned to remain at the margins of civil society."[11] Black reformers in Atlanta seized on New Deal programs to impose a vision of inclusion sustained by an elitist "uplift ideology" alien to the poorest working-class blacks in the city.[12] Black professionals' belief that racial inequality could be overcome by exemplary individuals leading the way oftentimes stigmatized those African Americans masses who did not conform to their standards of modesty, thrift, and temperance. Because of economic destitution, the latter could not meet such "politics of respectability." The uplift ideology was a call to reform individual behavior rather than to eliminate the unequal distribution of wealth. The reformers'

framework was at odds with that of an incipient local Left whose organizers sought to radically challenge the prevailing economic order, not to participate in the liberal reformist consensus of the era. Whereas Atlanta's
black reform elite incorporated positions of power and constituted a
"Talented Tenth" deserving of their inclusion into the polity, the black
working class remained at the margins of civil society. As the gulf within
black Atlanta widened during the early years of the New Deal, poor local
blacks' grievances were up for grabs. The Communist Party thus came
across as the working class's civil rights alternative to the NAACP, which
was more in tune with the black elite's interests.[13]

These tensions were exposed in 1931 when NAACP leader Walter White
published an editorial in *The Daily Worker* dismissing African American
women who had joined the Communist Party, calling them "ignorant and
uncouth victims who were being led to the slaughter by dangerous bold
radicals."[14] His vitriolic take was a reaction to communists' sudden appeal
to African Americans in the wake of the Scottsboro Boys' case, which
exposed the split and strained relationship between the CP and the
NAACP. In 1931, nine unemployed African American young men had
been wrongfully accused of the rape of two southern white women while
hoboing on the Southern Railway freight line between Chattanooga and
Memphis. Taken off the train at Scottsboro, Alabama, they were hastily
condemned to the death penalty (with the exception of the youngest). The
trials of the Scottsboro Boys became indeed such a cause célèbre, interna-
tionalizing the shame of Jim Crowism, that "*Scottsboro* has become short-
hand for Communist involvement in the South."[15]

The Scottsboro case and the national campaign orchestrated by the
communist-led International Defense Fund (ILD: the legal arm of the CP
that was founded in 1925 and defended the Gastonia strikers) propelled
many black radicals to join the party. That Walter White seemed to be
derisive of the boys and their families deepened the gulf between the
NAACP's middle class members and the black leftists.[16]

William L. Patterson, an African American born in California in 1891
who became a national leader of the Communist Party USA and presided
over the ILD's defense of the boys, exerted a tremendous influence on
black radicals. His contention that "every Negro worker and toiling slave
on the land breathes freer because of the activities of the ILD" and his

dedication to exposing American racism in the international arena at a time when the United States was committed to combatting Nazi Germany abroad, struck many chords.[17] In Harlem, Trinidad-born activist Claudia Jones joined the Young Communist League (YCL) to defend the innocent black boys from Alabama. Georgia-born sharecropper Hosea Hudson too became a member of the Communist Party that year, after he met a black communist who participated in the struggle to free the nine victims. Notably after the Scottsboro case, Marxian calls for a worker-led revolution exerted substantive influence on Georgia's and Alabama's working class, reshaping their vision of a black insurgency. A devoted Communist activist, Hudson settled in Atlanta from 1934 to 1937 and wrestled to convince the middle-class Black Mecca that a radical interracial coalition of the downtrodden was the best vehicle for black advancement:

> The Negro people will always be struggling and will always face setbacks until the time comes when all of us along with our white [working class] friends can join the ranks and organize the masses in [our] own defense. We'll continue to get a lot of lip-service from the higher-ups and from certain liberals, but struggle and unity remain our only real weapons.[18]

Unity with white workers was more than ever a hard sell. Confronted by autonomous black laborers who competed for jobs, a white working class, monitored by the white elite, reinforced Jim Crow practices during the 1930s, rendering class solidarity across racial line virtually impossible. Moreover, white supremacist practices remained labor's Achilles' heel despite the creation of the CIO in 1935, which however failed to gain traction in Dixie.[19] Yet, interracial unionizing did develop in the South, oftentimes with help from radical organizations. The United Mine Workers, under the umbrella of the CIO, successfully organized black and white miners in many southern states. The communist-sponsored Sharecropper's Union in Alabama, created in 1931, exerted considerable influence in the Deep South and in Arkansas; the socialist Southern Tenant Farmers Union (STFU), founded in 1934, spread throughout the South. Both impacted Georgian workers and sustained Atlanta's radical revival of the 1930s, despite the repressive Red Scare policies in place, such as when city officials used the "insurrection statute" against any individuals found in possession of communist literature seeking to incite workers' revolt.

To some degree, the unleashed brutality of the white resistance was reflective of leftist organizations' relevance to many Atlantans.

The Communist Party successfully made inroads in black working-
class Georgia by appealing to the scores of agricultural workers unable to
secure full-time jobs during the Depression. On the national level, the
CPUSA in 1930 launched an Unemployed Councils program to demand
an unemployed insurance bill and to provide jobless workers with substantive relief, regardless of their race.[20] Despite federal redistributive
policies and WPA employment, reliance on local administration almost
always entailed racial discrimination and southern blacks were often
purposely excluded from relief rolls. By organizing the poor and the jobless across racial lines, both the Communist Party and noncommunist
popular movements, notably A. J. Muste's Unemployed Leagues, spearheaded a large number of militant interracial unemployed organizations
whose scope "harkened back to the interracial struggles of Bacon's rebellion."[21] They inspired many mass movements to come, including King's
1968 "impatient Army of the Poor."[22]

The Workers Alliance of America (WAA) was formed in 1935 as a
merger of predominantly socialist and communist-led unemployment
councils, unemployment leagues, and independent state organizations
throughout the country. Harbinger to the 1960s National Welfare Rights
Organization, the WAA sought to organize and represent WPA workers,
whose dignity, they demanded, had to be recognized as "independent
citizen-earners rather than dependent paupers."[23] Uniting the poor and
the unemployed across the color line was for all these progressive organizations the most pressing endeavor. In addition to addressing poverty and
disempowerment, they not only challenged white supremacy but also
deceptive New Deal policies, particularly the Agricultural Administration
Act and Social Security provisions, which worsened vulnerable folks' predicament.[24] Federal agencies routinely enforced existing discriminatory
practices, *de facto* excluding African Americans from relief.

More straightforward, Georgia's governor Eugene Talmadge willfully
refused to fund relief or carry out welfare program reforms in his state.[25]
Despite the creation of WPA jobs in 1935 and massive federal financing
for public housing in Atlanta, jobless workers were more often than not
left to their own devices. Communist activists were thus critical in orga-

nizing social protest about unemployment conditions for blacks, but the Unemployed Councils they formed also addressed unfair housing evictions, provided food, and orchestrated marches to protest the restriction of social programs. In 1932, more than twenty thousand families were dropped from the relief rolls and hundreds of farmworkers (who had migrated to Atlanta in search of work) were arrested on charges of vagrancy. Hosea Hudson, like the many southern radicals who labored to organize the jobless in Atlanta and beyond, witnessed the ravages of black unemployment and the violence of white resistance.

Neither Hudson nor his comrades had expected the degree of repression that fell on them. The Unemployed Councils and the activists in general faced constant police harassment from Georgia's authorities. The local police used vagrancy laws as a pretext for breaking up the communists' meetings and arresting party agitators. Houses of suspected communists were routinely raided and workers of color were intimidated and harassed on a daily basis. Both the white supremacists of the Black Shirts, a militia created in 1930 and dedicated to eliminating "the doctrines of racial equality sponsored by communists among the Negroes of the South," and the courthouses orchestrated Atlanta's Red Scare.[26] The resentful white jobless workers of the Black Shirts engaged into terrorist attacks to expel the black workforce from the South. In Atlanta, they threatened to boycott major companies like Coca Cola unless it laid off its black employees. But their activities merely measured up to the institutional racial backlash.

The official repression was indeed unprecedented and criminal syndicalism laws were employed to target prominent communist members, as evidenced in the case of Angelo Herndon. An Ohio native, Herndon worked as a delivery boy and miner in Kentucky and Alabama where he embraced communism and became a zealous organizer. His personal experience of economic exploitation fed his radicalism. In his autobiography, which he wrote while imprisoned, he recalled how he came to realize the footprint race left on class:

> It was then that I fully became conscious of the inequalities of being a worker. They (white customers) used to refer to me unthinkingly as the "nigger boy" and sometimes would treat me with a callousness quite startling. If I knew what it was to be a "worker" I knew even better what it was to be a "nigger." The walls of race, color, and class now rose between me and the

hostile world outside. I wondered, in my confused, childish way, whether there would ever come a time when I would be able to scale them.[27]

In 1930, while in Birmingham, Herndon became active in the local Unemployed Council and was arrested for his communist sympathy. Yet, a year later, he was sent to Atlanta where unemployment, misery, and discriminatory and coercive policies had disheartened and angered jobless workers and their families. A year before his arrival, the "Atlanta Six" had been arrested for distributing subversive literature to black workers. Taking on the task, Herndon attempted to organize the unemployed. When local officials dropped more than twenty thousand families from the relief roll, Herndon led a march of many thousands of poor and unemployed Atlantans to a rally at the courthouse. The families he guided won their case, but Angelo Herndon was arrested in July 1932 on charges of attempting to incite insurrection. The ILD hired two black Atlanta attorneys, Benjamin J. Davis Jr. and John H. Geer, to defend the young communist. Ben Davis was a Georgia native who graduated from the high school program at Morehouse. Interestingly, he defined Morehouse, the institution that so thoroughly shaped King's mind a generation later, as a school "for the sons of the slave's field hands" whereas Atlanta University was home to the city's elite.[28] Davis joined the Communist Party while defending Herndon, whose trials lasted from 1932 to 1937. In 1933, the Southern Committee for People's Rights was created in Atlanta to offer a noncommunist alternative to the ILD. Emblematic of the Popular Front strategy in the south, it publicized the government's attempts to silence radicals, ignore civil rights violations, and deny justice to Herndon.

In February 1937, in the case *Herndon v. Lowry*, the U.S. Supreme Court overruled Herndon's prior sentence to twenty years on a Georgia chain gang. It was an uncontested victory for a southern Popular Front endeavor that coalesced labor, black organizations, and the CPUSA. Beyond Herndon's case, the radical egalitarianism defended during this period was significant. The Workers Alliance in Atlanta was a pivotal attempt to organize poor people regardless of color and constituted "one of the South's most promising experiments in interracial organizing during the New Deal."[29]

Mass demonstrations and communist involvement freed Herndon but exacerbated interracial divisions as the black working class's embrace of a leftist ideology put them on a collision course with black elite reformers' gradualism and respectability.[30] The NAACP, already embarrassed by the Scottsboro trials, objected to work with the Communist Party yet again and their entrenched animosity sometimes conflicted with the needs of the local community or the goals of the local branches, which they alienated. In Atlanta, unique in being home to a powerful middle class, the internal class-based conflicts translated into a debate on the most potent strategy to achieve freedom and equality. As Tomiko Brown-Nagin shows, black Atlantans who had achieved middle class and elite status sought to protect their gains while favoring litigation over protest. They also tended to dismiss economic rights in their fight for civil rights in the courts, bending toward negotiations and settlements with white leaders.[31]

Black workers, however, engaged in bottom-up initiatives, embracing street protests, sit-ins, negotiation, community action but also litigation.[32] The mobilization by Atlanta's black masses redefined pragmatism and legal as well as direct action campaigning. To a degree, the NAACP in itself was a synecdoche of Black Atlanta's disputes, particularly when a surge of working-class blacks joined it after the Second World War. E. D. Nixon, for instance, leader of the NAACP's chapter in Montgomery yet close to A. Philip Randolph as well as to union organizer Myles Horton, was "both radical and liberal."[33] Their classist framework infused Atlanta's black southern working class, which was dissatisfied with the black elite's calls to moderation and accommodation but also altered the NAACP.[34]

Class divisions within the African American population of Atlanta in the 1930s and 1940s not only shaped the legal and political strategies of activists in the city, thus impacting the cohesiveness of the movement. but also situated the dilemma of race and class at the center of Atlanta's battle for black freedom. Anyone born and raised in the Black Mecca was confronted by this question. Reverend Martin Luther King Sr., a city resident since 1918, student at Morehouse in 1926, and an active local leader of organizations such as the Atlanta Civic and Political League and the NAACP during the Herndon case, stood at the epicenter of the debates surrounding economic inequality, class contentions, and social democracy—especially because he was a devoted Social Gospel preacher.

SOCIAL GOSPEL AND CLASS STRUGGLE

As Kelley brilliantly demonstrates in his study of Birmingham's black communists, a "radical interpretation of Christianity" continued to thrive outside of the organized church.[35] Ironically, this radical, prophetic tradition of Christianity was a major factor in drawing blacks into the Socialist and Communist Parties and their affiliated mass organizations.[36] Neither W. E. B. Du Bois nor A. Philip Randolph repudiated Christianity wholesale for the sake of embracing socialism. On the contrary, their religiosity and sense of prophecy shaped their call to a Universalist humanism. Born in the African Methodist Episcopal (AME) church tradition, Randolph inherited his radicalism from a theology of liberation and of paramount social concern. It was an African Methodist Episcopal church minister, Reverdy Ransom, who founded the black Social Gospel movement in the 1890s, and Ransom's faith in a Christian democratic socialism left a heavy print on AME teachings. As Cynthia Taylor writes, "Randolph's conversion to socialism was a natural evolution from the social gospel message of his parents' African Methodism."[37] Similarly, King Sr. too was predisposed to care for justice. Not only had he witnessed the social protest and leftist organizing that had shaken Atlanta, but he was a self-proclaimed preacher of the poor. By virtue of his family's immersion in Social Gospel principles, King Jr. felt from the outset of his life bound to the wretched of the earth.

The influence of the prophetic radicalism of the Social Gospel on King has been consistently explored, with scholars pointing to the complicated nexus between American Social Gospel's early thought and socialism.[38] A progressive theology, combined with social justice politics, nourished and shaped King's calling, which he defined eloquently when, as a nineteen-year-old first-year student at Crozer's Theological Seminary, he predicated: "My mission is to deal with unemployment, slums and economic insecurity."[39] To King Sr. and his son, the Church had to be concerned with the material conditions of its fellow Christians and thus they had a duty to preach the Social Gospel of justice.

The Social Gospel movement sprang from an aborted Reconstruction and a deceptive Gilded Age. Although Christianity had always elicited concern for social and economic justice, Social Gospel, along with

Progressivism and Populism, coalesced around the same urgent need to diagnose and denounce the ills of an American society undergoing industrialization and urbanization and their collateral social injustices. Interestingly enough, it is in the pages of a white Christian socialist community's journal in Georgia that the words "Social Gospel" are found for the first time in the 1890s. Christian socialists laid the groundwork for a movement which not only espoused social justice but, in the spirit of social democracy, "conceived the federal government as an indispensable guarantor of constitutional rights, struggled with industrialization and economic injustice."[40]

Social Gospel thinkers' works were critical to King's theological education. His usages of "masses" and "classes" terminologies might have come from his critical encounter with prominent Social Gospel theologians, primarily Walter Rauschenbusch and Reinhold Niebuhr, whose works he studied extensively in college. Walter Rauschenbusch (1861–1918), leader of the Social Gospel movement in the Unites States and who explicitly embraced socialism while discarding dogmatic Marxism, profoundly shaped King's economic and social views and "left an indelible imprint" on him.[41] Social Gospel theology can be captured by Rauschenbusch's claim that "[capitalism] is unchristian as long as men are made inferior to things, and are drained and used up to make profit."[42]

Conceiving Christian doctrine in social terms, socialist Christians like Rauschenbusch and Niebuhr reviled the violence of capitalism and called on ministers to explicitly address poverty, unemployment, labor rights, and welfare policies. Rooting their social critique in the Bible, they dramatically altered the claim that Christianity and socialism were antithetical. Many "radical religionists," social gospelers but not exclusively, affiliated themselves with the Socialist Party, providing it with well-read theologians able to organize, mobilize. and educate. They did so much that the Socialist Party has been seen "as an important milieu for theology."[43] Indeed, just as the Eugene Debs era witnessed the creation of the Christian Socialist Fellowship (CSF) in 1906, so Norman Thomas was contemporary to the Fellowship of Reconciliation, both groups emblematic of Christian socialism.

Protestant Christianity moved leftward during the Depression. Many clergy members supported the Socialist Party in the 1930s, mostly attracted by the figure of Norman Thomas. Born in 1884, Norman Thomas was the son and grandson (on both sides) of Presbyterian ministers. After earning a degree from Princeton in 1905, he attended the Union Theological Seminary in New York. Seven years before joining the Socialist Party and rising to prominence, Thomas was ordained and became pastor in Harlem. During his entire life he contended that a Christian was "a man who passionately believes that in the spirit and inspiration of Jesus is to be found the solution of the problems of our collective life."[44]

A member of the Fellowship of Reconciliation (FOR), the pacifist clergymen sought to fuse the Socialist Party's agenda with Social Gospel principles, dedicating himself to the poor. The New Deal's shortcomings led to the radicalization of his Social Gospel liberalism, and, no longer a minister, Thomas repudiated President Roosevelt's policies on the grounds that they overlooked sharecroppers' predicament. He participated in organizing within the Southern Tenant Farmers Union. He emphatically harbored concern for black sharecroppers and attacked racial discrimination in industrial unions and federal policies. He appointed A. Philip Randolph and Frank Crosswaith to prominent positions in the party and became a major critique of Jim Crow and lynching.[45] Thomas's social Christianity as well as Randolph's fed the assumption that socialism was "the midwife and nurse to the Social Gospel."[46]

Unflinching on the necessity to organize the poor interracially, Thomas helped organize the Unemployed Workers Leagues and blazed a path to King's Poor People's Campaign. In 1964, upon receiving the Nobel Peace Prize, King stressed that Thomas should have had the prize. In a note he sent to the old socialist leader on his eightieth birthday, King wrote: "I can think of no man who has done more than you to inspire the vision of a society free of injustice and exploitation. . . . Your pursuit of racial and economic democracy at home, and of sanity and peace in the world, has been awesome in scope. It is with deep admiration and indebtedness that I carry the inspiration of your life to Oslo."[47]

Reconciling faith and left-wing affiliation, Thomas like King partially drew his thinking from Walter Rauschenbusch, the foremost theologian of the Social Gospel. Rauschenbusch dedicated himself to teaching the world that "Christianity has a mission to transform the structures of society in the direction of social justice," endorsing the new idea of "social structure."[48] Thomas was, however, neither an unqualified Marxist proponent nor a Socialist Party member. In his seminal book, *Christianity and the Social Crisis,* published in 1907, he defended a brand of nondogmatic socialism vehemently anticapitalistic, based on class solidarity and a solid faith in the advent in the Kingdom of God.

Like Rauschenbusch, Reinhold Niebuhr exercised considerable influence on early twentieth-century Christian social ethics. Niebuhr developed a critique of the Church as a conservative institution, blind to poverty and war. For him too, poverty raised questions about capitalism and the relevance of Marxism, which he never truly embraced. In 1931 however, he cofounded the Fellowship of Socialist Christians, an organization which exerted significant influence on Christians who grew up, like King, during the 1930s.[49] The newspaper Niebuhr co-edited with Norman Thomas, *The World Tomorrow,* theorized about the redemptive power of the American proletariat and the sealed fate of capitalism while reclaiming Jesus as a socialist. It was the first outlet to introduce nonviolence and satyagraha in the United States, publishing an article by Mohandas Gandhi in 1920. Chief spokesperson of the Fellowship of Socialist Christians, he entrusted the accomplishment of economic justice to left-wing parties. As did many in the years leading up to the Second World War though, Niebuhr grew disillusioned with Marxist parties in the late 1930s, particularly with the Communist Party. Conflicted about pacifism, which he ended up dismissing, he also left the FOR. He too would voice a scathing indictment of communism after the war. Yet, his articulation of Christianity and socialism was instrumental for American radical thoughts in the young twentieth century, unbinding Christian faith from the dominant liberal middle-class church mindset. After Rauschenbusch and Niebuhr, the structural issues of a class-divided society were to be read through the lenses of human nature and salvation.

Other figures stood at the intersection of religion and progressive politics, laying the ground for a radical civil rights movement. A.J. Muste, a committed pacifist, was a passionate advocate of "universal religion" as well. Raised as a Calvinist in the Dutch Reformed Church, he graduated from the Union Theological Seminary. But upon becoming a minister, he leaned toward Social Gospel. He became involved with labor issues during the First World War and launched the Conference for Progressive Labor

Action (CPLA) in 1929. The more dispirited with the Church he grew, the more involved with leftist movements he became. The CPLA helped the unemployed to organize and morphed into a radical and independent Marxist group in 1934, the American Workers Party. The latter merged with the secularist Socialist Party in 1936.

Muste's Christian faith proved so influential that he joined the Fellowship of Reconciliation to denounce the war—out of his rebirth of faith while in Paris. God's grace was revolutionary and pacifist to the core, devoted to love and justice, he claimed. Although he appropriated Gandhi's secular theory of nonviolence, Muste saw the Church as the key agent of change in the United States. To him, and he passed on this creed on to King, love included justice, thereby fastening religion to politics and the concern for social issues. Socialism was Jesus' most meaningful teaching and Christians had to be revolutionaries: "In a world of violence, one must be a revolutionary before one can be a pacifist; in such a world a non-revolutionary pacifist is a contradiction in terms, a monstrosity."[50] To him, economic exploitation and racial discrimination were offenses to Christian ethics. Such statements, along with an ethics of nonviolence, led to the formation in 1942 of the Congress for Racial Equality, which grew out of FOR. A defining figure on the radical Left, Muste inspired many social movements that praised his prophetic and spiritual dimensions, embedded in a dedication to the oppressed.[51] Martin Luther King Jr. credited him with the civil rights movement's emphasis on nonviolence. Bayard Rustin, who urged King to adhere to a strategy of nonviolence in 1957 but also relentlessly encouraged him to focus on job equity and economic justice, began his own militancy in the ranks of the Fellowship of Reconciliation. For black and white social gospelers alike, opposition to capitalism, war, and inequalities were biblical faith imperatives, a distinctive black Social Gospel tradition that laid the groundwork for civil rights activists' radical egalitarianism.

King paid homage in his autobiographical writings to the great white Social Gospel theologians who nurtured his thought. However, he substantiated his praise by stressing that they gave him "a theological basis for the social concern which had *already* grown up in me."[52] Indeed, if King was influenced by his formal training at the seminary and at Boston University, he was first and foremost born and raised in the black Social Gospel tradition. Books and classes provided him with an intellectual framework and curiosity which only substantiated his earliest sentiments, feeding his encompassing critique of an American "system" in which the words *exploitation* and *capitalism* became inseparable. Because the church was the most important institution in African American life and given that baptism originated in the working class, King was immersed in a spiritual framework which had its own tradition of care and dedication to the poor. He was profoundly molded by the social gospel he had always known, the one preached and lived in the black southern Baptist church.

Atlanta was home to the 1895 National Baptist Convention and, from 1897 to 1910, to Du Bois's language of spiritual prophecy and substantive equality. Not a social gospeler himself (he hardly defined himself as a Christian), Du Bois nonetheless influenced the movement tremendously, calling on the Black Church to break away from its conformism and its ministers to challenge the structural dimensions of racial inequality.[53] He radicalized the Black Social Gospel movement and gave it a socialistic edge. Prior to Du Bois though, a distinctively African American version of Social Gospel Christianity had already challenged the congregations to help the most vulnerable and to stand up against unemployment, lack of decent jobs, starvation wages, and substandard housing. But now was the time for the Black Church to forcefully reconcile sacred and social missions and to discard an entrenched conservatism, Du Bois chided.

Although the Black Social Gospel movement had been—like its white counterpart—diverse and conflicted since its inception in the 1880s, its defining feature had been to place racial reform at the forefront of its theology. Far from being unanimously affiliated to leftist organizations, its advocates were nonetheless overwhelmingly progressive with regard to racial justice. Although Gary Dorrien locates Booker T. Washington within the Social Gospel movement, most black Social Gospelers were also staunch critiques of capitalism. God must have wanted Christians to care for the dispossessed and all those "bearing the cross," black gospelers argued. Proselyte socialist ministers from Tennessee, George W. Woodbey and George W. Salter Jr., were the most unflinching in their attempt to fasten Social Gospel to Marxian socialism and labor unionism.[54]

But the communal aspiration of the black radical tradition translated mostly into a form of sui generis democratic socialism, noncommittal to left-wing parties or to a dogmatic Marxian framework.

Accordingly, King owed much of his radical edge to the role models who surrounded him while growing up in Atlanta, notably Mordecai Johnson and Benjamin Mays, two African American social gospelers who had espoused principles of democratic Christian socialism. Morehouse College president Benjamin Elijah Mays, Howard University president Mordecai Johnson, and also Boston University dean of the chapel Howard Thurman (author of *Jesus and the Disinherited*) were emblematic of the Black Social Gospel's egalitarian radicalism. Thurman's 1949 essay built on Rauschenbusch's defining statement on Jesus, who "proceeded from the common people. He had worked as a carpenter for years and there was nothing in his thinking to neutralize the sense of class solidarity which grows under such circumstances. The common people heard him gladly because he said what was in their hearts. His triumphant entry in Jerusalem was that of a poor man's procession."[55] Not only was Jesus poor, but he was a poor Jew and as such he was stripped of his citizenship and basic rights, rendering the condition of American blacks strikingly similar to his. To Thurman, Jesus was to be emulated inasmuch as "his message focused on the urgency of a radical change in the inner attitude of the people."[56] This radical reading of Jesus paralleled Du Bois's, who praised Jesus to the degree that he "befriended the marginalized, prayed to a God of the oppressed and taught that God was present in the poor and the oppressed."[57] Moreover, Du Bois defined Jesus as "the greatest of religious rebels," a radical whose message of liberation from an oppressive social order could only be carried out by the Black Church, a statement Thurman could have endorsed.[58] Tellingly, King kept a copy of *Jesus and the Disinherited* in his briefcase during most of his life.[59]

However powerful and influential, King's mentors could never surpass his father's moral authority in terms of molding his comprehension of what the ministry entailed. Baptist ministers and Social Gospel proponents in Atlanta's Ebenezer Baptist Church, King Sr. and his father-in-law Reverend A. D. Williams (who participated in the 1895 National Baptist Convention) were unmistakably devoted to the political arousing of their congregations along with a concrete commitment to the plight of the dispossessed. Williams, who instructed King Sr. that "whosoever carries the word must make the word flesh," provided for the material welfare of the unemployed during the Great Depression. King Sr. followed in his footstep, urging his congregation to register to vote, mobilize for the equalization of teachers' salaries in Atlanta, and care for the downtrodden and the underprivileged. Politically conservative and more favorable to free-market capitalism and liberalism, King Sr. nonetheless repudiated Christians' obliviousness to exploitation and espoused a vision of a "cooperative commonwealth."[60] Long before King Jr. rearticulated Harvard philosopher Josiah Royce's "beloved community" into a more radical black prophetic theology, King Sr. preached:

> Quite often we say the church has no place in politics, forgetting the words of the Lord, "The spirit of the Lord is upon me, because he hath [anointed] me to preach the Gospel to the poor; he hath sent me to heal the broken-hearted, to preach deliverance to the captives, and the recovering of sight to the blind, to set at liberty them that are bruised."
> ... God hasten the time when every minister will become a registered voter and a part of every movement for the betterment of our people. Again and again has it been said we cannot lead where we do not go, and we cannot teach what we do not know.[61]

King Sr. bequeathed his ability to reconcile Black Social Gospel tradition with elements of European theology and radical social thinking to his son.[62] It is therefore not surprising that a devoted social gospeler like King Jr. would read Marx's writings with the utmost interest. His major concerns over the ability of the current economic system to provide for the welfare of the poor predated his reading of Marx though, in a chronology akin to that of Du Bois's. King, like Du Bois, recognized that racism could not be separated from accumulated patterns of material inequality, historically exemplified by chattel slavery. But King, in his own time and his own faith, carved for himself a personal view on how progressive changes, aimed at achieving people's equal moral worth, occur.

4 The Torchbearer

Through an insistence that race was central to the way class works, social-ist- and communist-affiliated organizations provided an effective frame-work and a unique pulpit to express black grievances. Arguably, though many organizations including the NAACP began to agitate against pov-erty and racism after the Second World War, hardly any movements pro-vided the agency and voice to poorer blacks that leftist parties had in the 1930s.

FELLOW TRAVELERS

That King "refused to repudiate Marxism wholesale" is now established, historians pointing out his deep-rooted concern for economic structural inequality.[1] But King did not shy away from speaking his mind within his closest circle. While quarreling with Andy Young's centrism, he alleged: "You're a capitalist and I am not."[2] According to David Garrow, while talk-ing to his friends in the 1960s, the preacher admitted that "economically speaking he considered himself what he termed a Marxist, largely because he believed with increasing strength that American society needed a radical redistribution of wealth and economic power to achieve even a rough form of social justice."[3] He had entertained such ideas for a long time, formulating very early on the substance of his critique against capitalism and wealth inequalities. Rev. J. Pious Barbour, mentor and friend to the Kings, reminisced that when Martin was a young seminarian, he hinted at his socialistic leanings, defending that "Marx had analyzed the economic side of capitalism right" as "the capitalistic system was predicated on exploitation and prejudice, poverty."[4] In a letter he wrote to Coretta in 1952, King confided that he gravitated more toward socialism than toward capitalism but because of his reservations about Marxism, his public support of left-wing politics was hardly an option. A critical examination of his reflections on the flaws of Marxism are indicative of his tempered endorsement. However, that King eschewed using the word "socialist" publicly until his final days is arguably less an expression of his genuine reluctance than a prophylactic measure to avoid the stigma and the governmental harassment suffered by dozens of black radical activists.

The brutal repression of activists during the period was indeed consequential. Recent scholarship has debated the impact of witch hunts—the branding and targeting of those deemed "socialists"—and anticommunist fervor on the black liberation movement.[5] It is nonetheless widely accepted that Red Scare episodes and the consistent anticommunist rhetoric beginning in the 1920s impaired the struggle for civil rights, labeling black activists' demands for substantive equality "un-American" and "subversive." Southerners' paranoia over "Black Bolshevism" developed in the 1920s and 1930s, but Cold War politics in the 1950s allowed Dixiecrats to find national support and legitimacy for their portrayal of left-wing radicals as purportedly the most threatening danger to national security. Anticommunism became a proxy and a ploy to continue equating racial integration with subversion. In a telling fashion, black radical writers and activists summoned to testify before "loyalty boards" were asked, "Do you think an outspoken philosophy of race favoring equality is an index of communism?"[6]

Harassment of radical organizations and individuals skyrocketed during the Cold War. McCarthyism vilified any debates geared at addressing economic inequality and exploitation of blacks, mudslinging the very institutions dedicated to these issues. Most unions, including the CIO, were purged of leftists. The Southern Conference for Human Welfare disbanded in 1948, one of the many casualties of government antisubversive operations. Purges and intimidations were effective to the extent that, by the late 1950s, the radical wing of the black liberation movement was destroyed. Echoing Reconstruction, African Americans' advances toward full inclusion, notably in the aftermath of *Brown v. Board of Education,* were met by a fierce white reaction determined to roll back their gains and undermine the righteousness of their claims. Anticommunism provided a suitable ideological veneer. The postwar Red Scare crushed most progressive social movements, particularly in the South, "even more so when they defended racial equality."[7] Consequently, class-oriented civil rights politics and denunciations of economic exploitation tended to be abandoned.

Black voices who remained strident were tormented. Prominent radicals (including Paul Robeson, Claudia Jones, Ben Davis, Lorraine Hansberry) resisted the Cold War's pernicious consensus and strategized that, in response to such misrepresentation, they should continue precisely to voice a leftist critique of capitalism and imperialism. A delusional nation, blinded by anticommunism and red baiting, could not see its original sins, they argued. As a result, they suffered coercion, intimidation, and were sometimes subjected to exile.[8] Du Bois was the most notorious example. He ended his life in Ghana, unauthorized to come back to his home country. Lorraine Hansberry, a successful leftist playwriter who suffered from the anticommunist hysteria, gave a tribute to W. E. B Du Bois in 1964 in which she lamented the nefarious red-baiting that had forced Du Bois to expatriate. On the one hundredth anniversary of his birth, in February 1968 King would express similar dismay at his Carnegie Hall tribute to Du Bois:

> We cannot talk of Dr. Du Bois without recognizing that he was a radical all of his life. Some people would like to ignore the fact that he was a Communist in his later years. It is worth noting that Abraham Lincoln warmly welcomed the support of Karl Marx during the Civil War and corresponded with him freely. In contemporary life the English speaking world has no difficulty with the fact that Sean O'Casey was a literary giant of the twentieth century and a Communist or that Pablo Neruda is generally considered the greatest living poet though he also served in the Chilean Senate as a Communist. It is time to cease muting the fact that Dr. Du Bois was a genius and chose to be a Communist. Our irrational, obsessive anti-communism

has led us into too many quagmires to be retained as if it were a mode of scientific thinking.[9]

The blacklisting also targeted other prominent dissenters, forcing Langston Hughes to silence and marginalize the entire black cultural and literary left.[10] But most mainstream organizations sided with Cold War liberalism's rhetoric. Even socialists A. Philip Randolph and Ralph Bunche, who kept arguing that antidiscrimination measures would do little to redress black poverty and unemployment, stood as vibrant anti-communists. In 1951, Benjamin Mays left the Civil Rights Congress (which had been formed in 1946 by members of the National Negro Congress, the International Labor Defense, and the National Federation for Constitutional Liberties and which he had been a co-chairman of, all groups with strong communist ties), after sweeping charges of subversion launched by the House Committee on Un-American Activities (HUAC). The NAACP, which had emerged as a massive organization and the leading voice for African American civil rights after the war, joined the camp of liberal anticommunists and dismissed Du Bois, who was more and more drawn into leftist causes. Meanwhile, the Communist Party fell victim to its own internal contradictions, being an uncritical apologist of Stalinism and blind to the new militancy of black protest arising from the war and subsequent decolonization process.

The disrepute of the Communist Party harmed social democratic impulses in the United States and abroad, although with regards to the global national liberation movements and international calls for and social justice, it was neither the only player nor the central catalyst. Many struggles for economic justice, obscured by history, were in fact divorced from the Soviet Union, and grounded their claim in the American experience. Their "americanized" dissent is also a current that flowed toward King.

In the aftermath of the war, organizations sought to internationalize principles that had been defended by the New Deal and the Popular Front. In 1944, the International Labor Organization laid out its Declaration of Philadelphia. The ILO was created in 1919 as a part of the Treaty of Versailles and its constitution was drafted by a commission chaired by Samuel Gompers, head of the American Federation of Labor. Its aim was to build on the idea of social justice and workers' rights as a mean to achieve long-lasting peace. Its 1944 convention in Philadelphia reaffirmed key principles enshrined in its constitution: "All human beings, irrespective of race, creed or sex, have the right to pursue both their material well-being and their spiritual development in conditions of freedom and dignity, of economic security and equal opportunity" (article IIa). It also placed the attainment of social justice as central in any national or international policy or measure especially of economic or financial nature (article IIc). Hundreds of representatives of governments, employers, and workers from forty-one countries signed the Declaration of Philadelphia. The "welfarist spirit" of a declaration of international scope stemmed somewhat from Roosevelt's ideas on social justice.[11] It also captured the aspirations of internationalists like Du Bois, who viewed a universal human rights declaration of the oppressed as the key to combatting exploitation and racism.[12]

Not unlike the leftists of the 1930s, the diverse people who mobilized in Philadelphia in 1944 pleaded for a proactive federal government committed to providing all workers with the advantages of "the welfare state" (active full-employment policies, higher wages, and generous social benefits) and for more racially inclusive policies in order to achieve substantive equality. If the New Deal seems to have been, despite its limitations, in line with these demands, the United States' postwar liberalism would reject this Keynesian bargain once and for all, chiefly by virtue of its entrenched systemic racism.[13] Radicals and leftists had attempted up until the 1940s to enact systemic social change through a Marxist framework. But a stream of antitotalitarian social democratic activists, who gained an understanding of the intricate structural relationship between race and class in American society by drawing upon the 1930s radicals' achievements and limitations, also were to shape American radical egalitarianism.

Compellingly, the International Labor Organization was awarded the Nobel Peace Prize in 1969 for its dedication to universal economic justice and workers' rights, five years after King received the prize—and only months after the start of the Poor People's Campaign.

Like the PPC in the late 1960s, black social democrat initiatives in the 1950s were lumped together with communist activities and dismissed by

McCarthyism. This inflammatory atmosphere contextualized King's conflicted and complex perception of Marxian theory and socialism. Witch
hunts and Red Scare policies constrained black radicals' and the democratic left's rhetoric. In 1960, Du Bois lamented that McCarthyism had
had a nefarious effect on American democracy by vilifying all discussion
on socialism and communism.[14] It has indeed been a privileged means to
smear black discontent. Red- and black-baiters since Reconstruction had
portrayed integration as an "anti-American, Communist conspiracy."[15]
King's critique of communism, however, originated not from his fear but
from his spiritual and philosophical upbringing. A social gospeler, he was
convinced that a meaningful citizenship entailed equal access to those
social, cultural, and educational goods that enable people to develop their
human potential and that therefore they should be guaranteed access, as
a basic social right, to education, healthcare, housing, income security, job
training, and more. But, as a Christian and a humanist, he could not
embrace communism or refrain from having major qualifications about
Marxist tenets.

In fact, King belonged to a black tradition infused with powerful
streams of anticommunism and, as a Southern Christian, he had heard
that socialism and communism were socially disruptive and morally cor-
rupting to African Americans' religious ethos. Accordingly, he dismissed
the crude materialism of Marxism, in ways that distinguishes him from
Du Bois. What is more, whereas Du Bois was an admirer of the Bolshevik
revolution and grew to unapologetically praise the USSR, King utterly
condemned it. He excoriated an oppressive and godless regime. But nevertheless, drawing on the legacy of black radicals, he meshed his faith with
a radical vision of equality in such ways that he complicated and reframed
the prevailing religious-based anticommunist discourse. He certainly
stood out in the black middle-class environment he grew up in.

King Sr. recalled tense conversations with his son, pertaining to the
young man's critique of the free market and the soundness of the capitalist
system. "Daddy King" took issue with such dissent, bemoaning that, politically, his son "seemed to be drifting away from the bases of capitalism and
Western democracy that I felt very strongly about. . . . There were some
sharp exchanges; I may even have raised my voice a few times."[16] Very
early on indeed, King Jr. began to speculate that America's unfettered

capitalism was wrong. The Great Depression's economic ravages spared his family but hit his conscience. In his first book, *Pilgrimage to Nonviolence,* he recollected precisely when he "saw economic injustice firsthand, and realized that the poor white was exploited as much as the Negro." He rapidly grew to reason "that the inseparable twin of racial injustice was economic injustice" and that both were contingent upon the current capitalistic order.[17] In an early letter to Coretta, he wrote:

> I imagine you already know that I am much more socialistic in my economic theory than capitalistic. And yet I am not so opposed to capitalism that I have failed to see its relative merits. It started out with a noble and high motive, to block the trade monopolies of nobles, but like most human system it fell victim to the very thing it was revolting against. So today capitalism has outlived its usefulness. It has brought about a system that takes necessities from the masses to give luxuries to the classes. . . . Our economic system is going through a radical change, and certainly this change is needed. I would certainly welcome the day to come when there will be a nationalization of industry. Let us continue to hope, work, and pray that in the future we will live to see a warless world, a better distribution of wealth, and a brotherhood that transcends race or color. This is the gospel that I will preach to the world.[18]

In many of his early writings, King charged that inequality was the indictment of a capitalist economy predicated on an unfair distribution of wealth. He would never stop connecting his Christian faith to economic justice and the call for a commitment to more robust forms of democracy. The Social Gospel theology vindicated and substantiated his belief that the social welfare of the people, aimed at an inclusive beloved community, was a democratic imperative. Mays and Thurman further instilled in him an awareness of the global nature of oppression and exploitation, rooted in imperialism as an international expression of capitalism. At Crozer, Walter Chivers, his major adviser, encouraged him to explore the works of Walter Rauschenbusch and Reinhold Niebuhr, which impressed upon him the need to bind Christian brotherhood to concrete solidarity. Yet, he did not utterly concur with their political involvement. Hinting at Rauschenbusch's, he drew a clear line in the sand between the Church's commitment to economic and social justice and a specific partisan agenda.

"One should never identify the Kingdom of God with a particular social and economic system," he contended.[19]

While at Crozer, King read the *Communist Manifesto* and *Das Kapital*, grasping the concepts of materialism, class struggle, proletariat, exploitation, and the prospect of the disappearance of the political State. King's further insights on Marx's philosophy reflected the extent to which his attraction toward socialism was tempered by a clear-cut distinction between some of Marx's analysis and communism, an ideology he openly dismissed. At the merry age of twenty-three, in an academic paper, King deployed his critique of Marxism in terms that he would hammer throughout his life: the intrinsic materialistic ideology and humanist atheism required by communism were at odds with the sacredness of Man and his freedom:

> At the same time he [Marx] "turns Hegel upside down" by emphasizing the primacy of matter rather than spirit. So he was led to dialectically materialism. He became a thoroughgoing economic determinist. History is moving inevitably toward the classless society. Nothing can stop its consummation. Such a view destroys freedom, while the high Kantian motivation affirms it. We may conclude then that Marx' attempt to combine the Hegelian methodology with his Kantian motivation caused the flagrant contradiction in his thinking.[20]

But his rejection, which he substantiated in his student essays and in his later sermons and speeches, was dialectical. He meticulously separated the theory from the practice of communism, Marxist-inspired socialism, and Marxist-inspired bolshevism. Furthermore, many stages in Marx's thinking need to be distinguished as his early writings, chiefly the *1844 Manuscripts*, could be considered an independent corpus, insulated from the ideological system he would lay out later on.[21] The contentious issue of men's lack of agency within the underlying trend of historical materialism defended by Marx was particularly debated. Philosophers like Herbert Marcuse, who publicized a discordant reading of Marxism in the United States during the 1940s, argued that individualism was a feature of Marx's initial theory, individuals being the active agents of the advent of happiness once the age of reason is accomplished.[22] Whether or not these historiographical disputes reached Crozer, a critical reading of Marx taught King to grapple over the appropriate role of the State in achieving justice or the sources of exploitation in any system. Scrutinizing and balancing Marx's ideas was an intellectual requirement, not a prose-lyting attempt. Informed and well read, King sought to navigate the con-tradictions and limitations of communism while pointing to the flaws of capitalism. Reflecting on his discovery of Marxism, he concluded:

> In short, I read Marx as I read all of the influential historical thinkers—from a dialectical point of view, combining a partial yes and a partial no. Insofar as Marx posited a metaphysical materialism, an ethical relativism, and a stran-gulating totalitarianism, I responded with an unambiguous no; but insofar as he pointed to weaknesses of traditional capitalism, contributed to the growth of a definite self-consciousness in the masses, and challenged the social conscience of the Christian churches, I responded with a definite yes.[23]

If he abhorred the tyrannical nature, "deprecation of individual freedom," and the brute atheism advocated by communist countries—claiming in a 1962 sermon that "no Christian can be a Communist" whatsoever—he contrasted these defects with the evils of the purportedly opposite system. Whereas most Cold War liberals would articulate their castigation of com-munist regimes in ways that made the American economic and political system an irrefutable model, King refused to succumb to simplistic dichotomies. He boldly gave credit to communism for certain truths, pointing out that "however much is wrong with communism, we must admit that it arose as a protest against the hardships of the underprivi-leged," and went on to caution that "capitalism may lead to a practical materialism that is as pernicious as the theoretical materialism taught by Communism."[24] He therefore, implicitly, pleaded for a social democratic system, a synthesis of preexisting yet flawed regimes:

> My reading of Marx also convinced me that truth is found neither in Marxism nor in traditional capitalism. Each represents a partial truth. . . . The Kingdom of God is neither the thesis of individual enterprise nor the antithesis of collective enterprise, but a synthesis which reconciles the truths of both.[25]

He abided by this balanced view, unyielding that his faith was an insu-perable obstacle to a sincere endorsement of Marxian philosophy. He also remained emphatic that communist dogma and regimes denied the dignity of men, rendering them "means" rather than "ends." But he also expressed his concerns about capitalist countries' greed and neglect for the poor. Talking to the SCLC staff in 1966, he reiterated his dialectics:

> I always look at Marx with a yes and a no. And there were some things that Karl Marx did that were very good. Some very good things. If you read him, you can see that this man had a great passion for social justice. . . . [But] Karl Marx got messed up, first because he didn't stick with that Jesus that he had read about; but secondly because he didn't even stick with Hegel.[26]

As always, King then went on to talk about Jesus as his primary inspiration:

> Now this is where I leave Brother Marx and move on toward the Kingdom [of Brotherhood] . . . I am simply saying that God never intended for some of his children to live in inordinate superfluous wealth while others live in abject, deadening poverty.[27]

Upon launching the Poor People's Campaign, King stressed once again the urgency of a third way, beyond established ideologies, repeating his early claims: "The good and just society is neither the thesis of capitalism nor the antithesis of Communism, but a socially conscious democracy which reconciles the truths of individualism [Capitalism] and collectivism [Communism]."[28] Not a communist sympathizer by any means, he nevertheless used what was relevant in the Marxian diagnosis to call on the American economic system to restructure and redeem.

ON EXPLOITATION

If he would come to christen the Poor People's Campaign a form of "class struggle," usually King seldom talked about "class" or "classism." These words were not part of his vocabulary, no more than "proletariat," a term regularly used by Du Bois or by the socialist intellectual Michael Harrington. Du Bois used the terms "class" and "working class" while knowing good and well that race stood as their living denial. Arguably, neither Marx nor Du Bois understood "class" as a sociologic category—

although empirically grounded—but rather as a strategic framework meant to be performative, a process geared toward the emancipation of the oppressed. The notion of "class" allows for a group to *feel* that it is indeed a singular and symbolic social identity built on a "linked fate." Those who are dispossessed of the fruits of their labor and excluded from land ownership, who are in other words exploited, are to construct themselves as the revolutionary class. As E. P. Thompson illuminated, "the working class did not suddenly appear like the sun, it is fully engaged in its own formation."[29] African Americans leftists have hoped for a "probable class" to be fully inclusive and egalitarian.[30]

King would rather talk about "the poor," a generic category midway between Du Bois's proletarian words "classes" or "masses" and Gunnar Myrdal's 1963 liberal notion of "the bottom of society." But if he did not often talk in classist terms, he used the very concept that undergirds the idea of class, that is, the word "exploitation." His frequent interactions with labor unions leading up to the Poor People's Campaign were reflective of his attempt to build a "culture of solidarity" among those who were victims of an exploitative system.[31] In Duboisian fashion, he would argue:

> We have deluded ourselves into believing the myth that capitalism grew and prospered out of the Protestant ethic of hard work and sacrifices. Capitalism was built on the exploitation of black slaves and continues to thrive on the exploitation of the poor.[32]

Whether he read Edward Bellamy's *Looking Backward* or Michael Harrington's *The Other America,* King was compelled by the interplay of race and class, concurring that the material relations shaped by capitalism led to an economic exploitation that is at the heart of capitalist society. Harrington's 1962 book exposed the pervasiveness of poverty in a nation of plenty, offering a geography of American inequalities from the working poor in New York to the backwoods of Appalachia. Norman Thomas's heir, Harrington sought to awaken American consciences and to get the government to implement strong policies eradicating, not so much poverty itself, but the obliviousness to it. The extensive review published by the *New Yorker* in its January 19, 1963, issue, called "Our Invisible Poor," was widely read and, reaching the White House Council of Economic Advisers, is said to have been an inspiration to President John F. Kennedy's envisioned War on Poverty.[33] King purportedly commended Harrington in a humorous note, giving him credit for informing the nation that it had poor people.

Though not a Marxist in a dogmatic sense, King shared with leftist progressives the belief that, in order to build a just social democracy, the State should play a central role in ensuring the welfare of citizens. Government must be democratized with regards to racist practices and reoriented toward the protection of blacks—and beyond, toward the protection of the lesser-off. His educators transmitted to him such insights. At Morehouse, Benjamin Mays felt deeply that joblessness and poverty had to be taken care of by the government. By providing decent housing, health care, and education, Mays wrote and taught, the federal government would foster desegregation and democratize the country.[34] King also shared with French Catholic philosopher Jacques Maritain, whom he read at the seminary, that modern states were not yet fully democratized, and were still unable to promote the common welfare through their administrations and public affairs.

King's theological exploration helped him to comprehend the notion of "progress," whether or not ineluctable. The harmonious blend of theological claims, such as the quest for human liberation and the advent of a beloved community, and secular-based reasoning on the inner workings of a real democracy were central to Rauschenbusch. The theologian advocated a "communistic State" in which affluent people would not be able to dominate and subjugate through political power. King differed but remained dissatisfied with capitalism, predicting its decay. He also noted that racism was endemic to the American capitalistic order, too deeply rooted in the social structure of the nation.[35] In formulating these challenging views, he drew inspiration from earlier black radicals such as Du Bois and many socialist thinkers but also from Gandhi.

If he became mesmerized by Gandhi's philosophy of nonviolence and social change, King could not ignore the Mahatma's dismissal of profit-driven societies contingent upon structural imbalances that feed injustice. Capitalism was antithetical to Gandhi's social ethics. Although he never envisaged the expropriation of the rich through violence or state action nor a communist-inspired economic ideology, Gandhi entertained the prospect of an alternative system, based on nonpossession, nonviolence, village-communal life, and trusteeship. Justice and love were also governmental matters. The government should not limit itself to ensuring the free market and the respect of law but should actively propel economic and social justice. A notable example, India's affirmative action policies toward those he called Harijan ("children of God," a term meant to erase the stigmatizing names of the lower caste in India, the Dalits, commonly called the "untouchables") were praised by King when he visited India in 1957.

At Morehouse, Benjamin Mays had already taught him that the role of ensuring economic as well as social justice fell to the federal government. Here again, the black social gospelers who molded King's intellectual mindset at Crozer were his primary sources of inspiration. The State had to be compelled to enact redistributive policies, which entailed regulating a government behavior. The market too was to be regulated by the government, added Kenneth Smith, King's ethics professor at Crozer whose class "Christianity and Society" deeply challenged his thoughts. Another professor, George Davis, who introduced him to personalism and its emphasis on the moral shift from the individual to the social, protested state-sponsored capitalism as it reluctantly provided social protection and benefits to the poor and destitute. It was God's intent, Smith argued, that a true State within history would actively promote the masses' social welfare, which would foster equality and substantive citizenship, hence their "God given freedom."[36]

If the State had to be fought when it failed to protect its weakest and most oppressed citizens or to enforce democracy (which King understood as the letter of the Constitution), it also had to be entrusted with the power to counteract the nefarious effects of the free market and unbridled capitalism. Democratic socialists and egalitarian unionists were therefore natural allies, King joining A. Philip Randolph and Bayard Rustin in such a creed. Rustin, a former member of the Communist Party, reconciled his pacifism and his radical egalitarianism in the creation of the Congress on Racial Equality (CORE), with George Houser and James Farmer. Sent to Montgomery in 1955 to help King organize a truly nonviolent mass action, Rustin remained a close advisor and played a significant role in the Poor People's Campaign. Rustin had worked with Michael Harrington before the publication of *The Other America* and the two would reunite for the campaign, as King asked Harrington to write its blueprint. Undoubtedly, Rustin was the most notable advocate of democratic socialism in King's close circle. He theorized that a strong social democratic state could and should address the needs of the most disadvantaged citizens, renouncing individualistic notions of property and profit, but also that a doctrine of state's rights was needed in order to enforce the rights of black Americans. In 1956, Rustin explained how because "the mass of Negroes are workers and farmers" whose interests are "fundamentally allied to other workers and farmers," they should unite to forge a progressive coalition. Blacks, to Rustin as to Du Bois and later to King, were pivotal in that their "agitation . . . for jobs is bound to stimulate white workers to increase militancy."[37] Rustin worked closely with Randolph to connect the black liberation struggle with labor as "freedom cannot be sustained in the midst of eco insecurity and exploitation."[38] Although not the only leftist to be King's companion during his life, Rustin was certainly the most cogent ambassador for labor and secular socialist theories to the Southern Christian Leadership Conference. He helped King grasp the need to prioritize economic issues.

In the North, civil rights advocates had relentlessly fought for better economic conditions. Chief among them, the National Urban League led a struggle for the achievement of what has been called a "dual agenda," for social as well as economic justice.[39] But accommodationist in nature, the National Urban League sought to find common ground with municipal authorities and housing owners, staying clear of any radical or socialistic organizing. The uprising of Watts in the summer of 1965 and King's subsequent launching of the Chicago Campaign replaced economic justice at the forefront but in a more radical fashion. The racial militancy that King embraced in Chicago, however unsuccessful in its outcome, reconnected him to a black radical tradition infused with Marxist language and diagnosis.

In 1966, the SCLC allied with the Coordinating Council of Community Organizations to launch a campaign to end slums in the city and to open up decent housing to black residents. The Chicago Freedom Movement was a grassroots protest seeking the influence and visibility of the SCLC. In January 1966, King decided to bring his movement north and agreed to lead the Chicago fight. He moved into a rundown apartment in the ghetto of Lawnsdale with Coretta and their children to dramatize urban poverty and subjugation. After several months living with the ghetto's inhabitants and unsuccessfully participating in fair-housing protest marches into all-white neighborhoods, he wrote his last book, *Where Do We Go from Here* (1967), to a large extent the fruit of his experience in the Chicago slums. Much of its content stemmed from analysis he articulated while fully immerged in the post-Watts context.

In December 1966, he was invited by the Senate to give his expertise to the Subcommittee on Executive Reorganization of the Committee on Government Operations, which organized hearings to comprehend the recent urban uprisings. King's emphasis on economic justice compelled Senator Abraham Rubicoff to wonder whether the civil rights movement had "entered a different stage." mostly pertaining to economic and social issues. King answered in the affirmative but dodged the implicit assumption that racial inequalities were now subsumed under class issues, as though the two were not fundamentally entwined:

> As important as it is to improve the economic plight of the city dweller, we must not ignore that the struggle for equality is also a moral and political act. The aim is not only to improve the economic situation of the poor, but to provide the conditions for dignity and the exercise of rights. Economic improvement despite its importance, without full citizenship rights can be a bribe to the excluded rather than a gateway to the free society.[40]

Like Du Bois's before him, King's thoughts evolved toward a more Marxian-based approach to racial inequalities, moving away from strictly culturalist explanations of racial hierarchy. Yet, his dialectics is reflected into his rebuttal of the either/or fallacy. The concept of "institutional racism," more and more relevant to 1960s social scientists and which King used, precluded any satisfaction with the recent antidiscrimination legislations.[41] Tracing back the systemic nature of racial oppression to slavery, he pointed to its profound impact in shaping the social-political-legal structure of the nation.[42]

If King avoided the pitfall of decoupling race from class issues, he also instructed the senators about the common oppression suffered by poor whites and blacks, whether unemployed or underpaid and underworked, who "huddle in the big cities." Not talking about a "working class," let alone a "proletariat," King nonetheless repeatedly hammered at the "economic exploitation" at play, directly inherited from antebellum institutions. Describing the predicament of black children living in ghettos, he unraveled the continuity of the systemic deprivation:

> Already in childhood their lives are crushed mentally, emotionally and physically, and then society develops the myth of inferiority to give credence to his life long patterns of exploitation, which can only be described as our system of slavery in the twentieth century.[43]

"Exploitation" is not neutral term. Economic "oppression" refers to an asymmetrical situation in which some own property and have full ownership rights, whereas others are deprived of it and therefore doomed to sell the only thing they own, their labor. The term "exploitation" points to the condition in which the haves are rich *because* the have-nots are an exploited class. They make profit out of oppressed labor. The causality matters since it posits that only the appropriation of labor of the lesser-offs serves to enrich the ruling class. "Exploitation," rooted in production relations, is therefore intrinsic to the concept of class and economic relations in a capitalistic system.[44] King further substantiated his usage, denouncing the "ghetto tax," the higher rents and higher prices blacks had to pay to live in decrepit housing when compared to white suburbs. He also explicitly pointed to those making profit out of the ghetto: "Many retail business and consumer-goods industries deplete the ghetto by selling to Negroes without returning to the communities any of the profits," he remarked, later charging the rich and powerful who had a vested interest in concentrated poverty:

> You can't talk about solving the economic problem of the Negro without talking about billions of dollars. You can't talk about ending the slums without first saying profit must be taken out of slums. You're really tampering and getting on dangerous ground because you are messing with folk then. You are messing with captains of industry.[45]

Like Du Bois, King placed great emphasis on the structural and economic underpinning of racism while pointing to the exploitation of the poor white as well. Echoing Harrington's *Other America,* he reminded his audience that whites had a stake at reforming the economic system they lived in. Moreover, King, who had attended workshops at the Highlander Folk School in Tennessee, related to the leftist tradition of interracial union organizing. In 1957, he expressed his sense of solidarity and linked fate with labor, telling Highlanders that "the forces that are anti-Negro are by and large anti-labor." Speaking to a meeting of Teamsters union shop stewards in 1967, he reminded his audience that "Negroes are not the only poor in the nation. There are nearly twice as many white poor as Negro, and therefore the struggle against poverty is not involved solely with color or racial discrimination but with elementary economic justice."[46]

Although the scope of the role of leftist organizations and political parties with Marxist leanings in the black liberation movement is debated, the fact remains that a social democratic vision had for a significant period united their members and civil rights activists.[47] From E. D. Nixon to Bayard Rustin, people with roots in the leftist milieu of the prewar period suffused the post-1955 movement with demands for substantive justice including full citizenship for blacks, strong labor rights, full employment policies, and progressive taxation that could fund a radical welfare state. To them, the government also had to remedy past inequality and to forcefully eradicate poverty and the mechanisms that perpetuated it. But whereas most civil rights organizations addressed economic conditions, unemployment, and discrimination on the workplace, few called for a redistributive policy toward the poor beyond the mere enforcement of fair opportunities. While most of them sought to help African Americans with the job market, aware that most black families were yearning to be consumers and owners, they hardly challenged corporate capitalism. Mainline leaders would barely support King's lifelong claim that exploitation and nationwide poverty were the symptoms of a lethal defect in capitalism.

Following in the footsteps of Du Bois, King challenged the prevailing racial liberalism among progressives, "the idea that all Americans, regardless of race, should be politically equal, but that the state cannot and indeed should not enforce racial equality by interfering with existing social or economic relations."[48] The Poor People's Campaign King envisioned was more than a class-based movement open to progressive-minded liberals and reformists of good will. In 1961, speaking at the Negro American Labor Council King had already proclaimed, "Call it democracy, or call it democratic socialism, but there must be a better distribution of wealth within this country for all God's children." King's call harked back to late nineteenth century calls for a fully realized Reconstruction and a fair industrial democracy. At the dusk of his life, he envisaged a Poor People's Campaign as a nonviolent revolutionary mass movement, as subversive as the interracial General Strike Du Bois had praised or as the populist movements of the Progressive era.

The Poor People's Campaign would eventually see the light of day in 1967, as an attempt to build a coalition capable of pursuing the egalitarian agenda Douglass, Du Bois, and scores of radical egalitarians had in mind.

PART II   The Campaign

The Poor People's Campaign's singularity and radicalism cannot be comprehended without considering the different temporal rhythms within history which historian Fernand Braudel metaphorically called "the swell" of underground forces which he distinguished from the "foam" of events.[1] The first part of this book explored the "swell" that shepherded the Poor People's Campaign toward its realization, a long tradition of black American dissenters who, since Frederick Douglass, stressed class issues when framing the black liberation struggle and embraced the notion of structural forces. But the undercurrent thread of radical egalitarianism has been constantly challenged and reframed by the vicissitudes and vagaries of history. Although being acted upon, King and his contemporaries' agency is not to be downplayed. Not only would a deterministic approach to the Poor People's Campaign be inaccurate, it would be misleading. The substantial political changes generated by the major legislation of 1964–1965, and notably King's position with regard to Lyndon Johnson's politics, bred his conviction that something truly dramatic had to be done for the disadvantaged.

This part of the book does not describe in depth the fine details of the campaign, a task well undertaken by recent scholarly work, but instead it demonstrates that the campaign clearly illustrated King's understanding that racial inequality was embedded in class.[2] The Poor People's Campaign would thereby be the culmination of Martin Luther King Jr.'s social thought and unyielding commitment to a truly egalitarian society.

5 The Pauper

Arguably, although the 1964 Civil Rights Act was a remarkable achievement of the black insurgency, the voting issue was still unresolved and the urban uprisings that erupted during the summer of 1964 in New York, Philadelphia, Chicago. and other northern cities (heralding the widespread national civil disorders that would culminate with the outbreaks of sorrow following King's assassination in 1968) placed economic issues and the policing of the poor at the forefront. Young African Americans revolted in wrath against their conditions, which, despite legislative civil rights progress, had not been substantially altered. The newly adopted antidiscrimination Title VII policies (which established a Commission on Equal Employment Opportunity), yet to be enforced, could not adequately right structural wrongs, particularly with respect to employment and housing. The black urban poor, whose destitution was worsened by discriminatory policing, laid bare "the violence of poverty" and the alienation of those rendered invisible, voiceless, and utterly powerless. King understood that what the nation confronted was a poor people's insurrection.

In a November 1964 editorial entitled "Negroes Are Not Moving Too Fast," King called on President Johnson to fulfill his obligations: "Despite new laws, little has changed in his [the Negro's] life in the ghettos. The

Negro is still the poorest American walled in by color and poverty. The law pronounces him equal, abstractly, but his conditions of life are still far from equal to those of other Americans."[1] King had not lived the Chicago experience yet, but he already grasped the political economy of the north-ern ghettoes, clearly pointing out that the Civil Rights Act was incapable of addressing "the magnitude" of joblessness and the wretched housing conditions of the poor. Unblurred by the Civil Rights Act victory, he con-ceived the end of *de jure* segregation as the first step in a grander emanci-pation design which would address the structural side of inequality. Beyond the ongoing fight to abolish segregation, to secure voting rights, and to enforce antidiscrimination provisions, economic and class issues were *de facto* King's prime concern.

ECONOMIC JUSTICE AS A CIVIL RIGHT

This call for economic justice was nothing new to the White House. Up to 1964, the civil rights struggle mainly concentrated on the dismantling of Jim Crow laws and attitudes in the South, and questions of citizenship and segregation were put to the front. However, if most civil rights orga-nizations shared a similar race-centered agenda, it was complemented by a commitment to economic equity and job opportunities. Northern orga-nizations such as the NAACP, the Urban League, and CORE had consis-tently pushed for fair employment practices and economic uplift. They helped farmers and factory workers to get better job opportunities, through financing or training. Socialist leaders like A. Philip Randolph, Bayard Rustin, and, later, Martin Luther King Jr. had been aware since the early civil rights movement that economic progress was the sine qua non for substantial civil rights advances. No real enfranchisement could be reached without economic gain. But no economic gain was within reach in the Jim Crow framework. Besides, more than any programs, the real connection between civil rights organizations and the poor lay in the socioeconomic condition of the members of these organizations who dis-proportionately experienced poverty and economic disempowerment. John Lewis, who presided over SNCC's strong engagements on behalf of the southern poor, would later clarify that "people have said that the civil rights movement was a middle-class movement. . . . But, a lot of the people that made up the rank and file of that movement, the people that got arrested and went to jail, the people that participated in the marches, that stood in that immovable line, they were dirt poor."[2]

The 1963 March on Washington, for "Jobs and Freedom," was in this regard a pivotal moment. Despite the sanitized image of a gathering aimed at dismantling Jim Crow and at reaching national reconciliation, the main goal of this labor-organized and socialist-inspired demonstration was to shed a harsh light on "the economic subordination of the Negro" (in 1963, black workers earned 55 cents for every dollar earned by whites) and to advance a universal "broad and fundamental program for economic justice."[3] The brainchild of A. Philip Randolph and Bayard Rustin, both social democrats, the demonstration demanded not only the desegregation of schools and public accommodations in the South but, on an even grander scale, a "massive federal program to train and place all unemployed workers—Negro and white—in meaningful and dignified jobs at decent wages," which entailed minimum wage and labor protections. Full employment was to be reached through structural reforms: a two-dollar minimum wage (which entailed a raise of 85 cents, from the prevailing $1.15), the broadening of the Fair Labor Standards Act and a Federal Fair Employment Practices Act were demanded by marchers, who sought to be a "living petition."[4] Their plea for genuine equality, economic as much as social, was only partially satisfied by the landmark vote obtained a year later. It is also because the 1963 marchers were not fully heard that King labored to have another gathering of massive proportions in Washington, preceded by a dramatic journey toward its Mall. It would be more radical, more disruptive, and more explicitly class-based.

The common argument claims that the years 1964–1965 were a critical juncture in the history of the civil rights movement, for they marked the end of a consensual period and the dawning of protestors' radicalization. But the initial shift, to which activists responded, was President Johnson's fading sense of commitment to racial equality. Rendering African Americans free was a leap of unprecedented proportions and Johnson reasoned that he had done enough. Genuine equality would have to fall on someone else's shoulders. The Democratic president felt as did most liberals that the "race question" had been somewhat resolved and Johnson's skewed diagnosis propelled him to refocus his priorities. Although liberal Democrats in Congress had the votes necessary to pass his bills on domestic policies, he made sure he would not fall prey to conservatives' assaults, which led him to water down his egalitarian agenda and instead to engage in an anticommunism battle in Vietnam.[5] Before the war became an irreconcilable bone of contention between Johnson and King, the president's domestic policies or lack thereof in the realm of economic justice were subjected to critical scrutiny. The urban uprising added fuel to a simmering political detachment that contrasted with the ambitious agenda that initially prevailed.

Thus, the 1968 Poor People's Campaign cannot be understood without being traced back to 1964. That year, King articulated for the first time the core theme of the later PPC: an "Economic Bill of Rights for the Disadvantaged," whose overarching goal was to eradicate poverty and establish the notion of social citizenship. Beyond a commitment to full employment, the demand for an unconditional, non-withdrawable income paid to every individual as a right of citizenship was the antipoverty measure King pushed the most forcefully. A few months afterward, Johnson launched his War on Poverty, seemingly responding to civil rights' leaders demands for economic justice. If he did not take King's suggestions into account, he seemed to have heard his call for a GI Bill-inspired legislation to tackle inequality, and as well, the proposal from National Urban League president Whitney Young Jr. to launch another domestic Marshall Plan.[6]

It might then seem paradoxical that King called for a massive attack on structural inequality and envisioned a Poor People's Campaign exactly when the War on Poverty, the most impressive social welfare program since the New Deal, was being rolled out. But precisely because King had himself appropriated antipoverty activists' experiences and inherited a long social democratic tradition, he came to understand that even well-intended liberal policy makers would not spontaneously tackle the structural roots of racial inequality and class exploitation. Arguably, the PPC was bolstered by the disappointing outcome of Johnson's War on Poverty. With the Poor People's Campaign, King sought to achieve the core components of a *real* antipoverty policy: a true empowerment of the poor and massive structural reforms that were critically absent from Johnson's War on Poverty. If Johnson would prove to be truly concerned about the economic dimensions of racism, King expected to tackle the entanglement of capitalism and systemic poverty. Progressives thought that inequality stemmed from racist practices, but King proclaimed that they resulted from the nation's defining economic structure.

However, the PPC was by no mean a circumstantial byproduct of the Great Society: King had called for a "war on poverty" even before Johnson was elected. Moreover, King had offered the yet-to-be-elected president the blueprint of a true War on Poverty, which anticipated many of the limitations of Johnson's antipoverty initiatives. At the Atlantic City convention of August 1964, King urged the Democratic Party to adopt an "Economic Bill of Rights for the Disadvantaged" and issued a document substantiating his demand for a tangible redistribution of wealth. King explicitly exhorted the Democratic Party to move beyond formal rights to tackle critical economic issues plaguing the American poor. His address and his blueprint, rejected by the platform committee, has been forgotten and buried by the controversy that surrounded the convention, especially the Mississippi Freedom Democratic Party dispute.[7]

But King's 1964 proposals, which he also enunciated at the Republican convention earlier that summer, deserve attention. Most of them would form the backbone of the Poor People's Campaign. His choice of words, an "Economic Bill of Rights for the Disadvantaged of the Nation," was meant to struck a chord in the conscience of liberals. Reminiscent of Franklin Delano Roosevelt's 1944 "Second Bill of Rights," it sought to enshrine the "freedom from want" as a core democratic principle. Full citizenship, King declared, entailed good wages and the right to employment, decent housing, medical care for all, welfare protections, and good education. But he suggested that only the *right* to an income would ensure citizenship to those unable to secure a decent living. The last attempt of New Deal forces to implement this "freedom from want" was the 1946 Full Employment Act, enacted under President Harry S. Truman. Before its final revision, the act claimed that "all Americans able to work and seeking work have the right to useful, remunerative, regular, and full-time employment, and it is the policy of the United States to assure the existence at all times of sufficient employment opportunities to enable all Americans who have finished their schooling and who do not have full-time housekeeping responsibilities to freely exercise this right."[8] The government was charged with the responsibility to provide full employment. King demanded the fulfillment of this commitment. He called on the Democrats to take strong action.

He then fleshed out his Economic Bill of Rights, citing the 9.3 million families living below the poverty threshold of three thousand dollars per annum. He made clear that this figure should be legally declared a minimal subsistence floor "under which families would be entitled to receive direct payment to reach $3000." In addition to this economic safety net for families, King called for "free quality education" and "broad health services." Adding the need for a massive program to fight unemployment and slums, King estimated that an investment of fifty billion dollars over a decade would be required. Two years later, the Freedom Budget would make the same estimate, which suggests that King drew in large part from the ongoing work of A. Philip Randolph and Bayard Rustin to bring forth a precise budget to fight poverty. Rustin, who returned to King's inner council early in 1964, became one of his closest and most influential advisors and a key member of a task force named "The Research Committee." By the time of the Atlantic City convention, Rustin's class-based, labor-rooted analysis of freedom and equality permeated King's speeches on poverty. King sought to convey the idea that if black Americans were, by virtue of their long history of victimization, the epitome of exploitation, poor whites were poverty stricken too.

Consequently, he urged the Democratic Party to come to terms with "what can be done to make freedom real and substantial for our Negro citizens, and for millions of white citizens afflicted with poverty." In accordance with A. Philip Randolph and Bayard Rustin's analysis, King dismissed the idea of race-based social policies such as the "Marshall Plan for the Negro" put forward by National Urban League president Whitney Young Jr.[9] King favored universal economic programs which would benefit poor whites as well. Later, when presented with a "Negro Bill of Rights," King rejected the idea, reasoning that "many white workers whose economic condition is not too far removed from the economic condition of his black brother will find it difficult to accept a 'Negro Bill of Rights.'"[10] He made clear that his bill would be inclusive and that "while Negroes form a large percentage of America's disadvantaged, there are many more millions of white poor who would also benefit from such a bill." Race-conscious policies were for King, as for Randolph and Rustin, inadequate to wrestle with the economic issues faced by blacks. Politically, they also ran the risk of alienating Johnson, whose support was expected. As stressed in a December 1964 speech in New York, King intended to build "a broad alliance of all forces—Negro and white" to mobilize against economic injustice and nudge the party toward wealth redistribution on behalf of the poor. The question of whether such grassroots mobilization of the underprivileged would partner with Democrats or disrupt them remained to be settled. The dismissal of King's proposals by the platform committee vindicated the latter supposition. Other documents would be credited with the "rediscovery" of poverty by progressives and policy makers and the outcome in terms of public policy would be considerably different from what King suggested in 1964.

Civil rights leaders' advocacy for the poor was indeed reinforced in social sciences and political circles by a renewed concern for poverty. President John F. Kennedy had purportedly been struck by Michael Harrington's notorious 1962 book, *The Other America*, more precisely by its riveting review by Dwight McDonald in *The New Yorker*. The year Harrington's book was released, converging publications addressed hidden poverty in America, Gabriel Kolko's *Wealth and Power in America* and James Morgan's *Income and Welfare in the United States*, to name a few. Demands for antipoverty public aid programs and full employment had been constant since the end of the New Deal. As early as 1958, John Kenneth Galbraith's *Affluent Society* explicitly pointed to the pressing issue of wealth inequality. But the astonishing popularity of *The Other America*, an essay portraying the American dispossessed and the nation's inability to give them recognition, was indeed a wake-up call for an oblivious suburban nation. The commonplace argument crediting Harrington for a national "rediscovery" of poverty was so widespread that King jokingly teased Harrington when they first met: "Why, Mike, we never knew we were poor until we read your book."[11] But there was more than a wisecrack in this homage. Harrington's Christian socialism merged with King's Social Gospel. They first met in 1960 when Rustin, friend to both of them, asked Harrington to help organize a march in Los Angeles where the

Democratic National Convention was being held, in an attempt to deepen the party's commitment to equality. Harrington would later describe their political affinity: "[King] in the course of a much more profound political and intellectual journey than mine, come to a view of America and the world that I largely shared."[12] Not only would King give two major sermons named "The Other America" in 1967, but he would also ask Harrington to write the Poor People's Campaign blueprint. White, socialist and Christian, Harrington could bridge the divide between poor whites and blacks. He also had, by virtue of his fame, the capacity to compel Washington to act.

By 1964, alleviating poverty had become a prime concern not only for the federal government, which brought together experts and social scientist to address the issue, but also for many progressive individuals and institutions. Liberals, emboldened by the Kennedy administration, came to see poverty as worthy of public consideration. In the aftermath of the Civil Rights Act, liberal-minded policy makers came to mesh integration and economic fairness.[13] In October 1964, United Auto Worker (UAW) president Walther Reuther founded an antipoverty organization, the Citizens Crusade against Poverty (CCAP). A broad interracial coalition supported the CCAP's call for massive public spending and significant measures to "bring the disadvantaged back to the mainstream of American life." A "who's who of the labor union–liberal lobby," the CCPA also reached out to religious groups and grassroots organizers.[14] Notably, almost all black leaders endorsed Reuther's "crusade": King partook in this initiative along with Bayard Rustin, A. Philip Randolph, Whitney Young Jr., Dorothy Height, and John Lewis.

Whether or not freedom fighters were duly credited with the early 1960s' renewed national concern for poverty, their commitment to couching black liberation in economic justice terms was instrumental. As Johnson proceeded to carry out Kennedy's antipoverty initiatives, Bayard Rustin audaciously stated in *Commentary:* "It seems reasonably clear that the Civil Rights movement, directly and through the resurgence of the social conscience it kindled, did more to initiate the War on Poverty than any other single force."[15] Social democrats like Rustin had bound civil rights issues to the labor struggle, adamant that unions and their Democratic allies in Congress were at the same time the vanguard of fed-

eral efforts to expand policies for the poor and a key obstacle to implementing effective policies.[16]

Other activists distrusted such strategy. More than any other civil rights
groups, SNCC remained unremittingly dismissive of top-down federal initiatives. But it had relentlessly brought forward the lingering economic
origins of black disadvantage in a post–Jim Crow society. In accordance
with King, SNCC members had fingered the limitations of civil rights legislation in the daily lives of black workers, particularly in the rural South,
calling for policies capable of addressing the structural issues associated
with poverty. The idea of empowering impoverished communities of color
through grassroots organizing and participation also stood as a core principle of SNCC's militant deeds. Despite internal disagreement on strategy,
civil right groups and their progressive allies successfully pressured
Lyndon Johnson, who announced a "war on poverty" as a complement to
the civil rights bills.

THE WAR ON POVERTY AND ITS DISCONTENT

In his State of the Union message on January 8, 1964, Johnson declared
an "unconditional war on poverty." He did not shy away from addressing
racial inequality, underscoring that "many Americans live on the outskirts
of hope—some because of their poverty, and some because of their color,
and all too many because of both." The War on Poverty (WOP), set in
motion with the Economic Opportunity Act (EOA) of August 1964, was
granted a budget of one billion dollars by Congress in order to launch
major antipoverty programs throughout the nation. Accounting for about
1 percent of the total budget, the WOP was tied by tax constraints and its
scope thereby limited. Yet, it looked unprecedented. The entanglement of
these revolutionary policies on poverty and race, two dimensions of social
policy that have been intertwined throughout the history of the United
States, seemed to be acknowledged at last. For a short period it looked like
the federal government, both during Kennedy's and Johnson's administrations, grasped the structural nature of inequality and poverty. Expectations
were high, chiefly for African Americans who were disproportionately
represented among the poor.

Resuscitating New Dealers' ambitions, Johnson and Office of Economic Opportunity (OEC) director Sargent Shriver were however adamant about confronting Roosevelt's skewed compromise with southern states, which clung to their racial double standard.[17] Subsequently, beyond a massive expansion of welfare programs, the cornerstone of Johnson's war was its Community Action programs (CAP) and local agencies (CAA), entrusted with the responsibility to coordinate the antipoverty policies and provide direct services to the poor. Thrust by the OEO, CAP sought to ensure that local communities would not be excluded from social programs through racially discriminatory practices but rather able to co-organize federal action and to participate in their own uplift. Accordingly, Johnson cleverly bypassed southern states' obstruction to racial equality by circumventing local welfare authorities.[18] Although some historians contend that the War on Poverty was not intended primarily to address black poverty or to cater to black voters, with more than half the black population living in poverty in 1964, it is hard to decouple Johnson's poverty programs from his racial concerns.[19] If he strategically stressed that justice was to be for all Americans (not just blacks) in order to pass his Economic Opportunity Act in Congress and get public support, the underlying motive of racial equality was hard to conceal.

The intertwining of the civil rights bills with War on Poverty programs was indeed eloquently articulated by Johnson a year after their adoptions. On June 4, 1965, Johnson delivered a commencement address at Howard University, "To Fulfill These Rights," that was, in this regard, remarkable. Quite forcefully, Johnson envisioned acts of "corrective justice" for African Americans, by virtue of the legacy of their suffering. Undeniably, Johnson understood that economic justice could not be peripheral to the emancipation of blacks: "We seek not just legal equity but human ability, not just equality as a right and a theory, but equality as a fact and equality as a result." The speech pointed to the inherent limitations of formal justice absent the economic empowerment of black Americans:

> Thirty-five years ago the rate of unemployment for Negroes and Whites was about the same. Tonight, the Negro rate is twice as high. . . . From 1952 to 1963, the median income of Negro families compared to whites actually

dropped from 57 percent to 53 percent. . . . Of course Negro Americans as
well as white Americans have shared in our rising national abundance. But
the harsh fact of the matter is that in the battle for true equality too many—
far too many—are losing ground every day.[20]

Never before had a president seemed more aware of the scale of the problem of racial inequality. Johnson probably owed his insights to his assistant secretary at the Department of Labor, Daniel Patrick Moynihan, who
wrote the speech and who lobbied for a "second phase of the civil rights."
Boldly quoting Bayard Rustin, Moynihan argued that the major new challenge consisted of not "merely . . . removing the barriers to full *opportunity*" but of "achieving the fact of *equality*."[21] Moynihan's emphases
seemed to accurately capture the social democratic underpinning of the
civil rights movement. Johnson's Howard University speech sounded like
the more fitting answer to civil rights leaders' concerns about the substance of the formal equality bestowed on blacks by way of Constitutional
legislation. The speech was naturally widely praised by black activists as
Johnson's policy synchronized with lobbying efforts by civil rights activists
to bound voting rights and economic justice.[22]

King related to Moynihan's left leanings, especially since the assistant
secretary of labor's commitment to economic justice originated in the
social teaching of his Catholicism, which infused his rhetoric and at times
paralleled King's. "Men without work," Moynihan wrote in 1964, "are
deprived of an essential condition of human dignity."[23] He also supported
the guaranteed annual income which King had called for and they both
praised European welfare states.

Martin Luther King Jr. called President Johnson to commend the
intervention, hopeful that it would be followed by an announcement of
large-scale public policies on behalf of the disadvantaged. In a private conversation with King, Johnson reassured him, emphasizing that his eight
billion dollars of public spending for health care, education, and poverty
would directly benefit those who earned less than two thousand dollars a
year. With a wink he added: "You know who earns less than $2,000 a year,
don't you?"[24]

On paper, the War on Poverty seemed to be a promising and brave
attempt to tackle race-based economic inequalities. Johnson pushed

through an unprecedented amount of antipoverty legislation which, at its inception, accurately grappled with problems affecting low-skilled workers, most of them African Americans. With the specific purpose of promoting socioeconomic mobility and security, Johnson sent the Equal Opportunity Act to Congress in March 1964, legislation that vastly increased the scale and power of the federal government. Congress enacted major programs aimed at strengthening the American welfare state: Medicaid in 1965 along with Medicare and Head Start programs for early education.

The multifaceted dimension of poverty was addressed as a national concern, close to being co-orchestrated by the White House and most civil rights leaders. From 1964 to 1966, antipoverty activism therefore increased within black circles, from the National Urban League, NAACP, and CORE to the Southern Christian coalition and SNCC. The NAACP and the National Urban League (which received funds from the Office of Economic Opportunity) were closely involved with federal antipoverty policies, considering themselves somewhat as social service agencies in charge of advocating for the poor and defending the War on Poverty within the civil rights movement. Many organizations had an almost symbiotic relationship with Johnson's Community Actions programs. Some, such as the National Urban League, "considered the implementation of the War on Poverty Programs to be its responsibility."[25]

At the local level, the War on Poverty triggered an upsurge of grassroots democratic activism not only among poor blacks but also among poor Latinos and poor Appalachian whites as well. It also galvanized middle-class whites, particularly women, who—as the main recruits of community services programs—built grassroots interracial coalitions to voice their predicament.[26] Such a community of purpose is worth noticing, although in many instances whites were reluctant to be associated with what they perceived as programs designed for blacks. In many places in the South, the federal effort to implement antipoverty policies became a part of the ongoing struggle against segregation and white supremacy. Most programs favoring racial equality were undermined by the racial animosity they unleashed: Head Start programs in the Louisiana Delta[27] or Concentrated Employment Programs in Texas[28] fostered formidable local resistance and racial backlash. The War on Poverty oftentimes morphed into a war for African Americans' right to achieve substantive equality. It also allowed for race-conscious politics of resistance which cut across class lines. The NAACP supported the EOA throughout, which helped mainstream civil rights advocates to reach out to low-income communities. National Urban League president Whitney Young Jr., far from deploring the mixed results of Johnson's policies, sought to expand and tighten the relations between the organization and federal agencies.

Arguably, the War on Poverty had a catalytic effect on the organizing of black communities. The "maximum feasible participation" principle of the Economic Opportunity Act, which resonated so strongly with the spirit of empowerment embodied in the massive mobilization of the period, was immediately embraced. More than a thousand Community Action agencies (CAAs) ensured that African Americans would not be prevented from participating. The more educated and more informed of their rights they grew, the more politicized African Americans became. The urban poor expressed their sense of alienation through community action and the local agencies became their privileged sites of protest. Despite numerous attempts to undermine their participations, ghetto dwellers used the CAAs as means to obtain benefits, to make assertive claims of their rights, and to castigate local corruption. Undeniably, the War on Poverty increased opportunities for African Americans, providing them with unprecedented avenues to voice their concerns and to increase voter registration and minority office-holding.

Galvanizing the poor was not the sole accomplishment of the Great Society. The concomitant effects of desegregation and social welfare policies, which reinforced each other, decreased black unemployment and poverty: from 1961 to 1969, unemployment for nonwhites fell from 12 percent to 6 percent and from 1959 to 1974, black poverty plummeted from 55 percent to 30 percent. The Civil Rights Act compelled the federal government to make real the citizenship rights of black workers and employees.[29] New opportunities were open to African Americans as schools, hospitals, and many services were forced to desegregate. Federal money and power were *de facto* used to emancipate blacks from economic exploitation. Recent and compelling scholarship has also vindicated the far-reaching economic gains of the civil rights bills. For instance, the right to work in industries previously segregated (including public services) opened major opportunities for black workers, and the economic impact of such measures on the upward mobility of black Americans was significant in the South.[30] Examples abound of the ripple effects of the Civil and Voting Rights Acts on the economic life of black America.

But the War on Poverty fell short on Johnson's promise to wage a true war on economic disparities and injustices and never embraced the notion that economic security was also a civil right. It proved powerless to bring about real changes in the life of the poor, let alone the black poor. The fate of the War on Poverty, crippled by the premises on which it was built and struck by the fatal blow of the Vietnam War, laid the groundwork for King's most ambitious antipoverty campaign.

From the onset, the most radical civil rights activists had expressed their distrust about an antipoverty program which to them was too frail to be able to reach out to disinherited blacks, particularly in urban areas. In 1964, civil rights leaders meet during a summit on race to push for more assertive policies, notably a massive public-works program. Bayard Rustin warned the government that their social welfare policies, or rather lack thereof, was leaving a "trail of despair" in poor urban communities.[31]

Low-income communities in northern cities, most notably women of color living in concentrated poverty areas, were using the Community Action programs to also voice their discontent. Welfare rights and housing were thereby quickly addressed by some agencies, which would lay the groundwork for more specific organizing.[32] Social workers channeled the poor in demanding a fair share from the affluent society, which the War on Poverty was unable to provide. But quite often, disadvantaged residents in impoverished areas were *de facto* excluded from participating in Community Action programs. Many elected officials, notably Mayor Richard J. Daley in Chicago, were wary of a program which they perceived as a seedbed for subversion. In Los Angeles, concentrated areas of poverty were almost deprived of participation in social welfare programs although the unemployment rate in the 1960s would reach 30 percent, notably in Watts. When the latter erupted in August 1965, the relevance and efficiency of Johnson's policies were questioned. The president grew more and more convinced that to mitigate the effects of poverty, his social policies had to be compounded by reinforced policing and self-help programs so that behavioral patterns could be derailed. The idea of community participation lost its edge and funding for local agencies waned.

The "equal opportunity" welfare state eventually did little for the economic security of the black poor.[33] The government's antipoverty top-down effort alienated militant indigenous organizations uneasy with the underlying assumption that the poor had to be socialized, trained, and adapted to the job market. As soon as the Economic Opportunity Act was adopted, SNCC expressed its doubts about governmental commitment and grit and launched its own local antipoverty initiatives. In a venture with the Council of Federated Organizations (COFO) activities in Mississippi, SNCC established the Poor People's Corporation on July 20, 1965 to help the disadvantaged start cooperatives or other self-help programs, giving them technical and moral support.[34] SNCC also organized the Mississippi Freedom Union to support indigenous labor. Their community-based approach to combatting poverty, although short-lived, was not short of federal policy makers, notably Richard Boone, who intended to nationalize their technique to the North.[35] But arguably, although grassroots antipoverty work oftentimes intersected with federal actions, it underscored the flaws of the War on Poverty. By nature distrustful of state-funded welfare policies, SNCC was insulated from disappointment. Such was not the case for mainline organizations.

When President Johnson asserted in his July 1965 Howard University speech that "freedom was not enough," civil rights organizations were hopeful that the growing trend of racial economic disparities would forcefully be altered. But eventually, neither Rustin nor King turned out to be satisfied. The policies implemented fell short of the economic initiatives they had called for. Upon adopting the new legislation, Congress had explicitly stated that the EOA was limited in scope, specifying: "These are not programs to bring about major structural change in the economy, or to generate large numbers of additional jobs."[36] Far from New Deal policies, the War on Poverty downplayed income transfer and did not address the structural issues of low wages, low demand for labor, systemic racism on the labor market, and inadequate income support for those outside the labor market. Indeed, the expenditures under the War on Poverty represented only a small percentage of the total social welfare budget (Social Security, public assistance and housing, Medicare/Medicaid, etc.). Furthermore, the federal programs Johnson put in motion in order to avoid the southern hold that gutted New Deal policies, did leave great discretion to local authorities who, over time, curtailed the scope of the Community Action Program.

Central to Johnson's economic theory was the belief that poverty could not and should not be addressed through centralized administration and federal spending. In the footsteps of Kennedy's administration, he opted out of income redistribution and toward a less interventionist form of Keynesianism that emphasized overall economic growth through tax cuts. Tied by the Kennedy tax cut of 1964, Johnson refused altogether to raise taxes, create jobs, or transfer income in distressed communities.[37] To King, this form of regulatory liberalism fell short of the fair equalization of distribution needed. The nature and scope of the policies could not offset centuries of economic injustices. He lamented that the War on Poverty eschewed redistribution, relying instead on a gospel of corporate-led economic growth which neither addressed the realities of black urban experiences nor the transformation of the southern economic landscape, in which small farms were vanishing and low-wage jobs increasingly prevailed.[38]

The demise of industrial democracy after 1945 and the overall economic expansion that ensued reinforced the postwar assumption that, inasmuch as opportunities were fairly spread, a sustained economic expansion would "lift all boats." The effects, not the causes, of inequality could be addressed, to the extent that low-income individuals were responsive to the incentives offered. Relying on social engineering, Johnson favored job training over job creation, focusing on individuals' employability. Besides, the initial audacity of the War on Poverty—to be an integral part of the civil rights package—turned out to be its major liability. By targeting young blacks from urban ghettos, the job-training programs put the War on Poverty on a collision course with Dixiecrats, the main trade unions, and part of the northern working class.[39]

When civil disorders erupted in Harlem, Rochester, and other northeastern cities two weeks after the passage of the Civil Rights Act, Johnson attempted to quell his opposition by putting into motion his "war on crime" agenda. But his opponents blamed his antipoverty efforts toward inner cities. From the outset, the CAP had been controversial. But after the Watts uprising of the summer of 1965, the vocal participation of the poor was seen as subversive, aggravating the distorted perception that Johnson was running a racial agenda. Southern Democrats denounced the misuse of taxpayers' money to fund antipoverty initiatives "for blacks."[40] Initially supported by public opinion, Johnson's antipoverty programs became unpopular when they became associated with racial issues. Politically, this equation proved fateful: from 1966 on, southern Democrats in Congress refused to vote for the expansion of antipoverty budgets which they identified as civil rights measures by stealth.

Johnson's personal commitment to the Office of Economic Opportunity was also waning. In 1966, military expenditures skyrocketed while the OEO was chronically underfunded.[41] The retrenchment of Johnson's antipoverty policies were all too apparent when the Senate adopted a dwarfed appropriation request that same year. The Vietnam War induced a reign of austerity and the level of appropriation for the EOA kept declining.[42] King would ultimately issue a sobering evaluation of Johnson's promising initiative: "it did not take long to discover that the government was only willing to appropriate such a limited budget that it could not launch a good skirmish against poverty, much less a full scale war."[43]

But the macroeconomic and fiscal constraints which hindered Johnson's antipoverty policies were consequences of a deeper ideological defect, which fully came to light when the black urban poor rebelled. The rise of behavioral explanations for poverty dovetailed with budget constraints. From the White House standpoint, the structural disadvantages that afflicted poor young people, particularly in northern inner cities, were not seen as the primary cause of their social and economic predicament. The uprising provided a tragic subtext for the "culture of poverty" thesis, which already existed inchoately in War on Poverty policies. Chief among the post–Watts riots arguments was the white establishment's contention that the rioters were "culturally" drawn to violence and poverty, and therefore immune to economic redistribution. Liberals and conservatives blamed Johnson's naïveté with regard to local agencies meant to empower underprivileged communities.

The culture of poverty thesis struck a fatal blow to any efforts at bolstering the American welfare state. It has been misconstrued since anthropologist Oscar Lewis argued that the lower-class Hispanic families he observed in Mexico and New York had developed a subculture of their own in which matriarchy was a defining feature. Fruit of their isolation, such a culture of poverty stemmed from economic inequalities on which capitalistic nations thrived. It allowed the exploited to adapt and to make sense of their social exclusion, Lewis claimed. His point was not to blame them and he took issue with contemptuous interpretations of a "culture of poverty."[44] Likewise, Michael Harrington's 1962 *The Other America* suffered from conservatives' misreading of his essay, which also contributed to sanctimonious visions of "islands of poverty" sustained by a specific "culture." The othering of the poor by means of behavioral explanations discredited social welfare policies and to some extent vilified them.

Ironically, the author who was the most effective at undermining wealth redistribution and job creation to the benefit of the poor was the most ardent supporter of such policies in Johnson's circle. In March 1965, the Office of Policy Planning and Research at the Department of Labor produced a report entitled "The Negro Family: The Case for National Action." Named after its author, Daniel Patrick Moynihan, the document pushed for a broader and more aggressive War on Poverty, while opposing Community Action programs, which he deemed ineffective and likely to derail into an unbridled black activism. He called for massive full-employment policies in inner cities and worried that the scope of the War on Poverty was far from sufficient to address American economic inequality. Moynihan ambitiously regarded the European welfare state as a model to emulate and supported the idea of a universal guaranteed income.[45] His hope was to mobilize Washington against race-based economic inequalities.

But Moynihan's culturalist way of framing black poverty, pointing to the "deterioration of the Negro family" as the main cause of black poverty, percolated among liberal policy makers and journalists who, in the context of urban uprisings, seized on the idea that blacks were responsible for their own demise. By positing a nearly self-perpetuating "tangle of pathology" based on family structure, the report suggested behavioral defects were the issue to be fixed, not the racist structural and systemic dynamics.

White conservatives saw the report as scientific evidence that government efforts could never alleviate black poverty, and many liberals, revealing their ambiguities, began to doubt the relevance of economic solutions to the nation's racial tensions. Moynihan's careless rhetorical use of black "pathologies" (induced by the "matriarchal arrangement" of black life, out of line with the American mainstream) stressed the pattern of black dysfunctional families, blaming overpowering African American mothers, and assuming that working men, not women, should be the prime recipients of antipoverty "national action." His macroeconomic blueprint to achieve full employment was dismissed but his behavioral explanation of poverty as the product of black pathologies and crime led to the Law Enforcement Assistance Act of 1965, a punitive answer to poverty.

King initially subscribed to Moynihan's view, including to his controversial depiction of the pathological destructuring of the black family. He chiefly endorsed Moynihan's analysis of black disadvantage and saw the report as an opportunity to tackle inequality in northern slums. But he also quoted the report's "alarming conclusion that the Negro family is crumbling and disintegrating" and endorsed Moynihan's framework on the black family's fragility and its "matriarchal" patterns.[46] Beyond his concern about the black family, King also seemed to concur with Moynihan's description of black lower-class life when he used the metaphor of the "culture of poverty." In his 1964 address to the Democratic convention, King claimed that "Negroes are still at the bottom of the economic ladder . . . they are chained to the lowest rung by a double lock: one imprisons them on the basis of color while the second binds them to a culture of poverty." Like Moynihan, he sounded derisive of "people languishing on welfare rolls" and of "welfare-oriented policies" and argued that jobs would solve the dysfunctional pattern of the black poor. He prophesized that once full employment was reached, the decline in school dropouts, family breakups, crime rates, illegitimacy, swollen relief rolls, and other social evils would stagger the imagination.

Worse yet, he couched his understanding of the aggrieved black man in a masculinist framework, assigning women to the domestic sphere and dismissing their demands for recognition, both as wage-earners and as women, worthy of consideration beyond the boundaries of the family.[47] But his patriarchal and normative conception of the intertwining of the family structure and black male unemployment nonetheless diverged from Moynihan's reasoning.

He repudiated the behavioral framing of the urban marginalization and outbursts of discontent. The white power structure, not the "disorganization" of the black family, was what had crippled disadvantaged blacks, he asserted. To King, the poor black was not responsible for his extreme powerlessness and lack of jobs. In a speech to Planned Parenthood of America in May 1966 entitled "Family Planning—A Special and Urgent Concern," he dismissed the notion of an intractable "tangle of pathology" and challenged the premises of the Moynihan report. He hinted at it when deploring that "recently the subject of Negro family life has received extensive attention. Unfortunately, studies have overemphasized the problem of the Negro male ego and almost entirely ignored the most serious element." Neither male ego nor a black matriarchy could accurately explain poverty or familial breakups in inner cities: "Yet one element in stabilizing his life would be an understanding of and easy access to the means to develop a family related in size to his community environment and to the income potential he can command."[48]

King would later clarify his approach to the "culture of poverty" framework. In his October 1967 statement before the National Commission on Civil Disorders, he sought to reclaim Franklin Frazier's analysis: contrasting the southern white migrant's facilitated adaptation in northern cities, he described the "exploitation" and "discrimination" which awaited southern blacks, who were "left jobless, ignorant and despised." This situation bred a growing "underclass" in the cities, "as aptly described by E. Franklin Frazier in . . . his book on the Negro Family in the City of Destruction."[49] If Frazier was purportedly Moynihan's main source of inspiration, his socialist approach to cultural patterns was misconstrued. Frazier perceived black family structures as products of structural socioeconomic forces, not culture. If Frazier did talk about "family disorganization," it was from the standpoint of the black community's own standards. Frazier stressed adaptation rather than inherited traits, and believed disorganized behaviors were transitory. Even in the northern urban ghetto, "the city of destruction," the black poor would eventually rise. Like Du Bois, Frazier claimed that a "liberal and radical labor organization, attempting to create a solidarity between black and white workers" and better wages would transform the lives of the black urban youth.[50] By 1966, it became clear to King that the usages of "culture of poverty" arguments were reflective of a structural pattern of exploitation and poverty. In a fall 1966 speech, he publicly laid out what was henceforth SCLC's "newest and most urgent program": "to organize the poor in a crusade to reform society in order to realize economic and social justice."[51] The seeds of the Poor People's Campaign were planted.

Another dismissal of the cultural explanation of poverty came from labor unionist A. Philip Randolph, assisted by Bayard Rustin. They both challenged the Johnson administration's antipoverty efforts and, arguing that substantive social justice required government-sponsored economic rights and security, they suggested a new War on Poverty.[52] In October 1966 the Randolph Institute publicly presented a "Freedom Budget" concocted with leading progressive economists.[53] Its proclaimed goal was to eradicate unemployment and poverty within ten years, with a set of federal policies worth $180 billion over the decade. Pointing out that 34 million Americans were living in poverty during a time of "unparalleled prosperity," the budget provided seven objectives:

1. To provide full employment for all who are willing and able to work, including those who need education or training to make them willing and able.
2. To assure decent and adequate wages to all who work.
3. To assure a decent living standard to those who cannot or should not work.
4. To wipe out slum ghettos and provide decent homes for all Americans.
5. To provide decent medical care and adequate educational opportunities to all Americans, at a cost they can afford.
6. To purify our air and water and develop our transportation and natural resources on a scale suitable to our growing needs.
7. To unite sustained full employment with sustained full production and high economic growth.[54]

Despite what its critics saw as an amorphous set of demands, ill-fitted for tangible implementation, the Freedom Budget received an impressive show of support among progressives, including labor union leaders (Walter Reuther, I. W. Abel, David Dubinsky, and Albert Shanker);

prominent academics (Kenneth B. Clark, John Kenneth Galbraith, Gunnar Myrdal, Hylan Lewis, C. Vann Woodward, and David Riesman); civil rights leaders (Dorothy Height, Roy Wilkins, Floyd McKissick, Whitney Young Jr., John Lewis, and Vernon Jordan); and public figures (Ralph Bunche, Ossie Davis, Ruby Dee, Jules Feiffer, Father Robert Drinan, Burke Marshall, Benjamin Spock). King was among the strongest supporters of the Freedom Budget's intent and content, specifically its redistributive aspect. He pushed for an enhanced Freedom Budget, repeatedly advocating job guarantees through a government-provided "employer of last resort" program, which was already in his 1964 address in Atlantic City.

The Rooseveltian rhetoric of the budget was aimed at building consensus among progressives. But Randolph and Rustin failed to make the case for their Freedom Budget to the Johnson administration, which dismissed it as "socialistic."[55] If they managed to obtain a broad consensus among mainstream civil rights groups, they alienated the young radicals. SNCC expressed its discontent with the budget, although it had initially signed the proposal. But not only were SNCC activists committed to fighting poverty and organizing the dispossessed at the grassroots level and were deeply skeptical of the ability of the government to truly enact social change, much less to eradicate poverty, but they charged that the Freedom Budget only scratched the surface of the problem. The substance of their critique was grounded on a distinctive analysis of poverty and inequality, for which they blamed a deeply rigged tax system. An internal SNCC document called "Position on the Freedom Budget" read: "It seems to us that people are poor because 2000 families control 85 percent of the wealth in the country . . . in short, the Freedom Budget does not deal at all with the real problem: the fact that economic and political institutions of the United States have . . . resisted . . . efforts to redistribute the wealth of the society."[56] They also resented the budget's anti–Black Power innuendo and its lack of a firm standing on the Vietnam War issue, both things that King also took issue with. Moreover, Rustin's pragmatic approach to the Johnson administration—which he was careful not to antagonize— became an increasing bone of contention with King, who strategized that only civil disobedience and disruption would impel change. Despite Rustin and Randolph's faith in their collaboration with the Democratic administration, the urban uprisings and the war in Vietnam soured the relationship between black activists and the White House but also among black liberation groups.

If the foregrounded tension over the War in Vietnam crippled and eventually doomed the Freedom Budget, it was not the only source of dissension. Cooperation with Johnson and the relevance of moving from "protest to politics" and of entrusting liberals with substantive reforms were also divisive alternatives. The question of whether or not to publicly indict the war in Vietnam exacerbated and deepened tensions among civil rights leaders: while "moderate" organizations such as the NAACP and the National Urban League, were, like Rustin, reluctant to publicly oppose the war because of their pragmatic belief in Johnson's beneficence, SNCC, CORE and—although *mezzo voce* until 1967—King, openly excoriated the war, breaking with the Johnson administration and the Democratic Party.[57]

Despite regular meetings at the White House with black leaders, Johnson quickly backed away from the civil rights leaders' diagnosis of the socioeconomic cause of the urban uprisings. Notwithstanding a genuine awareness of the lack of jobs available to unskilled workers and the social consequences of this problem, federal policy makers eschewed structural reform, instead choosing to address poverty by focusing on behavior. The Freedom Budget but also King's repeated calls for full employment were nothing short of illusory. Yet, King sought to oppose the anxiety and punitive actions of the government, ushered in by the uprising, by stressing the federal government's fundamental responsibility to the poor. In a December 1966 speech entitled "The Violence of Poverty," King laid out his position with regard to the insufficient accomplishments of Johnson's antipoverty policies: "The Negro in America is an impoverished alien in an affluent society," he argued. He estimated that a third of black Americans were living in extreme poverty and lamented that the War on Poverty, while promising, failed to "carry out the mandate of the 1946 Full Employment Act, to raise the minimum wage [and to] initiate massive works-programs'" Only such policies could "light fires in the underprivileged black and white communities."[58]

In November 1966, King told a Howard University audience that African Americans needed to confront "basic issues between the privileged and the underprivileged." Beyond the influential Freedom Budget, 1966 marked a profound change in King's understanding of the poor's plight.[59] That year, he moved to a slum in Chicago, visited Marks, Mississippi where extreme poverty drove him to tears, and grappled with the growing appeal of Black Power activists. Addressing poverty and economic exploitation in more forceful ways while preserving his deeply held principles was the common thread of these events. Since Stokely Carmichael uttered the slogan "Black Power" during the "March Against Fear" in the summer of 1966 in Mississippi, SNCC's new radicalism challenged King's nonviolent political vision. Such a rift pertained mostly to the viability of the interracial coalition which Carmichael, increasingly disaffected with biracial politics since the rejection of the Mississippi Democratic Party's demands in 1964, no longer supported. It was telling however that his call for Black Power originated in the Mississippi Delta where, before the March Against Fear, Carmichael had toiled on behalf of the poor. King and Carmichael were opposed on several questions from 1966 onward but not on the centrality of economic exploitation in the black liberation struggle. If to Carmichael the path to substantive equality could not be interracial, King came to understand in Chicago that it not only had to be biracial but "pan-racial." In that respect, Chicago was decisive in elaborating the Poor People's Campaign, a prelude to a broader multiracial and labor coalition.[60]

CHICAGO AND THE MANY FACES OF THE EXPLOITED POOR

Chicago proved critically instructive. King knew poverty. But the exploitative southern sharecropping system was more comprehensible to the SCLC than the economy of northern slums. According to Rustin, it is only by moving to a dilapidated apartment in the Chicago slum of Lawnsdale and living among the urban poor that King fully understood how the political economy of cities explained black poverty. In the aftermath of the Watts uprising though, he had a glimpse of the specificity of northern poverty:

In the South, there is something of shared poverty, Negro and white. In the North, white existence, only steps away, glares with conspicuous consumption. Even television becomes incendiary, when it beams pictures of affluent homes and multitudinous consumer products at the aching poor, living in wretched homes. In these terms, Los Angeles could have expected riots because it is the luminous symbol of luxurious living for whites. Watts is closer to it, and yet farther from it, than any other Negro community in the country. The looting in Watts was a form of social protest very common through the ages as a dramatic and destructive gesture of the poor toward symbols of their needs.[61]

The West Side of Chicago was another tragic case in point and King contended that "the slum of Lawndale is truly an island of poverty in the midst of an ocean of plenty."[62] To him, inequality, that is the violence of someone's relative poverty in an affluent society, was the unsustainable ordeal of the American poor. Not only in American ghettos but in America as a whole, the humiliating effect of visible wealth inequality injured disadvantaged people's dignity, thereby impairing their status as citizens. During a December 1966 Senate hearing, King made clear that the obvious unequal distribution of wealth in the United States created an undercurrent of social unrest and was fraying the nation's social fabric:

> The rising affluence of America has benefited the better-off more than the poor and discriminated. Our income record is acceptable only if we wish to tolerate a society in which the richest fifth of the population is 10 times as rich as the poorest fifth, and in which the average Negro earns half as much as his white counterpart.[63]

The living conditions of the working class communities of color in Lawndale indeed left an indelible impression on King. He heard the pleas of poor people concentrated in chronically unaffordable, inadequate, and insecure housing and witnessed their ailments, which ran the gamut from unemployment to malnutrition to failing segregated schools to humiliating conflicts with welfare services and local police. Worse yet, as Tommie Shelby eloquently describes King's egalitarian concerns, he grasped that "black ghetto dwellers are fully aware of the opulence just beyond their reach, and this knowledge makes them miserable."[64]

King came to reframe his definition of "the poor" which, in a northern urban setting, was the epitome of political disempowerment as the local party machine ran the Community Action programs but rendered community action nonexistent. The poor people he lived with were mostly displaced southern agricultural workers, a group familiar to him but they concentrated within the boundaries of the city where they were kept isolated, excluded, and marginalized in singular ways. Their socioeconomic position reinforced their political disinheritance. Most residents were victims of the lack of decent-paying jobs but also suffered from inequitable social policy. As in a "domestic colony," King contended, they represented "a source of cheap surplus labor in times of economic boom" and so were exploited. Oppressed by the police and the welfare worker, confined to misery by design, they were ironically "blamed for their own victimization."[65] King clearly rejected the Moynihan-inspired rhetoric which singled out the urban poor as an "undeserving poor" whose cultural deficiencies condemned them to welfare dependency and crime. But urban northern poverty was not the only one he somehow "rediscovered" in 1966.

During the summer of 1966, as he joined James Meredith's "March Against Fear" in Mississippi, King and Abernathy visited Marks where the squalor of famished black kids left him tormented. Their eyes, he wrote, would haunt him. Deeply shocked by the invisibility of the poor, he felt the need for a dramatization of the dispossessed: "I don't think people really know that little schoolchildren are slowly starving in the United States, I did not know it."[66] If the most vulnerable of the poor took the faces of the Marks schoolchildren, it was in Chicago that King came to the realization of the systemic nature of poverty. Nowhere more than in a northern, economically depressed area did King understand that the misrepresentation of the poor was meant to deflect attention from the entrenched structural inequality. Arguably, the Chicago Freedom Movement and the Chicago Campaign were seminal, for they were the first explicit attempts to address the issues of exploitation and poverty outside the South. But more than a regional shift, they ushered in a new approach to the race and class dialectics and to the historical role of the poor.

Spanning September 1965 to the fall of 1967, the Chicago Freedom Movement was an attempt to organize the urban poor, building a grassroots movement of the dispossessed which would challenge landlords and their predatory practices, as well as public discriminatory practices.

A Union to End Slums was put in motion to organize poor tenants and confrontationally address the systemic nature of poverty. Here, the Marxist notions of "internal" or "domestic colonialism" undergirded King's antipoverty endeavors.[67] He also talked about "slumism" and "white power structure," loaded terms meant to point to the historical forces which, creating the plantation and the ghetto, ensured the perpetuation of the poor's powerlessness. Precisely because "power refused to acknowledge its debt to the poor" the haves-not should voice their dissent. Refusing to give in to black cultural-deficiency assumptions, which would explain concentrated urban poverty, King pointed to the structural mechanism leading to the spatial confinement and economic exclusion of blacks:

> These communities have become slums not just because the Negroes don't keep clean and don't care, but because the whole system makes it that way. I call it slummism—a bad house is not just a bad house, it's a bad school and a bad job, and it's been that way for three generations, a bad house for three generations, and a bad school for three generations.[68]

The overarching purpose of the Chicago Campaign was to empower poor people and to give them the political leverage to compel city hall into action. In doing so, the Chicago Campaign also exposed the limitations of Johnson's War on Poverty and suggested an alternative. The simmering discontent of black urban youth but also of poor families and welfare recipients had grown all the more salient, especially as their continued subordination and exploitation was organized by Richard Daley, the powerful mayor of Chicago and ally to the Johnson administration. The Chicago Freedom campaigners felt that the government's antipoverty initiatives and racial patronage were tools to reinforce the status quo and buy off black disaffection. Challenged by black power militants and gang members, King grasped that economic redistribution had to be conflated with power reallocation in ways that neither Rustin or Randolph's perspectives nor Community Action programs could insure. The Chicago Campaign included in their call to end the slums appeals for welfare rights, tenant's rights, and a denunciation of the exploitative practices at play in areas of concentrated poverty as well as the lack of jobs available to the residents. In a second phase, the Chicago Freedom Movement engaged in "open housing" marches to integrate all white neighborhoods as slum landlords anchored their practices on the scarcity of available housing for blacks.[69] Tenant-housing problems stemmed from poverty, unemployment, and the lack of decent housing—altogether, symptoms of what King repeatedly called "a large system of slum exploitation." The attempt to tackle housing inequities proved disappointing and the SCLC came to terms with the limits of community politics as not suited to tackle the structural roots of poverty.

The collaboration between the SCLC, which missioned James Bevel in Chicago, and Al Raby's Coordinating Council of Community Organizations could not truly challenge Chicago's power structure but it was a lesson and, as such, the breeding ground of the Poor People's Campaign. Pointing to the direct influence of the Chicago Campaign on the PPC, Al Raby recalled:

> I think that Chicago was an education for Martin, and in some ways was an education for those of us in Chicago who believed we were very sophisticated and knowledgeable. It was an education in terms of the conquerability of poverty in northern areas. He was certainly familiar with poverty in the South; I think it was an education in terms of resistance. You should remember that at the same time we were in the midst of the rhetoric of Black Power, and Martin, I think, was trying to say to the activists, that as the leader of the Poor People's March I am going to bring forward and make visible the rainbow nature of poverty in this country.[70]

The rise of Black Power occurred at the same time as King's interaction with disaffected young urban blacks in Chicago. They all exhibited greater militancy and demanded substantive political participation. King's plans for the PPC were deeply influenced by the young Black Power activists, who obviously were unconvinced by his abiding commitment to interracialism and strict nonviolence. Quoting Du Bois's *Black Reconstruction* and the populist episodes of the late nineteenth century, the authors of the seminal 1967 book *Black Power*—Stokely Carmichael and political scientist Charles V. Hamilton—dismissed any idea that such a coalition could be based on the racial asymmetry of power.[71] Their revolutionary message appealed more to Chicago's young blacks than did King's despite his best effort to talk to them. His will to challenge Black Power collapsed with his attempt to neutralize gang members. Lawrence Johnson, leader of the Conservative Vice Lords of Lawndale, recalled his meeting with King at his apartment. King expressed his understanding of the systemic oppression ghetto dwellers were enduring, telling them that the police "represented the establishment" and as such, had a power violence could not match.[72] Reaching out to West Side gang members and quelling their resentment and unrest was a major concern of his stay in Chicago. If the SCLC had attempted to work with gangs before, Chicago was the first attempt to organize, train, and hire them. The Blackstone Rangers, the Cobras, the Roman Saints, and the Vice Lords were the main street gangs of the Windy City. SCLC's James Bevel, Bernard Lafayette, and James Orange had some of them serve as marshals for the open-housing marches. Although unable to prevent the violence that eventually erupted in June 1966, King employed the bold move he would repeat during the PPC, willing to prove that young, disaffected, and dispossessed blacks could be a vanguard. Here again, he expected to confront the vilification of the urban poor.

If, to a certain extent, he grasped the young urban blacks' disempowerment and their subsequent assertive masculinity, he also reconsidered the relevance of poor black women, who had been engaged for a long time in welfare rights activism.[73] Johnson's War on Poverty, like Roosevelt's New Deal, had reignited intraracial tensions along class and gender lines. In the 1960s, just as in the 1930s, middle-class and professional blacks benefited the most from new job openings in federal agencies and social services by virtue of their status. Yet, grassroots poverty workers like welfare rights activists (mostly women) had been critical of the unfairness of these policies. Despite mainstream civil rights organizations' participation in the OEO, they fought for substantive equality in their own right. As Annelise Orleck put it, "the poorest of the poor, despite daunting obstacles, transformed themselves into effective political actors who insisted on being heard."[74] Welfare groups and poor single mothers involved in the Chicago Freedom Movement began to reframe King's representation of the type of poor suited to be the nonviolent vanguard, so much so that welfare rights women would come to spearhead and co-orchestrate King's PPC.

The seeds of the PPC were indeed rooted in Chicago. King and the people involved in the Windy City campaign understood that poor people had to get nationally organized.[75] Grassroots mobilizing and direct action at the local level were not to be dismissed but rather coordinated statewide. Welfare recipients, whom King interacted with for the first time in Chicago, had come to this conclusion too. In 1966 civil rights activist George Alvin Wiley organized several demonstrations for the poor and brought together a number of local organizations into a National Welfare Rights Organization whose goals were to shore up public assistance for the poor and provide them with adequate income, dignity, justice, and democratic participation. Their community organizing approach addressed poor families in working class communities in ways that tackled their immediate concerns and give them agency. If Wiley began by cooperatively pushing for a more expansive War on Poverty, he evolved as militant women radicalized the organization, demanding a guaranteed income and the recognition of poor people's voice and dignity through welfare reform.[76] So did King.

Like Randolph, King had defended job creation for men over "welfare dependency" and dismissed concerns over child welfare appropriations. But the indignities suffered by welfare recipients and the discretionary distribution of welfare benefits were now on his agenda. Estranged from mainline civil rights leaders, King also parted ways with Randolph's approach. The divergence between the unionist and King was explicit with regard to the guaranteed job or income, advocated by King as nothing less than a right, a reasoning tellingly absent from the Freedom Budget. The right to an income, be it welfare payments, was not endorsed by Randolph, who saw welfare as a privilege undermining the pride and dignity of the black man. His gendered approach to wage earning, consistent throughout Randolph's life, was shared by Rustin but abandoned by King.[77]

In an October 1966 speech, King called for a $4000 guaranteed annual income for all citizens, a drastic redistribution of wealth advocated by welfare rights activists. Most renters in Chicago's housing projects relied on public assistance to survive. As modest as it was, this source of income was at the same time indispensable and unfairly dispensed. King came to understand—if not the specifics of the welfare legislation—the reason why recipients, mostly women, resented the "man in the house rule" which deprived non–single women of welfare payments.[78] "We are tired of a welfare system which dehumanizes us and dispenses payments under procedures that are often ugly and paternalistic," he said during a multiracial rally in Chicago.[79] He would now talk about the "economic paternalism" of social welfare providers and his guaranteed income was now not only intended for the unemployed and the underpaid but also for poor single mothers whose domestic "work" deserved an income. The Chicago Campaign contextualized the elaboration of King's most significant book on substantive justice, which undergirded the PPC. *Where Do We Go from Here,* his last essay, laid the blueprint for the economic demands and philosophical imperatives that were needed to sustain a deep restructuring of the American political economy.

While in Chicago, King also gained a more complex understanding of the class-based nature of American racism. Not only did he come to oppose the cultural explanation of poverty and the government's outright condemnation of the uprising of an emergent black militancy, but he reasoned that, in order to counteract the misrepresentation of the poor, he had to move from an interracial cooperation to a multiracial one. Chicago arguably laid the groundwork for a radical multiracial organizing on behalf of the poor and the left-out. For the first time, the SCLC attempted to join ranks with Latino activists, Mexican Americans but also Puerto Ricans who—because of the racial make-up of the city—were to be significant allies.[80] As far as multiracial organizing, the SCLC was a latecomer by virtue of its southern origin, where racial animosity was almost exclusively between blacks and whites. But SNCC, implanted in the Southwest, had been supporting Cesar Chavez's United Farm Workers since 1965, binding the plight of southern sharecroppers to that of Mexican farmworkers. SNCC's ability to reach out to nonblack activists was particularly salient in Mississippi where, during the summer of 1965, hundreds of white students joined "Freedom Summer."

In the North, SNCC inspired many nonblack social movements, notably the Students for a Democratic Society (SDS), which was dedicated to addressing poverty as the central fact of Negro oppression and to organizing an "interracial movement of the poor."[81] An embodiment of the New Left, the SDS carved out a revolutionary program known as the Port Huron Statement. Drafted in 1962 by white radical students one year after the creation of the group, it demanded the expansion of public spending, the creation of jobs and housing to respond to automation, substantive equality for African Americans, and the immediate stopping of the war in Vietnam.[82] At the micro-level, the SDS labored to build solidarity among the poor from diverse racial and ethnic backgrounds. As for SNCC, its class and race framework paved the way for King's Poor People's Campaign.

SDS expected to launch a "new insurgency," bringing together blacks, students, radicalized unions, and middle-class liberals to force their political and cultural agenda through. To overcome alienation, they relied on automation, which "would lead to the possibility of a world of plenty [that] could give leisure to all," enabling direct democracy and bottom-up economic planning.[83] Tellingly, SDS activists picked Chicago in September 1963 to launch their Economic Research and Action Project (ERAP) in the hope that addressing economic inequality among the urban poor would create bonds of solidarity between Puerto Ricans, poor whites, and Native Americans. JOIN (Jobs Or Income Now) became the name of ERAP's Chicago chapter. They opened their main office next to the city's Unemployment Office, to be available to help the jobless poor obtain a check and get organized, actions reminiscent of the unemployment leagues of the 1930s. JOIN sought to address class-based issues without shying away from the reality of the poor white's prejudice and privilege. They attempted to organize in Chicago's uptown section, nicknamed "Hillbilly Harlem" by virtue of its predominant Appalachian population.[84] But securing full employment would not address the predicament of poor women, a limitation ERAP sought to solve by considering their specific issues and demands. They thus mobilized for decent housing, child care, and along with welfare rights activists, demanded a more participatory welfare state, more attention from overworked welfare caseworkers, and less intrusive welfare provisions. Because they were influenced by poor women and women of color overrepresented in the local Welfare Recipients Demand Action group, JOIN addressed the gender imbalance of many grassroots organizations. The chapter also managed to build solid relations between union-inspired organized poor residents and the United Packinghouse Workers and the Independent Union of Public Aid Employees. By 1966 though, ERAP had enjoyed only limited success. Yet, it did attempt to build "an interracial movement of the poor" that challenged liberal tenets and empowered the dispossessed with a radical dialectics of class and race.[85]

When King arrived in Chicago, SDS was already actively calling for, as their local chapter's acronym explicitly points to, "Jobs or Income Now," a slogan the PPC would appropriate two years later. A former CORE activist engaged in JOIN, Peggy Terry, and SDS cofounder Tom Hayden met with King and Carmichael to discuss interracial coalitions of the poor. Interestingly, white activist Peggy Terry was among those in Greenwood, Mississippi who, in June 1966, in response to Stokely Carmichael's question "What do you want?" chanted "Black Power! Black Power!" She carried her radical approach to race and class to Chicago and later to King's PPC. Fully committed to it, Terry organized Chicago's poor whites so that they joined the insurrectionary campaign in 1968.

Unsurprisingly, major figures of the Chicago Campaign would be crucial to the Poor People's Campaign: Bernard Lafayette would become the PPC's national director; Tony Henry, of the American Friends Service Committee (AFSC) in Chicago would preside over the Washington headquarters of the PPC; and Jesse Jackson (who lead "Operation Breadbasket" in Chicago) would become the mayor of Resurrection City.[86] At the end of an excruciating campaign which had not delivered as expected, King emphasized that however limited in its outcome, the campaign "forced" the " white power structure" to negotiate. To obtain real results, only a national campaign would persuade the dominant group to give up some of its privileges. The mixed results in Chicago breed a grander project. Tony Henry, poised to become the associate director and head of the PPC's Washington, DC office, recalled that "the concept of a campaign of poor people from all over the country attacking racial discrimination and other types of oppression finally began to take root and blossomed. What came out of that finally was the decision to bring poor people from all over the country to Washington DC."[87]

THE WAR IN VIETNAM AND THE POOR AS CASUALTY

King's experience and the new understanding he grasped in Chicago put him on a collision course with Johnson and the Democrats. From the SCLC standpoint, there was no doubt that the disappointing outcome of the Chicago Campaign stemmed from northern liberal whites' reluctance to enact substantive equality. What was exposed in Chicago was a northern brand of racism deeply entrenched in the structures and systems of northern cities. "Northern racial liberals," particularly city officials, promoted an uplift ideology that was purportedly egalitarian but refused to tackle the systemic racism and existing power hierarchies that, albeit far from Jim Crow, were nevertheless deeply embedded in northern urban life.[88]

While in Chicago, King also witnessed the defects of War on Poverty programs, the culturalization and criminalization of poverty, and the punitive turn which resulted from the urban uprisings. He was now deeply aware that racial inequality was embedded in economic structures, defiantly calling black poverty an "economic holocaust."[89] His experience in Chicago and his observation of urban discontent led him to share Bayard Rustin's Marxist definition of the riots as "outbursts of class aggression in a society where class and color definitions are converging disastrously."[90] But he made more complex Rustin's Old Left, labor-oriented vision by endorsing Black Power's and other new insurgents' notion that structural wealth inequality was embedded in *all* institutions. He incriminated the capitalist system, which "was built on the exploitation and suffering of black slaves and continue to thrive on the exploitation of the poor, both black and white, both here and abroad" and also called out for condemnation America's growing wealth inequalities.[91] In his December 1966 statement to the Senate subcommittee appointed to analyze the uprising, King was emphatic that not only poverty but inequality and the resentment it ushered in for those left behind had to be addressed:

> American cities are not the City of God nor the City of Man. They contain the residues of exploitation, of waste, of neglect, of indifference. The poor and the discriminated huddle in the big cities—the poor-houses of the welfare state—while affluent America displays its new gadgets in the crisp homes of suburbia.[92]

Embedding racial equality in an overarching program to correct economic structural wrongs was less than ever President Johnson's idea. Afraid of alienating his constituency, who came to equate the War on Poverty with "black riots," Johnson incrementally distanced himself from now controversial OEO programs (even the inoffensive Child Development

Group of Mississippi) and from civil rights leaders insufficiently accommodating for his taste.

The rise of revolutionary black nationalism, which attracted more and more young impoverished blacks, brought forward an assertive racial and class-based claim. Johnson and a significant part of the nation collapsed their militancy with their own fear of social chaos. Young urban black men were burdened with a presumption of guilt and dangerousness and any organization willing to give them a voice was dismissed. Along with welfare rights antipoverty activists and working-class blacks, Black Power leaders were deliberately excluded from Johnson's discussions of national civil rights policy. During his 1966 White House Conferences on Civil Rights, he expected mainstream black leaders to refrain from employing the use of protest and demonstrations and marginalized those who could speak on behalf of the poor.[93]

King's relationship with Johnson had been strained since the passage on the Voting Rights Act but such political maneuvering accelerated their disagreement. Yet, still hoping that a coalition with liberals, unions, and the White House would be supportive of wealth and power redistribution, King refrained from publicly condemning the escalating Vietnam War. In contrast to SNCC and antiwar students, he silenced his pacifism on the altar of progressive domestic policies. His economic agenda was actually being tenaciously advocated by a few within the Democratic Party. On August 18, 1967, at the SCLC convention in Atlanta, John Conyers, a Democratic congressman from Michigan, called for a $30 billion per year omnibus bill "to provide every American adequate employment, housing and education on a truly non-discriminatory basis." Conyers planned to introduce this "Full Opportunity Act" in the House of Representatives the following week. Echoing King, he contended that "piecemeal programs and patchwork legislation have proven totally ineffective . . . it is like applying a Band-Aid to a cancerous growth. Only a massive Federal Program can eradicate the ghettos and slums that have spread throughout the cities of America over many decades."[94] His bill would guarantee jobs by making the government "the employer of last resort." The minimum wage would be raised to two dollars an hour and workers would get better legal protection. A massive program of low-cost housing was proposed, as well as a comprehensive federal college loan program to provide higher

education to all. The bill also included the enforcement of antidiscriminatory laws in all economic areas.[95]

Despite the voices calling for radical institutional changes in policy,
Conyers's bill was no more successful for the disadvantaged than King's
Economic Bill of Rights. Yet King too kept pressing the White House for
job creation and economic justice. As the 1967 Chicago riots prompted
Johnson to implement emergency action, King urged him "to do as his
Hero FDR did" by setting up a WPA-type make-work program for the
poor. The Scripps Howard journalist who reported the interview in a
January 1968 article underscored King's comments: "I am not convinced
the statesmanship exists in Washington to do it. . . . I am convinced that
one massive act of concern will do more than the most massive deploy-
ment of troops to quell riots and instill hatred."[96] He repeated his call for
an Economic Bill of Rights for the Disadvantaged, a guaranteed income,
and suggested that a national agency should immediately be set up "to
give employment to everyone needing it." Incensed by the escalation of the
Vietnam War, King grew more and more distrustful of the White House.
While Randolph and Rustin still sought conciliation to foster progress,
King believed in social change through confrontation with Johnson and
Congress as it became clear to him that the War on Poverty would not be
broadened. Quite the contrary, the Vietnam War was torpedoing social
and economic justice.

By 1967, King willfully jeopardized a failing alliance with Johnson and,
despite Rustin and Randolph's opposition, pilloried Johnson's bellicose policy. The Vietnam War, which the SNCC and then King publicly denounced,
fractured the civil rights movement, with moderate groups such as the
NAACP and the National Urban League remaining silent on this controversial topic.[97] Most mainline leaders felt that the Black Freedom movement
should not get distracted by non–civil rights-related issues. King was
emphatic that the war was such an issue. SNCC had already repeatedly
pointed to the racial and classist inequalities which undergirded the draft, a
point later underscored by King. Blacks were disproportionately sent into
combat and disproportionately killed: less than 10 percent of American soldiers, they represented almost 20 percent of those killed in action.

Tellingly, King framed his indictment of the war as a welfare policy
issue. He saw the conflict in Vietnam not only as an immoral, unjust, and

destructive use of violence against mankind but also as a lethal blow to the nation's effort to become truly egalitarian. Poor and blacks were the major casualties of Johnson's many wars. At the April 1967 Riverside Church meeting, he explained how Johnson's War on Poverty was a war directed against the poor:

> There is at the outset a very obvious and almost facile connection between the war in Vietnam and the struggle I, and others, have been waging in America. A few years ago there was a shining moment in that struggle. It seemed as if there was a real promise of hope for the poor—both black and white—through the poverty program. There were experiments, hopes, new beginnings. Then came the buildup in Vietnam, and I watched this program broken and eviscerated, as if it were some idle political plaything of a society gone mad on war, and I knew that America would never invest the necessary funds or energies in rehabilitation of its poor so long as adventures like Vietnam continued to draw men and skills and money like some demonic destructive suction tube. So, I was increasingly compelled to see the war as an enemy of the poor and to attack it as such.[98]

Indeed, funding the escalating conflict against the Vietcong took precedence over social welfare interventions. The metaphorical War on Poverty was gutted as its budget was diverted by Congress to wage a real war abroad. Rightly so, King connected American belligerence to social justice at home. "We spend approximately $500,000 to kill every enemy soldier in Vietnam, while we spend only $53 per person in the so-called 'War Against Poverty,'" he bemoaned.[99] Less than two weeks after his Riverside Church speech on Vietnam, King told the 125,000 New York City's protesters who had marched from Central Park to the United Nations that the war had metastasized on American soil. The bombs in Vietnam explode at home, he said; they destroy the hopes and possibilities for a decent America.

King's severe statement would eventually be vindicated by Sergeant Shriver himself, who recognized that "the War Against Poverty was killed by the war in Vietnam—first of all, because of the lack of money."[100] For King, such an imperialist war, which he saw as draining funds from domestic policies, dramatically undermining social welfare policies and community participation, raised serious doubts about the antipoverty commitment of the government. By 1966, racially marginalized residents in central cities and low-income neighborhoods saw their expectations shattered upon realizing how deceptive the promotion of equal opportunities heralded by the OEO was. Indeed, as early as February 1964, President Johnson had vetoed a $1.25 billion unemployment plan for the urban poor, and with expanding military expenditures, the total antipoverty budget would not go significantly above $2 billion a year after 1966. This consequential change in priorities occurred at a time when structural exclusion and inequality had reached a tipping point. The shift of the industrial labor market from low-skilled jobs and its relocation to the suburbs was almost beginning to annihilate blacks' educational gains. In 1964, more than 20 percent of young black men under age 25 were unemployed nationwide.[101] According to an AFL-CIO report, although they made up only 12 percent of the population, black workers accounted for 36 percent of long-term unemployed Americans.[102] Despite the decrease in the national unemployment rate with the Vietnam War, it was still about twice as high for blacks (8 percent versus 3.7 percent for all Americans). Throughout the decade, wage inequality increased and black unemployment remained twice as high as for whites.[103]

Washington could not be a reliable ally to the poor, much less to the black poor, unless a strong social movement pressured elected officials, prompting them to take action. Vietnam was, as King told the audience in Chicago on November 11, 1967, an unjust and racist war which was eviscerating the domestic antipoverty programs:

> In the past two months unemployment has increased approximately 15 percent. At this moment tens of thousands of people and anti-poverty programs are being abruptly thrown out of jobs and training programs to search in a diminishing job market for work and survival. It is disgraceful that a Congress that can vote upward of 35 billion a year for a senseless, immoral war in Vietnam cannot vote a weak 2 billion dollars to carry on our all-too-feeble efforts to bind up the wounds of our nation's 35 billion poor. This is nothing short of a Congress engaging in political guerilla warfare against the defenseless poor of our nation.[104]

King also pointed to the double standard of Johnson's policies, which criminalized urban residents' use of violence but justified his own war. The extensive racial violence that erupted in Newark, Detroit, and dozens of other cities during the "long, hot summer" of 1967 moved Johnson further away from King's structural critiques of poverty. The spectacle of the urban uprisings prompted the apostle of satyagraha to restore the image of nonviolence while addressing the causes of the unrest: unemployment, poverty, and discrimination. A nonviolent gathering of poor people dedicated to peace and justice on Johnson's front porch would be the dramatization needed to gain momentum. On the heels of the urban uprisings, public opinion was open to policies aimed at eradicating slums.[105] Moreover, influential policy makers seemed supportive of massive redistribution on behalf of the urban poor.

In 1967, a "Crime Commission" chaired by Nicholas Katzenbach issued a report urging Johnson to strengthen his antipoverty initiatives, mainly in zones of segregated urban poverty, to prevent future civil disorders. Guaranteed income, new welfare regulations, and housing programs were offered as the most effective strategies to keep inner cities peaceful.[106] A year later, the Kerner Commission, which was formed in 1967 to explain the tide of riots, vindicated black activists by recommending massive job creation to curtail the ghettos' "frustrated hopes," Here again, a guaranteed minimum income was proposed. During the commission's hearings, King made the case that the interplay between race and class had to be grappled with: police brutality, certainly, but more than most, the economic roots of racial oppression were to blame. He forcefully asserted that the "underclass" uprising was caused by economic alienation and were therefore "environmental and not racial."[107] Years before, on his way to Chicago, he had already stated that "the economic deprivation, social isolation, inadequate housing, and general despair of thousands of Negroes teeming in Northern and Western ghettos are the ready seeds which give birth to tragic expressions of violence."[108]

Although several federal policy makers further echoed King in acknowledging that unemployment and subpar urban school systems were factors contributing to both poverty and revolt, Johnson stuck to his fiscal conservatism and his punitive approach to poverty. Congress, guided by a growing resentment among "white ethnic" democratic voters, undermined the antipoverty policies still standing with major budget cuts, claiming that rioters were being rewarded. For instance, days after the Newark uprising, conservatives derided a program aimed at eliminating slum rats through a $40 million grant by calling it the "the civil rats bill." Despite civil rights organizations' uproar, the program was voted down.[109] Though Johnson was not to blame for this setback, some have argued that the overall governmental disdain for pleas from black organizations to tackle joblessness amounted to acquiescing to "institutional racism."[110] Certainly, "had Johnson listened more carefully to blacks, he might have created jobs for those who desperately needed them."[111] Had he listened to King, he would perhaps have understood that effecting universalistic structural reforms would have benefited poor whites as well as blacks.

In December 1967, in a press conference announcing the Poor People's Campaign, King explained that the organizers "intend to channelize the smoldering rage and frustration of Negro people into an effective, militant and non-violent movement of massive proportions."[112] King couched his PPC framework in a language likely to struck a chord: social peace was at stake, and the nation was in a state of emergency, he contended. With such dramatic rhetoric, he hoped to tap into liberals' fears that collective urban violence would become a permanent feature in American life. The Poor People's Campaign would be a buffer to simmering discontent and poverty. As he would later write.

> We intend, before the summer comes, to initiate a "last chance" project to arouse the American conscience toward constructive democratic change. The nation has been warned by the President's Commission (on Civil Disorders) that our society faces catastrophic division in an approaching doomsday if the country does not act. We have, through this non-violent action, an opportunity to avoid a national disaster and to create a new spirit of harmony.[113]

The Poor People's campaign would, in King's mind, offer an alternative image to that of the badly off, burning city. But more than that, the campaign would gather all those who felt alienated by an unequal system: "Similarly, we will be calling on the swelling masses of young people in this country who are disenchanted with this materialistic society."[114] More than ever, King expressed a sense of urgency, an imminent threat to an oblivious nation.

6 An "American Commune"

The SCLC leadership met from November 27 to November 31 in Frogmore, South Carolina to discuss the campaign. Embattled and distressed by the surge of violence in and by his country, King expressed his qualified optimism, maintaining a hope that had become—in Du Bois's words—"not hopeless but unhopeful."[1] King eloquently shared his sense of his own limitations and that of the country, confiding that "everyone underestimated the amount of white bigotry" and the sturdiness of the "white power structure." He made clear that from now on, nonviolence had to "be adapted to urban conditions and urban moods." Thinking aloud, he suggested a "massive, active nonviolent resistance" to a "property-centered" and "profit-centered" system. To redeem it and to achieve a "person-oriented" society, a dramatic, dislocative, and disruptive yet nonviolence campaign had to be launched.[2]

The SCLC staff reluctantly agreed to organize an unprecedented civil disobedience campaign in Washington, DC, focused on jobs and income. The strategic outline was not only for a mass meeting in Washington but also a showcase of the campaigners' odyssey from all around the country to the capital. Hundreds of well-trained nonviolent activists would accompany the multiracial caravans of the disinherited and help them get settled on the Washington Mall where they would, through daily demonstrations at federal agencies, compel Congress to take action against poverty. The initial plan was to disrupt the daily functioning of the capital, for instance by staging sit-ins at the Department of Agriculture or the Department of the Interior. Nonviolent yet resolute, campaigners would settle on the Mall for as long as necessary. Moreover, the campaign would be truly and dramatically multiracial. Bernard Lafayette recalled:

> Well, the concept was this, once we had our staff meeting here in Atlanta, I stayed back after the staff meeting, and I said now, Dr. King, and he was sitting down . . . in the board room and I was standing up. And I said, now you say this is gonna be a poor people's campaign? He said, yes. I said, okay. I said, well there are other people who are poor. What about the Native Americans? He said yes, I wanna get the Native Americans involved. Well, we hadn't, up to that point SCLC had not really established a coalition with Native Americans, so I said, what about the Hispanics? He said yes, we wanna get them involved. And by this time, he is already clued into my next question. And he turned around and he looked up at me, and I said well what about the poor whites? Martin Luther King say, are they poor? I said yes. He said we want them involved.[3]

A NEW ALLIANCE

It was to be the most ambitious campaign ever envisioned by King. Bringing the poor to Washington, dramatizing their predicament, and forcing the elites to see them could be a game-changer with respect to social policy. King's goal was to petition the government for specific reforms aimed at securing jobs and income for all. Without renouncing the idea that race was a major factor in the mechanism of inequality and that it had to be dealt with as such, he nonetheless asserted that blacks shared common needs with other dispossessed groups. He announced that the campaign would be embryonic of a new progressive mass movement, "the beginning of a new co-operation, understanding, and a determination by poor people of all colors and backgrounds to assert and win their right to a decent life and respect for their culture and dignity."[4]

King was not the only one to have been awakened to extreme poverty in the midst of plenty by the spectacle of Mississippi's hungry children. Bobby Kennedy, then the senator from New York and who had accepted NAACP activist and lawyer Marian Wright's invitation to meet with the poor in Mississippi a year after King's visit, was choked by the famished children he saw. Wright, who was lobbying for the restoration of federal funding for children with the Child Development Group in Mississippi, would recall being pleasantly surprised to see a senator "profoundly moved by Mississippi's hungry children."[5] Also concerned about Cesar Chavez's farmworkers' struggle, the former attorney general came to believe in the necessity for a liberal progressive coalition able to end the war in Vietnam, address racial inequality, and wage a true war on poverty.[6] It would be his presidential campaign platform at the Democratic primary the following year. Arguably, Kennedy's visit was instrumental in putting Mississippi Delta child hunger on the national agenda and it sparked a coalition of individuals dedicated to waging a war against the violence of poverty.[7] In August 1967, Kennedy met with Wright in his Virginia residence. During the conversation, he purportedly suggested that she convinced King to "bring the poor people to Washington," which she did. The idea was already present in King's mind but upon Wright's 1967 hint, it crystallized.

The radical framework that sustained the Poor People's Campaign was at odds with many civil rights leaders' liberal thinking but also with some of their undertakings. Jesse Jackson for instance, who lead Operation Breadbasket in Chicago, advocated black economic power and fully embraced capitalism as a venue for black emancipation.[8] Such an obvious contradiction with King's socialist leanings did not go unnoticed but in fact reinforced many of King's friends' misgivings about the campaign.[9] According to Taylor Branch, "half his staff was revolting against it," asserting that "we are a black movement."[10]

Prominent leaders, including Bayard Rustin and Roy Wilkins, immediately dismissed the project while most SCLC leaders disagreed on the timing and relevance of such an unprecedented campaign. Yet, King's persuasiveness won them over and the plan was adopted. King announced the Poor People's Campaign on December 4, 1967, casting an unprecedented act of dissent which would disrupt the disempowering process of formal democracy and liberate the poor:

> We are still not free. . . . And you know why we aren't free? Because we are poor. We are poor. . . . What is poverty? . . . Poverty is being underemployed,

poverty is working a full-time job, getting only part-time income. Poverty means living in a run-down, dilapidated house. . . .

. . . now, we are tired of being on the bottom, we are tired of being exploited. . . . And as a result of being tired, we are going to Washington D.C . . . in order to say to this nation that "you must provide us with jobs or income" . . . And for 60 or 90 days, this nation will not be able to ignore or overlook the poor. And we are going to plague Congress, and we are going to plague the government, until they will do something. . . .[11]

The first step by the Poor People's Campaign would be the creation of a multiracial, nonviolent army of the dispossessed, made up of poor whites, Puerto Ricans, African Americans, Chicanos, and Native Americans. The thrust of the campaign was not only a mass meeting in Washington but a showcase of the poor's odyssey from all around the country to the capital. Trained to nonviolent techniques, several thousands of them would caravan from their regions to the capital, settling on the Washington Mall to get the nation to pay attention and compel policy makers to address the structural imbalance of wealth and power crippling the nation. The dispossessed would travel to the capital by car, bus, train, or mule wagon, stopping for local rallies, all the while performing spectacular acts of civil disobedience and civic disruption.

In the inception of the project, King gravitated toward a militant tactic of disruption and civil dislocation not only in Washington but in New York where Wall Street would be the target of specific actions.[12] After the settlement of the poor on the Mall in Washington for an undisclosed amount of time, the campaigners were to disrupt traffic, organize mass demonstrations and other public acts of civil disobedience, fill the jails, and spearhead a massive economic boycott. The campaign had to channel the exploited poor's anger, frustration, and longing for action. With the help of his advisor Stanley Levison, who was harassed by the FBI for his purported communist affinities, King drafted a road map to further actions. Named "The Crisis in America's Cities, an Analysis of Social Disorder and Plan of Action against Poverty, Discrimination and Racism in Urban America," it advocated for a disciplined urban disruption in the North, with Washington, DC as its main objective. Willing to move "from outbursts" of anger to "nonviolent insurrection," King presented massive civil disobedience as the only option. Sit-ins for jobs at factories, boycotts, and "thousands of unemployed youth camps" on the Washington Mall could have an "impact of earthquake proportion." Although he did not utterly dismiss coalition politics, the document stood as a clear repudiation of Rustin's accommodationist strategy, for it called for a disruption sufficient "to cripple the operations of an oppressive society."[13] Later, King was emphatic that the campaign would be "as dramatic, as dislocative, as disruptive, as attention-getting as the riots without destroying property."[14]

During the press conference announcing the campaign on December 4, 1967, when asked by a journalist if this campaign was to be "a more militant movement than ever before," King answered that "timid supplications for justice" did not solve problems. "We've got to massively confront the power structure . . . to dramatize the situation, channelize the very legitimate and understandable rage of the ghetto. . . ." By far, it was not meant to reenact the respectable coalition of the 1963 March on Washington.

The plan was a work in progress and many of the initial ideas were eventually modified for the sake of practicality. The upheaval of the democratic process was to be unprecedented. Structural reforms beyond anti-discrimination bills were becoming King's overriding design, which estranged many of his former supporters and allies. As Michael Eric Dyson puts it, the Poor People's Campaign "forced those who were used to thinking about race to think about class while forcing those who puzzled over economic inequality to talk about race."[15] King's egalitarian radicalism was predicated on a fierce critique of postwar assumptions.

The liberal approach to social change which had presided over the first half of the 1960s had ran its course. Chicago was a case in point and certainly altered King's strategic vision of social change. The journalist David Halberstam, in the August 1967 issue of *Harper's*, postulated that King was undergoing a "new radicalism[16] to the extent that he was not the "radical America felt comfortable to have spawned" any more.[17]

King still attempted to steer a middle course between the militant determination of Black Power activists and mainline civil rights leaders, the most moderate of whom were NAACP president Roy Wilkins and Whitney Young of the National Urban League. But when he publicly scolded the war in Vietnam, in line with SNCC's position, King alienated the moderates as well as Randolph and Rustin. Most were willing, like Rustin, to rekindle liberal enthusiasm and to reinvigorate a coalition of progressive-minded Democrats including President Johnson. To them, that King called for a "'massive dislocation" of federal agencies amounted to irresponsibility and lack of judgment. The dissenting identity of the Poor People's Campaign immediately put it on a collision course with most members of the liberal coalition that had sustained previous racial progress. The uncritical support by the AFL-CIO for the Vietnam War put the union at odds with the pacifist message of the Poor People's Campaign. Besides, not only was King unflinching on the war issue but he also made clear that absent a labor movement purged of its prejudice, no real change would be achieved. Despite his critical need for a strong alliance with labor to sustain the PPC, King refused to sacrifice his position on the altar of a liberal coalition. He publicly repudiated unions' support for the war in Vietnam on November 27, 1967, speaking at the National Labor Leadership Assembly for Peace in Chicago, pointing to the hollowness of labor's call for a stronger War on Poverty absent an outright denunciation of Johnson's bellicose policies in Southeast Asia.

Black freedom fighters, notably King, had always had a combative yet mostly trusting relationship with the White House. But King's indictment of the Vietnam War as well as his project for a national movement of massive civil disobedience blew open the divide between the freedom fighters. Although King included the Kerner Report's recommendations and Randolph's Freedom Budget at local rallies for the Poor People's Campaign, he expressed doubt about the relevance of such conciliatory initiatives and contended that the campaign could not run the risk of suffering a similar fate. It would be confrontational.

In contrast to Rustin and Randolph's patience with Johnson, King expressed more stridently his ardent longing for substantive equality. He made clear that if the American nation says "we are to have, life, liberty and the pursuit of happiness, then [the nation] must give us an economic base so that we can have life, liberty and the pursuit of happiness."[18] But it was not so much "liberalism" that he chided as it was the deceitful attitude of supposedly "liberal" allies. He also concurred with SNCC that poor urban communities were erupting *because* of their economic exploitation and unfair policing:

We believe that if this campaign succeeds, nonviolence will again be the dominant instrument for social change—and jobs and freedom will be placed in the hands of the tormented poor. . . . We intend, before the summer comes, to initiate a "last chance" project to arouse the American conscience toward constructive democratic change.[19]

His tone was at times as militant and defiant as Stokely Carmichael's. At the Kerner Commission's hearing, King fingered the "policy makers of the white society" who "created discrimination . . . slums . . . perpetuated unemployment and ignorance and poverty," who "violate welfare laws to deprive the poor of their meager allotments" and "so many of his police" who "makes mockery of the law" as "the slums are the handiwork of a vicious system of the white society."[20] King, however far from being as radical as Black Power activists with regard to strategy, also shared their fierce opposition to the war. The Poor People's Campaign was grounded on the idea that the conflict in Vietnam was a war waged on the poor because it undercut Johnson's Great Society programs. The domestic harmony he sought to restore with an empowerment of the dispossessed would remain hollow as long as the Vietnam War continued to be pursued. The campaign was to be, intrinsically, a vibrant indictment of American imperialism. Echoing the New Left, "welfare not warfare" was a chant reflective of his view.

The purpose of the Poor People's Campaign was subsequently not to participate in a political bargain with Democratic allies any longer, as King, like many, had grown disillusioned with the administration's Great Society. King's understanding of "liberalism" had always entailed, at odds with the core features of Cold War liberalism, an indictment of U.S. global hegemony and imperialism as well as of an individually uplifting ideology. "Reformism" to him meant integration on the basis of universalist values, but first and foremost, full equality and "radical egalitarianism."[21] It was to King what Norman Thomas called an "implicit religion," a deeply held creed.[22] Antipoverty activist Michael Harrington disagreed with King on his decision to merge the antipoverty and antiwar agendas, wary of alienating Johnson once and for all. But Harrington eventually supported the campaign. So would Rustin despite increasing disagreements, but only after King's assassination.

In a February 1965 *Commentary* article entitled "From Protest to Politics: The Future of the Civil Rights Movement," Rustin had called for the termination of street mobilization to engage in an alliance with the Democratic Party and their agenda. The politics of confrontation had to be abandoned altogether in favor of a renewed March on Washington coalition. He still expected much from the War on Poverty and his editorial sounded like an apology for the war in Vietnam. Rustin, subordinating his antiwar convictions to his political strategy, wanted to reap stronger antipoverty public policies, a strategy that entailed moderation and cooperation with the White House, labor, and liberal religious groups. In accordance with Rustin, King defended race as a framework from which to move toward a larger, more powerful democratizing force. King also concurred with Rustin's renewed call for social democratic measures, eloquently outlined in Rustin's argument that he could not see "how the movement can be victorious in the absence of radical programs for full employment, the abolition of slums, the reconstruction of our educational system and new definitions of work and leisure."[23] But King objected to the self-imposed co-option by the Democratic Party and the withdrawal from the streets. Whereas Rustin was dismissive of the "white backlash" theory, King on the contrary devoted more and more of his writings and speeches to the crippling effects of former civil rights supporters' withdrawal from the cause of blacks. An explicit rebuke to Rustin's insider strategy, king was willing to break with Johnson and, to paraphrase Rustin's description, to choose uncompromising "protest" over "participatory" politics. He downplayed electoral politics to renew his commitment to social mobilization and grassroots dissent:

> Everything Negroes need . . . will not magically materialize from the use of the ballot . . . in the future we must become intensive political activists . . . most of us are too poor to have adequate economic power, and many of us are too rejected by the culture to be part of any tradition of power. Necessity will draw us toward the power inherent in the creative uses of politics.[24]

On March 4, 1968, issuing a statement about the PPC, King repeated that "our experience is that the Federal Government, and most especially Congress, never moves meaningfully against social ills until the nation is confronted directly and massively. . . . This is why the SCLC will lead masses of people to Washington in aggressive nonviolent demonstrations."[25] Certainly King and Rustin clashed over strategic positioning with respect to the Johnson administration and mainstream unions, but with regard to the Vietnam War in particular, their discord was reinforced by their diverging understanding of race and class-based alliances. King, distancing himself from Rustin's classist framework, contended that racial misrecognition was—as much as economic alienation—at odds with an inclusive democracy. He rejected the racial division of civil rights activists' alliance with labor but did not repudiate Black Power's principle of economic self-sufficiency. The campaign rhetoric offered a trenchant analysis of race-based inequality while keeping the Duboisian perspective on poor white's collateral exploitation. Without renouncing the idea that race was a major factor in the mechanism of inequality and that it had to be dealt with as such, he nonetheless asserted that blacks shared common aims with other dispossessed groups. He engaged in a rapprochement with race-conscious Mexican Americans and included Native Americans' cultural pride in his plans. He was also willing, despite his strong qualifications, to reach out to Black Power activists.

King concurred with SNCC that a new phase in the black freedom struggle had to be propelled. A new promising liberal paradigm, undergirded by grassroots empowerment and multiracial poor people's protest, had been institutionalized through a real "maximum feasible participation" principle.[26] Transforming the poor into a revolutionary vanguard, calling for peace, jobs, guaranteed income, and group-based rights would challenge the postwar liberal consensus. In *Where Do We Go from Here,* King had made clear that traditional alliances with liberal-minded Americans were no longer viable, too narrow in scope and insufficiently reliable for the issues at stake: "We deceive ourselves if we envision the same combination backing structural changes in the society." Laying the groundwork for the Poor People's Campaign, he envisioned a new coalition: "The future of the deep structural changes we seek will not be found in the decaying political machines. It lies in new alliances of Negroes, Puerto Ricans, Labor, liberals, certain church and middle-class elements."[27]

Only such a diverse grassroots coalition could be of national significance. Ultimately, rather than relying on liberal-progressive forces, both the black and white middle class, and labor, the Poor People's Campaign was to be a loose association of the SCLC activists, Black Power dissidents, welfare rights women, socialist movements, and grassroots activists of various ethnicities. The SCLC appointed Bernard Lafayette to recruit the group of fifteen hundred people who would spearhead the Poor People's Campaign. Another Chicago-trained SCLC member, Billy Hollins, eloquently described how he laid the groundwork for the Midwestern caravan he would coordinate:

> I went up to Michigan and found some Native-Americans; I went to Indiana and found some poor white folks. I went to churches, I went to organizations, and I talked about the Poor People's Campaign. We're going to have some bus leaving, we're going to Washington, DC. This is Martin Luther King's movement—we always used Martin Luther King's name—you need to get on this bus—you need to be part of this thing! I was able to organize these people.... I did a lot of fund raising for all of this too. When it was time to go, I sent all the buses over to Jesse Jackson's place and let him kick it off.[28]

Coming from all parts of the nation, the campaigners would head toward the capital, each region coordinating its own "caravan." Nine convoys (trains, buses, cars, and spectacular mule wagons) would travel toward Washington, DC, stopping for rallies where they were likely to recruit more campaigners: the "Eastern Caravan," the "Appalachia Trail," the "Southern Caravan," the "Midwest Caravan," the "Indian Trail," the "San Francisco Caravan," the "Western Caravan," the "Mule Train," and the "Freedom Train." They would place a premium on the shared indignities suffered by the poor of diverse racial or ethnic backgrounds while illuminating the specificities of each group's demands. Mass meetings were held in each of the nine regions to mobilize grassroots organizations and coalesce them into a national network. In the South, the Alabama Poor People's Crusade was the template for such groups to recruit volunteers and foster enthusiasm among the poor. King himself crisscrossed the country to gather support and funding for a hard-sell campaign. Tom Houck, a Boston-born SCLC member close to the King family, was assigned the mission of soliciting volunteers for the Poor People's Campaign through the network of religious organizations the SCLC worked with.

Under the auspices of King, through active canvassing and recruiting, SCLC managed to gather hundreds of participants. In the early months of

1968, King toured the country, delivering speeches, meeting and negotiating with prominent Mexican Americans, Puerto Ricans, Native Americans,
and poor white activists. He also insisted on bringing into the fold the
most disaffected elements of the black working class and alienated young-
sters. If King met with traditional civil rights leaders in Washington, DC,
he brushed aside Rustin's or the NAACP's misgivings (and most mainline
leaders who distanced themselves from urban black convulsions) by
reaching out to welfare rights activists and SNCC leaders H. Rap Brown
and Stokely Carmichael. He met with them as early as February 1968, less
in the true hope of convincing them to join the campaign than as an
attempt to prevent their outright opposition to it. King emphasized the
role of grassroots organizing in order to articulate local issues with the
overarching national scheme, pointing to the militancy sustaining
the campaign. The upheaval of the democratic process was indeed to be
unprecedented. The first march of the Poor People's Campaign was scheduled for April 1, 1968, with all marchers arriving at the Mall encampment
by April 22.

In March 1968, King led a planning symposium, called the "Minority
Group Conference Meeting," in Atlanta in order to bind the cause of blacks
with others' own issues, given the extent to which nonblack accomplished
freedom fighters intended to remain autonomous. Mapping out a new
coalition, he presented them with a plan in which each group's grievances
would be channeled through Washington, blending issues of cultural recognition (central to Chicanos and Natives) and universal antipoverty policies. This new alliance was built upon the radical activism spurred on the
ground by the War on Poverty, particularly by the National Welfare Rights
Organization. For the first time, a true multiracial gathering was taking
place, propelling the struggle for freedom and equality to an unprecedented dimension and scope. In revolutionary fashion, poor whites were,
along with groups of color, considered an exploited minority whose grievances had to be voiced.

The SCLC promised an egalitarian and grassroots campaign, reflected
in the choice of elected agents and spokespersons who would represent
each of the five ethnic groups, especially in the formation of a Poor People's
Organizing Convention, with an equal share from each group, who would
oversee the election of five main spokespersons. The five elected ethnic

spokesmen were Hank Adams for Native Americans, Cornelius Givens for African Americans, Reies Tijerina for Mexican Americans, Dionicie Paden for Puerto Ricans, and Ted Wulpert for poor whites.[29] This convention would also serve as a planning committee tasked with defining the commonalities of each ethnic group. Bernard Lafayette was King's pick for coordinating the campaign, a choice anchored in Lafayette's long commitment to local organizing, with James Bevel in Nashville and in New York against the war, with SNCC in Birmingham and Selma, and with the SCLC in Chicago. The pacifist Quaker organization which had hired him in 1963, the American Friends Service Committee (AFSC), would prove instrumental in reaching out to Latinos and Native Americans.[30] The SCLC also laid out the idea for a Committee of 100 made of an equal representation of each group who would elect its own representatives. The final committee instead comprised one-third steering committee members and two-thirds poor people recruited from each group. Its purpose was to be a multiracial poor people's delegation, entitled to initiate lobbying efforts once in Washington, chiefly at the Departments of Justice, Labor, Health, Education, and Welfare, and Housing and Urban Development. The SCLC also invited eighty nonblack representatives to join together for a one-day meeting to discuss the campaign and define its purpose and its content with regard to each group's priorities.

The steering committee which emerged out of the Atlanta symposium represented the minority groups, equally endowed with responsibility. The National Welfare Rights Organization stood for black Americans, Reies López Tijerina and Rodolfo "Corky" Gonzales for Chicanos, Grace Moore Newman and Haleong Balentine for Puerto Ricans, Peggy Terry and Bob Fulcher for poor whites, and Tillie Walker and Mel Tom for Native Americans.[31] After the March 14 Minority Group Conference Meeting, each ethnic and racial group formed caucuses which eventually agreed to participate to the campaign and went on to elaborate a steering committee in charge of its oversight and of the election of the committee of 100. A vanguard delegation, the committee would represent the poor (who made up two-thirds of the total) and were sent to Washington to lobby every agency and department who had a stake in poverty. The goal was to compel Congress, which was on the hook for implementing a "new

economic deal for the poor."[32] For King, such lobbying efforts in the traditional sense were meant to give the poor an interlocutor, someone to talk
to and to be listened to:

> A delegation of poor can walk into high official's office with a carefully, col-
> lectively prepared list of demands . . . and if that official says: "but Congress
> would have to approve this" or "But the president would have to be con-
> sulted on that," you can say, "All right, we'll wait" and you can settle down as
> long as necessary.[33]

POOR WHITES

King, very early on, expressed his hope that poor whites would also join him,
as their economic oppression was linked to and entwined with blacks' subjection. He was convinced that a real, from-the-bottom-up war on poverty
entailed an interracial class-based coalition. In 1958, he already contended
that a class-based struggle was to be envisioned: "Whites and Negroes have
mutual aspirations for a fairer share of the product of industries and farms.
Both seek job security, old-age security, health and welfare protection."[34] A
decade later, he was still adamant that the switch toward economic justice
entailed a class-based coalition: "At this level, Negro programs go beyond
race and deal with economic inequality, wherever it exists. In the pursuit of
these goals, the white poor became involved, and the potentiality emerges for
a powerful new alliance."[35] King was aware that white workers viewed blacks
as potential competitors and resisted cross-racial solidarity. Yet, he sought to
challenge this false assumption. He drew on Du Bois's "symbolic wage" analysis, which convincingly purported to explain how whiteness was designed
as a means of dividing the working class along racial lines by persuading the
white working class that its skin color was a privilege and a piece of cultural
capital it ought to cling to. Echoing Du Bois, King contended that "there are,
in fact, more poor white Americans than there are Negro. Racism is a tenacious evil, but it is not immutable. . . . White supremacy can feed their egos
but not their stomachs."[36]

He subsequently demanded that poor Appalachians be an integral part
of the Poor People's Campaign. In "The Drum Major Instinct," a sermon

he gave in Atlanta a couple of weeks before the opening act of the campaign, he recalled his encounter with a bitter poor white:

> And I said, "You are put in the position of supporting your oppressor, because through prejudice and blindness, you fail to see that the same forces that oppress Negroes in American society oppress poor white people." (*Yes*) And all you are living on is the satisfaction of your skin being white, and the drum major instinct of thinking that you are somebody big because you are white."[37]

But the nagging question of labor's reliability had grown more salient and, in opposition to Rustin and Randolph, King questioned the Popular Front style of alliance, despite its success in 1963. The "class struggle" King advocated could not work under the patronage of the liberal establishment as evidenced by AFL-CIO president George Meany's support for President Johnson's war policies, a position aggravated by his statements accusing antiwar activists of being "victims of Communist propaganda."[38] Echoing the New Left, King came to believe that building a bridge to liberal institutions was the same as building a bridge to imperialism. Moreover, he had grown skeptical about the egalitarian commitment of mainstream unions. At a September speech at the national convention of the New York-based union District 65, he lamented that labor's "sporadic and limited support" amounted to "inconsequential contributions to civil rights"; he added, "We have talked many times about Negro Labor unity and the multitude of mutual interest we have . . . yet this has not vitalized a consistent unity of action."[39]

United Auto Workers president Walter Reuther, though holding a less dovish position than George Meany, eventually called for a peace settlement in Vietnam. He stood as an exception that proved the rule, being also a longtime supporter of the NAACP and of King's campaigns. He would endorse and supply funding for the Poor People's Campaign but overall, labor would not be the channel through which interracial solidarity would be sustained.

King looked to alternative sources of class-based interracial camaraderie. White social justice activists were present, notably Carl Braden of the Southern Conference Education Fund and Richard Boone of the Citizens Crusade Against Poverty, both of whom attended the March 1968 planning symposium. Despite FBI intimidation, King asked white Christian social-ist Michael Harrington to draft the blueprint of the Poor People's Campaign.

The SCLC also invited white socialists Tom Hayden and Myles Horton to the symposium table, betting on their class-based and integrationist militancy. Hayden, cofounder of Students for a Democratic Society, was not only one of the main voices of the antiwar protest, but an advocate of racial equality. A Freedom Rider, he worked at building an "interracial movement of the poor" in 1964 when SDS joined a community-organizing project in Newark. He publicly denounced police brutality in housing projects. His presence at the symposium was therefore in line with King's emphasis on the structural sources of inequality. They both advocated a re-evaluation of the productivist model of an advanced industrial society and, as did many New Left representatives, Hayden denounced "corporate liberalism," the close and nefarious collaboration between the liberal state and corporate America, extensively overlapping his anticapitalistic cri-tique with his antiwar position. Through Hayden, King sought to reach out to the young white dissenters of the countercultural movement who shared his antiracist, anti-imperialist, and anticapitalistic sentiments. For King, as for Harrington or Haden but mostly following on the heels of W. E. B. Dubois, empowering the poor entailed a confrontation with free-market ideology. Targeting the foundations of racial inequality demanded combatting the logic of class inequality in American capitalism.

Equally significant was the presence of educator and socialist activist Myles Horton in Atlanta. An Appalachia native, he was, like King, influ-enced by the social thought of theologian Reinhold Niebuhr and was com-mitted to liberating the poor through popular participation and education. He had founded the Highlander Folk School in 1932 in Monteagle, Tennessee where he aided striking workers but also provided integrated workshops on racial equality and labor rights. Although the working poor of southern Appalachia were his main constituency, Horton connected in the early 1940s with the newly created CIO in order "to build a broad-based, racially integrated, and politically active southern labor move-ment."[40] Horton defended a colorblind notion of the American proletariat. He was, therefore, forcefully engaged in the civil rights struggle and, in 1957, hired Bernice Violanthe Robinson as the first Citizenship School teacher to help illiterate blacks to register to vote. She would join SCLC in 1963, merging the two institutions. In addition, Horton enrolled the Highlander Folk School in the SNCC Mississippi Freedom Summer Project and the Southwide Voter Education Internship Project. The Highlander Folk School was a hotbed of interracial camaraderie and workers' solidarity. Representatives from progressive unions such as the United Auto Workers, but also civil rights activists such as Ella Baker, Septima Clark, NAACP member Rosa Parks, SCLC's James Bevel and Ralph Abernathy, attended the school's workshops and meetings. At Horton's invitation, King himself was welcomed as a guest speaker in 1957. The FBI, which had labeled Highlander Folk "a communist-training school" for years, seized on Horton and King's relationship to discredit the Poor People's Campaign, and J. Edgar Hoover actively propagated the rumor that it was instigated by subversive anti-American agitators.[41] Nevertheless Horton actively participated in organizing the journeys of hundreds of poor white folks to Washington. Like King, the socialist Christian intended on binding together the urban and agrarian underclasses.

The plight of the displaced white worker was epitomized by Appalachian workers who had migrated to midwestern cities where they experienced the scorn and stereotyping echoing racist tropes on shiftlessness and criminality. As poor whites, often dubbed "hillbillies," they faced disenfranchisement and exploitation. In Chicago, white activist Peggy Terry—who attempted to organize them through an interracial group called JOIN (Jobs Or Income Now)—would actively participate in the PPC, eager to get poor whites to embrace class-based solidarity.[42] Invited to the symposium and elected to the steering committee, Terry was to be one of the most ardent voices of the white poor. Asked to talk on their behalf during the launching rally of the campaign, she would claim: "We, the poor whites of the United States, today demand an end to racism, for our own self-interest and well-being, as well as for the well-being of black, brown and red Americans who, I repeat, are our natural allies in the struggle for real freedom and real democracy in these, OUR, United States of America."[43]

While interracial alliances had been major elements of the civil rights revolution, such a focus on poor whites and their commonalities with poor people of color was truly revolutionary. More unprecedented was the scope of the class-based union King envisioned, for King made his most dramatic gesture toward Latino groups.

LATINOS AND NATIVE AMERICANS

In October 1967 in Albuquerque, New Mexico, prominent Mexican American and African American leaders met to contemplate further collaboration. The annual conference of the Alianza Federal de Pueblos Libres was an unprecedented gathering of black and brown activists: New Mexican activist Reies López Tijerina, José Angel Gutiérrez of the Mexican American Youth Organization, Bert Corona of the Mexican American Political Association, David Sánchez of the Brown Berets, and Rodolfo "Corky" Gonzales of the Crusade for Justice interacted with Ron Karenga of the United Slaves (Us) organization—a Los Angeles–based Black Power group—Dave Dennis of the Congress of Racial Equality, Ralph Featherstone of the Student Nonviolent Coordinating Committee, Walter Bremond of the Black Congress, and Anthony Akku Babu of the Black Panther Party.

The representatives eventually agreed to sign a "Treaty of Peace, Harmony, and Mutual Assistance," a solemn pledge to interracial struggle. The treaty stated that "for the first time the old myth of coalition for mutual self-interest is exploded and we move into the area of mutual respect," an indirect insight into the deep divisions and competing self-interests keeping the groups apart. By 1967, the idea of building a black-brown coalition with Hispanics had been entertained with limited success. Mexican American and African American civil rights struggles rarely meshed and racial divisions among dissenters have been an impediment to the growing leftward shift in the 1960s. The War on Poverty further intensified the competition between blacks and Latinos, with each group battling for scarce governmental funds.[44]

Besides, both groups held a binary vision of race, as deployed in the Jim Crow South. Up until the late 1960s, most Mexican Americans self-identified as white and stayed clear of any identification with the black struggle. The framework of race prevented attempts to build a united movement between the two communities. Despite occasional attempts at coordination and cooperation, bridging that cultural gulf proved difficult, each group developing its own strategy to undermine the mechanisms of the specific discrimination they faced.[45] Black and Hispanic communities worked simultaneously but separately to challenge racial discrimination and segregation. On the other hand, most black civil rights organizations shared the pervasive idea that building interracial coalitions (that is, black and white) would provide the most effective strategy to enact social change. But the shifting ground of race led more and more Mexican American leaders and organizations to move from classifying themselves as racially "white" during the early stages of the civil rights movement to "brown", that is, an ethnic minority.[46]

Cesar Chavez's organizing illustrated that rearrangement. Since 1965, Chavez's United Farm Workers had successfully organized the farmworkers of California's Central Valley to reclaim justice from the powerful local agribusiness. The farmworkers had begun their first strike against grape growers in Delano in September 1965. Nonviolent and inspired by the black liberation struggle, the UFW had a class-based understanding of its struggle and was willing to merge its struggle with African Americans and build multiracial alliances. A predominantly Mexican American labor union, the UFW attempted to reach out to black freedom fighters, pointing to their common economic exploitation and disenfranchisement and to the existence of individual "bridge leaders" who were "willing to not only recognize commonalities, but . . . act on them."[47]

Only CORE and SNCC had contacts with Californian farmworkers. SNCC proved particularly committed to uniting with them, in contrast with King and the SCLC, who were unwilling to get involved in labor disputes. The NAACP and the National Urban League would not jeopardize their relations with local businesses which the UFW protested and, although the National Urban League formally supported the "grape boycott," the middle-class, urban, and East Coast orientation of these organizations precluded a real rapprochement with the UFW. Besides, its leadership had developed a strong relationship (including financial ties) with labor unions, most notably with the Teamsters Union, while Chavez had connections with the AFL-CIO. Also, the SCLC had done poorly in supporting Hispanic farmworkers and failed to grasp the need to advocate for economic justice in the Southwest. King remained distant despite Chavez's attempts to reach out to him. On September 22, 1966, shortly after the UFW merged with the AFL-CIO, Martin Luther King eventually sent a telegram to Chavez. The note was supportive but uncommitted:

> As brothers in the fight for equality, I extend the hand of fellowship and good will and wish continuing success to you and your members. . . . The fight for equality must be fought on many fronts—in the urban slums, in the sweat-shops of the factories and fields. Our separate struggles are really one—a struggle for freedom, for dignity, and for humanity. You and your valiant fellow workers have demonstrated your commitment to righting grievous wrongs forced upon exploited people. We are together with you in spirit and in determination that our dreams for a better tomorrow will be realized.[48]

Bay Area SNCC members, however, allied with the National Farm Workers Association (NFWA) and provided a fruitful training in nonviolence, hailed by Chavez. Interestingly, white civil rights activists in the Southwest worked as effective go-betweens and alliance builders for African Americans and Mexican American farmworkers, laying the groundwork for future multiracial coalitions.[49]

Chicago changed King's perspectives. In *Where Do We Go from Here,* he acknowledged that

> in a multi-racial society no group can make it alone. It is a myth to believe that the Irish, Italians, and the Jews . . . rose to power through separatism . . . group unity was always enlarged by joining in alliances with other groups such as political machines and trade unions.[50]

Despite the still contentious alliance in 1967 between Chavez and the AFL, which was vocally supportive of the war in Vietnam, the SCLC came to terms with the potentiality of an alliance with him. The SNCC-NFWA coalition was disintegrating by 1967 and new multiracial alliances were envisioned. On March 5, 1968, laying the groundwork the Poor People's Campaign, King sent another telegram addressed to "Cesar Chaves [sic], United Farm Workers, P.O. Box 120, Delano, Calif."

> My colleagues and I commend you for your bravery, salute you for your indefatigable work against poverty and injustice, and pray for your health and your continuing service as one of the outstanding men of America. The plight of your people and ours is so grave that we all desperately need the inspiring example and effective leadership you have given.[51]

That month, King missed his planned meeting with Chavez, but Andrew Young, who had visited Chavez in Delano the prior month, obtained his positive answer. Chavez himself would ultimately not participate in the campaign (only a UFW representative would be present at the March 14 minority symposium) and so the two men never met.[52] Beyond the geographical constraint, the reason for such a missed opportunity was SCLC's tardiness to work on black-brown solidarity, as SNCC had suggested.

In Chicago however, and while planning the PPC, King reached out to two prominent Chicano leaders, Corky Gonzales and Reies Tijerina. On August 31, 1967, Chicago hosted a National Conference for New Politics, a gathering of antiwar and civil rights leaders of all races and ethnicities. King attended the event, along with Black Power activists, Latinos leaders, and white pacifist students. He met with Gonzales and Tijerina, who talked to him about the denial of their land which was, as for Native Americans, the primary cause of their poverty. After a fruitful conversation with the black leader, they both would endorse the campaign and attend the minority conference organized by King for March 14, 1968.

Reies López Tijerina, a pastor and activist based in northern New Mexico, had always fought to put the national spotlight on land issues, demanding the repatriation of the territories confiscated by the American government under the 1848 Treaty of Guadalupe Hidalgo.[53] Founded in 1963, his grassroots organization Alianza Federal de Mercedes (Federal Alliance of Land Grants) worked to organize Mexican American and Native Americans families who had been dispossessed by a "land-grant movement." The group lambasted the government's confiscation and, echoing black radicals' vindication of the sanctity of property rights with respect to the "twenty acres and the mule" that were never given to freedmen, called for tangible redistribution.[54] On October 22, 1966, Tijerina led the armed occupation of Echo Amphitheatre Park, in northern New Mexico, which had been the land grant of San Joaquin del Rio de Chama and was now U.S. National Forest land, and was subsequently jailed. Challenging the binary framework of race, he defined his people as "Indohispano." This pan-ethnic label was intended to resist the racialization of people of Mexican descent (that is, through an American racial frame) but also to claim kinship with Native American groups.[55]

Native Americans were also present at the symposium and through the figures of Hank Adams, a fishing rights activist from Montana, and Tillie Walker, a Denver-based social worker. They voiced their concerns about the restrictions on their fishing rights, their land rights, and more than most on the cultural recognition they too were deprived of. Other Native American representatives were present, notably National Indian Youth Council founder Mel Thom, Rose Crow Flies High of North Dakota's Three Affiliated Tribes, the Sioux Council's Ray Berry, Cecil Corbett of Arizona's Indian Ministries, Thadis Oxendine of the Lumbee Indian Citizens Council in North Carolina, and several members of the eastern band of the Cherokees.[56] At odds with mainstream black organizations' demands for integration and assimilation, most Native Americans dismissed a white society destructive of their culture and resources. At the height of the Poor People's Campaign, Mel Thom would claim "the right to separate and equal communities within the American system."[57] Thom provocatively launched the slogan "Red Power!" Natives' wholehearted participation in the campaign underscored its dissident undertone.[58]

Indigenous populations were natural allies to the Chicano struggle, and Tijerina stood as their most ardent advocate during the Minority Group conference Meeting, chiefly as it related to their rights to self-determination and restoration of land rights. He repeatedly argued that his group should march shoulder to shoulder with the American Indian Movement. By stressing the nonwhite indigenous aspects of Mexican American working-class culture and by emphasizing a form of "cultural resistance," Chicano groups accorded with Native Americans in ways which were more problematic to mainline African American groups.[59]

When he joined King for the Minority Conference Group Meeting, Tijerina bragged that it was he "who began the coalition philosophy between the brown and black people and the Indian people and the good whites."[60] Undeniably a cultural nationalist, and responsible for an armed clash with New Mexico state authorities, Tijerina was a militant voice. Nevertheless, he was King's interlocutor of choice, which again suggests that the campaign was meant to be radical.

Corky Gonzales, founder of another Chicano civil rights and cultural movement, the Crusade for Justice, also attended the planning symposium. Crusade for Justice was based in Denver and had organized many mass demonstrations to protest police brutality and the Vietnam War. Rooted in antipoverty work, Gonzales was active in the Southwest's antipoverty program and had been appointed chairman of Denver's War on Poverty. Gonzales worked on voter registration for the John F. Kennedy presidential campaign and successfully registered thousands of Mexican Americans. Temporarily close to the Democratic establishment, he received a Ford Foundation grant as well as public Office of Economic Opportunity (OEO) funding to assume the role of community organizer among low-income Latino youth in Denver.[61]

Witnessing institutional racism against Latinos, Gonzales came to dismiss coalition-based politics. A fiery leader of the Chicano Movement, he captured its spirit, complexity, and longing with his 1967 poem "Yo Soy Joaquin" ("I am Joaquin"). For him as for Tijerina, racial categories were inadequate to grasp the substance of "La Raza," a mixture of Indian, European, Mexican, and American strands. The indigenous component which constituted "La Raza" was neither an identification with the black struggle movement nor an endorsement of whiteness. Gonzales deployed a pacifist, nationalist, and redistributive political framework that paralleled the Black Power movement. In Los Angeles, the two groups symbolically bonded in 1966 when young Mexican Americans formed the Young Citizens for Community Action in East Los Angeles. That group would later mushroom into the Brown Berets group, a nationalist organization which, emulating the Black Panther Party, emphasized the right of self-determination and defense against police aggression. The BPP mentioned poverty-stricken whites, Latinos, Asians, and Native Americans from the outset and many self-defined Chicanos shared their overarching common aims.

The basic analytic framework put forward by the late 1960s Chicano movement, focusing on the commonalities like poverty, health, or police violence between blacks and Latinos, suggested class politics. Black and Chicano groups' agendas were tightly focused on the economic conditions of their constituents as well as their racialized status. However, although Gonzales and his agenda of a "plan for the barrio" (better housing, education, barrio-owned businesses, etc.) were perfectly in tune with King's blueprint for the ghetto, Gonzales voiced his concern that Latinos' specificities would be overshadowed by blacks' worldview and that the

Latino cause would be belittled by the SCLC. Bert Corona, Mexican labor organizer and community activist, acknowledged that King "understood" the specificity of Hispanic experience and reassured Tijerina that King was "now committed to all the poor peoples" but they both feared that the campaign would be a black-led endeavor.[62] Echoing black radical activists' distrust of coalition-building, Chicano groups feared that cross-racial initiatives would ultimately become co-opted by others. They repeatedly expressed their concern over what they perceived as black leaders' patronizing attitude. The SCLC leadership style was particularly rebuked by both Tijerina and Gonzales and would prove to be a constant obstacle to the Poor People's Campaign black-brown coalition.[63] Similarly, Native American leader Tillie Walker lamented: "I think the biggest problem [is] that this is a black movement. And this is the biggest problem that we've faced throughout the whole campaign."[64] Indeed, King mostly used a black freedom movement framework and although he moved toward a multiracial scheme, his rhetoric failed as he oftentimes omitted "brown" groups.

Yet, despite these tensions and the Farm Workers union leader Cesar Chavez's absence, the minority conference in Atlanta was one of the few occurrences of such an alliance at the national level, at odds with the traditional chasm between Latinos' and African Americans' quest for freedom and equality. Such solidarity was illustrated by Puerto Ricans, mostly from New York City, who were widely represented at the meeting: Grace Mora Newman, Gilberto Gerena Valentin, Ruben Collier, and Elodio Mendez attended, following in the footsteps of the Puerto Rican activists who had developed cross-racial civil rights collaboration in post-WWII New York. From the 1950s to the late 1960s, they chose to align themselves politically with African Americans, sharing the stage with prominent African Americans such as Frank Horne, Bayard Rustin, and Kenneth Clark. Voluntary hospital workers in New York, overwhelmingly black and Puerto Rican, were notoriously underpaid, exploited, and worked in an environment of racial hierarchies, as janitors, nurses' aides, and orderlies while supervisory and management positions were predominantly held by whites.[65] Under the leadership of female hospital workers, a strike was launched in 1959, followed by a campaign which lasted until

1963, for union representation and collective bargaining rights. The NAACP and King supported Local 1199 of the Drug and Hospital Workers Union from its inception, which also demanded pay standards comparable to other industries and a significant improvement in working conditions. In 1965, the union achieved a significant milestone when collective bargaining rights were granted to hospital workers. Local 1199 had endorsed King's struggle since the Montgomery boycott and would enthusiastically join his 1968 campaign. That year, they won a minimum $100 weekly salary for their twenty-one thousand hospital workers, a victory hailed by King, who lauded their multiracial organizing: "You have provided concrete and visible proof that when black and white workers unite in a democratic union like local 1199, they can move mountains."[66] If their struggle was oftentimes race-framed, Local 1199 activists exemplified labor-civil rights collaboration and solidarity among minority workers.

Like Mexican Americans, Puerto Ricans had a conflicted racial self-identification and if, ultimately, Puerto Ricans refused to assume a wholly "black" identity, the idea of a linked fate between Puerto Ricans and African Americans and the construction of a shared space to develop platforms for community development and social protest in New York City laid the groundwork for the Poor People's Campaign coalition.[67] Puerto Ricans, like Mexican American activists, were transitioning from efforts to become fully integrated into the dominant culture to an activist agenda that stressed their separate identity. The Latino activists present at the March 1968 conference underscored their cultural pride, bringing forward the previously derogatory label "Chicano" as a defiant term that amounted to a repudiation of previous generations' desire to integrate the American mainstream.[68] Another leader, José Angel Gutiérrez, embodied such dissent. Months before the gathering in Atlanta, which he attended, Gutiérrez founded the Mexican Youth Organization (MAYO), committed to fostering cultural pride and heritage. Joining a multiracial campaign could not be at the expense of these nationalist dimensions. Martin Luther King Jr. and Ralph Abernathy's attempts to bind Latino groups' demands to the black struggle therefore translated into the incorporation of demands for land rights but also for the cultural recognition of the campaign objectives. King spoke on their behalf during the conference when he expressed his thanks: "This is a highly significant event, the beginning of a new cooperation, understanding, and a determination by poor people of all colors and backgrounds to assert and win their rights to a decent life and respect for their culture and dignity."[69]

Moreover, as publicized in SCLC's March 15 official statement, questions regarding Latino groups' quest for an identity and an affirmation of their cultural heritage were clearly addressed:

> At the meeting of minority group leaders in Atlanta, representatives of each group talked about the poverty and oppression of their people and the rich culture and heritage they cherish. There were songs and stories of the poor white miner, the Mexican-American migrant worker, the Negro slave, the Puerto Rican worker, the proud original American—the Indian.[70]

The document concludes with a Duboisian analysis of the process through which "established powers of rich America have deliberately exploited poor people by isolating them in ethnic, nationality, religious and racial groups," an artificial division campaigners would no longer tolerate.[71] If the SCLC statement hinted at a poor white cultural heritage, the makeup of white representatives at the conference was reflective of a more class-based approach to identity.

The campaign was not limited to establishing racial equality in a superficially inclusive society through an equal representation of racial groups across the rungs of class hierarchy. Neither was it a reductionist class-based movement, dismissive of the racial and ethnic underbelly of economic oppression. It tackled economic inequality *and* the embeddedness of racism in the unfair distribution of resources, wealth, and power. Such a call for a radical egalitarian democracy was evidenced by King's outreach to Black Power militants and by the defining presence of the race- and gender-conscious welfare rights activists. Both groups held a strong understanding of the political economy of racism in the United States. King was committed to maintaining an increasingly fractious black united front, from black nationalists to secular unionists like Randolph and Rustin, from the black Left (that often fused elements of black nationalism with Marxism) to his own quarreling group of Christian social democrats.

REACHING OUT TO BLACK DISSENTERS: BLACK POWER AND WELFARE RIGHTS ACTIVISTS

King could not envision a campaign that would not include SNCC and the other emerging voices of black radicalism. The National Welfare Rights Organization's radical "vision of citizenship" and its disruptive lobbying for new legislations on behalf of the poor laid the groundwork for King's last campaign.[72] The convergence of King's economic demands and the welfare rights' struggle was a core element of the Poor People's Campaign, as evidenced by the AFL-CIO's dismissive comment on the campaign as "welfare-oriented."[73] The welfare rights organization, which had organized dramatic poor people's marches as early as 1966, was the trailblazer and King its torchbearer. By and large, the NWRO augured King's last crusade.

Indeed, both King and the NWRO called for a "bill of rights for the poor," a guaranteed income, a higher minimum wage, and redistribution of wealth. The National Welfare Rights Organization stood as the epitome of this new empowerment of the poor in the 1960s. Mostly a northern movement (with a significant outpost in California), the NWRO was an instrumental medium for King, who sought to connect the SCLC with the northern urban poor. But more importantly, the activists substantiated the campaign philosophy, as they had developed a radical critique of poverty that revealed how gender and race determined poverty and inequality, and they regarded welfare as a right. King, predisposed to patriarchy as a leader, gradually came to terms with the issue of women's low-wage labor and unpaid domestic labor.

To protest the traditional stigma attached to welfare since its creation in 1935 (as Aid to Dependent Children, later AFDC), poor women, chiefly black women, who benefited from welfare programs, organized themselves to contest welfare policy which was obviously shaped by class, race, and gender. In stark contrast to the respectability of Social Security, welfare programs were stigmatized and, as recipients became increasingly single, feminine, and black after the war, welfare clients were maligned. Black single mothers became the utmost "undeserving poor" and oftentimes were treated as such by condescending caseworkers. In 1963, Johnnie Tillmon, herself a recipient, organized one of the first local welfare rights group in her California community in Watts. Three years later, George Wiley, an assistant professor of chemistry at Syracuse University and former associate national director of CORE, sought to conciliate grassroots antipoverty action with progressive academic circles. In January 1966, he met in Syracuse with several antipoverty workers and civil rights leaders, notably Cesar Chavez, Beulah Sanders, and Columbia sociologist Richard Cloward, who pointed to the centrality of welfare policies with regard to poverty efforts. Activists and Columbia University School of Social Work professors, Cloward and his partner, Frances Fox Piven, had worked for Mobilization for Youth (MFY), a social welfare program in New York's Lower East Side which focused on empowering welfare recipients. Since the early 1960s, Cloward and Piven had articulated a theory of disruption led by poor people themselves, propelled by "cadres of aggressive organizers" who would lead "demonstrations to create a climate of militancy." George Wiley was the perfect pick for their organizing effort toward a rebellion of the poor. He would bring their initiative to national prominence and bind it to the black liberation struggle.

In May 1966, Wiley had left his faculty position and founded the Poverty/Rights Action (P/RAC) center in Washington, DC, of which he became national director, to coordinate welfare activists organizing. P/RAC organized the first "poor people's march" in June 1966 as hundreds of welfare recipients marched from Cleveland to Columbus Ohio, a 155-mile "Walk for Adequate Welfare," joined along the way by unions, churches, civil rights leaders, and elected officials. Not merely passive recipients of public relief, welfare recipients were transformed into radical civil rights activists. The first statement of P/RAC read: "Our rights are not for sale. We are not willing to sell our rights as American citizens, our right to dignity, our rights to justice, our right to democracy . . . our goal: jobs or income now! Decent jobs with adequate wages for those who can work, adequate income for those who cannot work."

In a formal statement of testimony before a Senate subcommittee on urban affairs given that same year, which laid the groundwork for his last book, King called for a federal government guarantee of a minimum annual income for the poor. Not only were Wiley's "poor people's march" demands in accordance with King's in *Where Do We Go from Here,* but welfare activists too hoped to gain political leverage with a grassroots poor people's movement capable of influencing Congress. On August 8, 1966, scattered welfare groups formed a National Coordinating Committee of Welfare Groups, which coalesced to produce the National Welfare Rights Organization. As much a child of the long civil rights movement as of Community Action programs, the organizing of poor recipients of public aid were instrumental in the struggle for substantive equality. As African American families comprised 48 percent of the 806,000 welfare recipients in 1960, with single mothers over-represented among the recipients, the organization developed an egalitarian framework whereby material conditions infused definitions of race, class, and gender. As Premilla Nadassen argued, women welfare rights activists, the diamond point of the NWRA, "adopted political positions based on a material understanding of the hierarchies of race, class, gender, and sexuality," forging a unique form of "multiple consciousness" rooted in the black liberation movement.

At the poor people's convention held in 1966, women of color voiced their discontent with the leadership and management of the antipoverty programs, and expressed their expectation for a truly democratic process. Expanding the notion of "rights," they demanded economic security and empowerment. Johnnie Tillman was among the hecklers who abrasively confronted Sargent Shriver and, committed to organizing welfare recipients, she would join Wiley in the National Welfare Rights Organization. To her, the poverty program was a "laugh" because "when all the money is spent, the rich will get richer and I will still be receiving a welfare check."[74] Ironically, the War on Poverty enabled poor communities to point to the limitations of EOA policies and to find an avenue to express their grievances beyond the circle of traditional civil rights groups. As Wiley noticed, "the poor are developing a voice . . . someone is going to have to listen to them."[75] The War on Poverty had promised much but delivered too little. The purpose of the NWRO was not only to dramatize the plight of the poor and to get them get eligible on the welfare rolls but also to compel the federal government to offer more generous benefits and, further down, to disrupt the fiscal arrangements to the point where Congress would have to adopt a "guaranteed annual income," set at a dignified and adequate level. But their major concern was the criminalization of the welfare recipient and subsequent dismantling of poor people's safety net.

Scholars/activists Richard Cloward and Frances Fox Piven theorized about welfare recipients' politics of disruption in an editorial published in 1966 in *The Nation*, "A Strategy to End Poverty," which was widely circulated. Their main assumption was in line with Wiley's, that "a placid poor get nothing, but a turbulent poor sometimes get something." Through a "crisis strategy," eligible poor families, organized in a robust welfare rights movement and helped by dedicated legal services lawyers, would overload the system and foster the replacement of an inadequate welfare system with a guaranteed income. Challenging the vilified and racialized state-imposed category of "welfare recipients," low-income women of color sought to offer a counter-representation of the poor, one that resisted further disempowerment and dehumanization.

More and more, welfare policies were being rolled back as part of a backward trend to contain what was perceived by officials as a "negro problem." The idea that social programs targeting low-income urban African Americans would diffuse the unrest before outbreaks of violence was certainly prevalent among liberal policy makers. Despite major accomplishments in increasing the level of benefits and securing women's entitlement to state support, welfare rights activism could not halt the rollback. The criminalization of urban social programs in the context of budget cuts translated into harsher requirements for welfare recipients. The Kerner Commission, while stressing unemployment and police harassment, blamed the welfare system as one of the causes of the "social disorganization" that fueled the uprisings. Far from expanding "fair work" initiatives as requested by civil rights organizations, Congress reformed AFDC requirements in 1967 and moved toward workfare while freezing social expenditures. Congress enacted a Work Incentive Program which considered amendments to the Social Security Act to penalize mothers of children born outside marriage or mothers deserted by their husbands. The amendments proposed to freeze federal aid to the states for such mothers, denying additional funding to states that increased the proportion of unwed or single mothers in their caseloads. Such policies infuriated the National Welfare Rights Organization, which was closely tied to the civil rights movement. It organized nationwide protests against the antiwelfare rhetoric and the increased surveillance of the poor that permeated President Johnson's social policies.

The antiwelfare backlash crippled his antipoverty policies but was not particularly at odds with Johnson's personal viewpoint. Among the justifications he provided to sustain his War on Poverty, he argued that it would help young Americans "escape from squalor and misery and unemployment rolls where other citizens help to carry them." The racial innuendo was clear as, in the mid-1960s, the unemployment rate for blacks was more than twice that of whites: 41 percent of nonwhites fell below the poverty line and 48 percent of welfare recipients were black. American social policy had hardened racial lines and encouraged racial stereotypes since the 1930s, but President Johnson's fiscal conservatism in the context of racial turmoil further relegated inner-city black residents to a delegitimized welfare system while simultaneously blaming them for their dependence on public assistance.

The black urban poor had been pathologized since Kennedy's administration, but when America's black inner cities erupted, a self-righteous, punitive approach to welfare prevailed. The stigmatization and belittlement attached to welfare recipients since the 1950s had undergirded and justified tightened requirements, but as urban disorders escalated, the federal government engaged in a simmering "war on crime" in which law enforcement and welfare authorities became partners—intertwining social welfare with social control. More than ever, racial stereotypes of "unworthy blacks" exposed the scaffolding of ghetto exploitation and welfare arbitrariness. Welfare activists like Wiley naturally indicted urban renewal programs and police brutality, which they identified as byproducts of federal backsliding on poverty and racial equality issues. The retreat of most welfare provisions and the harsh treatment received by the poor at government offices were their main concerns, but their economic demands also touched on the issues of a minimum wage and full employment. A chief concern, beside welfare policies and fighting the stigma of being a recipient of such benefits, was the implementation of a guaranteed annual income. The NWRO's May 1966 platform read:

> It is our purpose to advance a strategy which affords the basis for a convergence of civil rights organizations, militant anti-poverty groups and the poor. If this strategy were implemented, a political crisis would result that could lead to legislation for a guaranteed annual income and thus an end to poverty.[76]

By 1966, these were proposals King could have embraced and they would become the central component of PPC demands. Indeed, as Piven put it, the welfare rights impulse manifested as a "version of the Civil Rights" which "had come to the Northern slums and ghettos." Despite their common ground though, the National Welfare Rights Organization was unsuccessful in its attempt to reach out to the Black Freedom movement: from 1966 to 1968, the SCLC rejected most of its pleas for support. Some black leaders were outright hostile. According to Piven, when the welfare rights activists contacted National Urban League president Whitney Young, he retorted that he would "rather get one black woman a job as an airline stewardess than to get twenty black women on welfare." In 1964, at the Democratic convention, King had pointed out that the black man "does not want to languish on welfare rolls," but instead would "rather have a job," and that poor blacks were bound "to a culture of poverty."

Although his use of the phrase "culture of poverty" most certainly stemmed from Gunnar Myrdal and Michael Harrington (who saw it as the result of economic deprivation, certainly not as an essential feature or intrinsic deficiency of the black poor) and did not carry the negative undertone it would have a couple of years later, King may have vacillated on the definition of work and "idleness." A man of his time, he was bombarded by negative labeling of welfare and stereotypical depictions of unworthy black single welfare-reliant mothers, which became the norm among many whites in the mid-1960s. As welfare rights activist Betty Mandell deplored, "The NAACP, the Urban League and other middle class black groups chose not to ally with welfare rights group advocating a guaranteed annual income, preferring instead to emphasize jobs" and the Johnson's philosophy of "hands-in rather than hand-outs."[77]

"Not alms but opportunity" remained the National Urban League's explicit motto until a more militant Whitney Young took over as the league's president. Since Reconstruction, black elites and black reformers had espoused an ethos of respectability, employing more than most a language of racial uplift infused with class bias and disdain for the black urban poor. Even middle-class black caseworkers were biased against the black dispossessed. The SCLC was not immune to such an inclination, but from 1966 onward, King clearly stated that intraracial class prejudice and notions of disreputable poor blacks was to be eradicated. Along the same line, he underscored in an address to the SCLC staff in May 1967 his longing for a more comprehensive struggle pushing for the reallocation of wealth and power:

> We have been in a reform movement . . . But after Selma and the voting rights bill, we moved into a new era, which must be the era of revolution. We must recognize that we can't solve our problem now until there is a radical redistribution of economic and political power . . . this means a revolution of values and other things.[78]

King came to understand the lopsided nature of social policies that implicitly imbued antipoverty reasoning with racialized (thus stigmatizing) assumptions. Race obviously trumped class in the management of social welfare distribution. Antiwelfare policies, particularly those involving the surveillance of recipients, were inscribing criminality onto every aspect of the lives of disinherited African American families. The NWRO reframed the debate, arguing for the "right to an income" to replace ubiquitous yet prejudiced concepts of worthiness and deservedness. Within this frame of analysis, single mothers were entitled to their own income and the patriarchal concept of family wage was defiantly challenged. Such *aggiornamento* is crucial to capturing the revolutionary nature of the Poor People's Campaign.

Certainly, King could not entirely expunge his personal views or his long-held assumptions about black manhood and gender unequal roles. In an interview on the television program "Face the Nation," King was asked about the supposed disintegration of the black family and the high levels of black children born out of wedlock. Utterly rejecting the assumption of a structural cultural problem specific to black people, he pointed to the way economic deprivation destroyed families: "I think if we look at it thoroughly, it goes back to the economic realm. So many Negro man end up deserting their families because of economic insecurity . . . they ended up in situations where illegitimate children emerge and I don't think any answer to that problem will emerge until we give the Negro man his manhood by giving him the kind of economic security capable of supporting his family."[79]

But under the guidance of the NWRO, he made strides toward a greater understanding of poor people's multifaceted predicaments, particularly as they relate to women. By 1966–1967 King had fundamentally reconciled with a female-oriented welfare rights activism. In *Where Do We Go from Here,* he denounced the "arbitrary power" of abusive welfare bureaucrats who "often humiliate or neglect" the recipients. During his Soldier Field Rally in Chicago on July 10, 1966, King debunked the racism undergirding social policies: "We are tired of a welfare system which dehumanizes us and dispenses payments under procedures that are often ugly and paternalistic."[80] His usage of "we" in this sentence reflects his understanding that welfare was a civil rights issue but also indicates his identification with black women, who formed the bulk of the welfare rolls. Where Rustin blamed black poverty on class structure and a changing labor market, King clung to the framework of exploitation and structural racism:

> Poor people are victimized by a riotous Congress and welfare bureaucracy. Lawlessness against persons exercising civil rights continues. The insult of closed housing statutes is preserved and sanctified by white society. Flame throwers in Vietnam fan the flames in our cities. Children are condemned to attend schools which are institutions of disorder and neglect. The lives, incomes, the wellbeing of poor people everywhere in America are plundered by our economic system. No wonder that men who see their communities raped by this society sometimes turn to violence.[81]

He therefore became a supporter of the welfare rights movement, lambasting middle-class disdain for any measure called "welfare" for the poor but "subsidies" for everyone else. He mocked the better-off's proclivity to demonize anything as "socialist" when the American economic system was in fact "socialism for the rich and rugged free enterprise for the poor."[82] The Poor People's Campaign would champion redistributive welfare policies and a guaranteed income, decent minimum wages, and public jobs. King's economic agenda also included a visionary call for social services jobs (which King called "human services jobs"). Byproducts of Community Actions programs, these nonskilled jobs provided poor communities with day care, health and welfare services, employment programs, and the like to the poor without stripping them of their agency. Resurrection City would be a laboratory for their implementation.

But welfare rights activists were unimpressed by King's late commitment to their cause, relying instead on more radical militants. In January 1967, Wiley met in Washington with Carmichael, who sought to create a radical Black United Front, but Wiley, who had also attended a New Left meeting, eschewed a nationalist strategy. Multiracial in their scope, NWRO activists had locally organized numerous inclusive marches and rallies that foreshadowed Poor People's Campaign rhetoric, as illustrated in a 1967 issue of its information brochure, *Now!:* "Most NWRO groups are located in the ghettos and barrios of major US cities but there are also groups located in rural areas of the South, Appalachia and the Mid-West. NWRO includes substantial numbers of low income whites, Puerto-Ricans, Mexican-Americans, as well as Negroes in its membership." Appealing to the poor of all races and ethnicities was the key to sustaining a strong and effective antipoverty social movement. From its creation, the architects of the movement pointed to the necessity for a broad class-based coalition of the dispossessed:

> The prospects for mass influence are enhanced because this plan provides a practical basis for coalition between poor whites and poor Negroes. Advocates of low-income movements have not been able to suggest how poor whites and poor Negroes can be united in an expressly lower-class movement. Despite pleas of some Negro leaders for joint action on programs requiring integration, poor whites have steadfastly resisted making common cause with poor Negroes.[83]

Despite their common ground, when King, along with Ralph Abernathy, Bernard Lafayette, Andrew Young, and Al Simpson, asked the NWRO to support his Poor People's Campaign at a Chicago meeting in February 1967, they were confronted by NWRO activists, who refused to be submissive foot soldiers. Resenting King's lieutenants' attitude, George Wiley, Johnnie Tillmon, and thirty leaders of the group, mostly women, called into question King's commitment and knowledgeability on current pressing issues. Etta Horn opened fire, bluntly asking him: "How do you stand on P.L. 90–248?" Andrew Young came to King's rescue: "She means the Anti-Welfare Bill, H.R. 12080, passed by the Congress on December 15, and signed into law by Lyndon Baines Johnson in January." Tillmon and Beulah Sanders, two key figures in the welfare rights movement, grilled

King too: "'Where were you last October, when we were down in Washington trying to get support for Senator Kennedy's amendments?" before holding up a copy of the NWRO pamphlet on the Kennedy Welfare Amendments.

Unconvinced by his answers, Tillmon lectured King: "You know Dr. King, if you do not know about these questions, you should say you don't know and then we could go on with the meeting." Shaken by such an outright blow, King conceded: "You are right Miss Tillmon, we do not know anything about welfare. We are here to learn."[84] Pressed by AFDC mothers, King added NWRO concerns about current antiwelfare laws to the campaign's demands. Welfare rights activists bred his leftward maturation, elucidating the violence of the contempt harbored by the middle class toward them and the mechanisms through which poverty was gendered, including social workers' coercive regulation of AFDC mothers. At the end of the meeting, the SCLC agreed that their demands would become the campaign's ones. It would call for the repealing of the welfare freeze law of 1967, and would advocate for a national guaranteed income and the appropriation of federal funds to create millions of public jobs. On March 25, as the Poor People's Campaign's organization was on the move, King sent a telegram to the Pennsylvania's Welfare Rights Organization which read: "Pennsylvania AFDC grants of 71 percent of a starvation standard are a shame and a disgrace. I strongly support your demonstration."[85] The NWRO's powerful disruptive lobbying techniques inspired King as he laid the groundwork for the campaign. Moreover, on a more personal level, they awakened him to the double bind of poor black women, notably mothers who, insofar as their work was unpaid, were working poor too.

King's desire to build a revolutionary grassroots mass movement of poor people entailed a shift in strategy. Andrew Young reckoned that "the civil rights movement up until 1968 anyway, was really a middle-class movement.... Cesar Chavez and George Wiley had poor people's movements."[86] But for the Poor People's Campaign, King modeled his plans on theirs and somewhat followed the NWRO road map, including reaching out to Black Power activists.

Wealth redistribution had been main feature of the young black members of SNCC since its inception. John Lewis's speech at the 1963 March on Washington, although truncated and watered down, had been considered controversial because of the uncompromising tone of his economic demands. But in 1968, his words resonated with the Poor People's Campaign: "We need a bill that will provide for the homeless and starving people of this nation. We need a bill that will ensure the equality of a maid who earns five dollars a week in the home of a family whose total income is 100,000 dollars a year. . . . My friends, let us not forget that we are involved in a serious social revolution. By and large, politicians who build their career on immoral compromise and allow themselves an open forum of political, economic and social exploitation dominate American politics."[87] SNCC then proceeded to implement economic progress in the Deep South. The Mississippi Freedom Labor Union, for instance, had a membership of more than a thousand and organized strikes for wage raises, free medical care, and accident insurance involving at times upward of seven hundred of the most impoverished workers in the Delta.[88] It was small wonder that Mississippi, a state canvassed by SNCC workers, would stand as the crucible of the Poor People's Campaign. Both the Mississippi Freedom Democratic Party and the Child Development Group of Mississippi, a community action group created in 1965 to run a series of Head Start programs, were pioneers in their commitment toward eradicating poverty.[89]

In May 1966 Stokely Carmichael replaced John Lewis as chairman of SNCC, a move that signaled a shift in the student movement from an emphasis on nonviolence and integration toward black militancy. Out of that strategic discord, the student group (about to become the Student *National* Coordinating Committee) eventually announced that it would not march with the Poor People's Campaign in Washington, DC. Marginalized, Lewis nevertheless attended the Chicago planning symposium. Sure enough, King's appeal to Lewis was related to SNCC's new political orientation. Carmichael's successful call for Black Power, flourishing in 1968, had certainly compromised SNCC's relationships with the SCLC. But it would be inaccurate to argue that King and SNCC were utterly estranged in the wake of Carmichael's repudiation of nonviolence and interracial cooperation (Carmichael did oppose the decision to expel whites from the organization). Not only did Lewis remain close to King and willing to collaborate, but Carmichael himself was to personally approve of the Poor People's Campaign.

Beginning in February 1967, King and Carmichael engaged in a rapprochement, both on the issue of Vietnam (Carmichael had urged King to voice his opposition to the war for a long time) and on the PPC. When King announced his plan to gather three thousand people on the Mall of the nation's capital to dramatize poverty, Carmichael endorsed the campaign. Over the phone, he initially expressed his unconditional support for King's endeavor. King and Carmichael met several times in private, assessing their commonalities. In February 1968, Carmichael promised to support the nonviolent march and the camp-in.[90] But they continued to hold different views on the political purpose of the campaign and eventually, SNCC's official position was neither to endorse or condemn the campaign.[91] The two men would meet one last time along with Jesse Jackson, who was also reluctant to support King's idea of a poor people's crusade. Carmichael had in fact another coalition in mind, the one he sought to build among black radicals, closing the gap between SNCC and the Black Panther Party. Interestingly, he also connected with Reies Tijerina, who had been in contact with both the Panthers and King, and was fully engaged in the PPC. Many local chapters of Black Panthers, whose 1966 "10 steps platform" also stressed the urgent need for full employment and decent housing, ultimately participated in the campaign. Embarrassed, the SCLC staff urged King not to publicize his bond with Black Power activists, for they feared antagonizing liberal whites and middle-class institutions.

But whatever their personal bonds and intellectual communalities, Carmichael and King differed more and more on strategy. After relinquishing the SNCC chairmanship and becoming prime minister of the militant Oakland-based Black Panther Party, Carmichael eventually defended the exclusion of white radicals from the Panthers and from SNCC as well. Young proponents of the Black Power creed were now deeply distrustful of a coalition predicated on the American liberal creed. Besides, he grew more and more dismissive of socialism and Marxism, arguing that none of these ideologies were fit to "speak to the problem of racism," which came first, before any form of exploitation.[92] On the contrary, SNCC, now under the leadership of James Foreman, riddled its critique of racism in the United States with stances on economic exploitation, a Marxian-inspired framework which could have dovetailed with King's radical egalitarian framework analysis. But the internal fracturing of the organizations rendered their convergence unrealizable. In *Where Do We Go from Here*, King unraveled at length his opposition to the concept of "Black Power," favoring instead a class-based framing of the struggle for liberation.

> One unfortunate thing about Black Power is that it gives priority to race precisely at a time when the impact of automation and other forces have made the economic question fundamental for blacks and whites alike. In this context a slogan "Power for Poor People" would be much more appropriate than the slogan "Black Power."[93]

While the Poor People's Campaign defended a universal set of antipoverty measures, it nonetheless emphasized the primacy of the black condition and shared Black Power's call for the reappraisal of black working class manhood. King had regularly mocked the misgivings of some better-off African Americans, who, "through some education and a degree of economic security floated or . . . swam out of the back waters" and have "forgotten the stench of the backwaters."[94] Their obliviousness to their "underprivileged brothers" left the latter alienated from them and resentful.[95] Chicago edified him.

But his visit to Marks, Mississippi, from where the first Poor People's Campaign caravan was expected to depart, seared southern poverty in his conscience. Thus, while it was originally scheduled to begin on April 22, King postponed the start of the Poor People's Campaign. In the midst of his whirlwind organizing of the campaign, he naturally acquiesced to the demands of local organizations to support the Memphis sanitation workers. Their fight for decent wages and collective bargaining rights were strikingly consistent with the campaign, and was to be its prologue. Andy Young hinted at the congruence of the two campaigns and called Memphis "a necessary stepping stone to Washington."[96]

The sanitation workers' condition in Memphis indeed illustrated how race and class intersected as the disregarded menial sanitation work was exclusively carried out by black men. The appalling working conditions and the denial of basic bargaining rights were embedded in a racial order in which the Memphis white elite was set in opposition to the African American workers in the city. For years, garbage collectors in Memphis had tried to improve their working conditions. In 1964, the AFSCME (American Federation of State, County and Municipal Employees, the biggest public-sector union in the United States) launched a local union: Local 1733. It was chartered but the city would not sign any contracts.

Led by Mayor Henry Loeb, Memphis officials resisted the challenge posed by the black working class, which endangered the racial arrangement that had prevailed in the city. Loeb tightened city labor policies and enforced black Memphians' exploitation. By 1968, the city population was 40 percent black, most of them trapped in poverty and low-paying jobs. Almost 60 percent lived in poverty—10 percent above the national average, four times as high as the rate of poverty among the white families of Memphis.[97] Enduring starvation wages and subjection, the garbage collectors were exploited in ways reminiscent of plantation-like conditions.[98]

But on February 1, 1968, the death of two sanitation workers accidently crushed in their faulty garbage truck sparked the protest which had been simmering for years. On February 12, more than 1,100 workers launched a strike for job safety, better wages, and benefits, and union recognition. The workers demanded not only significant improvements in pay, work conditions, and the right to unionize but first and foremost dignity. The strikers in Memphis exemplified how the workplace had, against all odds, been perceived as a space of empowerment for black workers.[99] More than a labor dispute, the strike therefore exposed entrenched patterns of discrimination and beyond, the exploitation of workers absent government-sponsored protection and mass collective action. Although they got initially no formal support from the AFSCME, workers carried out their mobilizing with the support of the local AFL-CIO, the NAACP, and the SCLC.

Despite organizing city-wide boycotts, sit-ins, and daily marches, the garbage workers were initially unable to secure concessions from municipal officials. Reverend James Lawson, pastor of the Centenary Methodist Church, called on King to join their fight. Dr. King came to Memphis on March 18, 1968, and addressed thousands of people at the Bishop Charles Mason Temple. The speeches he gave there captured the philosophy of the new revolution for economic rights he intended to launch with the PPC.

He empathically channeled the frustration and discontent of a working class he did not belong to but could identify with and addressed the middle-class disdain for the working class in Marxian undertones:

> You are demanding that this city will respect the dignity of labor, so often we overlook the work and the significance of those who are not in professional jobs, of those who are not in the so-called big jobs. But let me say to you tonight that whenever you are engaged in work that serves humanity and is for the building of humanity, it has dignity and it has worth.[100]

He laid out a systemic analysis of economic exploitation affecting the working class, for "it is a crime for poor people to live in this rich nation and receive starvation wages." Fingering the policy makers and the corporate world, which he called the "power structure," he spoke with populist fervor: "Do you know that most of the poor people in our country are working every day? And they are making wages so low that they cannot begin to function in the mainstream of the economic life our nation. . . . You are here to demand that Memphis will see the poor."[101] He also described the exploitative inner workings of the American capitalistic system:

> My friends, we are living as a people in a literal depression. . . . Now the problem is not only unemployment. Do you know that most of the poor people in our country are working every day? And they are making wages so low that they cannot begin to function in the mainstream of the economic life of our nation. These are facts which must be seen, and it is criminal to have people working on a full-time basis and a full-time job getting part-time income.[102]

Arguably, the Equal Employment Opportunity Commission (EEOC) established on July 2, 1965, and the other antidiscrimination policies pertaining to employment enshrined in the Civil Rights Act under Title VII had been positive achievements for workers. But they barely scratched the surface of the unequal distribution of American wealth. "Our struggle is for genuine equality, which means economic equality. For we know that it isn't enough to integrate lunch counters. What does it profit a man to be able to eat at an integrated lunch counter if he doesn't earn enough money to buy a hamburger and cup of coffee?"[103] To those "who are tired of being overworked and underpaid" but willing to join the next phase of the civil rights struggle, King promised "the rest of freedom and economic security."[104]

Michael Honey cogently demonstrates the extent to which his involvement in Memphis was reflective of King's plans for a new phase of the civil
rights movement, enmeshing it with the most progressive labor organizations. Despite his 1959 support for the hospital workers in Local 1199 and
Walter Reuther's reformist mindset, King's hopes for a labor–civil rights
coalition had not been seriously crippled. However, they were not fore-
closed as many small unions opposed the war in Vietnam and enforced
inclusive policies within their ranks. Much in the footsteps of A. Philip
Randolph and Bayard Rustin (who came to Memphis on March 14), King
foregrounded the socioeconomic hardship and political disinheritance of
the male black worker:

> We are tired. We are tired of being at the bottom. We are tired of being
> trampled over by the iron feet of oppression. We are tired of our children
> having to attend overcrowded, inferior, quality-less schools. . . . We are tired
> of smothering in an airtight cage of poverty in the midst of an affluent
> society. . . . We are tired of our men being emasculated so that our wives and
> our daughters have to go out and work in the white lady's kitchen, leaving us
> unable to be with our children and give them the time and the attention that
> they need. We are tired.[105]

While these words could have been perfectly in tune with the Poor
People's Campaign rhetoric, it is worth noting that King pointed to the
racial component of exploitation and social neglect, arguing that inequalities of wealth and power did not stem simply from the misapplication of
liberal democratic ideals but from racial stratifications intrinsic to the
American liberal creed. For all the class-based rhetoric of King's speeches,
the issues clearly at stake were race and gender, as black masculinity was
an integral part of the recognition black workers sought to be granted.[106]
Although many women endorsed the Memphis protestors' slogan "I am a
Man," interpreting it as a "gender neutral call for human rights"[107] and an
inclusive call for "justice" and "freedom," a male-centered rhetoric prevailed.[108] King understood that for the strikers and their families in
Memphis, manhood and freedom were conflated. During his April 3
speech, he called for the strengthening of black institutions and black
businesses, providing yet another insight on his economic justice framework which, placing the universal poor at the center of the fight, was

nonetheless informed by the race-based nature of American capitalism. Hopeful that he would win over the young disaffected ghetto dwellers who embraced a belligerent approach to Black Power, he reenacted his Chicago outreach toward gang members. He expected to recruit them as marshals for the PPC. To a certain extent, what King defended in 1968 was what Michael Eric Dyson has called an "integrationist embrace of Black Power."[109]

Black Power activists actually participated in and at times disrupted the peaceful protest in Memphis. When the March 28 march degenerated into an outbreak, with participants at the tail of the parade breaking storefront windows, the city officials blamed young Black Power activists, particularly a local group named The Invaders. Sixty people were injured, one killed. Although the FBI admitted that the activists did not initiate the "riot," the local gang was deemed responsible for the escalation of coercive policing.[110] Civil disturbance narratives overshadowed the garbage collectors' demands. Mayor Loeb claimed that his decision to place the city under martial law was justified by the lawlessness of some protestors, a line of argument already being mobilized in Washington to dismiss the Poor People's Campaign. King, afraid that the strike would turn sour again, returned to Memphis on April 3 to rekindle the appeal of nonviolence. The groundwork for the PPC was already lagging, and he knew that its success was predicated on his ability to restore peace in Memphis. He announced he would lead another march alongside the sanitation workers on April 5 and spoke at the Mason Temple that night, giving what would be his last speech.

His assassination the following day sparked anger, frustration, outrage, and urban uprisings that spread like wildfire throughout the nation. Hopes and plans were in shambles and although some voices called for a "Marshall Plan" for America's burning cities, the Poor People's Campaign's economic plea was drowned out.[111] Arson, looting, and crime monopolized the media and officials' attention. As the date for opening the Poor People's Campaign loomed, they fearfully condemned the project of gathering hundreds of young black males in Washington. The racial unrest spurred by King's death was met with further counterinsurgent policing. Rumor had it that rioters pretending to support the campaign were instead planning on burning down the capital.[112] Lance "Sweet Willie"

Washington, the leader of the Memphis Invaders, who had decided to join the Poor People's Campaign in Washington, was willing to prove them wrong: "They ask us, 'Did ya'll come here to burn?' Now we did not come here to burn, (*No!*), we come to make ya'll *learn* (*Yeah*), that's what we come up here to do!"[113]

If the Memphis sanitation workers were, by geographical constraint, peripheral to the Poor People's Campaign, "Sweet Willie" Washington's maturation was reflective of the continuities and distinctness of the two campaigns. If both campaigns mingled class- and race-based oppressions, they contrasted in their interracial and gendered dimensions. The Memphis protest was suffused with a claim for the recognition of black manhood which white supremacy had denied. Although he embraced this framework, King sought to expand the scope of the struggle. The economic reconfiguration King hoped for could not be initiated by an all-black male workers' strike, however proletarian and illustrative of poverty and exploitation. The Memphis strike was less King's last campaign (to which the Poor People's Campaign would be a byproduct of, as most historians have argued) than a remarkable occurrence in a long history of civil rights unionism that drew on the social experiments and expectations of the late nineteenth century.

To begin with, the Poor People's Campaign voiced more explicitly the concerns of working-class black women, a shift due to the pivotal role played by the National Welfare Rights Association. It also reflected the ethnic and racial diversity of those hurt by poverty. More and more poor people were unemployed—whether welfare recipient or nonunionized—and traditional organizations could not reach out to them. Something bold, dramatic, and inclusive had to be launched that would fuse class, gender, and race in a populist call for justice. Only an interracial and mixed-gender movement of the underprivileged and dispossessed could compel the nation to see the ravages of poverty and to accept a restructuring of their economic, social, and political system.

The Poor People's Campaign organizers therefore expected not only to build bridges across gender and racial divides but also to reconcile the demands and perspectives of African American radical activists across a range of political orientations. Audaciously, the campaign built on the unexpected kinship already established between welfare-reliant mothers and Black Power groups.[114] Black and brown women, many young northern blacks and even prominent SCLC figures (including James Bevel and Hosea Williams) appropriated the nationalistic rhetoric that had thrived since 1966.[115] Chicano movements also reached out to Black Power activists, stressing their commonalities. Their radicalism as to how to articulate a framework of class, race. and gender-economic oppression infused the Poor People's crusade.

7 A Counter-War on Poverty

King's death was paradoxically both crippling and reinvigorating. Arguably, it plunged the nation into an emotional storm, which ultimately benefited the campaign. The Poor People's Campaign was seen as a fitting tribute to the deceased leader and gained traction with grassroots organizations, which enthusiastically offered to participate. However, Ralph Abernathy, *de facto* in charge of the movement, was overshadowed. Absent King, the Poor People's Campaign seemed to lack leadership and charisma. Responding to press criticisms about his inability to fill the void, Abernathy replied:

> if you're trying to make Martin Luther King outa me, I got news for you . . .)
> I'm gonna be nobody but Ralph Abernathy. . . . I don't speak for the press.
> I'm not concerned about the press, I'm concerned about my people. All I
> want to do is to get my black people together, and to get my Mexican-
> Americans, and my American Indians, and my Puerto Ricans and get all of
> them together; that's all—and the poor white people in the Appalachia
> areas, that's all I want to do is to get them together.[1]

He announced on April 17 that the SCLC would move ahead with the Poor People's Campaign but that its official start would be postponed to

May 12. Hundreds of volunteers throughout the country were on the starting line and contributions were flooding in; a dozen committees were dedicated to preparing all the infrastructures needed for the encampment, from free schools to health services and transportation. By the end of March, the SCLC had benefited from the endorsement of five major religious groups in Washington and from a reluctant NAACP. Major religious groups also endorsed the campaign (notably the Washington Jewish Council and the Interreligious Committee on Racial Relations) as well as local Washington unions such as the Washington Teachers Unions and the National Association of Social Workers. Significant allies came forward including informal support from the Peace Corps, Volunteers in Service to America (VISTA), and the Young Men's Christian Association (YMCA).

Senator Robert Kennedy, who had decided to run for the presidency, became the strongest supporter of the PPC, which he had indirectly initiated. He managed to appeal to many young dissenters, disaffected by President Johnson's record on war, equality, and economic justice. He met several times with Cesar Chavez, obtained the endorsement of John Lewis and even of some Black Panthers. By all measures, the month of April saw the campaign's agenda gaining steam.

CITIZENSHIP FOR THE POOR: A NEW ECONOMIC BILL OF RIGHTS

In 1964, King had called for a class-based "Economic Bill of Rights for the Disadvantaged" to achieve a truly egalitarian citizenship.[2] The right not to be poor was a human right and he had urged a nation as rich as the United States to reform itself:

> The Constitution assured the right to vote, but there is no such assurance of the right to adequate housing, or the right to an adequate income. And yet, in a nation which has a gross national product of 750 billion dollars a year, it is morally right to insist that every person has a decent house, an adequate education and enough money to provide basic necessities for one's family.[3]

In 1968, the Poor People's Campaign took up his proposal and carved out a social welfare agenda comparable in scope to the Marshall Plan. The PPC's economic fact Sheet, which the SCLC issued in January 1968 as an internal document, underscored the unequal distribution of power and access to resources between the poor of all races and the white majority. Intentionally vague in its early stage, to avoid any petty bargaining with Congress, the Economic Bill of Rights called for "a meaningful job at the living wage for every employable citizen; a secure and adequate income for all who cannot find jobs or for whom employment is inappropriate; access to land as a means to income and livelihood; access to capital as a means of full participation in the economic life of America; [and] recognition by law of the right of people affected by government programs to play a truly significant role in determining how they are designed and carried out."[4] Later on, the SCLC articulated more precise demands, including $30 billion for antipoverty policies, full employment, guaranteed income, and the annual construction of 500,000 affordable residences. The minority groups present in Atlanta in March had further substantiated the "cahiers de doléances" they intended to bring before Congress.[5]

On April 28, the multiracial committee made a spectacular entrance to the federal capital. Vic Charlo and Mel Thom, members of the National Indian Youth Council (NIYC), Latino organizers José Ortiz, a Puerto Rican from New York City, and Maria Varela, a land rights activist in New Mexico, along with SCLC members, welfare rights activists, and white coal miners vehemently claimed a right to a job, a living income, and a right to speak up. Their demand for an "Economic Bill of Rights for the Disadvantaged" offered a counter-hegemonic explanation of poverty, bringing forth a structural critique of corporate liberalism and pointing to the paradox of a welfare system that benefited most those who needed it the least and dehumanized the truly disadvantaged.

The advance guard for the caravans soon to gather on the Mall, the Committee of 100, composed largely of poor people, arrived in the capital as ambassadors with a streamlined and collectively approved version of SCLC's bill of rights and began its lobbying effort on April 29. It presented the bill to Washington's officials in an established usage and orderly manner, a display of their cooperative spirit. The committee strived to carve out a space of dissent while maintaining an ongoing dialogue with the federal government, allowing for a conversation between poor people and high-ranking officers that sought to bridge the gap between disempowered and dispossessed citizens and policy makers. The labor-inspired delegation granted officials ten days to respond to their demands:

1. Adequate jobs for the unemployed and the underemployed.

2. Welfare payments brought up to realistically defined minimum subsistence levels with removal of qualifications that tend to be punitive and to break up families.

3. Basic minimum income guarantees for all Americans.

4. The firm and final establishment of school desegregation and quality of education for all Americans

5. A massive program of building and renovation to provide decent housing for the poor and those Americans who live on minimum, fixed income.

6. Adequate medical and dental care for all Americans.

7. The elimination from the law enforcement and judicial systems of whatever forms of discrimination against minority groups and poor people now exist.[6]

A true distribution of governance entailed the recognition of the right of poor people affected by social welfare programs to actively elaborate them, participating as full citizens in the inner workings of participatory representative democracy. Challenging the myth of equal opportunity, the committee underscored the entanglement between racial subjugation and class status. The campaign's substantive "lobby-in" was to be disruptive in form and content, faithful to King's expectations: "It ought to be a continuing, massive lobby-in," he had told his staff in March 1968, for "pressureless persuasion does not move the power structure."[7] The committee invited itself to various federal agencies, including but not limited to the Department of Justice. It specifically reached out to governmental agencies created by Johnson to oversee welfare programs (the Departments of Health and Human Services, Housing and Urban Development, Labor, Agriculture, Education, and the Office of Economic Opportunity), pushing for massive federal investment in housing and employment policies, including a guaranteed income. The multiracial committee also added group-specific demands that were collectively requested, with a particular emphasis on land rights, as the necessary "access to capital as a means to full economic life of America."[8]

Unsurprisingly, their rhetoric and strategy were met with political resistance, mass-media contempt, and overall suspicion. Despite the pan-ethnic makeup of the participants, the national press marginalized non-black participants throughout the campaign, belittling its revolutionary class-based framework.[9] Conservative congressmen vented their disdain for the campaign's demands with regards to economic equality, especially deriding the guaranteed income, about which Senator Russell Long of Louisiana lashed out: "If they think they are going to push us into bank-rupting this country to pay worthless people to be more worthless, they are making a mistake."[10]

On April 22—the date on which King had initially intended to present the campaign's demands to Congress—NWRO activists were arrested while holding a vigil on Capitol Hill and calling for a "living Memorial" to King in the form of a guaranteed income and public-job-creation program as well as the repeal of antiwelfare legislation. The judge assumed that they were in reality expressing their support of the riots which were enflaming the nation. The FBI's smear campaign (whose first step was to spread rumors that if welfare recipients were to join the campaign, their checks would not be paid) gave ammunition to Southern congressmen who fiercely opposed a campaign they dubbed "mob rule." Ralph Abernathy was nonetheless granted a temporary permit by the National Park Service for the encampment to settle for six weeks on the Washington Mall, on a site symbolically adjacent to the Lincoln Memorial.

The participants staged nonviolent protests as King had planned: fol-lowing his vision, they remained on government agencies' premises and asserted that they would not depart as long as the White House, Congress, and federal institutions ignored their plight. On April 29 at the Department of Justice, Ralph Abernathy called into question the government's com-mitment to fighting discrimination, explaining that blacks as well as Mexican Americans routinely faced employment discrimination (particu-larly in the Southwestern farming industry) and arbitrary police beating. If Abernathy and Andy Young presented a soft-spoken face, a more militant call to action was made by Ray Robinson, an antiwar Alabama native who had been supportive of King since 1963 and would later die mobilizing on behalf of Native Americans.[11] The NWRO black activists demanded the repeal of antiwelfare provisions but also policies to stop Native Americans' mistreatments. Peggy Terry, talking on behalf of poor whites, expressed her shame and resentment toward the prejudice shared by most Southern whites.[12] Attorney General Ramsey Clark acknowledged their visit but eschewed any substantive answer.

That same day, the delegation met with Secretary of Labor William Wirtz, asking him for bold measures to fight unemployment, notably what King had called for, a system of guaranteed income in which the government would be the employer of last resort. On-the-job training programs and better wages were also a major concern as the poor present were working poor. Cleveland Robinson, president of the American Negro Labor Council and one of King's advisors on the labor movement, talked on behalf of black workers. A member from the Ponca tribe of Oklahoma, Martha Grass, pointed out the lack of educational opportunity and resources available to Indians, condemning them to misery; welfare activists, notably George Wiley, and white unemployed coalminers added their voices to a call for dignity and empowerment of the poor.[13]

Later, Ralph Abernathy, Corky Gonzales, welfare activists, Appalachians, Southwestern workers, Puerto Rican activists, and more than a hundred others gathered at the Department of Agriculture to demand free food stamps, school lunches, and distribution programs to tackle hunger and malnutrition. Moreover, the disrupters demanded the protection of farmworker's rights to unionize and lampooned the federal subsidies to corporate agribusiness. Also in the spirit of Cesar Chavez, they brought up the issue of the green-card strikebreakers who undermined Mexican workers' rights. Agriculture Secretary Orville Freeman, illustrating his contemporaries' bias against the poor, replied by pointing to the damaging side-effect of food stamps, claiming that the poor would be inclined to misuse the program, and he mocked their initiative, dubbing it a "publicity stunt."[14]

On April 30, the delegates disrupted the offices of HUD (Housing and Urban Development) where they reviled the pervasiveness of the "culture of poverty" narrative that stigmatized the poor while ignoring their legitimate and ardent need for decent housing. They asked for a five-year program to tackle the lack of affordable housing and the discrimination at play, which penalized both black Americans and Latinos. They suggested that these groups should be hired by construction companies to build and rehabilitate low-income housing. At each of their appointments, the protestors stressed with indefatigable drive that poor people had not only a right to decent amenities and jobs but that their participation in the process of policy-making was a requirement.

At the Senate Committee on Manpower, Employment and Poverty, a delegation led by Abernathy eloquently demonstrated that, were the poor to be given a real opportunity, they would prove eager to work wholeheartedly toward a more just nation. But, as Abernathy boldly reminded the senators, the systemic inequality created by the policies enacted had to be challenged. He forcefully pointed to the double standard of a government which gave "tax advantages to the richest and most powerful corporations in the world" while it was unable to "provide a job that pays a living wage, a decent house, the food to make a child healthy and strong."[15]

On the day the delegation of the poor disrupted HUD, the activists also headed to the Department of Health, Education, and Welfare (HEW) where they lashed out at the OEO, which "had failed" the poor by rendering them dependent upon local officials, thus gutting the participation of poor communities. The demeaning yet ubiquitous notion of the idleness of the poor was all the more intolerable, they claimed, in that it justified the demise of the EOA's "maximum feasible participation" principle. Because of such misrepresentation, they argued, the scope and autonomy of Community Action programs had indeed been critically curtailed. Local organizing was either depicted as a seedbed for subversion or as an ineffective endeavor in need of cooptation. Bernard Lafayette, the campaign coordinator, eloquently demanded that the government provide the poor with health care, whether by expanding Medicare to all people or by giving universal access to health care centers organized and administered by trained poor people. Such jobs, along with a guaranteed income, would provide the framework for income maintenance, skill development, and community service protection for health care and education. These were spaces of a high cultural sense of empowerment and the department was asked to sustain grassroots efforts to "permit poor black, brown and white children to express their own worth and dignity as human beings."[16]

Interestingly, this demand echoed King's earlier call for "human services jobs" to be developed in the ghettoes. In *Where Do We Go from Here?* he had laid out his vision for Public Service Job Assurance, in which human services (all forms of work in social care) could be "the missing industry that will soak up the unemployment that persists in the United States":

> The human services—medical attention, social services, neighborhood amenities of various kinds—are in scarce supply in this country, especially in localities of poverty. The traditional way of providing manpower for these jobs—degree-granting programs—cannot fill all the niches that are opening up.... The growth of the human services should be rapid. It should be developed in a manner insuring that the jobs that will be generated will not primarily be for professionals with college and postgraduate diplomas but for people from the neighborhoods who can perform important functions for their neighbors.[17]

King had perceived that human services jobs could not only tackle unemployment in dispossessed communities and provide them with much needed care, but they would also spearhead a "person-oriented society" which, borne out of a "revolution of value," would cure the nation from its materialism. During their impromptu meeting at the HEW, NWRO activist specifically pointed to the lack of childcare services, which rendered the welfare policy's work requirement unjust and immoral. They claimed that the social policies at play were about norm enforcement rather than poverty alleviation and were infused with underlying racialist aims. The "man in the house rule" was exposed as a racially coded and gender-discriminating provision. Poverty was not only framed as an insidious form of violence but also as an exploitative form of domination. One version of the campaign statement read that the poor were "the captives, the colonized of the colony, consigned to an island of abject poverty from the mainland of power and decision . . . the poor are trapped in poverty because they are voiceless and powerless; the most militant poor have resorted to retaliatory violence in their demands for economic justice . . . they have looted stores as they have been legally looted by the greed of the business world."[18]

At the Department of the Interior, which activists visited on May 3, members of the Committee of 100 met with Secretary of Interior Steward L. Udall but focused their attention on Commissioner of Indian Affairs

Robert L. Bennett. Native American spokesperson Mel Thom denounced the forced "Americanization" of native children, reviled a "paternalistic" and "colonialistic system," and demanded the right to "separate but equal communities," reservations free to self-govern—altogether a much more radical phrasing of the demands of the civil rights movement than the government was accustomed to. Moreover, on this day Native Americans were supported by Chicanos and black Americans, who expressed their common sense of invisibility and neglect. Reservations, barrios, and ghettos were exposed as an American shame, spaces of exploitation and oppression.

After a meeting with Dean Rusk at the State Department, where the committee asked chiefly for the protection of the land rights of "Spanish-speaking people" and Native Americans, Abernathy announced to the press that "the poor" were "no longer divided" and that the time had come for a "people's power." Portraying antipoverty programs as efforts toward domestic pacification, black, white and brown poor challenged the conventional views of the impoverished and showed an unprecedented united front. The common thread of all the meetings was the demand for a real empowerment of the poor, which had been falsely promised by the EOA.

The opening act of the participants' dramatic militancy was the Mother's Day Parade on May 12, born out of the intense negotiations between the SCLC and the National Welfare Rights Organization. Although led by Coretta Scott King, the parade, which brought together five thousand individuals, was orchestrated by the National Welfare Rights Association. Ralph Abernathy, embattled but stalwart, channeled King's ambition, telling the crowd: "We come with an appeal to open the doors of America to the almost fifty million Americans who have not been given a fair share of America's wealth and opportunity, and we will stay until we get it."[19]

The Mother's Day march in Washington, DC, hoped to jump-start the movement by enlisting the support of "black women, white women, brown women, and red women—all the women of this nation—in the campaign of conscience" to end poverty.[20] Moving through the low-income areas of the capital, the marchers demanded their Economic Bill of Rights as well as the end of punitive welfare regulations and the freeze in social expenditures. Echoing the voice of her diseased husband, Mrs. King lambasted a "Congress that passes laws which subsidize corporations, farms, oil companies, airlines and houses for suburbia. . . . But when it turns to the poor, it suddenly becomes concerned about balancing the budget."[21] Ethel Kennedy, Robert Kennedy's widow, attended the march, reminding the participants that her husband was supportive of the campaign, so much so that his funeral procession had marched through Resurrection City days before. The Mother's Day Parade was a success. While many of the protesters came simply for the march, others decided to stay.

On May 21, demonstrators began picketing at the Capitol, the Departments of State and Agriculture, and other agencies which had a bearing on poor people's lives. The Office of Economic Opportunity was the only agency truly supportive of the campaign. The protestors engaged in almost forty demonstrations, peacefully presenting their demands for welfare, housing, and jobs to governmental agencies. On May 23, more than twenty people were arrested outside the Capitol for protesting without a proper permit, but Jesse Jackson rushed to intercede on their behalf.[22] A week later, four hundred protestors demonstrated in front of the Supreme Court to oppose its decision to uphold a ban on fishing which hurt the Native American population from the state of Washington. Pretending that rocks had been thrown, the police arrested many protestors and the press once again portrayed the Poor People's Campaign as a site of insubordination and violence. The *Washington Post* portrayed the protestors as ruthless "hippies," one of them having purportedly "splash[ed] about in one of the pools"; while others "lowered the flag" or screamed "obscenities, flailing and kicking."[23] In addition to the demonstration at the Supreme Court on May 29, a group marched on May 30 to the Department of Agriculture and on June 4 to the Attorney General Ramsey Clark's office to condemn the new fishing rules and ended up being brutally molested by the police. Although only hundreds out of the three thousand poor gathered in Washington participated in these actions, the dramatic retaliations by police reinforced the shared sense of unity of purpose by Chicanos, Native Americans, and poor blacks.

Jesse Jackson, initially opposed to the campaign, turned out to be the most ardent supporter of welfare rights and poor people. The SCLC's young preacher called welfare "dehumanizing" and demanded not only the repeal of the 1967 antiwelfare bill but also an end to all the mistreatments endured by welfare recipients. On May 28, Jackson, the newly elected mayor of Resurrection City, organized a march of hundreds of poor people to the Department of Agriculture where they demanded fair labor standards in agriculture, cheaper food stamps, and the end of indecent agricultural practices. They went on to ostentatiously have a meal at the department's cafeteria. Jackson held up the consolidated lunch check, collected the money he was given, added a few hundred dollars more to cover the bill. Then, according to Daniel Schorr, the CBS journalist appointed to cover the campaign, he emphatically declared that the pending $292.66 bill was little compared to the government's debt to the poor.[24] Jackson subsequently claimed he was sending the bill to "whoever owes the other will pay," theatrically adding through a megaphone: "This government owes us a lot. And they've just begun to pay a little bit of it with this lunch."[25]

On May 30, a thousand marchers followed Abernathy to the Department of Agriculture. Native Americans made a dramatic visit to the Supreme Court on May 31, wearing tribal costumes and chanting traditional hymns, in order to raise the judges' attention to their violated rights. On June 1, 150 Appalachian whites demonstrated outside the office of West Virginia senator Robert Byrd, who was a vocal opponent of the campaign, while another group protested the indictment of the Chicano group the Brown Berets. Later that month, another Mexican American contingent protested the "inadequate and racist school systems in this country" in front of the Department of Education, demanding the recognition of Chicano's culture and heritage.

Although far from the massive disruption and civil disobedience King had envisioned, the sallies to governmental agencies were nevertheless dramatic. From May 21 to June 6, actions involving 50 to 500 people took place on a daily basis; 900 people simultaneously protested. Congressmen seemed at times open to the protesters' claims, as illustrated by the African American senator from Massachusetts, Edward W. Brooke, chair of the informal congressional committee in charge of negotiating with the PPC, who pledged to help residents reaching out to Congress through hearings held onsite.[26]

But the poor crusaders faced considerable challenges and resistance. The assassination of Bobby Kennedy on June 6 struck a terrible blow to the campaign. Besides, as the FBI kept demonizing the campaign, more and more officials and mainstream journalists expressed their misgivings or took an outright hostile stand, undermining the campaign's already waning popularity in public opinion. The Republican candidate to the presidency, Richard Nixon, publicly urged Congress not to give in to the campaign's "demands." Absent the charismatic figure of King, the encampment failed to garner media interest and was quickly misrepresented. Although fifteen members of Senator Brooke's ad hoc committee visited Resurrection City to attest to their interest, it was now obvious that Congress was not willing to act. The Fair Housing Act, the last block of the civil right legislation, which Johnson signed on April 11, 1968, casting it as a "tribute" to King, would be the last step Congress was willing to take toward inclusiveness.[27] But the much awaited mule train was still on its way and protestors remained hopeful that they would regain momentum.

RESURRECTION CITY: A PEOPLE'S DEMOCRACY

During the second half of May, the caravans began to convene in Washington. As imagined by King, a dissenting shantytown was occupying the nation's most iconic national public space, framing Resurrection City as an alternative order where the poor, through acts of civil participation and dissenting presence, would reclaim their full meaning and power.

The "city of hope" King had imagined was never meant to be the campaign's raison d'être but a staging ground for further protest actions. It was designed not to be a sit-in, but rather a "live-in" with thousands of demonstrators settled on the site. King's advisor Stanley Levison had stated that the Poor People's Campaign would be somewhat a reenactment of the 1932 Bonus March, which saw 15,000 to 20,000 First World War veterans marching on the Capitol and camping on the Mall to demand payment immediately of cash bonuses promised to them in 1945, But another episode compellingly foretold the Poor People's Campaign. The Coxey's Army march of 1894, also named the "Hobo Army march," or, as they christened themselves, "the Commonwealth Army of Christ," was composed of unemployed workers from Ohio. Jacob Coxey, who lead the march to Washington, sought to shed light on American poverty and

demanded a massive federal government investment plan including public jobs to alleviate it.[28] During their five weeks march toward the capital,
hundreds of protestors coming together from forty different processions
received massive public support. The Coxey family foreshadowed the
PPC's mule train by traveling in open horse-drawn carriages. Only five
hundred people eventually reached Washington but their makeup was
extraordinary: black, white, native Americans, men, and women joined
hands and remained united until Coxey's arrest for trespassing and the
"army's" subsequent dispersion.[29] Unable to convince Congress, Coxey's
populist march nonetheless reshaped public opinion on the need to solve
economic hardships and to care for the lesser-off.[30]

Symbolically, the first caravan of the Poor People's Campaign left from
the Lorraine Motel in Memphis, where a massive rally was held, and
headed toward Washington on May 2, 1968, followed throughout the
month by eight other multiracial caravans. Poor whites from the Southwest
as well as West Virginia, Tennessee, and Kentucky were represented by
the "Appalachian Trail" caravan while poor African Americans departed
from the small Mississippi Delta town of Marks, embarking on a dramatic
"Mule Train", a procession which captured most of the media attention.
The mule train highlighted the spirit of the campaign, as "a symbolic protest of the limits on poor people's mobility" and a theatrical exhibition of
their determination to be heard.[31] It made its way from Marks to Atlanta,
Georgia, where the campaigners boarded trains to arrive on time in
Washington.[32] The "Southern Caravan," comprised of Mexican Americans
and poor white southerners also made its way through the Deep South up
to the capital. They joined the "Eastern Caravan," containing some eight
hundred people, the "Western Caravan" including Mexican Americans
and Indians from New Mexico and Oklahoma, and the "Indian Trail"
which had departed from Seattle.

The Quaker AFSC provided most of the financing for the transportation of remote groups and also for their food and lodging. Each caravan
stopped in several cities along its way, picking up more participants. Each
was sustained by regional grassroots organizing and reflected the diversity
of the poor people involved. The Western caravan, although mostly
Hispanic and led by the prominent Chicano figures Corky Gonzales and
Reies Tijerina, also included Black Panther Party members, a contingent

of Californian Brown Berets, and Native Americans. Although nonblack groups strived to remain as central and visible to the campaign as African Americans, solidarity and equal representation were their mantra, a point underscored by an editorial in the *New Republic:*

> New Left radicals, black power advocates, American Indians, Mexican Americans, white Appalachians, and middle class whites in large cities. They want money—but something else, too. They want more control over their environment. . . . To these radical conservatives (or radical reconstructionists) the main issue in America is repossessing political and economic self. That is why they want new forms of community government.[33]

Ralph Abernathy and campaign coordinator Bernard Lafayette welcomed the statewide delegations which eventually settled on the Washington Mall, inaugurating Resurrection City on June 12. The legal encampment was being tepidly tolerated by Congress, wary about further disruptions of federal agencies, ongoing demonstrations, and visible acts of civil disobedience in the wake of King's assassination. Accordingly, a thousand National Guardsmen and eight thousand federal troops were assigned to protect the capital, standing on reserve in case of yet more civil unrest.[34]

Abernathy launched the multiracial "American Commune" with a statement evocative of King: "Here we will build a *Koinonia,* a community of love and brotherhood. Throughout the entire period from May 13 to June 24, American Indians, Puerto-Ricans, Mexican Americans, white poor Americans from the Appalachia area of our country and black Americans will attempt to live altogether in this city of hope."[35] As a tribute to the looting of Indian land, he asked a young Native American girl's permission to use the acres between the Washington Monument and the Lincoln Memorial devoted to the encampment. He also repeatedly pointed to the historical dimension of the campaign, which sought to resume the radical egalitarianism of the young American Republic:

> All our citizens would start out equal because they would arrive at Resurrection City in equal need: No one would have a larger house or a fuller stomach merely because of what he or she had inherited. . . . No one would need an extra push because no one would have a head start. No one

would be greedy and no one would be envious. We would all be back on the frontier, where liberty and equality were not mutually exclusive ideas, but achievable goals.[36]

This indeed was to be an experimental city, sketched by architect John Wiebenson and designed to accommodate 500 to 2,500 persons in 650 square-foot plywood and plastic-sheeting huts.[37] The A-frame cabins with wooden flooring were cheerfully constructed by volunteers and poor people themselves, who would christen their "streets" and decorate the cabins. The makeshift city was managed by several committees in charge of food, sanitation, transportation, and medical and legal services. It was barely finished when the campaigners arrived, still lacking sustainable plumbing and electricity. As 3,000 poor people kept pouring in, outnumbering expectations, District of Columbia schools and churches stepped up to shelter the marchers until Resurrection City was in a livable condition. But the shantytown would still be more desirable than the squalid neighborhoods many of the marchers had just fled. It also had an undeniable utopian flavor. Photographer Jill Freeman, who participated in the campaign, recalled: "If you forget about things like traffic lights and dress shops and cops, Resurrection City was pretty much just another city. Crowded. Hungry. Dirty. Gossipy. Beautiful. It was the world, squeezed between flimsy snow fences and stinking of humanity."[38] Schoolteachers, lawyers, and social workers volunteered to provide the residents with services they had hardly benefited from before. One participant described the mushroomed city and its ambitious institutions:

> Still further on was City Hall, a larger plywood structure, the nerve center of the camp. Here all announcements were posted outside where teenagers and children milled around. . . . Beyond the City Hall the wooden walk-ways stopped, and one had to wade a quarter of a mile in the deepening mud, passing the common plywood latrine, to get to the site of the Day Care Center and its adjacent empty Freedom School tent.[39]

Resurrection City would be granted its own zip code (20013), its own mayor (Jesse Jackson), and a local government, but most importantly it would provide its inhabitants with three dining facilities offering free meals, and a medical tent as well as a cultural center named Many Races

Soul Center. The multiracial workshops and seminars (which many nationalist Chicanos and Puerto Ricans attended along with Black Power activists) offered an in-depth reflection on the entangling of poverty and "identity." Participants were also provided with a wide array of social services, from child care to shelter, modeled on the poverty and social service support provided by the NWRO (counseling to get emergency food stamps and housing relief, job training, help with health care, social security, and welfare checks from the administration).[40] Part of the War on Poverty and the 1964 EOA, Community Action agencies were also purveyors of such relief for the poor, but as the government decreased its funding for anti-poverty programs in 1966, it also increasingly imposed requirements for welfare recipients. The social services provided in Resurrection City were therefore designed as an act of resistance on the part of the poor and an experiment aimed at being implemented nationally. Resurrection City's social services also got their inspiration from social democratic countries such as Sweden, which had impressed King during his 1964 trip to receive his Nobel Prize. Almost 1,000 residents would benefit from free medical care and medical examinations during the six weeks of the encampment's existence. Sixty children would be enrolled in a universal day care program, notably a Head Start program at the Coretta Scott King Day Care Center, which not only provided them with quality schooling but allowed their parents to participate in daily demonstrations.[41]

The Poor People's University (PPU), modeled on the egalitarian Mississippi Freedom Schools, sought to foster self-consciousness and to empower students. Although at a distance from the shantytown (lectures were held at the American University's downtown campus), twenty-five successful lecture series and various workshops were organized in Resurrection City. Issues of race, class, and poverty were thoroughly discussed.[42] The city also launched its own newspaper, *True Unity News*, and somehow established its own police, made up of "marshalls" selected from the ranks of the "street kids" King had invited: the Blackstone Rangers from Chicago, the Invaders from Memphis, and the Commandos from Milwaukee. In policing as well as in construction or social welfare services, demonstrators took an active part in community life. Aimed at being a radical democracy, the shantytown was organized around three communities of 1,000 participants which comprised four neighborhoods of approximately 250 people each, divided into sixty-person blocks. Each of these units were to be equally endowed and represented.

During its six weeks of existence, Resurrection City provided its inhabitants with an unprecedented cross-racial understanding. Latinos, for instance, who settled in the nearby Hawthorne High School with most of the Appalachian caravan, came to terms with white poverty. Despite this relocation, which rendered Resurrection City mostly all black, and regular bickering among the groups, a sense of solidarity beyond racial affiliation emerged, symbolized by a shared space and a shared purpose. "This is no longer a civil rights thing," commented Reverend James Bevel. "This is economic. We intend to force the power structure of this country to divert more energy—and by that I mean money—into getting 40,000,000 Americans into this nation's economic mainstream."[43] On June 12, the campaign released a list of fifty "doléances" pertaining to food stamps, commodity distribution, school lunch and breakfast programs, the anti-poverty program, and the Elementary and Secondary Education Act.

Beyond day-to-day acts of protest, campaigners sought to raise the nation's awareness through a massive rally in front of the Lincoln Memorial, a tribute to King, and a demonstration of their self-righteousness. Initially planned for May 30 but postponed to June 19—*Juneteenth,* the date for celebrations marking the end of the Civil War, and thus the enforceable end of slavery—a "Solidarity Day" gathering was organized to once again demand an Economic Bill of Rights for the Disadvantaged. The culmination of the campaign, this march to the Lincoln Memorial attracted between 50,000 and 100,000 people. Reminiscent of the 1963 March on Washington, the sunny day was filled with songs, prayers, sermons, and rousing speeches. Benjamin E. Mays and Wyatt Tee Walker, both prominent figures of the long civil rights movement, UAW's Walter Reuther, among other union leaders, attended the event where they heard Mexican American leader Reies Tijerina, Native American activist Martha Grass, and also Eugene Joseph "Gene" McCarthy, the antiwar Democratic candidate running against President Lyndon Johnson for their party's presidential nomination. Michael Harrington attended the march and the following day gave a speech in the ramshackle encampment to castigate the rich corporate farmers and home builders who hypocritically lectured the poor, telling the latter "to stop asking for handouts" while themselves accepting subsidies.[44] Abernathy too sounded radical, demanding that

> no child go hungry . . . that no citizen be denied an adequate income . . . that no human being be deprived of health care . . . that no American be denied the opportunity of education . . . and that this murdering of people end in America, in Vietnam, and the world.[45]

He also chastised an American society which, albeit Christian, tolerated wealth inequality:

> I see nothing in my Bible about the riches of the world or this nation belonging to Wilbur Mills or Russell Long; nor do they belong to General Motors, the grape growers in California, the cotton kings in Mississippi, and the oil barons in Texas. But I read in my Bible that the earth is the Lord's and the fullness thereof, and there is no need of God's children going hungry in 1968.[46]

But, as on Mother's Day, Coretta Scott King gave the most electrifying speech. She opened it by reading aloud a telegram sent to her by Ethel Kennedy, calling for a memorial to their late husbands in the form of a federal antipoverty program. She then pointed to the alienation of the poor, stressing the "rumbling discontent of the downtrodden, and dispossessed" who "had no participation in the life of this nation." Capturing the spirit of the Poor People's Campaign, she reminded her audience that "they have come to Washington to dramatize the desperateness of their plight in the richest nation in the world." Ending the war in order to reallocate the funds was her "call to conscience." The protestors' purpose was to fight "the triple evil: racism, poverty and war," with racism being the root of all evils. Deploying the complex entanglement of race and class, Mrs. King addressed a "class structure" which ensured that "poor whites are impacted as well" by the violence of poverty. But if the majority of the U.S. poor were white, poor minorities faced specific difficulties, for only whites had the privileged capacity to get rid of the stigma once wealthy. Racism and classism were both byproducts of a violence etched in the American social fabric. She therefore called for an urgent revolution of value which would eradicate the nation's consent to violence:

> I must remind you that starving a child is violence. Suppressing a culture is violence. Neglecting school children is violence. Punishing a mother and her family is violence. Discrimination against a working man is violence. Ghetto housing is violence. Contempt for poverty is violence.[47]

Stressing the role of mothers and women, she urged them to "become the soul of this country." A convergent feminist call was put forth by other female speakers, notably National Council of Negro Women president Dorothy Height and American Indian activist Martha Grass. An article from *The Worker* argued: "Some may call it 'Soul Power,' others may scream 'Black Power,' and yet others may say 'Poor Power,' but whatever the phrases may be, it was crystal clear that above all else, there was 'Woman Power.'"[48]

But for all its substance, Solidarity Day failed to eclipse the shortcomings of the campaign. Most media chided the organizers for what they saw as a second-grade March on Washington, unable to reenact the discipline and scope of the 1963 landmark event. In a vitriolic article named "Solidarity and Disarray," *Time* portrayed Resurrection City as "an ill-housed, ill-fed, self-segregated, absentee-run slum afflicted with low morale, deepening restiveness and free-floating violence."[49] The following day, the police fired several canisters of tear gas into the camp on the ground that provocateurs had infiltrated it. A couple of days later, authorities claimed that some Resurrection City youths had thrown fire bombs at passing motorists and urged the SCLC to terminate the campaign. Although two hundred troublesome street gang members had been excluded on May 22, the leaders of the campaign could not indeed eschew skirmishes and harassments within the encampment, duly reported by the press. A black electrician who worked as a security marshall during Solidarity Day reportedly told the *Washington Post*, "if the leaders there don't do something soon, this is going to be known as blood city instead of Resurrection City."[50]

Arguably, the campaign suffered from a profound lack of planning and organization. Designed to accommodate several hundred residents, Resurrection City was quickly overwhelmed by newcomers, approximating three thousand at its peak. Bernard Lafayette, in charge of its logistics, struggled to finance the ever-expanding shantytown. Not only was the infrastructure insufficient but the summer of 1968 was particularly rainy. By the end of May, the ill-equipped encampment was flooded and transformed into a soggy slum that alarmed health officials. Evacuation plans were made every other day. Sanitation was a constant concern for the interracial medical team, who worried about the outbreak of contagious disease in such an environment. One nurse recalled, "the mud, the depth of the mud and how these people survived in the rain, the leaks, the mud, the cold and the dreariness."[51] The heavy rain transformed the "city of hope" into a muddy swamp and crippled every single aspect of the residents' daily lives. These conditions fueled editorials that kept maligning the campaign, with the support of infiltrated FBI agents.[52] Negative and dismissive articles, seizing on the picturesque images of squalid poverty in the shantytown, sustained the "othering" of the poor, while simultaneously blaming activists for the sorry state of the residents. Andy Young mitigated the gloomy depiction offered by mainstream media, ironically pointing to its double standard:

> When medical examinations we provided revealed that a large number of people were suffering from medical problems, the press saw an "epidemic," not the deeper truth that poverty and health problems go hand in hand. It was as if the doctor who discovered a cancer was blamed for it.[53]

Though five hundred people resisted the harsh environment and remained on the premises, the conditions undeniably bruised the enthusiasm and resilience of the poor residents. Young, critical of the misrepresentation offered by the press, nonetheless acknowledged that Resurrection City was "almost a microcosm of an overcrowded big city ghetto. Our staff became weighed down by the problems of housing, feeding, and governing."[54]

Beyond logistic shortcomings, the scope of the campaign turned out to be disappointing. Whereas King had envisioned massive demonstrations, only a couple of hundred of the poor, out of the three thousand, were mobilized. Somehow, King had foreseen the lack of involvement, deploring to his staff at the beginning of 1968, "There's no masses in this mass movement."[55] Life in Resurrection City was also rendered galling by the internecine tensions and clashes. Only a portion of Resurrection City residents were truly committed to nonviolence, and some were willing to express a more radical and disruptive form of militancy. Admittedly, King had met with Carmichael, who had promised not to interfere with the campaign. But Black Power's appeal and call for more militant action had always been potent for the campaigners and stood at odds with Abernathy's ongoing negotiations with the White House and congressional leaders. Abernathy, who invited Vice President Hubert Humphrey to visit the camp, resorted in effect to the conventional ties with Democrats that King himself had dismissed. In its June 13 issue, the *New York Times* ran a piece explicitly pointing to this contradiction:

> Mr. Abernathy's difficulties with militant leaders, and the confusion caused by mismanagement of the campaign, has complicated extensive behind-the-scenes efforts by the Johnson Administration to guide the poor people's demonstration . . . the Administration has sought to stage-manage the Poor People's Campaign for what Government officials believed were shared objectives. [56]

The SCLC, already discredited when its staff relocated to the Statler-Hilton Hotel on June 7, was obviously losing control of the mismanaged city. As the expiration of Resurrection City's permit—June 24—was looming and media misrepresentation of the campaign exacerbated tensions, more and more physical altercations with outsiders occurred at the outskirts of the camp. Abernathy was blamed for the violent attitude of some of the participants. Almost two hundred black militant residents, coming mostly from Chicago and Detroit gangs, had actually been expelled after incidents with journalists and white residents. But the boundaries of Resurrection City, marked by fences which separated "outsiders" from "insiders," were spaces of clashes between young black men and "outsiders" and among the security marshalls themselves. They were not fully dedicated to nonviolence, although they signed a formal pledge to it (as did every participant), and their predictable display of resentment alienated journalists and bystanders who already held negative views of the campaign. Irremediably, the shantytown remained an isolated island, disconnected from its environment.[57]

But the tensions that undermined the campaign the most were between the SCLC and the other ethnic and racial groups. At the micro level, each group ended up self-segregating, with most Native Americans settling at St. Augustine Episcopal Church in southwest Washington while Mexican Americans were sheltered at Hawthorne High School. They grew particularly resentful with their lack of space in the framing and managing of the campaign. Despite their early warnings, Gonzales and Tejerina lamented the SCLC's top-down leadership style, which resulted in a lack of consideration for their suggestions, and made clear that the PPC was a black-led campaign.[58] Tijerina deplored what he saw as a double standard:

> Lights are given to rangers and to security to use at night and we don't get anything. They are given two way radios to operate and we don't get anything of that kind. They get new clothing and we don't get any of that kind, we get nothing but used clothing. The Negroes get special things in Resurrection City that we don't even share. . . . Two days ago I tried to move into Resurrection City and I ran into trouble. Everybody wants me out of Resurrection City.[59]

Tom Houck, speaking on behalf of the Native Americans, expressed similar grievances with regard to SCLC's overcontrol. If some Native Americans' decision to settle at the nearby Hawthorne High School with Mexican Americans rather than in Resurrection City per se smacked of intracoalition squabbling, it nevertheless turned out to be a critical experience of interracial bonding. The school was ill equipped and far less visible than Resurrection City. Yet, Latinos, Native Americans, and whites interacted no less, if not more, than in the shantytown on the Mall. Rudy Gonzalez, the son of activist Corky Gonzalez, confided: "I had never seen poor whites before. I mean dirt poor. Some hardly had shoes."[60] At Hawthorne, the unlikely diverse congregation gathered and shared experiences, planning communal demonstrations, including the one in front of the Supreme Court over Native fishing rights that led to a brutal beating of some demonstrators by police. A symbol of multiracial poverty as well, Hawthorne was spared from the chaotic life in Resurrection City.

Even within the ranks of the black groups, internal conflicts were raging. The most telling example related to the role assigned to Bayard Rustin, who had been asked by Abernathy to orchestrate Solidarity Day as masterfully as he had the March on Washington. The nomination was problematic for Rustin, who had been dismissive of the disruptive philosophy of the campaign from its inception and who remained adamant that it would further alienate the progressive coalition he forged in 1963.

On January 29, 1968, Rustin had sent a detailed three-page memorandum to King to convince him that a strategy aimed at efficiency rather than at principles be adopted. To him, another failure after the Chicago Campaign would be lethal and a victory had to be obtained by any means. Accordingly, he had then reasoned that wide "economic justice demands" be downplayed or postponed as some measures were "not necessarily expected to be obtained now, such as guaranteed income for those who cannot work and public works at decent wages . . . for those who can," as opposed to specific demands for "jobs, housing, welfare, and passage of a strong civil-rights bill." Beyond realizable demands, he had argued, the campaign should refrain from antagonizing Washington. Like NAACP executive secretary Roy Wilkins and SCLC prominent member Marian Logan, Rustin had been concerned about King's tactics and doubted the SCLC's ability to contain violence:

> Given the mood in Congress, given the increasing backlash across the nation, given the fact that this is an election year, and given the high visibility of a protest movement in the nation's capital, I feel that any effort to disrupt transportation, government buildings, etc., can only lead, in this atmosphere, to further backlash and repression.[61]

King had shared Rustin's concern for the "racial exhaustion rhetoric," a discursive form of resistance to further racial egalitarian legislation which spread across party lines.[62] But he had stuck to his idea that the campaign needed to be disruptive and demanding. But after King passed away, Abernathy needed Rustin's organizing experience to carry the leader's last crusade forward. Called to the rescue, Rustin stood in a strong position to negotiate and unflinchingly asked for an uncontroversial and pragmatic framework. He also demanded that there would be no disruption of government functions on Solidarity Day and that only a set of fourteen "specific concrete demands" would be presented. On May 24, Rustin was appointed as national coordinator of the campaign. Soon thereafter, he publicly reiterated that there would be "no disruption of government functions" and that "the mobilization will not content itself with defining general social goals. It will make specific demands which can, and must be, immediately translated into law by congressional action and Executive order."[63] Willing to strike a deal, Rustin took it on himself to reframe the campaign's demands in a more reformist fashion, with the hope that they would come across as achievable by middle class liberals and labor. He boiled the campaign's demand down to a mobilization "call", a list of specific "attainable" demands, which Congress and the president could enact immediately.

Silencing the antiwar component of the campaign and drastically narrowing the scope of the policies expected, he published an updated version of the Economic Bill of Rights in the June 5 issue of the *New York Times:*

1. Recommit to the Full Employment Act of 1946 and legislate the immediate creation of at least one million socially useful career jobs in public service;

2. Adopt the pending Housing and Urban Development Act of 1968;

3. Repeal the 90th Congress's punitive welfare restrictions in the 1967 Social Security Act;

4. Extend to all farm workers the right—guaranteed under the National Labor Relations Act—to organize agricultural labor unions;

5. Restore budget cuts for bilingual education, Head Start, summer jobs, Economic Opportunity Act, Elementary and Secondary Education Acts.

Obliterating nonblack demands for justice, the strategist erased claims for land rights and fishing rights and he softened the tone of the campaign by silencing issues of police brutality and American imperialism. He also sounded dismissive of welfare recipients, outlining an economic program which would spare black people "from prison or welfare."[64] Outraged by Rustin's initiative, Ralph Abernathy removed him from the campaign on June 7. He replaced him with Washington Urban League director Sterling Tucker, appointed as organizer of the Solidarity Day march. Two years before, Tucker had put forth a plan to bring more economic rights to African Americans eager to achieve full equality.[65] But to some observers, notably to Tom Kahn, who was a Socialist close to Rustin and an organizer of the campaign, Rustin's dismissal sealed the fate of the campaign for he stood as the only valid interlocutor to many congressmen.[66] Although a notorious Social Democrat, Rustin came across as a trustworthy centrist whose moderate views contrasted with King's late extremism.

However, on June 11, the SCLC shortened the initial list of economic demand to shovel it into a set of bills ready for passage: the Clark Emergency Employment Bill and the pending housing bill, the repeal of the compulsory work requirements of the 1967 Social Security Amendments, legislation guaranteeing collective bargaining rights for farmworkers, increased appropriations for food stamp and commodity programs, and legislation providing a guaranteed income.[67] But such a pragmatic move was ineffective: a Louis Harris national survey conducted on June 10, 1968, revealed that only 29 percent of whites were supportive of Solidarity Day while 61 percent held negative opinions about it. The racial breakdown was striking as 80 percent of African Americans embraced the march.[68] The Poor People's Campaign was obviously failing to achieve guaranteed jobs and income. This lack of tangible result, which demobilized participants, combined with the indifference of public opinion, proved fatal. As the permit for Resurrection City came to a close, blatant disorganization and disturbances within the camp irrevocably crippled the campaign's politics.

Wary about incidents spreading throughout the city, Mayor Walter Washington of Washington, DC, declared a curfew. Anticipating the official expiration limit, the police decided to storm the camp firing tear gas, as a retaliation for rocks allegedly thrown at them. Such a display of violence against the remaining poor residents infuriated SCLC leader Andrew Young, who fumed: "It was worse than anything I saw in Mississippi or Alabama. . . . You don't shoot tear gas into an entire city because two or three hooligans are throwing rocks."[69] The "city of hope" was closed on June 24, 1968. At dawn, Abernathy tried to conjure the camp's gloomy fate, not without bravado and a sense of the tragic: "No matter what happens to me or to Resurrection City, the Poor People's Campaign will go on" and he asked the remaining residents to join him that day for another visit to the Department of Agriculture.[70] He had unsuccessfully tried to bargain with city officials for a peaceful dismantlement of the camp, but authorities began clearing up the camp and, after the intervention by bulldozers, the tents were leveled and the remaining occupants arrested. A couple of hours before the final assault, Abernathy led two hundred protestors to the Capitol, in a desperate attempt to enact social change. As they were heading back, their shelters were swept away. Abernathy and his comrades were arrested and jailed. Eventually, 288 residents were arrested and remained in jail for twenty days. Disheartened but still militant, they defiantly boarded the jail buses, singing along with the Freedom songs broadcast over the city's intercom system.[71]

The journalist Daniel Schorr, witnessing the final hours of Resurrection City, described its last jolts:

> On the last day, there was a march up the Capitol Hill, all planned apparently in advance for them to be stopped by the Capitol Police for trying to get in without a permit and then they were all going to be arrested. And they knew they were all going to be arrested. They were led up there by the Reverend Jesse Jackson, who had meanwhile returned from Chicago. And I walked up and down the line with him as he would say to these people, "I am somebody. Repeat after me: I am somebody." And then they chanted with him, "I am somebody." And saying, "I am somebody," they arrived where they were stopped by the Chief of Police who told them that they would be arrested. They submitted quietly to arrest. They were identified. They were somebody. . . . The cameras were there, their dignity was there, as Jesse Jackson had said, "I am somebody." They were somebody.[72]

OUTLIVING RESURRECTION CITY

However ill-fated the encampment, the activists attempted to keep the campaign going. On June 25, a multiethnic group convened at Hawthorne High School. As Abernathy was still in jail, Andrew Young represented African Americans. He met with Hank Williams, Reies Tijerina, and representatives of the Highlander Folk School and the welfare rights organization. They agreed on the idea that a "Poor People's Embassy" should be formed and entrusted with the mission to carry on the campaign's lobbying efforts. A planning committee was formed in July and it envisioned a permanent presence in Washington. It would fill the void of current federal agencies by providing the poor the services they would have suggested themselves. It would also serve as the headquarters of a national movement expecting further local actions. After several gatherings, the interracial coalition watered down its political ambitions, focusing on educational and cultural programs. Members of the SDS and of local chapters of the Black Panthers joined the remaining coalition. Re-enacting the intercultural and pan-racial exchanges that had developed in Hawthorne High

School and in Resurrection City, the embassy perpetuated the revolutionary nature of the campaign, that of a movement fusing class-based and
nationalist "intra-ethnic identity politics."[73]

As an incubator of interracial activism, the PPC also inspired some of
the participants to pursue their efforts to sustain the coalition once back
in their respective home regions. Andrew Young would come to reflect:

> Looking back, I can see that it marked the emergence of a broad based pro-
> gressive coalition: poor people who were black, white, brown, and red; reli-
> gious leaders; union leaders; peace activists. Jobs, peace, and freedom
> would be linked, sustained through a loose shifting, but persistent coalition
> of organizations. Among the people gathered were some who would go on to
> head organizations and become members of Congress and elected officials
> from small Southern communities.[74]

Indeed, the most radical among the campaigners returned home with a
desire to continue the complex fight initiated by the PPC.[75] One city stood
out in such endeavor. By 1968, Chicago, the most racially residentially segregated city in the country, had indeed grown to become the most innova-
tive setting for the interracial organizing of the poor. Since the mid-1960s,
grassroots movements like JOIN Community Union had brought together
southern migrants, student radicals, civil rights activists, and welfare
recipients to fight for housing, health, and welfare.[76] But after 1968, it was
the upcoming Black Power movement that proved instrumental in the
continuation of a radical call for interracial struggles on behalf of the
dispossessed.

In 1969, Illinois Black Panther chairman Fred Hampton's speech,
"Power Anywhere There's People," laid out in revolutionary terms King's
urgent call for a multiracial working-class unity:

> We got to face some facts. That the masses are poor, that the masses belong
> to what you call the lower class, and when I talk about the masses, I'm talk-
> ing about the white masses, I'm talking about the black masses, and the
> brown masses, and the yellow masses, too. We've got to face the fact that
> some people say you fight fire best with fire, but we say you put fire out best
> with water. We say you don't fight racism with racism. We're gonna fight
> racism with solidarity. We say you don't fight capitalism with no black capi-
> talism; you fight capitalism with socialism.[77]

Field secretary for the local Black Panther Party, Bobby Lee labored to reach out to the Appalachian group the Young Patriots for the sake of initiating cross-racial alliances. Hampton endorsed Bobby Lee's initiative and named the nascent interracial alliance the "Rainbow Coalition."[78] Convinced by Lee, the Patriots held several meetings with him to negotiate the terms of a white, black, and brown Rainbow Coalition consisting primarily of the Black Panther Party, the Young Patriots, and the Young Lords. But, as antiwar and revolutionary activists, they also appealed to New Left white students from SDS along with Illinois Black Students Unions. Women were represented by female members of the Black Panther Party, joining their voice to the mobilization of the poor. The move was explicitly inspired by the Poor People's Campaign. Doug Youngblood, a Young Patriots founder and former Resurrection City resident, predicted its endurance:

> The Poor People's Campaign isn't going to end when the big march is over and all the speeches are orated. It isn't going to end when we have to move out of the wooden city. I firmly believe that what is taking place in Resurrection City will someday result in change of power that we are all working so hard for . . . Black, White, Mexican, Puerto Ricans, Indians, the entire spectrum of poverty is there talking and learning and it may not be radical enough for some, but to me it is one of the most radical events I've ever been a part of.[79]

Carrying forward the Poor People's Campaign approach, the Rainbow Coalition attempted to surpass the attachment of ethnicity in the construction of class consciousness which hitherto had hindered interracial solidarity. Understandably, a class-centered approach to emancipation somewhat entailed downplaying racial nationalism and enhancing interracial unity.

Peggy Terry, who represented Uptown Poor Whites during the Poor People's Campaign and gave an eloquent speech on Solidarity Day, stood as the most visible embodiment of the long-lasting kinship between the PPC and the original Panthers-led Rainbow Coalition. Eldridge Cleaver, minister of information for the Black Panther Party, picked her as vice president when he ran as the presidential candidate of the Peace and Freedom Party (PFP) in California in the fall of 1969. Tellingly, Corky

Gonzales, another major leader of the campaign, appeared as PFP's vice-president on Utah ballot. Not only was the California-based PFP mostly white when created in June 1967 but Cleaver also reached out to SDS white activists.[80] Echoing the Poor People's Campaign, their candidacy revolved around the demands for an immediate withdrawal from Vietnam, poor people's solidarity across the color line. and black liberation.

Jakobi E. Williams rightly observed that many members of the Rainbow Coalition, influenced by King's late work, eventually adopted a class-based ideology, which complicated the rhetoric of black nationalists.[81] In Chicago, as Lee would later point out, the Rainbow Coalition was eager to transcend identity politics (conceding however that many inhabitants of Hillbilly Harlem were racist) to focus on the overarching communality, which was poverty:

> The Rainbow Coalition was just a code word for class struggle. Preacherman [Patriots' leader] would have stopped a bullet for me, and nearly tried. . . . When I went to Uptown Chicago, I saw some of the worst slums imaginable. Horrible slums, and poor white people lived there. . . . It wasn't easy to build an alliance. I advised them on how to set up "serve the people" programs— free breakfasts, people's health clinics, all that. I had to run with those cats, break bread with them, hang out at the pool hall. I had to lay down on their couch, in their neighborhood. Then I had to invite them into mine. That was how the Rainbow Coalition was built, real slow.[82]

Picking the first anniversary of King's assassination to hold their first press conference, the members of the Rainbow Coalition demanded that "the city's poor . . . stop fighting each other and tearing up their own neighborhoods" and claimed that "it was time for poor people to claim their rightful place, leading movements for revolutionary change in Chicago and beyond."[83] In July 1969, flaunting the Confederate flag, the Young Patriots joined a three-day Black Panther Party's reunion in Oakland named the "Conference for a United Front Against Fascism." Hampton tolerated the Patriots' subversive exhibition of the Confederate flag for the sake of solidarity: "If we can use that to organize, if we can use it to turn people, then we need to do it."[84] At the invitation of the Illinois Panthers, representatives of the Communist Party, the Farm Workers Union, and Students for a Democratic Society also attended the event.

The expanding Rainbow Coalition now also included the Chicago-based and self-identified hillbilly group Rising Up Angry. Young Patriot's leader William "Preacherman" Fesperman claimed the need for fraternity and interracial solidarity:

> We come from a monster and the jaws of the monster in Chicago are grinding up the flesh and spitting out the blood of the poor and oppressed people, the blacks in the South Side, the West Side; the browns in the North Side; and the reds and the yellows; and yes, the whites—white oppressed people.[85]

This grassroots radical union of the poor was illustrative, albeit circumscribed, of a "community organizing approach that addressed poor people's immediate concerns—health, welfare, housing, jobs, drug addiction and police violence—while paying strategic attention to civil rights and multiracial coalitions."[86] The Panther-led coalition in Chicago was continuing the Poor People's Campaign's attempt to tackle structural inequalities through interracial coalitions although at the micro-level. Many among its members had been youth organizers and leaders of Martin Luther King's Chicago Freedom Movement. From 1968 to 1973, their radical organizing worked on behalf of the city's disadvantaged populations. Socialistic and internationalists, the black, brown. and white members of the original Rainbow Coalition entwined race and class in order to highlight their interrelatedness, not to mutually dissolve them. This coalition indeed "rested on the contention that theirs was a struggle to overcome race—by going through race (and not around it)."[87]

On the national scale, the NWRO, which co-orchestrated the PPC, continued to stand as the most vocal advocate of social welfare for the poor, regardless of their gender and race. In the wake of the campaign, it continued to call for the government to play a greater role in mitigating economic and social inequalities, deploring the retrenchment of welfare policies that deepened the political and social isolation of the poor and exacerbated racial animosity. George Wiley, like King, rightly argued that material inequalities translated into unequal capacity for political participation and demanded corrective public policies for the poor. Despite the NWRO's internal tensions and a crippling lack of funding, welfare activists continued to combat the vilification of the poor, most notably poor women of color.

In 1972, Johnnie Tillmon replaced Wiley as the NWRO's new executive director and refocused on poor single mothers of color, while he kept advocating for a large multiracial coalition of the poor.[88] Expanding his concern to nonrecipient underprivileged groups, Wiley envisioned a broad populist "Movement for Economic Justice" to obtain redistribution of wealth and power, which he launched just months before his death. Although both the NWRO and the Movement for Economic Justice lost momentum and support and were ultimately shut down in the mid-1970s, the concept of a "right to welfare," akin to King's advocacy for a "right to an income" was pioneering and would be vindicated in many regards.[89]

Indeed, these ideas were not quixotic. Ground-breaking scholars have upheld King's class-based analysis, some of them still advocating for the kind of structural reforms he called for in the late 1960s. From Gunnar Myrdal to William Julius Wilson, a radical redistribution of income has been demanded to curtail the growing gap between the American haves and have-nots. What was also truly revolutionary in the intellectual foundation of the Poor People's Campaign was its paralleling of structural unemployment, structural racism. and the underlying crippling of the American social fabric by a consent to inequality. King's analysis of the intertwining of egalitarianism, substantive justice, and democracy proved prescient and insightful with regard to the intellectual debates and social issues of our time.

The next part re-examines the Poor People's Campaign's intellectual underpinning and appraises the extent to which the ideas it embodied resonate with the works and insights of scholars and thinkers who continue to engage with the public-policy conversation, giving a sense of urgency and political importance to racial and wealth-based inequality. Whether contemporaries of King or not, these intellectuals and their theoretical frameworks help us to grasp the accuracy and modernity of the Poor People's Campaign.

PART III The Vision

The accuracy of King's diagnosis of the indispensable structural reforms needed to address poverty, segregation, housing, transportation, and decaying infrastructures in urban areas can be assessed through its confrontation with prominent contemporary scholarship, some of which predated King and some of which emerged in the late 1970s. Whether he consistently read academic books or not, King was assuredly receptive to state-of-the-art scholarship in the realm of racial and economic equality, oftentimes quoting economists, psychologists, and sociologists such as Gunnar Myrdal, John Kenneth Galbraith, E. Franklin Frazier, Kenneth Clark, and many other progressive minds. Apart from mainstream thinking, which exerted a dominant influence on social policies, these intellectuals tackled black conditions in terms of political economy and structural reforms. Analyzing the Poor People's Campaign in light of their contributions to our understanding of race and class inequality therefore illuminates its intuitiveness.

Tellingly, King called upon social scientists to play an active role in debunking the biased assumptions upon which racial inequality was built. He believed their empirical research could disprove whites' behaviorist and prejudiced views on black Americans. On September 1967, King gave the Distinguished Address at the American Psychological Association's convention, a speech printed in the *Journal of Social Issues* after his death. He explicitly missioned social scientists to participate in the struggle for racial equality:

> In the preface to their book, "Applied Sociology" (1965), S. M. Miller and Alvin Gouldner state: "It is the historic mission of the social sciences to enable mankind to take possession of society." It follows that for Negroes who substantially are excluded from society this science is needed even more desperately than for any other group in the population.
>
> For social scientists, the opportunity to serve in a life-giving purpose is a humanist challenge of rare distinction. Negroes too are eager for a rendezvous with truth and discovery. We are aware that social scientists, unlike some of their colleagues in the physical sciences, have been spared the grim feelings of guilt that attended the invention of nuclear weapons of destruction. Social scientists, in the main, are fortunate to be able to extirpate evil, not to invent it.
>
> If the Negro needs social sciences for direction and for self-understanding, the white society is in even more urgent need. White America needs to understand that it is poisoned to its soul by racism and the understanding needs to be carefully documented and consequently more difficult to reject.[1]

8 Facing Structural Injustice

The Poor People's Campaign's diagnosis of the race and class dialectics at play in the country echoed and anticipated many academic works on urban poverty and structural inequalities, notably with regard to a class analysis of black social conditions.

Uprooting Concentrated Disadvantage

A core tenet of the Poor People's Campaign was its understanding that poor communities of color (and poor whites to a lesser extent) were more vulnerable to economic exploitation because of their spatial isolation. Under the guidance of King and welfare rights activists, the campaign grasped the plight of the urban poor and the multidimensional dynamics of the American ghetto. King had indeed identified the lack of decent-paying jobs, affordable housing, and efficient transportation as the main obstacle to African Americans' economic integration. On December 15, 1966, during a Senate subcommittee hearing, he laid out his analysis on the persistence and meaning of ghettos:

The new era of abundance finds us not only with proliferating ghettos, but it finds us enmeshed in confused commitments and distorted values. . . . Is there evil in America today? Not in the sense of the systematic physical extermination of a people but in the sense of the destruction of hope, after the raising of expectations, the forced separation of the poor, whether black or white, from the rest of society, the confinement to poverty and squalor of millions of Americans. To be born a Negro in an American city, for most of us, means to be "under" the main stratum of our society—to be underemployed, or unemployed, or underpaid; to be undereducated and ill housed; to face illness and perhaps death, undercared for; to face a life of little hope, entrapped by both color and need.[1]

King's use of the word "under" echoed the debates in which he was engulfed when reflecting on the ghetto, in which "underclass" was a successful yet deceptive concept. A contentious word, "underclass" captured long-held assumptions about dispossessed groups outside of and alienated from the mainstream of society. In America, the term has mostly smacked of social "unwantedness."[2]

Although E. Franklin Frazier depicted a "lower class culture" in the 1930s, it was Swedish Social Democrat economist Gunnar Myrdal who first used "underclass" to describe the increasing polarization of American society. These terms were not pejorative in intent. Likewise, King did not intend the concept of "underclass" to serve as a generic label for a host of cultural and behavioral traits that supposedly differentiated a certain segment of the poor from the rest of society. Rather, he echoed liberal scholars of the 1960s, notably Lee Rainwater, Eliott Liebow, and Ulf Hannerz, who, while depicting the behavioral dysfunctions of black ghetto dwellers, downplayed a deterministic cultural explanation, instead favoring a macro-structural economic analysis.[3] But Kenneth Clark's work stood out as the most relevant with regards to King's perspectives.

Pioneering black social scientist and civil rights activist Kenneth Clark insightfully tackled the enduring "culture versus structure" binary vision with regards to ghetto poverty. Clark did stress the psychological dimensions of black lives in inner cities, which stemmed from the powerlessness of these communities. But he charged that the ghetto was the epitome of premeditated "institutionalized of powerlessness," pointing to the patronizing policies of urban planners, federal agencies, and social services, which sustained residents' isolation, poverty, and subordinate mindset.[4]

The "tangle of pathology" he deplored, which disorganized black families,[5] was not curable merely by tepid jobs creation, much less by behavioral reform. In the wake of the uprising in Newark, Clark did begin developing a social democratic critique of racial inequality, particularly as it pertained to urban segregation, pointing to the nefarious effects of a capitalistic system which fueled a colonial order in the ghetto. Greed was, he reasoned, the engine of racialized urban dynamics. King concurred with Clark that exploitation and subsequent alienation—in their Marxist sense—led to urban unrest and that capitalism and racism were Siamese twins.

Clark's perceptive dissatisfaction with the outcome of civil rights legislation somewhat provided King with the intellectual ammunition needed to challenge the liberal status quo. In a class-based perspective, Clark noted: "The masses of Negroes are now starkly aware of the fact that recent civil right victories benefited a very small percentage of middle-class Negroes while their predicament remained the same or worsened."[6] In accord with Clark, King had never been blind to the limited achievements of the civil rights' movement. Before he even set foot in Chicago, he conceded: "What little progress has been made—and that includes the Civil Rights Act—has applied primarily to the middle-class Negro. Among the masses, especially in the Northern ghettos, the situation remains about the same, and for some it is worse."[7]

Clark substantiated his class-based approach to black urban poverty by calling into question affluent blacks' dismissive attitude toward ghetto dwellers. King, although less abrasive than Clark, came to agree and lamented the kind of privileged black who "acquires the white man's contempt for the ordinary Negro . . . more often at home with the middle-class than he is among his own people, and frequently his physical home is moved up and away from the ghetto."[8] Quoting explicitly sociologist E. Franklin Frazier's *Black Bourgeoisie*, King deplored the enduring tendency "of the upwardly mobile Negro to separate from his community, divorce himself from responsibility to it, while failing to gain acceptance in the white community," a pattern particularly acute when inner cities erupted.[9]

Also in consonance with Clark, King pleaded for an extensive plan to address the ghetto's economic exploitation, powerlessness, and cultural dysfunctions.[10] He also dismissed behavioral rhetoric, contending instead that "dislocation in the market operations" and "the prevalence of discrimination," not individual deviance or cultural inaptitude, condemned black Americans to poverty and social ills.[11] Poor urban blacks' isolation stemmed from racialized structural forces somewhat related to the mechanisms of imperial dominance, he claimed. King borrowed Du Bois's and Clark's "domestic colonialism" metaphor. The latter relied on it to frame black urban poverty in terms of space and powerlessness, institutions and market forces purposely locking African Americans in areas of exploitation, poverty, and social isolation. Indeed, as sociologist Robert Blauner demonstrated in his seminal 1969 article on the American ghetto, many people gain from its existence, "owners of ghetto housing and small businesses, privileged white workers protected from black competition, employers who play upon each race's hatred against the other, and all who gain when society's dirty work is done cheaply by others." Blauner, versed in Marxian theories, eloquently titled his article "Internal Colonialism and Ghetto Revolt."[12]

Marxist thinkers inaugurated the metaphor of the "internal colony." W. E. B. Du Bois had recurrently applied it to African Americans. In 1944, he described America's slums as "internal colonies" and talked about the "semi-colonial status" of African Americans.[13] Not only were blacks "super-exploited" and subjected to an organized racial division of labor but their political dependence and subjugation were reminiscent of the status of colonial subjects in Africa and Asia. Communists' project to help African Americans build their own nation within the United States was grounded in the "internal colony" paradigm. Nonleftist black radicals also endorsed the analogy. In 1964, Malcolm X argued that "America is a colonial power. She has colonized 22 million Afro-Americans by depriving us of first-class citizenship, by depriving us of civil rights, actually by depriving us of human rights."[14] While in Chicago, King, who according to Rustin fully came to terms with the political economy of social inequalities, adopted this contentious terminology. He professed: "The slum is little more than a domestic colony which leaves its inhabitants dominated politically, exploited economically, segregated and humiliated at every turn."[15]

The common historical oppression and fate of black Americans and colonized nations of color has been emphasized from du Bois to Clark and

King. To some extent, in their use of the "domestic colony" analogy, Clark and King acquiesced to Frantz Fanon, who framed white supremacy as a world-wide phenomenon. Clark echoed Fanon as to the ability of violence to improve the psychological health of oppressed groups and to the collateral liberating effect of urban rebellions. To King—who rejected Fanonian methods of violent resistance[16]—and most activists in the PPC, deliberate segregation and poverty bred each other, rendering acts of revolts inevitable: "The unemployment of Negro youth ranges up to 40 percent in some slums," King fumed, adding: "What hypocrisy it is to talk of saving the new generation—to make it the generation of hope—while consigning it to unemployment and provoking it to violent alternatives."[17]

Overt Fanon-inspired activists further substantiated the relevance of the "domestic colony" framework. In 1967, Black Power theoreticians Stokely Carmichael and Charles Hamilton too used the metaphor to describe black Americans' predicament in their manifesto, *Black Power: The Politics of Liberation in America*. The Black Panther Party, revisiting Du Bois's Marxist internationalism, made clear that low-income urban communities of color were "colonized":

> Our black communities are colonized and controlled from the outside—The politics in our communities are controlled from outside, the economics of our communities are controlled from outside, and, we ourselves are controlled by the racist police who come into our communities from outside and occupy them, patrolling, terrorizing, and brutalizing our people like a foreign army in a conquered land.[18]

Neither nationalists nor separatists, Clark and King nevertheless used the case of the mechanics of the ghetto to underscore the degree to which concentrated urban poverty was etched in the nation's institutions. If racism sustained the ghetto, socioeconomic forces were factored in to a decisive extent. They therefore demanded a massive reallocation of wealth and resources, designed and overviewed by the government.

Confident that Johnson's War on Poverty would tackle urban ghettos' disadvantage, Clark drafted a blueprint for an ambitious antipoverty initiative, Harlem Youth Opportunities Unlimited, known as HARYOU. It called for a $110 million budget for the neighborhood's schools, early

childhood education, adult education, job training, and drug rehabilitation programs, along with community control of social services. As a way
out of the "colony," the empowerment of the oppressed stood at the core of
Clark's plan. To him, poverty was not an individual failure, but rather the
collective responsibility of the entire nation. The Poor People's Campaign
similarly called on the government to address inequalities of outcome:
"the true responsibility for the existence of these deplorable conditions,"
campaigners claimed, "lies ultimately with the larger society, and much of
the immediate responsibility for removing the injustices can be laid
directly at the door of the federal government."[19]

Ultimately, Clark grew disillusioned with President Johnson's liberal
approach to race and class, which jettisoned wealth redistribution.[20]
Shaken by the urban uprisings of the second half of the 1960s, and mirror-
ing King's *aggiornamento* in Chicago, Clark witnessed the degree to which
the decade's uprisings walled off black families in urban communities that
were vilified and pathologized. Ghettos were seen as sites of violence and
urban problems to be contained, not as spaces of injustice. By the late
1970s, Clark came to cast the federal government as a critical accomplice
to the perpetuation of the ghetto, fingering, as did the National Welfare
Rights Organization, the condescending management of poor people by
bureaucrats.[21]

King explicitly dealt with exploitation in the ghetto but took the vital
step of expanding that analysis to the question of ownership power.
Slumlords were in fact not the sole perpetrators of systematic exploitation
in the ghetto. Institutions partook in the process of urban exclusion, linking prejudice with power. Echoing Du Bois and socialist radicals, he
bound the underdevelopment of the ghetto to the political economy of
capital accumulation: "We are called upon to help the discouraged beggars in life's marketplace. But one day we must come to see that an edifice
which produces beggars needs restructuring . . . when you deal with this,
you begin to ask the question, 'Who owns the oil?' You begin to ask the
question, 'Who owns the iron ore?'"[22] "For Negroes," he added, only a revision of property rights could ensure that "the emancipation from slavery
. . . will finally be attained."[23]

The PPC's Economic Bill of Rights and King's late writing called for
drastic structural reforms, addressing dispossession through joblessness

and lack of public resources in the American ghetto. In an article published postmortem in *Look*, King wrote:

> We call our demonstration a campaign for jobs and income because we feel that the economic question is the most crucial that black people, and poor people generally, are confronting. . . . There is a literal depression in the Negro community. When you have mass unemployment in the Negro community, it's called a social problem; when you have mass unemployment in the white community, it's called a depression. The fact is, there is a major depression in the Negro community. The unemployment rate is extremely high, and among Negro youth, it goes up as high as forty percent in some cities.[24]

In another interview published after his death, he complicated his socioeconomic analysis with a provocative depiction of the racism at play in the process leading to urban segregation and isolation. Contrasting the easiness with which low-skilled immigrant workers could find jobs in the late nineteenth and early twentieth centuries, he contended that not only had these jobs disappeared because of the structural transformation of the urban economy, but that opportunities for blacks had mostly vanished because whites refused to share power. Moving further, he explained the urban upheaval with arguments that squared with the Kerner Commission's findings: most young black males were deliberately either unemployed or "underemployed," and this economic discrimination, along with police harassment, were combustive materials:

> A Negro who has finished high school often watches his white classmates go out into the job market and earn $100 a week, while he, because he is black, is expected to work for $40 a week. Hence, there is a tremendous hostility and resentment that only a difference in race keeps him out of an adequate job. This situation is social dynamite. When you add the lack of recreational facilities and adequate job counseling, and the continuation of an aggressively hostile police environment, you have a truly explosive situation. Any night on any street corner in any Negro ghetto of the country, a nervous policeman can start a riot simply by being impolite or by expressing racial prejudice. And white people are sadly unaware how routinely and frequently this occurs.[25]

Johnson's War on Poverty and the 1968 Fair Housing Act forbade state and local governments from sending federal housing money in ways that perpetuated segregation. Taking into account the demands of civil rights leaders, Johnson, who created the Department of Housing and Urban Development in 1965, was willing to pay tribute to the late King by including the construction or rehabilitation of twenty-six million housing units (six million of which were for low-income communities) in the Fair Housing Act. Despite Congress reluctance, the bill was passed on April 11, 1968. But the actual implementation eventually fell short of expectations. Owing to senators' gutting of the bill, "residential segregation followed directly from inherent weaknesses that were built into the act as [the] price of passage."[26]

Whether ghetto or barrio, in small southern places like Marks, Mississippi, or the projects of Washington, DC, racial and poverty concentrations have reinforced pre-existing inequalities. Like *The Other America* in 1962, the Poor People's Campaign challenged the racialized assumptions on poverty, not only in regard to black ghetto residents but also in regard to poor whites from Appalachia, oftentimes held in contempt and objectified if not racialized.[27]

Three years after the PPC, Robert Blauner expanded its line of thought, demonstrating how "race affects class formation and class influences racial dynamics in ways that have not been adequately investigated."[28] Had it not been obscured by the racial fatigue of the late 1960s and 1970s, the campaign's analysis of the dynamics of American inequality, as it relates to socioeconomic relegation, would have accordingly been reappraised.

The Rising Significance of Joblessness

Among the clairvoyant analyses laid out by King when reflecting on the Poor People's Campaign, one directly foresaw what contemporary urban sociologists named the "spatial mismatch" hypothesis. It posits that the lack of available jobs for inner city residents and their inability to reach the suburbs where entry-level jobs were being relocated could greatly account for the high unemployment rate in the ghetto. Since 1945, the concentration of jobs has continuously decreased in central cities and increased in the suburbs. In a vicious cycle, the hypothesis contends, residential segregation has expanded black unemployment and vice versa. Sociologist William Julius Wilson insisted in *The Truly Disadvantage* that inner-city "social dislocation" stemmed from such spatial and racial mis-match, a major illustration of the "economic structure of racism"[29] affect-ing the African American "underclass."[30]

In 1968, King clearly intuited that the structural shifts experienced by the American economy and patterns of discrimination locked poor blacks in the ghetto. He demanded policies capable of creating jobs in inner cities and rendering suburban jobs accessible to them by public transportation. In a 1968 interview for *Playboy*, he hinted at the nefarious combination of the lack of jobs for low-skilled workers, an underdeveloped mass transit system, and employment and housing discrimination which merged to exclude blacks from economic integration. His emphasis on jobs creation in the ghetto along with the construction of a mass transportation system spoke to a subtle analysis on the relatedness of high black unemployment and the geography of jobs:

> When you go beyond the relatively simple though serious problems such as police racism, however, you begin to get into all the complexities of the mod-ern American economy. Urban transit systems in most American cities, for example, have become a genuine civil rights issue—and a valid one—because the layout of rapid-transit systems determines the accessibility of jobs to the Black community. If transportation systems in American cities could be laid out so as to provide an opportunity for poor people to get to meaningful employment, then they could begin to move into the mainstream of American life. A good example of this problem is my home city of Atlanta, where the rapid-transit system has been laid out for the convenience of the white upper-middle-class suburbanites who commute to their jobs down-town. The system has virtually no consideration for connecting the poor people with their jobs. There is only one possible explanation for this situa-tion, and that is the racist blindness of city planners.[31]

This insightful hypothesis was articulated for the first time in 1965 by Harvard economist John F. Kain, in a paper entitled "The Effect of the Ghetto on the Distribution and Level on non-White Unemployment in Urban Areas."[32] This pioneering article pointed to the spatial mismatch between low-skilled jobs and poor urban areas as a result of the relocation of these jobs to the suburbs, a pathbreaking framework vindicated by later works, notably by Harvard sociologist William Julius Wilson. Announcing Wilson's research, Kain also argued that the lack of a public mass transit system deepened the isolation of blacks in disadvantaged areas, rendering them unable to reach suburbs where jobs opportunities were abundant but from which they were barred. Most low-income whites did live in the suburbs, which vindicated the civil rights' call for integration in northern cities.

In the aftermath of the Watts uprising, the California governor's study group known as the McCone Commission considered Kain's contention that inadequate transportation was contributing to high rates of unemployment among the black urban population. The McCone Report unequivocally pointed to the damaging effects of subpar educational and transportation resources in Los Angeles's disadvantaged areas. During the commission hearings, Kain strongly advocated for a reorganizing of California's bus service, and suggested massive public subsidies to lower the cost of fares. In 1968, the Kerner Commission recommended yet again the creation of improved transportation links between ghetto neighborhoods and new job locations in the suburbs to link black unemployed young workers with employment concentrations. King's concurrent and comparable call for ambitious urban policies aimed at bringing jobs back into inner cities was and has been consistently corroborated.

King's insights on poverty have notably been substantiated by prominent sociologist William Julius Wilson. The Harvard professor has deeply reframed our understanding of the complex dynamics of urban disadvantage and concentrated poverty. An advocate of economic justice, he claims that the dynamics of class and race were underestimated by civil rights leaders. He nevertheless concedes that Bayard Rustin and to some degree King expressed prescient concerns:

> these perceptive civil rights advocates recognized in the 1960s that removing artificial barriers would not enable poor blacks to compete equally with other groups in society for valued resources because of an accumulation of disadvantages flowing from previous periods of prejudices and discrimination, disadvantages that have been passed on from generation to generation. Basic structural changes in our modern industrial economy have compounded the problems of poor blacks. . . .[33]
>
> [But] just as the architects of the War on Poverty failed to relate the problems of the poor to the broader processes of American economic organization, so too have the advocates for minority rights failed in significant numbers to understand that many contemporary problems of race . . . emanate from broader societal organization.[34]

Notwithstanding the fierce debates that surrounded the publication of *The Declining Significance of Race* in 1978, Wilson accurately nailed a process which Rustin and King outlined, that race alone could not explain the situation of black Americans. King frequently contrasted the fate of affluent black Americans to that of ghetto residents who not only were mired in intractable poverty but forgotten by mainstream leaders. It is now widely known that African Americans have become increasingly divided into two economic worlds, one middle class whose gains in terms of wealth and power have been real and substantial since the 1960s while a large share of blacks has been increasingly left out and marginalized. The Poor People's Campaign hinted not only at the issue of a widening intraracial wealth gap but also at inequality as a plague for all.

Wilson and the PPC agenda square in many regards, chiefly with respect to their job-centered approach to fighting racial inequality. They both reframe the race versus class dichotomy, highlighting how the dynamics of class and the structure of the economy account for the subordination of poor people of color. They both see socioeconomic issues as critical to racial progress. In an article in *Look* published just after his assassination, Dr. King wrote that "We call our demonstration a campaign for jobs and income because we feel that the economic question is the most crucial that black people, and poor people generally, are confronting."[35] He further explained:

> Our whole campaign, therefore, will center on the job question, with other demands like housing that are closely tied to it. We feel that much more building of housing for low income people must be done. On the educational front, the ghetto schools are in bad shape in terms of quality and we feel that a program should be developed to spend at least ten thousand dollars per pupil. Often, they are so far behind that they need more and special attention, the best quality education that can be given.[36]

Despite civil rights legislation, King and Wilson both argued, race and class subordination were intersecting through structural unemployment and poverty, thus dramatically plaguing dispossessed blacks. To them, full employment policies were the main path toward racial equality, regardless of the perpetuation of racial prejudice and discrimination. Echoing the Freedom Budget and King's views on oppression, Wilson contends that "a system of racial discrimination over a long period of time can create racial inequality, a system of racial inequality that will linger on even after racial barriers come down. That is because the most disadvantaged blacks victimized by decades and centuries of racial oppression do not have resources that allow them to compete effectively with other people. They are at a disadvantage."[37]

Interestingly, both King and Wilson hinted at the thesis of a culture of poverty, which they dismissed while giving credence to the concept of a black "underclass," singled out from the rest of society. "There is a fire raging now for the Negroes and the poor of this society," King observed. "They are living in tragic conditions because of the terrible economic injustices that keep them locked in as an 'underclass,' as the sociologists are now calling it."[38] King also contended:

> Now we realize that economic dislocations in the market operations of our economy and the prevalence of discrimination thrust people into idleness and bind them in constant or frequent unemployment against their will. Today the poor are less often dismissed, I hope, from our consciences by being branded as inferior or incompetent. We also know that no matter how dynamically the economy develops and expands, it does not eliminate all poverty.[39]

In 1965, King had already promoted a set of WPA-style policies: "We must develop a federal program of public works, retraining, and jobs for all—so that none, white or black, will have cause to feel threatened. At the present time, thousands of jobs a week are disappearing in the wake of automation and other production efficiency techniques. . . . Black and white, we will all be harmed unless something grand and imaginative is done."[40]

Wilson, who regards Michael Harrington as one of his personal heroes, faulted the liberal policy makers who engineered the War on Poverty programs for their misestimating of the degree to which the structural changes in the U.S. economy impacted the lives of poor blacks, notably in inner cities. Paving the way for Wilson, Randolph, Rustin, and King grasped that the erosion of well-paying jobs for low-skilled workers had to be corrected in order to prevent inner cities from sinking into structural poverty. Although poor of every stripe were instrumental in the coalition that sustained the Poor People's Campaign, the urban black poor stood out as a unique embodiment of the nexus of race and class. Within the framework of economic disadvantage and disempowerment, the dispossessed of the inner cities were the case in point of institutional racism and structural unemployment. Like King, Wilson advocated an ambitious redistributive agenda, including public jobs, guaranteed income, a European-style "welfare system,"[41] and an interracial coalition.[42]

Despite these commonalities, Wilson blamed the civil right movement for its neglect of the masses, and for falling prey to a narrow middle-class framework. But had Wilson paid more attention to the Poor People's Campaign, his severe criticism might have been mitigated. Indeed, King had seen the effects of postwar economic restructuring on the American working class. The PPC stemmed from this observation. In *Where Do We Go from Here*, he argued:

> Economic expansion alone cannot do the job of improving the employment situation of Negroes. It provides the base for improvement but other things must be constructed upon it, especially if the tragic situation of youth is to be solved. In a booming economy Negro youth are afflicted with unemployment as though in an economic crisis. They are the explosive outsiders of the American expansion. . . .
>
> The quest of the Negro male for employment was always frustrating. If he lacked skill, he was only occasionally wanted because such employment as he could find had little regularity and even less remuneration. If he had a skill, he also had his black skin, and discrimination locked doors against him. In the competition for scarce jobs he was a loser because he was born that way.[43]

Appealingly, King singled out Chicago, where Wilson taught for 25 years and which inner neighborhoods Wilson relentlessly studied, as the epitome of American inequality. In 1967, his portray of the Windy City was a judicious assessment of the drift between the haves and have-nots: "This is truly an island of poverty in the midst of an ocean of plenty, for Chicago now boasts the highest per capita income of any city in the world. But you would never believe it looking out of the windows of my apartment in the slum of Lawndale."[44]

TOWARD AN AMERICAN WELFARE STATE

Gunnar Myrdal and Social Democracy

When King went to Stockholm in 1964, one of the people he was eager to meet was Gunnar Myrdal, the Swedish economist whose monumental *An American Dilemma* (1944) had greatly influenced his views on race as a social, moral, and psychological problem in the United States. While pursuing his dissertation at Boston University, King became familiar with the economist's work and would frequently point to the Myrdalian thesis about the decisive inner tension of the white American, split between his ideals and his deeds. In 1966, as King and Harry Belafonte toured European capitals on behalf of the SCLC, the Swedish government organized an outstanding, cheering reception which impressed the visitors. The Swedish Royal Opera House hosted the expensive event whose sponsoring committee was headed by Gunnar Myrdal himself, who supervised the Martin Luther King Fund.[45] The two men deeply respected and influenced each other.

In 1937, the Carnegie Corporation had appointed Stockholm University professor Gunnar Myrdal (1898–1987) to direct a monumental study dedicated to computing every indicator pertaining to black America. With the help of seventy-five contributors, including Ralph Bunche and Kenneth Clark, the massive and comprehensive data-loaded report, issued in 1944, stood as a ground-breaking indictment of the history of race relations in the United States.[46] Debunking the myth of the biological inferiority of black Americans, Myrdal insisted that their situation stemmed from whites' prejudice and discriminatory practices. He pointed to a toxic "social environment" by which social, legal, and economic institutions condemned blacks to social exclusion through a vicious circle in which white prejudice and black poverty self-perpetuated themselves.[47] The most provocative idea of Myrdal's line of argumentation posited that democratic egalitarianism was not necessarily racially equalitarian and, on the contrary, that race was the means through which it could solve its obvious contradictions.[48]

Although an economist by trade, Myrdal framed race relations in the United States as a "moral issue" rather than a socioeconomic one, eclipsing the latter in favor of a speculative assessment of Americans' commitment to their democratic ideals, primarily equality. The discrepancy between what Myrdal called the "American Creed" and the virulence of racism was not sanitized. However, he contended that, by virtue of an egalitarianism embedded in its Constitution, America would necessarily realize its equalitarian potential, by fully endorsing its liberal ethos. The inconsistency between whites' ideals and practices was destined to be solved, he argued, prophesizing a significant leap toward racial progress.

Several thinkers devoted to racial equality have pointed to Myrdal's misestimation of Northern racism. To them, his faith in the capacity and desire of white Americans to overcome the national "dilemma"—even as black inner cities erupted—amounted to naïveté and sweet talk. Published in the mid-1960s, Kenneth Clark's *Black Ghetto* stands as a corrective to Myrdal's insightful analysis of structural poverty.[49] By couching the conditions in black inner cities in the language of colonialism, Clark underscored the role of an entrenched and unremitting white racism as a permanent hindrance to racial equality. Like King, he mitigated Myrdal's faith in American liberalism, pointing to his delusional optimism. During the *Commentary*-sponsored 1964 symposium on "Liberalism and the Negro," Myrdal contended that the cost of even substantive racial equality would be accepted by whites once they realized that it benefited the entire society:

> The civil rights things don't cost very much. But improving the real situation of Negroes and poor people generally would cost money. Now, as an economist, I think I can prove that in the end it wouldn't cost money, because it would mean the utilization of wasted resources, and the utilization of wasted resources has to make a society richer. Still, there is all this superstition about the budget in this country, and getting around it really presents a messy problem.[50]

Indeed, whatever his qualifications about the ability of the American government to spearhead an egalitarian reallocation of resources and wealth, Myrdal trusted Americans to endorse a liberal uplift ideology and to foster black emancipation, belittling along the way blacks' agency. Attending the event, Clark expressed a discordant position, doubting the commitment of whites to good will: "With all due respect to my friend and former colleague and boss, Professor Myrdal, I have come to the conclusion that so far as the

Negro is concerned, the ethical aspect of American liberalism . . . is primarily verbal."[51]

In *Stride Toward Freedom,* King commended Gunnar Myrdal for pointing to the moral issue at stake in racial inequality and he would frequently allude to the book's title, "An American Dilemma."[52] But, at odds with Myrdal, King refuted the belief that ideals of equality and racial tolerance were so deeply etched into the American ideology that the moral conflict borne out of prejudice was unsustainable. The discord between the so-called American creed and lasting discrimination was indeed egregious in 1968. In line with Clark's critique of Myrdal's views King would have probably also shared Ralph Ellison's 1944 rebuke of the "dilemma" framework. Ellison, in a sharp review of Myrdal's book, questioned his "refusal to locate the American ethos in terms of its material manifestations, or to point out how it is manipulated." Ellison further wondered about Myrdal's usage of the American ethos "to disarm all American social groupings by appealing to their stake in the American Creed, and to locate the psychological barriers between them" while also using it "to deny the existence of an American class struggle."[53]

If blind to class struggle, Myrdal was nonetheless a true Social Democrat whose ideas on wealth redistribution and equality were in accordance with King's. Before being appointed by the Carnegie Foundation, Myrdal had been a regular advisor to Social Democratic governments in Sweden which had commissioned him for policy recommendations on issues pertaining to the improvement of the welfare state. The "institutionalist" framework he deployed in *An American Dilemma* was consistent with his scholarship on poverty and inequality, factoring in such noneconomic factors as culture, beliefs, and distribution of power in his holistic approach to social organization. Myrdal eventually became—alongside John Kenneth Galbraith—the world's most renowned institutional economist.[54] Interestingly enough, his economic views on race relations mirrored his economic theories, dismissing a liberal laissez-faire perspective in favor of a federally sponsored set of regulations aimed at remedying racial inequality.

Long before they became a "social model," the Scandinavian countries were characterized by an extensive prevalence of the state in the functioning of the economy, a focus on class compromise through strong unionization, and a focus on equality. To reach this goal, workers, producers, and

consumers could organize and bargain in large units to act as market coun-
tervailing forces. Sweden illustrated Myrdal's contention that greater
income equality was congruent with sustained economic growth.[55] Myrdal's
economic theories, which won him a Nobel Prize in 1974, rested on
Keynesian assumptions which nurtured social democratic thought.
Succinctly, the latter puts a premium on proactive employment policies on
the grounds that workers who enjoy a gainful job have a bargaining power
which provides them with the perspective of better wages and working conditions but also with a social recognition, thereby accelerating the process of
democratization.[56] Sweden came to epitomize the progressive assumption
that a welfare-state government should be accountable for the universality
of social rights, a position that Gunnar Myrdal embraced to the fullest.[57]

King's discovery of the Scandinavian welfare state impressed upon him
how effectively the state could foster solidarity and economic justice. He
immediately claimed that America "had much to learn from Sweden's
Democratic socialist tradition."[58] He later reflected that the social ills that
plagued the United States were nonexistent in Scandinavia:

> As we journeyed around Scandinavia we saw no poverty. We saw no one in
> need of health care who couldn't get it, medical care who couldn't get it. We
> saw no slums. We saw no lack of quality education. And I said to myself if
> these small countries in our world can solve these problems, certainly the
> United States with a national gross product this year of more than $700 bil-
> lion can solve the problems so that nobody will have to live with poverty.[59]

King praised Sweden for what Myrdal called the "created harmony" of
a society where unfettered capitalism was seen as detrimental to the
common good.[60] More specifically, Myrdal defined the welfare state as a
system dedicated to improving the lot of "the less privileged groups in
democratic society"—for instance, by providing "social housing."[61]

In tune with Myrdal's economic reasoning, King contended with basic
social-democratic premises:

> We have so energetically mastered production that we now must give atten-
> tion to distribution. To a degree we have been attacking the problem by
> increasing purchasing power through higher wage scales and increased
> social benefits. But these measures . . . come only as a consequence of orga-
> nized struggles.[62]

As "those at the lowest economic level—the poor white, the Negro, the aged—are traditionally unorganized and have little or no ability to force a growth in their consumer potential," increasing their income would foster their purchasing power while such increased demand could boost the economy.[63] To King, although only a comprehensive full-employment policy could successfully tackle unemployment and poverty, the maldistribution of income was equally a political, moral, and economical misdeed. Income-based redistribution programs were the primary means through which equality could be reached. This assumption guided King's defense of social-democratic policies to address poverty and citizens' welfare.

Willing to go back to an era when providing economic security for families and workers was seen as incumbent upon the state, the Poor People's Campaign challenged the liberal creed in free market values. Equal opportunity was insufficient, it argued, for inequality was created by the rules of the market, not abstractly independent from them. More than income security, social democracies provided their citizens with free universal education and health care, a progressive policy entertained by both Presidents Roosevelt and Truman as part of the Social Security Act, but which they failed to get through. The Economic Bill of Rights put forth by the Poor People's Campaign revived the demand, as King was emphatic that "of all the forms of inequality, injustice in health care is the most shocking and inhuman."[64] Here again, Myrdal's class-based approach, articulated in this passage, stood in consonance with the Poor People's Campaign's:

> Prejudice will continue to exist even if the legal and institutional basis for it is removed. . . . But on the whole, what is needed, of course, is to lift all the poor people at the bottom, the people I call the "underclass" or the submerged group, out of poverty and everything that poverty implies. . . . Improving the lot of this whole submerged group has become a very acute problem for America, and it is only in that larger setting that the Negroes will be able to achieve anything more than formal equality.[65]

Wealth inequality was indeed the plague that the Poor People Campaign perceptively fingered as the damaging product of years of neglect for class and race entanglement. Not only Myrdal but John Kenneth Galbraith inspired King's late trope of "poverty in the midst of plenty," opposing the "affluent" to the "poor":

All too many of those who live in affluent America ignore those who exist in poor America. In doing so, the affluent Americans will eventually have to face themselves with the question that Eichmann chose to ignore: How responsible am I for the well-being of my fellows? To ignore evil is to become an accomplice to it.[66]

Over the past decade, concerns about wealth inequality and the entrenched racial wealth gap have become prominent in public debates. These concerns may be traced back to the 1960s where a handful of luminaries, including the PPC's architects and participants, denounced the growing wealth gap that had begun to undermine the American democracy.

John K. Galbraith and the Perils of Inequality

Many black liberation leaders have pointed to the rising economic inequalities between black and white workers and, by the late 1960s, many accurately took notice that the corollary political double standard was a major rebuke to the post-1965 democratization process.[67] The Poor People's Campaign more broadly warned Washington about the peril of inequality, proclaiming that it would continue to severe the social fabric of the nation absent a strong egalitarian set of redistributive policies. During the campaign, the SCLC issued a pamphlet which included a comparison of the annual incomes between the rich and the poor in order to document the institutional nature of racism and economic exploitation. Having demonstrated the need for change, the pamphlet concluded by emphasizing the hypocrisy of poverty in one of the wealthiest nations in the world.[68]

The Progressive Era and the 1930s were periods of concern about the economic and political implication of the obvious disparities in wealth in the United States, which the government attempted to solve through its defense of progressive taxation.[69] But, as Americans in the post–Second World War era enjoyed an unprecedented standard of living, the overarching liberal assumption of the period, which undergirded the War on Poverty, was that economic growth would solve poverty and inequality. By the late 1960s, not only was the concern for poverty sidelined but very little attention was paid to the changing structure of U.S. income inequality, except in progressive circles. John Kenneth Galbraith, one of the most renowned economists of his time, made quite an impression when he published *The Affluent Society* in 1958. The book exposed the fallacy of the liberal assumption on economic growth and demonstrated that the market alone was failing to provide certain key goods that defined a secure economic life—health, housing, and education. As the nation was grappling with persistent racial and economic injustice, the Canadian-born economist reminded Washington that it fell on the state to provide low-income and poor citizens with such goods.

Galbraith's indictment of poverty and inequality was to progressive thinking in the 1950s what Michael Harrington's *The Other America* would be in the 1960s: an exposé of the underbelly of American prosperity. They both fingered its underpinnings as responsible for the growing social divide between the majority of privileged citizens and the dispossessed. The American government played, in fact, a lesser role in mitigating economic insecurities than did other democratic nations, putting less-skilled and lower income workers in a vulnerable position, especially since welfare provisions were being retrenched. Galbraith contrasted the affluence of the private sector with the misery of a public one, which was in dire need of investment, chiefly with regards to education, employment, and antipoverty programs.

An adviser to President Kennedy (but not to President Johnson), Galbraith advocated for public policies capable of tacking the contradiction of entrenched poverty in an era of opulence. In his book, he championed the idea that "economy security" was to be reached for American workers and alerted his audience to an overlooked yet rampant widening gap between the haves and the have-nots:

> Inequality has fallen off the political landscape in the US in recent years. Some measure of increased redistribution has been achieved through the progressive income tax implemented at the end of the Second World War. However, inequality remains acute. Although a large part of the working class has become more affluent, it is often not appreciated the extent to which an underclass has remained poor in the midst of these broader gains.[70]

Deriding the current wisdom, he argued that growth would not solve poverty but redistribution would, if adequately implemented. An affluent America was suffering from residual islands of poverty, which required a set of proactive measures to be eradicated:

to guarantee a decent income to all (for example using the negative income tax) and to restore the social balance by increasing public spending, recognizing that localities with more poverty require significantly more investment in all public services (e.g., education, healthcare, law enforcement) to compensate for households' inability themselves to invest in their children's future—this is required in order to guarantee children growing up in poverty to enjoy the same opportunities to economic success that those born into more affluent families are given.[71]

In *Where Do We Go from Here,* King quoted Galbraith and endorsed his policy recommendations. He also appropriated Galbraith's catchphrase, recasting it as "poverty in the midst of prosperity," to illustrate his plea on behalf of the poor. In 1966, he called out an American unegalitarian system: "We must see still by the millions we have many, many people perishing on the lonely island of poverty in the midst of a vast ocean of prosperity.[72] His emphasis on the corrosive effect of wealth inequality on blacks' sense of civic belonging was also foregrounded in his last book: "It is not only poverty that torments the Negro" he wrote, "it is the fact of poverty amid plenty."[73]

"Poverty in the midst of plenty" belied the myth of "the rising tide that would lift all boats" and, echoing Galbraith, King rejected exhortations to hard work and self-reliance, instead contending that poverty was structural. He mocked the bootstrap metaphor, pointing out that it was "a cruel jest to say to a bootless man that he ought to lift himself by his own bootstraps."[74]

Through his interactions with labor, King had gained a particular awareness of the deleterious effects of structural changes like automation on low-skilled workers, pointedly connecting hardcore joblessness to poverty and swelling wealth inequities. "Automation," he reasoned in 1961, "can be used to generate an abundance of wealth for people or an abundance of poverty for millions as its human-like machines turn out human scrap along with machine scrap as a byproduct of production."[75] Whereas Galbraith warned about the "social imbalance" resulting from wealth inequalities, King, at the press conference announcing the Poor People's Campaign, deplored a creeping "social insanity":

Affluent Americans are locked in the suburbs of physical comfort and mental insecurity. Poor Americans are locked inside ghettos of material privation and spiritual debilitation. And all of us can almost feel the presence of a kind of social insanity which could lead to national ruin.[76]

During a talk at Stanford University in 1967, King blended the economist's statement with Michael Harrington's metaphor of the "two Americas" to give a remarkable address to a nation oblivious to its disadvantaged half:

> There are literally two Americas. One America is beautiful for situation. And in a sense this America is overflowing with the milk of prosperity and the honey of opportunity. . . . But tragically and unfortunately, there is another America. This other America has a daily ugliness about it that constantly transforms the buoyancy of hope into the fatigue of despair. In this America millions of work-starved men walk the streets daily in search for jobs that do not exist. . . . In this America people are poor by the millions. They find themselves perishing on a lonely island of poverty in the midst of a vast ocean of material prosperity.[77]

Acquiescence to poverty was, like that of segregation, sustained by a "two America" framework in which the privileged refused to give up some of their advantages.

> American cities are not the City of God nor the City of Man. They contain the residues of exploitation, of waste, of neglect, of indifference. The poor and the discriminated huddle in the big cities—the poor-houses of the welfare state—while affluent America displays its new gadgets in the crisp homes of suburbia. . . .
>
> The rising affluence of America has benefited the better-off more than the poor and discriminated. Our income record is acceptable only if we wish to tolerate a society in which the richest fifth of the population is 10 times as rich as the poorest fifth, and in which the average Negro earns half as much as his white counterpart.[78]

Inequality has indeed been the untold story of an opulent postwar American economy. The confluence of race and class has resulted in staggering racial economic inequalities. African Americans' wages, salaries, and overall wealth have lagged behind whites persistently throughout the period, despite the improvement bolstered by the civil rights legislation. The unequal distribution of resources has persisted and to some degree worsened.[79] As Michael K. Brown demonstrates, "real black median family income doubled between 1947 and 1972, as did the median income of white families. Black families gained relative to white families; the ratio of median family income increased to 59.5 percent from 51.2 percent. Yet the absolute median income gap between black and white families increased over this period by almost $5,000, a 35 percent gain for whites."[80]

Defining the middle class as those whose income lies between two-thirds and four-fifths of the median white male income, economists James P. Smith and Finis R. Welch noted that in 1960, 64 percent of whites and 59 percent of blacks belonged to that category, whereas only 12 percent of whites fell below the threshold while 39 percent of blacks did.[81] A decade later, 66 percent of blacks and 71 percent of whites were considered of middle class but the income gap was still stark: 9 percent of whites fell below as opposed to 24 percent of blacks. As far as the most privileged households are concerned, 25 percent of white families belong to the top third of the income scale but only 5 percent of black families. Examining the census data further, Smith and Welch also pointed out that where the majority of white workers in 1960 hold high school diplomas and 10 percent a college degree, 80 percent of black workers had not finished high school, and less than 3 percent were college graduates.

Harrington's, Galbraith's, and Myrdal's late works (the latter published *Challenge to Affluence* the same year as Harrington's pamphlet) stand as explicit vindications of the PPC demands, calling for an ambitious anti-poverty "Marshall Plan" including universal policies such as direct job creation and income guarantees along with measures aimed at alleviating black conditions. Galbraith perceptively understood that even in a growing economy, poor people could not access good education or housing, much less bequeath any wealth or educational opportunities to their children. That African Americans, because of spatial segregation, were doomed to this disadvantage whatever their economic position would be demonstrated decades later by state-of-the-art scholarship.[82] It is therefore somewhat astounding that King perceptively grasped the limitations of the "affluent society" and its connection to racial segregation in high-poverty neighborhoods as well as the perils of wealth inequality.

But Galbraith and his line of thought were dismissed by both Presidents Kennedy and Johnson. He failed to sway their economic policies and tax cuts, economic growth and behavioral approach to black poverty—targeting the employability of the unemployed—which prevailed among policy makers. Johnson's Council of Economic Advisors had initially endorsed a structural framework to address poverty, issuing a report which made clear that economic growth and incentives to work would hardly scratch the surface of unemployment, notably in inner cities. However, despite ongoing demands from activists and progressive scholars, redistributive social programs were brushed aside. The nefarious influence of the conservative reading of the Moynihan Report notably crippled Johnson's antipoverty legislation, which "began with a structural analysis and ended up with a service-based strategy."[83]

King not only adopted his analysis of insular poverty from Galbraith but also the main remedy the economist advocated, namely the guaranteed income. "We must create full employment or we must create income," King contended in 1967.[84] The idea was not new to welfare rights advocates nor to civil rights activists devoted to economic justice.[85] Sadie Tanner Mossell Alexander—the first African American woman to earn a PhD in economics in 1921—and Bayard Rustin had long pushed for its implementation.[86] In the late 1960s, the NWRO was the most fervent proponent of the guaranteed income, breaking sharply with other organizations committed to civil rights and social justice by decoupling a right to a decent income from access to wage work. Pioneering a strong understanding of social rights, the architects of Solidarity Day regarded a "Guaranteed Adequate Income" (GAI) as "an unconditional citizenship right, essential to equal respect, and an appropriate touchstone of equality in an affluent nation."[87] Their influence on King proved instrumental. Urging him to understand the degree to which women on welfare endured humiliation and oppression, welfare recipient activists updated his normative views of family wage and females' work, and he conceded the major contribution of their organizing.[88]

As Felicia Kornbluh points out, by the late 1960s, the idea of the guaranteed income, defined as the idea that the government should guarantee that no one's income would fall below the poverty level, was embraced across the political spectrum, gaining momentum among conservatives. Indeed, economist Milton Friedman,[89] Senator George McGovern, and President Nixon—once he was elected in 1969—pushed for what they perceived as an alternative to the bureaucratic social welfare system, "a kind of anti-New Deal and anti-War on Poverty."[90] The conservatives' goal was to replace all social security benefits, which explained the NWRO's strong opposition to President Nixon's version of the guaranteed income.[91] However, their understanding of what they framed as a "Negative Income Tax" had little in common with Galbraith's and King's vision of a redistributive policy aimed at tacking the structural and unfortunate consequences of America's postindustrial two-tier affluence. In stark contrast to their suggestion that the Guaranteed Adequate Income would manage poverty and foster individual responsibility, King, in step with leftist feminists, saw it as an instrument of "reparation" for the wrongs of racial capitalism.[92] "We have deluded ourselves into believing the myth that capitalism grew and prospered out of the protestant ethic of hard work and sacrifice" he stated in 1967, but "the fact is that Capitalism was built on the exploitation and suffering of black slaves and continues to thrive on the exploitation of the poor both black and white."[93]

Providing the poor with jobs and income would not only be just, it would restructure the political economy of the nation, by redistributing wealth, power and agency to the poor. "The way to end poverty is to end the exploitation of the poor," he asserted.[94] For all the social progress fostered by the guaranteed income if properly carried out, in the minds of the Poor People's campaigners it had to be combined with other social programs pertaining to education, health, and housing. They chiefly demanded a full employment strategy which would translate into a job guarantee policy, often referred to as the "Employer of Last Resort" framework, an idea that Randolph's and Rustin's Freedom Budget had unsuccessfully lobbied for. In 1968, King went further by demanding that the public jobs created would provide a socially valuable service to communities of color, which were hardly served by the private sector or other government programs. In a 1967 telegram to President Johnson, King was emphatic that the magnitude of young urban blacks' joblessness had to be addressed and treated as a national and urgent priority:

> Let us do one simple direct thing—let us end unemployment totally and immediately. In the depression days the nation was close to prostrate on the brink of bankruptcy, yet it created the WPA to make millions of jobs instantly available for all existing levels of skill. The jobs were tailored to the man, not the man to the job in recognition of the emergency. Training followed employment, it did not precede it and become an obstacle to it.

I propose specifically the creation of a national agency that shall provide a job to every person who needs work, young and old, white and Negro. Not one hundred jobs when 10,000 are needed. Not some cheap way out. Not some frugal device to maintain a balanced budget within an unbalanced society.

I propose a job for everyone, not a promise to see if jobs can be found. There cannot be social peace when a people have awakened to their rights and dignity and to the wretchedness of their lives simultaneously. If our government cannot create jobs, it cannot govern. It cannot have white affluence amid black poverty and have racial harmony.[95]

That the government should provide everyone with a job has been a social democratic demand since the New Deal, regularly advocated by progressives. In 1966, A. Philip Randolph and Bayard Rustin outlined their Freedom Budget under the guidance of Keynesian economist Leon H. Keyserling. It called "for a government-sponsored job guarantee for those ready and willing to work, a guaranteed income for those who cannot or should not be working, and an increase in the minimum wage to lift the working poor and their families out of poverty."[96] The Freedom Budget inspired King to keep on demanding full employment and job guarantee, entailing millions of public service jobs and public works: "We should be demanding," Rustin stated, the "immediate passage of an accelerated public works program."[97]

Echoing Rustin but also liberal economist Galbraith, King expressed his concern about the weakness of a public sector expected to provide jobs to the dispossessed:

The expansion of private employment and nonprofessional opportunities cannot, however, provide full employment for Negroes. Many youths are not listed as unemployed because in despair they have left the labor market completely. They are psychologically disabled and cannot be rescued by conventional employment.... A high percentage of these jobs is in public employment. The human services—medical attention, social services, neighborhood amenities of various kinds—are in scarce supply in this country, especially in localities of poverty. The traditional way of providing manpower for these jobs—degree-granting programs—cannot fill all the niches that are opening up. The traditional job requirements are a barrier to attaining an adequate supply of personnel, especially if the number of jobs expands to meet existing need.[98]

He also stressed that people who were pulled out of poverty with these jobs would gain a purchasing power that could be transformed into political empowerment.

Primarily concerned by inequality, King hoped that the guaranteed income would prove effective at reducing the disparities in the distribution of income among the entire population. In "Where do We Go from Here?" he clarified: "if we want to ensure that the guaranteed income operates as a consistently progressive measure . . . it must be pegged to the median income of society, not the lowest levels of income" and "must automatically increase as the total social income grows."[99] He clearly spelled out his vision of a program which could not only solve poverty but would curtail the stigmatization of welfare recipients.

The right to an income demanded by the Poor People's Campaign was far more an integrated concept of economic citizenship than a "right to a job." It is worth noting that the right to an income eschewed the gendered distinctions attached to the wage work ethic that contemptuously ignore the care-giving work provided by most women. Housework and care for children and other persons had hardly received any social recognition under the elaboration of the American welfare system. Unpaid work was denied the status of "work," thereby no compensations, benefits, payments, or rights were to be given to housewives and mothers. As only males received wages and were considered breadwinners, only they were granted full citizenship. A basic universal income had the ability to "assist democratization" for it "can help break the long-standing link between income, marriage, employment and citizenship."[100]

As Alice Kressler-Harris argues, "attaching economic rights to care . . . provides a language to inscribe caring rights into the larger economic structures," a point made by the welfare rights activists who combatted the 1967 Welfare Reform Bill and its work requirement for recipients but also by PPC's set of demands.[101] The "right to earn" is another way to name the guaranteed income. All citizens would have equal worth and democratic standing, regardless of their occupational status. Regular payments secured one's full citizenship, insulated from the vagaries of an unstable labor market. Both the guaranteed income and the public job guarantee eschewed the stigmatization of the poor, chiefly black families headed by females, who were demeaned by programs establishing male-based means requirements. Furthermore, truly universal and yet fitted for the black poor, they would work as an employment safety net "for those for whom traditional jobs are not available."[102] Black economically depressed residents, oftentimes in such despair that "they have left the labor market completely" would be the prime beneficiaries of "special workplaces where irregularities can be accepted," which would provide "real jobs," not training.[103]

Myrdal's and Galbraith's imprints also shone through King's call for an economic transition from mass production to distribution on the grounds that not only was consumer culture "debilitating" but because the lesser-off in society had little purchasing and bargaining power, they were "becoming poorer." King quoted Galbraith's estimation that establishing the guaranteed income would cost $20 billion annually, barely the cost of the war in Vietnam, he pondered. He remarked on the irony and hypocrisy of a society prone to shame the relief client but ignoring the extent to which "the wealthy who own securities have always had an assured income." In the spirit of the Poor People's Campaign, King underscored the inclusiveness of a policy which aimed to be not just a "civil rights program," but rather a universal antipoverty policy able to unite black and white poor in a fierce coalition.[104] To him, such a "coalition of an energized section of labor, Negroes, unemployed and welfare recipients" could usher in "a breakthrough to a new level of social reform" and not only achieve "the total elimination of poverty," but also "profound structural changes in society.[105]

That King couched the late phase of the civil rights revolution in terms of economic equality conjured an American social-democratic tradition which climaxed with the New Deal but was increasingly perceived as outlandish in the aftermath of the Second World War. The American welfarist liberalism of the mid-twentieth century, began to lose ground in the 1950s and by the time civil rights legislation was passed, it had almost utterly disintegrated. The Poor People's Campaign revived an antiquated American populist and egalitarian tradition.

Advocates for guaranteed income received ample support from legal scholars. who argued that a "right" to an income was constitutional. Columbia's Center for Social Welfare Policy and the Law (CSWPL) helped bring the case of welfare restrictions to the Supreme Court: *Goldberg v.*

Kelly would be a major victory. In 1970, the court indeed argued that welfare benefits were "a matter of statutory entitlement," and condemned states' discretionary policies with respect to welfare benefits rights.[106] Some claimed that the Supreme Court was moving toward a social rights philosophy, by means of "constitutional rights pertaining to the status of being poor."[107]

As inequality was slowly becoming the most irksome of American problems, few officials were eager to comply with the PPC's demands and to support a set of policies aimed at eradicating such intractable racial and, increasingly, wealth inequality. From the Freedom Budget to the Poor People's Campaign, radical civil rights egalitarian's call for full employment therefore sounded unfortunate and untimely, a point King clearly grasped:

> It was obdurate government callousness to misery that first stoked the flames of rage and frustration. With unemployment a scourge in Negro ghettoes, the government still tinkers with half-hearted measures, refuses still to become an employer of last resort.[108]

King and the campaigners' call was no more successful at enacting the guaranteed income and a full employment offensive strategy than the 1966 Freedom Budget. Nevertheless, the idea gained momentum and translated into further initiatives. The Poor People's Campaign, which substantiated the demand with a comprehensive Economic Bill of Rights, permeated academic debates and conversely was inspired by it. Its policy relevance and enduring salience proved explicit on May 27, 1968, with the circulation of a statement written by 1,300 economists from 125 universities, urging the passing of a bill to guarantee an income to everyone, whether they worked or not. The first paragraph opened with a reference to the Poor People's Campaign and the Kerner Commission, to buttress its perspective.[109] Among the economists involved, John Galbraith but also Robert Lampman, Paul Samuelson, James Tobin. and Aron Watts stood out as the most prestigious signatories. The petition was sent to Congress but the bill failed.

The conservative resurgence that manifested in the post-Johnson era was indeed suffused with an "ethnic revival" which flourished at the expense of racial equality. Former leftists shifted to the right in the late

1970s and developed a neoconservative ideology whose prime objective was to erase the legacy of both the New Deal and the Great Society and to tailor an American identity rooted in the free market, government distrust, and an individual work ethic. For them, as for conservatives, bolstering the welfare state became tantamount to handing out underserved benefits to blacks at the expense of hard-working whites. They also harped on the threat of urban uprising and fingered black radical egalitarianism as the culprit. Many concluded that blacks' radical call for racial equality was to blame for the fracturing of liberals and the dismissal of Great Society liberalism. They thus justified the racial fatigue already rampant in the late 1960s, which spiraled into outright racial resentment, mostly stemming from white ethnics.[110]

Democrats and other progressives eventually yielded to the widespread rebuttal of Keynesian policies as they pertained to racial equality. Daniel Moynihan, once in tune with King's call for redistributionist governmental policies, epitomized such drift.[111] His appointment on December 10, 1968, to conservative President Nixon's White House staff as assistant for urban affairs hardly raised highbrows, although Richard Nixon was notoriously hostile to social programs. At the 1968 Republican national convention in Miami Beach, Moynihan had actually charged: "For the past five years we have been deluged by government programs for the unemployed, programs for the cities, programs for the poor. And we have reaped from these programs an ugly harvest of frustration, violence, and failure across the land." Now was the time, he added, "to quit pouring billions of dollars into programs that have failed in the United States."[112]

Despite the liberal-sounding title of his book, *The Politics of a Guaranteed Income,* Moynihan called for work requirements and work incentives in exchange for meager welfare payments, a substantial curtailment of hard-won rights for welfare recipients. As reported by the *New York Times,* he plainly ridiculed the National Welfare Rights Organization, a key PPC architect, for its call for a guaranteed income of $5,500 or $6,500 a year.[113] Accordingly, Congress and the White House consistently refused to lift the load of poverty through redistributive federal programs. The rise of Richard Nixon and George Wallace in 1968 accelerated the retrenchment of social welfare policies, which were increasingly derided by the public. The disrepute and "racialization" of welfare policies initiated—and then reinforced—the misrepresentation of the poor as black and undeserving. The general distaste for the dependent was aggravated by white resentment triggered by affirmative action policies.

In the 1970s, civil rights and economic justice advocates attempted to unearth a redistributive tradition, buried beneath the dominant doctrine of "benign neglect" on the subject of race and poverty.[114] As the Nixon administration was increasingly deriding Great Society programs, the Black Congressional Caucus raised the issue of structural unemployment.[115]

In 1978 two liberal legislators, Senator Hubert Humphrey (D–Minn.) and Representative Augustus Hawkins (D–Calif.), put forth a bold full-employment bill which included a job guarantee, the creation of a Job Guarantee Office, a Standby Job Corps, and the changing of the name of the United States Employment Service to the United States Full Employment Service. An $8 billion domestic "Marshall Plan," the Humphrey-Hawkins Full Employment and Balanced Growth Act argued that the federal government had to "translate into practical reality the right of all Americans who are able, willing and seeking to work to full opportunity for useful paid employment at fair rates of compensation." Humphrey wrote his argument in a plea which was tellingly read aloud at Ebenezer Baptist Church:

> Fourteen years ago Dr. Martin Luther King Jr. shared with us his dream for America. That cherished dream of what our nation could and should be became our dream as well. We come together to recommit ourselves to the struggle to reach the promised land which he described from the mountain-top. . . . I will never deceive you, and I believe you know it. This legislation is a must. It is no miracle cure, but it is an indispensable step toward economic justice. We must keep up the fight. If we do, I assure you [it] will be worth every effort you make.[116]

As Helen Ginsburg observed, Hawkins—a representative of the structurally impoverished Watts ghetto of Los Angeles—sought to intertwine universalism and targeted policy, cognizant that only radical measures could cure the structural unemployment plaguing inner cities. Although he was "deeply committed to equality for all people and to a broad interpretation of full employment as a human right," he "did not see the bill as simply an anti-recession measure or another jobs program." His bill intended to

address the intractable joblessness of the American poor through the revivi-
fication of the idea of a "legal, enforceable right to employment."[117]

Coretta King Scott actively lobbied for Hawkins' bill, dubbing it—like
the NWRO years before—a "tribute" to her late husband. She echoed his
defense of the Poor People's Campaign:

> When we first started marching 22 years ago, we were talking about simple
> rights, dignity in civil rights. Now we are fighting for economic rights. We
> have legislation for civil rights and legislation that speaks to political rights.
> Now we are trying to get legislation for jobs.[118]

In 1977, she co-chaired the National Committee Action Council, a
broad-based group made of forty labor, civil rights, religious organizations, women, and social welfare organizations campaigning for full
employment legislation.[119] To them, the bill represented a direct continuation of the civil rights insurgency of the previous decades, as stated by
Andrew Young, then the chief U.S. delegate to the United Nations:

> Somehow we are the bridge as black Americans between the "haves" and the
> "have nots" of the world. We are beginning to build the kind of economic
> bridges that will enable the dream of Martin Luther King to be fulfilled in
> worldwide manner.[120]

The Humphrey-Hawkins bill was signed into law by President Jimmy
Carter in October 1978. But, re-enacting the weakening process that had
doomed Truman's bill, Congress emptied out the initial version, discarding
the right to a job. A conservative coalition thwarted the bill's effort to enact
full employment policies. Eventually amputated and sapped, the original
proposal remained however a topic of debate among progressives.[121]

Consistent with the belief that class was key to tackling African
Americans' condition, William Julius Wilson was a staunch supporter of
the bill as originally written, because it offered a social-democrat response
to the structural cause of American poverty. To him, it would have allevi-
ated the joblessness plaguing inner-city communities and, in accordance
with the Poor People's Campaign's intent, was politically sound for it presented itself as a universal class-based policy able to "bridge over the racial
divide."[122] In devising the strategy and tactics which, through a broad-
based movement, would make plausible a real redistribution of economic

and political power, Wilson drew on Rustin's liberal strategy. The PPC, in a more trenchant perspective, demanded that access to decent jobs, housing, and education become a "right." The "Economic Bill of Rights for the Disadvantaged," the cornerstone of the campaign, suggested that the right to work was a fundamental prerequisite for social justice and should be regarded as more legitimate than property rights. The "social citizenship" entailed by the Economic Bill of Rights confronted the liberal paradigm of equal opportunities and fair treatment.

9 A "Right Not to Starve"

LEGALIZING EQUALITY

AN ECONOMIC BILL OF RIGHTS
FOR THE DISADVANTAGED

To fully come to terms with the meaning of the policy repertoire of the Poor People's Campaign, it might be valuable to question King's late position toward the mainstream American belief in economic freedom. Indeed, an "Economic Bill of Rights for the Disadvantaged" conjured ideas of equality of outcome and entitlement to economic security, and stood as a rebuke of American values. However, from the early days of the republic African Americans have experienced that the equal rights creed was nothing but a fallacy as long as the government ignored class inequalities which condemned them to second-class citizenship. The federal government's withdrawal from Reconstruction's effort to untie this knot was a case in point. Similarly, the political economy of postwar America with its laissez-faire perspective reinforced the nexus of race, class. and civic status.

The Poor People's Campaign articulated the extent to which accelerated capitalism and social neglect revoked social citizenship within the liberal framework. The protestors demanded that the government enforce substantive equality through policies capable of reversing the degradation of the poor, protecting them from the crippling effects of the free market. Accordingly, the campaigners argued that a constitutional *aggiornamento* could buttress a new social contract. Moving toward an egalitarian social-welfare liberalism required a new understanding of "rights." Indeed, if citizens had a *right* to a living wage and decent homes, it was subsequently the moral obligation and legal duty of the government to provide them. The Poor People's Campaign was less about political rights than about economic justice, which entailed a reframing of the notion of citizenship.

The PPC's "Economic Bill of Rights for the Disadvantaged," although vilified and portrayed as un-American by media covering the campaign, may be traced back to the high tide of American progressivism. The New Deal's political order had hoped to usher in "a more expansive understanding of rights, fostered and sheltered by a centralized welfare State."[1]

President Roosevelt first articulated his idea for an Economic Bill of Rights in 1932, during a speech to the Commonwealth Club: "The task of Government in its relation to business is to assist the development of an economic declaration of right, an economic constitutional order. . . . Every man has a right to life; and this means that he has also a right to make a comfortable living." He came to push for a second bill of rights, which would metaphorically enshrine economic security in the Constitution. Framed as a "right," it required an unflinching national commitment and specifically entailed proactive federal policies, adopted by Congress and implemented throughout the country. In January 1944, Roosevelt presented his Economic Bill of Rights during his State of the Union message, in which he deemed it as "sacred" as the "Bill of Rights of our Constitution itself." He was emphatic that "a new basis of security and prosperity can be established for all, regardless of station, race, or creed." The revolutionary bill included "the right to a useful and remunerative job in the industries or shops or farms or mines of our nation," "the right of every family to a decent home," "the right to a good education," and "the right to adequate medical care and the opportunity to achieve and enjoy good health." The eradication of poverty, not the achievement of prosperity through economic growth, was the goal to reach, Roosevelt asserted. Predating King's rhetoric, the president claimed:

It is our duty now to begin to lay the plans and determine the strategy for the winning of a lasting peace and the establishment of an American standard of living higher than ever before known. We cannot be content, no matter how high that general standard of living may be, if some fraction of our people—whether it be one third or one fifth or one tenth—is ill-fed, ill-clothed, ill-housed and insecure.[2]

Roosevelt concluded that "all of these rights spell security. And after this war is won we must be prepared to move forward, in the implementation of these rights, to new goals of human happiness and well-being."[3]

Jim Crow proved instrumental in bringing down the Second Bill of Rights. Dixiecrats allied with Republicans in Congress to dismantle all the social rights envisioned by Roosevelt.[4] The elections of 1938, which saw Republicans regaining seats and Democrats disavowing the president, had already stalled his agenda. Thereafter, he renounced working for reforms on the domestic front and turned his attention to the war effort.[5] He died just a year after announcing his Economic Bill of Rights.

Still, Harry Truman picked up the torch and defended his predecessor's ambitious bill. Talking about "economic freedom," President Truman expected to enshrine economic rights in the framework of freedom. His full-employment bill of 1945 stated that "national policy and programs for assuring full employment" were urgent. Also known as the Wagner-Murray bill, it contended that "all Americans able to work and seeking work have the right to useful, remunerative, regular and full-time employment. And it is the policy of the United States to assure the existence at all times of sufficient employment opportunities to enable all Americans . . . to freely exercise this right."[6]

According to the new president, not only were Americans "entitled to an opportunity for useful and remunerative, regular and full time employment" but also to decent homes and universal health care. Therefore, Truman proposed an ambitious plan of federally financed affordable housing construction and the establishment of a European-style national health care system. Ultimately, the gutting of the bill by Republican congressmen left little of its initial content. Passed in 1946, the Employment Protection Act neither referred to the "right to a job" nor to "full employment." Truman's triumphant election in 1948 and his Fair Deal program marked the beginning of a "new liberalism," seen by many observers as a tamed and watered-down version of New Deal liberalism.[7] Buttressing a market-driven economy had become a priority for liberals and, by the late 1950s, the "grand postwar Keynesian bargain" (full employment and generous benefits to workers through a coalition of liberals and labor) had begun to disintegrate.[8]

As Americans renounced reconciling the sanctity of individual freedom with an enforced administrative state, the national experiment with social democracy was eclipsed.[9] The Poor People's Campaign sought to resuscitate a New Deal-inspired reformism but with the major qualification that the campaign was also an attempt to redeem the state from the discriminatory policies which had undermined it. Although African Americans became "a significant constituency in the Democratic electoral coalition" in the 1930s and "helped to alter the party's center of gravity," New Deal "universalistic" programs had fallen victim to Southern prejudice.[10]

King's last campaign was nonetheless infused with the Rooseveltian sentiment that "human rights," not solely "civil rights," had to be America's new frontier.[11] It is worth remembering in that regard that the term "human rights" was coined by Frederick Douglass to define the scope of fundamental rights of the enslaved. Until the Cold War divorced international human rights and domestic civil rights, the idea that the government had to ensure people's dignity by granting them economic, social, and political rights was commonly advocated. The PPC belonged to a substantive history of the U.S. struggle for domestic human rights.[12] Though radical, the campaign's demands were not alien to the United States.

But a truly progressive and egalitarian liberalism was a hard sell after 1945. The PPC's call for wealth redistribution infringed on property rights, a core tenet of the postwar "new liberalism."[13] In 1955, Harvard political scientist Louis Hartz identified English philosopher John Locke's liberalism as the core feature of contemporary American identity. The Lockean liberal consensus, he argued, was premised on a natural rights philosophy which consecrated property. Both Gunnar Myrdal and Hartz defined liberalism as the dominant ideological thread in American history. But whereas Myrdal saw the American creed as a dedication to equality, Hartz argued that property rights (and its related beliefs in social mobility, individual freedom, and popular democracy) were etched in the fabric of the nation. Radicals, and black radicals in particular, had challenged these rights, for they had justified the protection of bondage over the defense of human dignity and black personhood. If American liberalism had to be equated to sacrosanct property rights, African Americans could not be liberals. King regularly quoted nineteenth-century economist Henry George's views, who attributed economic inequality to land ownership patterns. King shared his qualifications with regards to property rights:

> I am aware that they are many who wince at the distinction between property and persons who hold both sacrosanct. My views are not so rigid. A life is sacred. Property is intended to serve life, and no matter how much we surround it with rights and respect, it has no personal being. It is part of the earth man walks on; it is not man.[14]

The Poor People's Campaign embodied King's core principle that the poor's inalienable rights supersede the rich's claim to property. He therefore opposed the consensual liberal dogma of property rights. To Hartz, the contractarianism inherent in the American political system was predicated on this "agreed-upon quiescent consensus."[15] It explained, he asserted, why Americans grew estranged from Europeans particularly with regard to socialism and the welfare state.[16]

Indeed, a decade before the publication of Hartz's essay, British economist Sir William Beveridge's influential essay in Europe, "Full Employment in a Free Society," had clearly defined economic security as a right. He subsequently stated that the responsibility to create full employment fell to the government, and his plan set the foundation for postwar social rights activism. What had previously come to be known as the "Beveridge Report," released in 1942, gravitated toward a social-democratic system, advocating a social security system (free health service, social benefits insurance) and full-employment policies, and was pivotal in laying the groundwork not only for the British but also other European welfare states.[17] Myrdal and other progressive thinkers and policy makers would substantiate a cradle-to-grave welfare security systems in their respective countries.

Unquestionably, Hartz was right to assert that self-reliance and equal opportunity were principles that have run deep in American society. State-sponsored social and economic rights legislation have always been unpalatable to American policy makers, as have the constitutionalizing of economic rights. As far as universal social rights, America has indeed remained distant from the European comprehensive welfare-state template. Hartz however overlooked that, arguing that through a flawed but consequential New Deal, the United States elaborated its own welfare state, hinting at the prospect of an Economic Bill of Rights. He also failed to mention that the New Deal program was exported to other nations, and thus was not a foreign import.[18] Ironically enough, Roosevelt and Truman castigated the very individualism Hartz regarded as the utmost American ethos. Besides, he glossed over the racial hierarchies upon which the American nation had been constructed and defined and which obviously contradicted the liberal paradigm from the outset.[19] Hartz was nonetheless widely praised in the 1960s and earned much credit for capturing the era's Zeitgeist: the belief that American democracy was based on an individualistic "society of owners" from which class and social resentment were absent but where liberal values were self-evident.

From the New Deal to the Poor People's Campaign, the dissenting idea of an Economic Bill of Rights, which would have anchored poverty in class relations, was never seriously reconsidered despite the growing domestic income gap, the Freedom Budget, and Article 23 of the UN Universal Declaration of Human Rights, which defined a job as a "right."[20] The redefinition of citizenship entailed by the Poor People's Campaign broke with the dominant definition of inclusion in the polity to suggest that economic justice and egalitarian principles should be the core element of a substantive citizenship. It outlined an alternative narrative to the American ethos and citizenship, one in which commitment to combatting economic inequality was crucial.

ON SOCIAL CITIZENSHIP

The concept of "social citizenship," elaborated in 1949 by British sociologist T. H. Marshall (whom Beveridge appointed as tutor on social work at the London School of Economics in 1925) turned out to be an intellectual vindication of postwar European welfare systems. In *Citizenship and*

Social Class, Marshall questioned how the opposing principles of equality of citizenship and class inequality of market capitalism "could grow and flourish side by side in the same soil" and charged that they were at odds, if not at war.[21] Addressing the inherent contradiction in capitalistic societies between the egalitarian imperative embedded in democratic nations and their economic inequalities, he suggested that only equal entitlement to universal rights, including fair and equal access to civil, political, and social rights, gave substance to citizenship. Social rights were the key to the limitation of capitalistic market forces, a democratization process he called "class abasement." To resist the classist dynamics of free-market societies, a social citizenship had to include a set of "universal rights," "from the right to a modicum of economic welfare and security to the right to share to the full in the social heritage and to live the life of a civilized being according to the standards prevailing in the society."[22]

Marshall piercingly pointed to the income gap, for it undermined democratic principles. Structural economic inequalities and citizenship were at odds, he suggested, and modern democracies should move beyond individualistic "civil rights." Presaging the PPC's main argument, Marshall argued that material inequalities subverted free and equal deliberation. Therefore, an equal capacity for political action entailed a substantial equality of result and stood as a precondition for a truly democratic process.[23] King too asserted that citizens should claim political but also economic and social rights to substantiate a civic identity undermined by their ascriptive economic and racial status. Hard-won social rights could make consequential indents in unequal capitalistic systems, modify their core meaning, and shape a new class system with new inequalities. "Anticipating Rawls," Pateman observed, Marshall nailed the "significant difference between the new social divisions and the old social class system, with its hereditary privileges" and hypothesized that "the new inequalities could be seen to have a legitimate basis and were in accord with social justice."[24]

The Poor People's Campaign was less about political rights than about economic justice, which entailed a similar reframing of the notion of citizenship. It indeed articulated its proposals in terms of social citizenship, whereby welfare benefits and income were legitimate rights. But whereas Marshall's principles fit the framework of a traditional liberal democracy, favoring "equality of status" over equality of outcome, King orchestrated the PPC out of distrust and disappointment. His faith in the American promise of equal opportunity had always been tempered by his belief that untrammeled free-market capitalism was inductive of poverty and inequality, hollowing out the democratic premise of equal citizenship. However, he renounced anchoring black emancipation and full citizenship rights for African Americans in American ideals and Constitutional principles unless the latter were amended and the structures of the country revised. The Poor People's Campaign precisely pointed to the shortcomings of the liberal definition of citizenship because, to use Abernathy's words, "there is no constitutional right not to starve."

> It is a constitutional right for a man to be able to vote, but the human right to a decent house is a categorically imperative and morally absolute as was that constitutional right. It is not a constitutional right that men have jobs, but it is a human right.[25]

King never forcefully settled for a strong centralized state, rather endorsing a Jeffersonian-inspired democracy, but he nevertheless advocated for an intensively active social-democratic state "in which all of the citizenry could enjoy the full benefits of their God-given freedom."[26] He hoped that the Poor People's Campaign would bring about a truly redistributive federal government dedicated to simultaneously enforcing civil, social, and economic rights:

> As important as it is to improve the economic plight of the city dweller, we must not ignore that the struggle for equality is also a moral and political act. The aim is not only to improve the economic situation of the poor, but to provide the conditions for dignity and the exercise of rights. Economic improvement despite its importance, without full citizenship rights can be a bribe to the excluded rather than a gateway to the free society.[27]

The campaign not only related the plight of the American poor to the question of human rights but it gave new objectives to the unfinished "rights revolution" at home, asserting that there is no citizenship without income. Compellingly so, a recent resurgence of claims for universal income and economic rights has shaped philosophical economic and political debates.[28] Public intellectuals have given cogent arguments in support of an institutional restructuring toward social rights and more broadly, toward substantive justice and equality. The interrelatedness between citizenship and income was for instance explored in political scientist Judith Shklar's work, which somewhat elaborated a philosophical foundation—if not a validation—for an Economic Bill of Rights. In her 1989 Tanner Lecture, "American Citizenship: The Quest for Inclusion," Shklar traced the genealogy of an American citizenship deeply molded by slavery. She shrewdly pointed out that, given the tormented history of labor in America, "earning is implicit in equal American citizenship." Applying somewhat Marshall's concepts, by endorsing his claim that capitalistic democracy was inherently at war with itself, Shklar relocated his concept of "social citizenship" in ways that sustain King's egalitarian and reformist insights. Earnings, in the sense of paid work, has been sine qua non prerequisite for citizenship. "We are citizens only if we 'earn,'" she argued. She traced back the implications of this equation to the early American Republic:

> The individual American citizen is in fact a member of two interlocking public orders, one egalitarian, the other entirely un-equal. To be a recognized and active citizen at all he must be an equal member of the polity, a voter, but he must also be independent, which has all along meant that he must be an "earner" a free remunerated worker, one who is rewarded for the actual work he has done, neither more nor less. He cannot be a slave or an aristocrat.[29]

If first-class citizenship is predicated on a gainful job, every American should be granted "a right to remunerated work."[30] Debating whether such a right is constitutional or metaphorical misses the point, she claimed. Only a proactive egalitarian public policy could substantiate this right to full citizenship: "Instead of thinking about rights at all, one should think in terms of general policies designed to eliminate unemployment and to raise the standard of living of the poor."[31]

If Shklar declined to endorse an Economic Bill of Rights, she nevertheless couched American citizenship in terms of unalienable social rights, starting with the right to a status-inducing job. Not every job is equally rewarding and accessible. Lack of opportunity to earn is as problematic as a low-paying job. Quoting William Julius Wilson, she recommended that public jobs be generated in ways that structural unemployment in isolated areas be addressed: "the minimal political obligation must be the creation of paying jobs geographically close to the unemployed and offering them a legally set minimum wage and the chance of advancement."[32]

Without uttering the word, she hinted at the guaranteed income idea. She also came to the understanding that an inclusive American citizenship entailed reforming the liberal doctrine. To concede a "right to earn" on the ground that it constitutes one's citizenship suggests that formal political right, such as civil rights, are nullified absent economic self-sufficiency and the social standing attached to income.

For King as well as for Shklar, whatever the means to achieve citizenship as equality, the overarching purpose is to accomplish justice.

SPHERES OF JUSTICE

John Rawls's *Theory of Justice* was published only three years after the Poor People's Campaign and has since been regarded as the greatest work of contemporary political philosophy. A witness to the civil rights movement and a theorist of civil disobedience, equality and liberalism, Rawls defended a new liberalism framed around the principle that a just society should be designed to improve the lot of its least fortunate members. Justice, he claimed, was to be the overarching purpose of an ideal well-ordered society. With Rawls, the least advantaged—epitomized by the poor—was the stepping-stone upon which democratic institutions shall be built. Interestingly enough, Rawls was defining his notorious "difference principle" for the first time as Resurrection City was dramatizing poverty and while the campaigners were demanding an Economic Bill of Rights. If Rawls elaborated a social justice theory beyond the basic liberal creed of equal opportunity, his position with regard to social citizenship is still under interrogation. Nevertheless, his theorization of "justice as fairness" echoes King's call for "substantive equality" and his premium on equality versus inequality in relation to equal citizenship resonates compellingly with the ideas raised by the Poor People's Campaign.

In a classic liberal framework, Rawls revisited the contractarian premises of modern democratic societies and imagined how the ideal democratic society could be elaborated. Asserting that justice was the core value to be translated into forthcoming institutions, he theorized about an "original position" where a member of the parties about to design their political order ignored "his place in society, his class position or social status; nor does he know his fortune in the distribution of natural assets and abilities, his intelligence and strength, and the like. Nor, again does anyone know his conception of the good, the particulars of his rational plan of life, or even the special features of his psychology."[33] Behind this "veil of ignorance," each person would freely, rationally, and ultimately fairly decide which principles should prevail, in accordance with the justice requirement. Behind the veil, people's choice would be insulated from personal prejudice. Thus, the social order to be established through the upheld institutions should preserve freedom while favoring justice.

Rawls's *Theory of Justice* attempted to reconcile the liberal framework of free-market societies with the moral imperative of equality and justice. Citizens should possess a fair share of primary social goods, including wealth, basic liberties, and equal opportunities. Rawls clearly contended that only a society inherently concerned with "the least of these" was satisfactory with respect to democratic requirements but also sustainable. His *Theory of Justice* suggested the degree to which pursuit of profit and growth without justice, cooperation, and reciprocity had become an exhausted endeavor. To some extent, Rawls put forth a secular version of the Poor People's Campaign concerns. But for Rawls, freedom supersedes equality. To him, basic liberties are sacred and cannot be curtailed whatsoever, even for the sake of economic equality.[34] Nevertheless, if the first principle of a just society—"the principle of greatest equal liberty"—posited that "each person is to have an equal right to the most extensive total system of equal basic liberties compatible with a similar system of liberty for all," the second postulated that "social and economic inequalities are to be arranged so that they are both to the greatest benefit of the least advantaged, consistent with the just savings principle, and attached to offices and positions open to all under conditions of fair equality of opportunity."[35] In other words, for Rawls the realization of justice is the paramount purpose for which to determine the institutions and rules that are to govern the upcoming society.

Rawls, also a proponent of civil disobedience, sounded like an ardent defender of civil rights and egalitarian liberal democracy. He further contended that "no person can have self-respect as a free and equal citizen if they are subject to coercive public power due to their inferior social or public status."[36] He also seemed to favor an extensive interpretation of "rights." In his framework, a bill of rights stands as the fundamental guarantee to substantive citizenship, which implied much more than the right to vote. An equal citizenship entailed not only that citizens have equal basic rights but also that they are endowed with a sense of self-respect, reflected by the public recognition of their worth and social standing.[37] This principle spoke directly to the insurgent poor people of 1968, notably the welfare rights activists, who demanded to be granted their dignity and social worth. A consensual agreement on the difference principle and on each person's equal citizenship was therefore an absolute prerequisite.[38]

If self-respect is the most important primary social good an equal citizen is entitled to, economic security and material standing accounted for citizenship. Echoing Roosevelt's and King's Economic Bill of Rights, Rawls pointed to "the basic wants of individuals," which would undermine one's citizenship if not fulfilled. Some have argued that it would not be unsound to speculate that Rawls stood in defense of a minimum guaranteed income.[39] Tommie Shelby professed that Rawls intended to implement a truly egalitarian society that would surpass the capitalistic welfare state, which hardly scratched the surface of entrenched inequities.[40]

The question though of whether Rawls defended the constitutionalizing of social and economic rights remains unresolved.[41] As Chris Armstrong compellingly showed, Rawls, in the footsteps of Marshall, "tried to integrate a concern for economic equality into the framework of liberal citizenship."[42] Arguably, Rawls claimed that the position defined by one's place in the distribution of income and wealth was as instrumental to assessing the justice of a social system as her position of equal citizenship.[43] He also pointed to the relevance of the notion of fraternity in the democratic interpretation of the two principles. His framework was supportive of a redistributive society and outlined the social democratic vision of an ideal polity chiefly concerned about the fairness of the consequences of income distribution. Individuals' relative place in the distribution of income and wealth would determine the extent to which they could benefit from an unequal distribution of assets and resources. In *Political Liberalism,* Rawls clarified the centrality of economic security for a fair democratic deliberation:

> the first principle covering the equal basic rights and liberties may easily be preceded by a lexically prior principle requiring that citizens' basic needs be met, at least insofar as their being met is necessary for citizens to understand and to be able fruitfully to exercise those rights and liberties. Certainly any such principle must be assumed in applying the first principle.[44]

Nonetheless, he took issue with the kind of welfare-state political economy the PPC called for, dismissing welfare rights and cash transfer. He seemed to reject the very idea of universal entitlement to social and economic rights, whatever the weight of income over one's social status. He attempted to overcome the dichotomy between capitalism and collectivism, preferring the ideal system where ownership *ex ante,* not redistribution *ex post* would prevail. Whatever the interpretations of the scope of the "difference principle" or of his concept of "justice as fairness" as a whole, he favored a "property-owning democracy," which fell in squarely with an Economic Bill of Rights.[45]

Likewise, Rawls's wholehearted faith in liberalism and in the genuine moral commitment of individuals in terms of racial equality attracted the same criticism as was leveled at Myrdal's. As a Baptist, King himself was deeply convinced that the sinfulness of men was an anthropological trait and that only through education and the enforcement of the law could it be uprooted.

The 1968 campaigners were never content despite benevolent if noncommittal support from agencies and liberal officials. They doubted the full compliance of Americans of good will with their professed egalitarian creed. Accordingly, the tone of the late King is at odds with Rawls's idealism. Robert Michael Franklin guessed that "Rawls would, no doubt, press King to be realistic and cautious about the extent to which the state can affect how persons, unequal in many regards, freely use and misuse their distributions to create even worse inequalities. Equality of opportunity can be effectively guaranteed by government action, but equality of outcome is an exceedingly unwieldy, perhaps impossible, end-state to guarantee in a democratic society."[46] Franklin also compellingly estimated that King would dissent from Rawls's moderation, pointing to Rawls's unqualified faith in the "rational, detached, autonomous and fully formed persons behind the veil," instead of deploring that "the principles of justice selected in the original position offer little hope of significant structural change."[47] Rawls's work, however, vindicated the Poor People's Campaign's argument on the centrality of wealth inequality in any reflection on justice and citizenship. Both defended a conception of justice blending freedom, nonviolence, and substantive equality.[48] Rawls offered a strong answer to the main plea made by the campaign: he suggested a society of mutual interdependence where no one would be oblivious to the plight of the dispossessed.

Nevertheless, another question unsettled Rawls's readers, who wondered about the extent to which his principles bore on race.[49] The sparsity of Rawls's comments on race-related issues struck many critics, who contended that his color-blind "eyes wide shut" paradigm was profoundly defective.[50] Among those who articulated the harshest rebuke of the philosopher, critical race scholar Charles Mills stands out. He has lambasted classic liberalism for its entrenched bias toward people of color and castigated Rawls for silencing it. He incriminated the philosopher for he "had next to nothing to say in his work about what has arguably historically been the most blatant American variety of injustice, racial oppression" and for ignoring "remediation of the legacy of white supremacy."[51] Mills claimed that Rawls hardly challenged the fact that, within the liberal framework he endorsed, nonwhites have been historically fashioned as unworthy of equal justice, subpersons unfit for citizenship. He further prosecuted Rawls's silence on the racial order which resulted from implementation of classical liberalism as reflective of his *white* perspective.[52] Along the same lines, some regretted that Rawls shielded the Constitution from any accusations of inadequacy with regard to racial justice and that he made no specific or explicit reference to any antidiscrimination principle in the basic structure of a well-ordered and just society and limited his corrective apparatus to the uniformity of rights.[53]

Rawls has made clear that he was not concerned with nonideal situations, where racial injustice did occur. His principle of equal citizenship entailed that people's class position—not their race—determined their status. He presumed that as racism would be unanimously resented, no specific qualification to the general principle should be adopted. In accord with Myrdal, Rawls took for granted that Americans care about their egalitarian conviction to the point where they believe that racial discrimination is reprehensible. His liberal conception of justice, "fairness," stemmed from the assumption that the moral convictions of the parties were foundational and non-negotiable once upheld—among them, the shared belief that everyone was a person of equal respect, regardless of race. Both the constitutional architecture and the "background culture" which sustained the newly defined social contract should reflect an inclusive understanding of full citizenship.

Shelby observed that Rawls hinted at the possibility of racial discrimination and took as self-evident that "in a democratic constitutional regime, such treatment would be ruled out by the requirements of equal citizenship," reaffirming that "racial discrimination is incompatible with justice as fairness."[54] Besides, Shelby pointed to the universality of Rawls's general principles, ahistorical and nonspecific. In such a framework, race is irrelevant. Many scholars argued, however, that Rawls neglected non-ideal situations, which lead him to contradict his egalitarian plea. Moreover, through his silence on the combustible issue of affirmative action policies, he seems to reject any form of compensatory justice based on past wrongs. Systemic racial discrimination, inherited from the past, has nevertheless proven to be active in the perpetuation of blacks' disadvantage, violating the principle of fair opportunity. The legacy of past discriminations might therefore require corrective justice and reparative treatment such as those demanded by the several ethnic groups of the Poor People's Campaign.

Myrdal and Rawls, as well as the vast majority of liberals, stuck to their unflinching refusal to envision preferential treatments for blacks, but such was not the case for King. He was a universalist and a humanist who nevertheless had come to understand the limitations of American liberalism. For all the needed interracial solidarity and the social-democratic framework he envisioned, class could not and must not eclipse race as an explanation of wealth inequality. He called for a race-conscious remediation:

> Special measures for the deprived have always been accepted in principle by the United States. . . . Throughout history we have adhered to this principle. It was the principle behind land grants to farmers who fought in the

Revolutionary Army. It was inherent in the establishment of child labor laws, social security, unemployment compensation, manpower retraining programs and countless other measures that the nation accepted as logical and moral. During World War II, our fighting men were deprived of certain advantages and opportunities. To make up for this, they were given a package of veterans rights, significantly called a "Bill of Rights." . . . In this way, the nation was compensating the veteran for his time lost, in school or in his career or in business. Such compensatory treatment was approved by the majority of Americans. Certainly the Negro has been deprived. . . . This [law] should be made to apply for American Negroes. The payment should be in the form of a massive program by the government of special, compensatory measures which could be regarded as a settlement in accordance with the accepted practice of common law.[55]

That Rawls defended a nonhistoricized difference principle implied that the question of rectificatory justice stood outside the purview of his concern.[56] We might deplore his framework. But, from a philosophical standpoint, his hypothetical consensual contract was not supposed to be relevant to the realm of public policies. Besides, as Brandon Terry rightly observed, the philosopher purposely challenged his readers by insulating them from deflecting contemporary controversies. "The refusal to invoke race or racial incidents," Terry contended, "may be more profitably understood as his attempt, perhaps in the end misguided, to remove his audience in the early 1970s from the cacophony of battle and all the contingencies of history that often dominate immediate perceptions."[57]

Moreover, Rawls eventually addressed his omissions. In *Justice as Fairness,* he attempted to assuage readers who might have wondered about his eloquent silence on race in a period infused with it. His explanation validated Shelby's explanations:

It is natural to ask: Why are distinctions of race and gender not explicitly included among the three contingencies noted earlier? How can one ignore such historical facts as slavery (in the antebellum South) and the inequalities between men and women resulting from the absence of provisions to make good women's extra burden in the bearing, raising, and educating of children so as to secure their fair equality of opportunity.[58]

In his 2001 reassessment of his 1996 book, he goes on to acknowledge that "Justice as Fairness and any liberal conception of justice would be seriously defective should they lack the resources to articulate the political values essential to justify the legal and social institutions needed to secure the equality of women and minorities."[59] This statement echoes King's profound qualifications with regard to liberals' commitment to substantive justice.

FOR A "TRULY LIBERAL" LIBERALISM

One of the main arguments raised by detractors of the Poor People's Campaign pointed to its unwillingness to follow the liberal course of the civil rights conversation, resorting instead to disruption and radical demands for wealth redistribution. From Douglass to Du Bois and King, the word "radical" has carried a substantial democratic meaning in black American political thought. As Nicholas Bromell has demonstrated, the black thinkers' objective was perhaps not to overthrow the U.S. constitutional democracy, or its political culture and practices, but to *radically* reinterpret them "to shift the conversation of U.S. politics onto new ground."[60] Liberalism, a sociopolitical custom that had enforced injustice and wealth inequalities, was subsequently to be *radically* redefined.

The Poor People's Campaign exposed the fault lines within the former liberal coalition and dismissed the transactional framework of mainline civil rights leaders. Until his last days, he bemoaned the stubborn prejudice of ordinary whites toward blacks. To a degree, he died disillusioned with white America, including liberals.

Such a dissenting position remains in the optic African Americans have historically endorsed.[61] Their strong egalitarian plea and their communal tradition never exactly fit the liberal framework, so much so that, according to Michael Dawson, "we cannot view black political thought as fully situated within American liberalism."[62] A high point of black political thought, the Poor People's Campaign embodied the vexed relation between discriminated groups and an evolving American liberalism whose definition has been also contingent on historical periods.

Although they have "strained at the boundaries of the American creed," black Americans have indeed redefined a natural rights liberalism and affirmed a vision of justice deeply rooted in American principles and its fundamentals on political freedom and equality before the law.[63] King probably would have concurred with Ralph Bunche, instrumental to Myrdal's research, that "the objectives which minority groups traditionally struggle for are the tenets of social justice embraced by 18th century liberalism, with its democratic creed of liberty, equality and fraternity."[64] True, such equalitarian conceptions of American liberalism remained an inspiring ideal. To Frederick Douglass and W. E. B. Du Bois, the liberal American tradition was mostly an aspirational spiritual emancipation. Yet Du Bois clearly warned about a misconstrued understanding of the significance of "liberalism" because it meant not "to concentrate on economic well-being and forget freedom and manhood and equality."[65]

But the racialization of citizenship in the American Republic—"the price for diluting antebellum class antagonism," explains Antoine Joseph— was reconciled with the doctrine of classical liberalism, which also decoupled political, social, and economic rights.[66] By the time of Reconstruction, liberals had obviously failed to sustain a commitment to equal citizenship for black people. King, following after Thoreau and Du Bois, perceived that the American Republic's liberalism was troublesome because the racial order defined its politics and social relations. To Du Bois, liberalism meant "self-ownership," not a vague promise of inclusion. African Americans' "double-consciousness" arise from the blatantly contradictory claims of race and rights.

In the broad scope of the postwar era, "liberal" became an adjective attached to "consensus." It referred to a system of democratic governance trying to strike a bipartisan balance between the pursuit of free-market growth and its citizens' welfare, while abstaining from addressing the structural causes of unequal opportunities. Liberals were quick to adopt a behavioral framework, pointing to individual deviances to explain poverty, thus exonerating the American democracy as a system from any responsibility.[67] The "racial liberalism" that prevailed then was defined by Lani Guinier as a system of thought which "emphasized the corrosive effect of individual prejudice and the importance of interracial contact in promoting tolerance" while securing "white middle-class sympathy."[68] Reasoning that the great racial divide plaguing the nation was mainly an issue of individual prejudice, racial liberalism was thus unable and unwilling to envision the structural reforms which many black activists knew to be indispensable. With such a framework in place, liberals who dominated the racial conversation in the aftermath of *Brown v. Board of Education* "redefined equality not as a fair and just distribution of resources but as the absence of formal, legal barriers that separated the races."[69]

Although civil rights had become a central plank of the liberal "consensus," the democratic-liberal American ideology enshrined private property, opposed a strong central state, and claimed the autonomy of the individual. Each of these core principles has been at odds with a black experience of systemic failure to provide *fair* equality of opportunity to African Americans. To silence their distrust, the ideological opposition to Communism which unraveled abroad and at home required that the civil rights movement fully endorse the anticommunist rhetoric including supporting free-market economy and imperialism.[70] To a degree, domestic racial progress was thought to be Cold War policy.[71] Black radicals had to sweeten their severe critique of the American political economy with an apparent deference to American principles. Many, including Du Bois and King, were recalcitrant and refused the trade-off.[72]

As King and radical black leaders saw it, white liberals failed to address the unequal distribution of power and resources that had perpetuated blacks' subordination long before 1965. For all the support antidiscrimination legislation had garnered, middle-of-the-road liberals declined to reform the institutions which bred the bleak economic and social situations they endured. As early as 1966, King had parted ways with Bayard Rustin and many black liberals who were still hoping to craft a new political landscape, which they understood as a "realignment" of the Democratic Party with leftist groups. The price to pay was not only to repudiate Black Power radicals (which King refused to do) but to reject any act of disruption on the streets, reasoning that only a broad New Deal-like coalition of civil rights sympathizers would be effective. King declined the Faustian bargain.

Moreover, he neither believed in the ability of capitalism to fairly spread affluence nor in the deep commitment of liberals to economic justice and racial equality in absence of massive social mobilization. In his annual update on civil rights for *The Nation* magazine in 1966, King deplored the "hardening of opposition to the satisfaction of Negro[s]" that should "be anticipated as the movement presses against financial privilege. . . . Conflicts are unavoidable because a stage has been reached in which the reality of equality will require extensive adjustments in the way of life for some of the white majority."[73]

When Northern liberals proved obviously reluctant to integrate their neighborhoods and to address race in terms of economic inequality, the "liberal consensus" was exposed as a myth.[74] King confessed his delusion with white liberals:

> There is not even a common language when the term "equality" is used. Negro and white have a fundamentally different definition. Negroes have proceeded from a premise that equality means what it says and they have taken white Americans at their word when they talked of it as an objective. But most whites in America in 1967, including many persons of goodwill, proceed from a premise that equality is a loose expression for improvement. White America is not even psychologically organized to close the gap— essentially it seeks only to make it less painful and less obvious but in most respects to retain it. Most of the abrasions between Negros and white Liberals arise from this fact.[75]

King's distrust was affirmed, first and foremost, by Congress' gutting of the War on Poverty under the Johnson administration despite the agitation of progressive black insiders. For instance, in 1965, as a firsthand witness to the Watts riots, Democratic congressman from California Augustus F. Hawkins publicly voiced his concerns over the inability of War on Poverty programs to truly empower the poor and to come to terms with the ravages of joblessness. King could not agree more and expressed his "wholehearted" support for Hawkins's dissenting views. Indeed, the total antipoverty budget would not go significantly above $2 billion a year after 1966. Although the national unemployment rate decreased significantly with the War in Vietnam, it was still about twice as much for blacks (8 percent versus 3.7 percent for all Americans). In a private letter to Hawkins, King expressed hope, too, that America would, at last, understand "the economic shipwreck" in which the American poor were forced to live.[76]

"There is a pressing need for a liberalism in the North that is truly liberal," King charged, witnessing former allies' faint-heartedness.[77] He also doubted that "opportunities" and mere "rights" would mean anything as long as racial discrimination and predatory capitalism would underlie the country's refusal to address poverty. In late 1967, Representative John Conyers Jr. of Michigan introduced the Full Opportunity Act, a $30 billion aid program which included items that provided for an income maintenance program, a raise of the minimum wage, a guaranteed employment agency in the Labor Department, a college loan program, a massive low-income housing plan, and better enforcement of equal opportunity legislation. His bill would also provide three million jobs for the unemployed, mostly in inner cities. His bill was indeed designed to aid the ghettos:

> The only way we can deal with the staggering problems of Negro Americans and other disadvantaged groups is through comprehensive and massive programs . . . it is obvious that patchwork legislation is totally outdated. There are many fine programs in existence, but due to their inadequate funding and scope they don't even begin to answer the needs of millions of American people. . . . The Full Opportunity Act attempts to deal with all the interrelated problems of the poverty and degradation of life in the ghettoes by assuring every American a full opportunity to have adequate employment, income, housing and education, free of any trace of racial discrimination.[78]

The bill was said by King to come "close to what we're talking about" but yet again garnered little support in Congress.[79] In stark contrast with Rustin, King resented liberals' unwillingness to target the economic inequality wrought by decades of systemic racism and their reliance on a "culture of poverty" rhetoric which allowed for liberalism to hinder, through its dismissal of redistributive social welfare programs, any real leap toward a more equitable and fair nation. The Poor People's Campaign sought to oppose postwar liberals' assumption that divorcing class from race and shifting away from class-based issues would not undermine civil rights progress.[80]

Many participants pointed to the white "backlash" which had been developing to explain the disappointing outcome of the Poor People's Campaign, and this claim is consistent with recent scholarship.[81] King himself used this abrasive term and worried about conservatives' efforts to denigrate the politics of inclusive democracy after 1965, which fostered a climate in which African Americans felt more and more alienated from American political life and distrustful of American institutions.[82] Michael

Harrington was emphatic that the root problem was that "America knows how to abolish poverty but doesn't want to do it." If, in a social-democrat framework, King pointed to affluent whites' reluctance to share wealth and power with dispossessed groups as the major hindrance to real equality, he also pointed to the intractability of American racism:

> Yet the largest portion of white America is still poisoned by racism which is as native to our soil as pine trees, sagebrush and buffalo grass. Equally native to us is the concept that gross exploitation of the Negro is acceptable, if not commendable. Many whites who concede that Negroes should have equal access to public facilities and the untrammeled right to vote cannot understand that we do not intend to remain in the basement of the economic structure.[83]

By 1968, the New Deal coalition was nothing but a relic from the past, and the transformative aspiration of liberalism had surrendered to white resentment and racial fatigue. The liberal coalition was far from being unanimously committed to racial progress, and Northern urban whites, the backbone of the liberal consensus, had relentlessly resisted racial equality.[84] The Poor People's Campaign, notably its welfare rights activists and Black Power groups also took aim at liberals' increasingly punitive approach to urban disadvantage and their cultural explanation for poverty.

An activist, PPC organizer and SCLC staff member, Tom Kahn reflected that the campaign urged liberal America to see the off-putting spectacle of dire poverty and racism and to be confronted with its contradictions:

> The affluent majority, once shown the face of poverty, can react in alternative ways . . . while one approach to the problem is to work for guaranteed jobs and income, another is to conclude from recent events that the poor are their own worst enemy, and that they must be repressed into respect for the law and order.[85]

Because racism was neither a matter of psychology nor a question of an American creed to be unleashed, liberalism was deeply flawed. It relied on the assumption that individuals not structures were to be fixed. Its defenders exonerated it from its collusion with capitalism, oppression, and imperialism. The "political framework of liberalism," Sheth Falguni observed, "which promises equality and universal protection for 'all,' depends on people to *believe* those promises, so that racial discrimination, brutality, violence, dehumanization, can be written off as accidental . . . rather than part of the deep structure of liberalism."[86] Indeed, as King saw during his lifetime, theoretical liberalism did not translate into a truly egalitarian politics, which explained the deterioration of King's faith in the American liberal tradition.

Conclusion

The memory of King's clarion call for economic equality through interracial camaraderie, embodied by the Poor People's Campaign, quickly faded away. To keep the consensual image of the prophet untarnished, the campaign was decoupled from its instigator. If historians have recently recaptured King's defense of unionization, his commitment to economic justice and human rights, his radical indictment of America's sins, the Poor People's Campaign has not received its deserved attention. The sorry closing of Resurrection City belied the campaigners' accomplishments. Although far from what was expected, their lobbying efforts were not negligible: food programs in 1,000 of the neediest counties in the nation, expansion of the school lunch program, agreement by the Department of Labor to create 100,000 jobs by December, the hiring of 1,300 people in 33 states' employment agencies, the agreement from the Justice Department to enforce rules against using "green card" farmworkers as strike breakers, and an Interior Department agreement to develop community control in Native American programs.[1]

As the first massive interracial protest on behalf of the poor to demand social welfare policies, minorities rights, redistribution of wealth, and anti-imperialist internationalism, the Poor People's Campaign's nature and aim were far larger than suggested by the few muddy square miles on which the campaign was staged. As miners' canaries, the residents of Resurrection City warned the nation about the subterranean tremors announcing the plague of inequality. "Right here in America," King warned, "one-tenth of one percent of the population controls almost 50 percent of the wealth. Some changes must take place here."[2] His jeremiad was hardly heard.

Notwithstanding the academic insights sketched out in this book, the current situation for the poor in America, the inextricable entanglement of race and class dynamics currently at play, and the dramatically rising tide of wealth inequality of the past decades bitterly vindicate the analysis and indignation of the 1968 poor campaigners. Tellingly, in an unexpected editorial in the *New York Times* entitled "How Dr. King Shaped My Work in Economics," Nobel Prize recipient Joseph Stiglitz paid homage to the black leader, writing that King's inspirational dedication to economic justice molded his own scholarship and politics. An economist committed to closing the gap between the haves and the haves-not, Stiglitz reminded his readers that, ahead of his time, King "was right to recognize that these persistent divides are a cancer in our society, undermining our democracy and weakening our economy."[3]

The alarming reality is that, in light of all the empirical data on poverty, inequality, and race available today, the campaigners are still right. Such clairvoyance is likely to explain the suppression of the Poor People's Campaign from the mainstream narrative of the civil rights movement. The latter has concentrated on the achievement of basic citizenship rights, "extolling the resilience of democratic liberalism."[4] Dismissed as a "failure," the Poor People's Campaign contradicts the tale of civic reconciliation, which had to be a triumphant episode. While the campaign demanded something that was beyond an abstract political-rights discourse, the nation complacently embraced the belief that it had reached a post–civil rights era. To compound the problem, King was in the process of becoming a national icon, joining the pantheon of white men who made the country great and good. Fitting the "romantic genre"[5] which tended to permeate the civil rights narrative, the Washington Mall had to remain a site of memory, celebrating the nation's atonement of the 1963 March on Washington.[6]

To cast doubt on the validity of the lingering protest coming from minority groups, the year of 1968 has been portrayed as a period of chaos, public disorder, and violence. Misleadingly, the complex dialectic of race and class that the campaign put forth has been erased. It contradicted the emerging argument about the demise of civil rights activism due to its derailment into "identity politics" and nationalism. The Black Panthers and the New Left were vilified and delinked from the civil rights movement. The Chicano movement was seen as a peripheral, southwestern phenomenon.[7] The welfare rights movement fell victim to the anti-redistribution backlash of the Nixon era and to the swelling contempt for poor single mothers of color. Policing blacks, the poor, and the insurgents on cultural grounds came to constitute the chief public policy for it was averred that they, not the unfulfilled promise of equality, were to blame for the unfinished Second Reconstruction.

Philosopher Richard Rorty's *Achieving Our Country* captured this convenient rhetoric.[8] The progressive trend which emerged after 1965 would have "permitted cultural politics to supplant real politics" and would have neglected the "declining economic condition of American workers," he wrote. Rorty was joined by sociologist and former activist Todd Gitlin in deriding the activists of the late 1960s, who had purportedly pitted social justice against economic justice and spurred the demise of a fractured Left.[9] Rorty and Gitlin echoed the neoconservatives of the late 1960s, who incriminated minority groups for their exaggerated "cultural demands," which were said to have torpedoed an inclusive political and social framework. Twisting the argument, neoconservatives blamed the white backlash on their never-ending cultural demands. Aggrieved liberals specifically lambasted the Black Power movement with its focus on reclaiming black cultural power and self-determination and wished the disadvantaged had not turned away from "universal" economic issues. Worse yet, truncating the late civil rights struggle, they misrepresented 1968 as the year of cultural nationalism and a race-centered approach to equality, opportunistically ignoring the Poor People's Campaign. The latter indeed contradicts their framing of the late 1960s as the unfortunate divorce of racial disparities from economic inequality. Ironically enough, upon launching the campaign, King was asked whether he remained true to his Christian roots while engaging into "radical class politics."[10] At the same time, liberals' "race-neutral" calls for economic reform—rolling back the tide of the Great Society's egalitarian policies—thwarted any possibility of achieving equality and justice for the poor.[11] Daniel Patrick Moynihan, once a champion of redistribution and economic justice, frequently contributed to antiwelfare publications in the 1980s, endorsing their "color-blind" defense of individual merit. He embodied many liberals' *volte-face.*

Failing to grasp that the ending of legalized discrimination did not adequately address the poverty that was more than ever pervasive in African American communities, the prosecutors of "identity politics" overlooked the long history of cultural-pride assertions and demand for recognition.[12]

At odds with mainstream wisdom, Resurrection City was in fact illustrative of the nurturing relationship between race-based and class-based politics. During the campaign, Corky Gonzales's "Plan Del Barrio" blended cultural Chicano nationalism with the assertion of a common economic fate with urban blacks. A blueprint for the campaign's *doleances,* the document pointed to the inclusive tax reform issue, pleading that "all citizens of this country share in the wealth of this nation by institution of economic reforms that would provide for all people, and that welfare in the form of subsidies in taxes and pay-off to corporate owners be reverted to the people who in reality are the foundation of the economy and the tax base for this society."[13] In Resurrection City and in Chicago, assertions of cultural pride and class-based struggle were dynamically entwined, providing a significant example of universal identity politics, which neither restricted the civil right movement to class-based issues nor derailed it into narrow group politics. Jesse Jackson reasoned that, as an enactment of solidarity, the campaign was an idea capable of disentangling the language of poverty from race:

> In our wallowing together in the mud of Resurrection City . . . we were allowed to hear, to feel and to see each other for the first time in our American experience. This vast task of acculturation of pulling the poor together as a way of amassing economic, political, and labor power, was the great vision of Dr. King. . . . History is on our side. . . . Resurrection City cannot be seen as a mudhole in Washington, but it is rather an idea unleashed in history.[14]

King's interracial Poor People's Campaign offered an alternative to the facile dichotomy between social and economic justice. It was an attempt to anchor poverty in the realm of universalism *and* a demand for cultural recognition. It was race- and ethnic-conscious *as well as* class-conscious. It refused to choose between economic equality and specific antidiscrimination demands. The poor insurgents declined to de-emphasize what was distinctive about their cultural identification and yet advocated interracial solidarity. They challenged a nation for its lack of structural answers to their debasement and their undemocratic disempowerment and yet, reclaimed their full citizenship. Such an interwoven and self-reinforcing position should serve, they believed, as a vessel for democratic egalitarian politics. They could not have been further removed from a narrow-minded "identity politics" framework. Their strategy was not farfetched, although perhaps quixotic.

As philosopher Nancy Fraser convincingly contended, a true emancipation required both redistribution and recognition. She denounced the false dichotomy between class-oriented politics such as the New Deal and difference-oriented ones such as civil rights. Taking issue with Rorty's analysis, she offered a compelling synthesis that validated the campaign:

> overcoming class injustice may well require joining a politics of recognition to a politics of redistribution. At the very least, it will be necessary to attend carefully to the recognition dynamics of class struggles in order to prevent these from generating injustices of misrecognition in the process of seeking to remedy injustice of maldistribution.[15]

An Economic Bill of Rights for the Disadvantaged was nothing if not compatible with a "politics of difference" insofar as they both pertain to the recognition and dignity of the marginalized. Economic exploitation had to be viewed through the lens of racism and vice versa. While in Memphis, among the sanitation workers whose basic rights had been denied, King repeated that "all labor had dignity." Because they have been the derivative victims of the nation's history of systemic injustice, the non-black dispossessed were allies. The Poor People's Campaign was a claim for the recognition of all poor people's dignity, with or without a job, welfare recipient or not, white or not. Its main purpose was for the American poor to be seen and recognized because misrecognition and obliviousness had deprived them of their basic right, a right to their dignity. The latter involved also that their cultural specificities be deemed worthy. Economic justice and cultural fairness had to be articulated, for the confluence of race and class has shaped American inequality.

The equal dignity of all citizens, regardless of their class, gender and race, is premised on a universal and egalitarian tenet but, as philosopher Charles Taylor demonstrated, "it asks we give acknowledgment and status to something that is not universal shared." If "a liberal society must give *these* rights equally to all . . . it can nevertheless provide some with 'privileges and immunities' provided to certain groups that are less fundamental."[16] Taylor's words capture what King had in mind when he suggested special compensation for black Americans, a specific Marshall plan within a universal redistributive policy.[17] To compensate for centuries of unpaid wages and exploitation of black labor, he contended, the government had to adopt the Bill of Rights for the Disadvantaged, which could remedy past injustices, including those concomitantly inflicted upon poor whites, Native Americans, and Mexican Americans.[18]

We can only speculate but it is not unreasonable to wonder about the shape of contemporary America had the campaign been considered in a different light by the nation. It can be argued that the inability to forge a political movement that is as much about class as race and gender rights could have been precluded. Moreover, had its class-based pan-racial demands been heard, the welfare backlash and the fragmentation of progressive coalitions along racial and gender lines would perhaps have been deflected. Lastly, had King's more radical and dialectical grasp of the nexus of class inequality in a racialized democracy been considered, the political splintering of the working class along racial lines could, perhaps, have been prevented.[19]

Fifty years after his death, King's revolutionary intuition that a highly redistributive welfare state would promote racial equality has been swept away by the dual tide of growing antiwelfare rhetoric and a rolling back of the social state. However, the poor people's case for a universal welfare state and its call for a class-based alliance of the dissatisfied across the color line is still compellingly being made today. Groups ranging from supporters of Bernie Sanders to Black Lives Matter activists or Moral Mondays participants in North Carolina have reignited the hope for substantive equality. In one of the nation's most conservative states, Moral Mondays dissenters have attempted to challenge policies highly detrimental to the poor, but also to women, racial and ethnic minorities, and LGBT communities. Rev. William Barber, leader of the Moral Mondays movement and whom Cornel West compares to Dr. King, resurrects the spirit of the latter when he reminds local officials that it is a moral duty to care for the sick and establish justice for the poor. Barber, who brought poor people from all stripes to Washington in May 2018, has explicitly cast his struggle in the footsteps of the late King, eloquently arguing that it is about time that we resume the unfinished work of the Poor People's Campaign:

> Fifty years ago, Dr. Martin Luther King called for a "revolution of values" in America, inviting people who had been divided to stand together against the "triplets of evil"—militarism, racism, and economic injustice—to insist that people need not die from poverty in the richest nation to ever exist. Poor people in communities across America—black, white, brown and Native—responded by building a Poor People's Campaign that would demand a Marshall Plan for America's poor.
>
> ... This is why I hear the Spirit calling us to build a new Poor People's Campaign.[20]

Notes

EPIGRAPHS

Upper: Quote from Martin Luther King, Jr., in Jose Yglesias, "Dr. King's March on Washington, Part II," *New York Times Magazine,* March 31, 1968. https://timesmachine.nytimes.com/timesmachine/1968/03/31/103473891.pdf

Lower: Quote from Ann Heppermann and Kara Oehler, "This Weekend in 1968: The Legacy of Resurrection City," Weekend America, May 10, 2008. http://weekendamerica.publicradio.org/display/web/2008/05/08/1968_resurrection

FOREWORD

1. Bayard Rustin, "The Blacks and Unions," *Harper's,* May 1971, p. 74.

2. Martin Luther King, Jr., "Showdown for Non-Violence," *Look,* April 16, 1968, p. 24.

3. James S. Fishkin, *Justice, Equal Opportunity and the Family* (New Haven: Yale University Press, 1983).

4. Ibid., p. 17.

5. Ibid.

INTRODUCTION

1. Quote from Nadine Eckhardt, *Duchess of Palms: A Memoir* (Austin: University of Texas Press, 2009). A staffer for President Lyndon B. Johnson, she married and worked with Texas Democratic representative Bob Eckhardt.

2. One notable exception is Thomas F. Jackson, *From Civil Rights to Human Rights: Martin Luther King, Jr., and the Struggle for Economic Justice* (Philadelphia: University of Pennsylvania Press, 2007), 335.

3. Michael K. Honey, *Going Down Jericho Road: The Memphis Strike, Martin Luther King's Last Campaign* (New York: W.W. Norton, 2007).

4. "The State of Working America," 12th ed. (Washington, DC: Economic Policy Institute, 2011).

5. Dylan Matthews, "Poverty in the 50 Years since 'The Other America,' in Five Charts," *Washington Post*, July 11, 2012.

6. Drew DeSilver, "U.S. Income Inequality, on Rise for Decades, Is Now Highest since 1928," Pew Research Center, December 5, 2013. http://www.pewre search.org/fact-tank/2013/12/05/u-s-income-inequality-on-rise-for-decades-is -now-highest-since-1928/

7. Quoted in Genevieve Fabre and Robert O'Meally, eds., *History and Memory in African-American Culture* (New York: Oxford University Press, 1994), 4.

8. Lani Guinier and Gerald Torres borrowed the metaphor of the caged canary miners carried with them into tunnels to detect polluted air to demonstrate how racial issues foreshadow dangers that imperil the entire nation. *The Miner's Canary: Enlisting Race, Resisting Power, and Transforming Democracy* (Cambridge, MA: Harvard University Press, 2002).

9. Martin Luther King, Jr., "The Time Is Always Right to Do the Good Thing," Address to Syracuse University, July 15, 1965. http://www.thekingcenter.org /archive/document/mlks-address-syracuse-university

10. Martin Luther King, Jr., Press Conference announcing the Poor People's Campaign, December 4, 1967. Martin Luther King, Jr., Papers Project. https:// kinginstitute.stanford.edu/publications/papers/unpub/671204–003_Announc ing_Poor_Peoples_campaign.htm.

11. Martin Luther King, Jr., *Where Do We Go from Here: Chaos or Community?* (Boston: Beacon Press, 2010), 37.

12. According to the 1963 Survey of Changes in Family Finances, the average wealth of a black family amounted to $18,892, compared to $136,221 for a white one. Calculation of the Urban Institute, "Nine Charts about Wealth Inequality in America." http://apps.urban.org/features/wealth-inequality-charts/

13. King, *Where Do We Go from Here*, 586.

14. The National Advisory Commission on Civil Disorders, chaired by Governor Otto Kerner of Illinois and hence informally known as the Kerner Commission, was appointed by President Johnson to answer three questions in the wake

of the "riots": "What happened? Why did it happen? What can be done to prevent it from happening again?"

15. I borrow these words from Daniel Geary, *Beyond Civil Rights: The Moynihan Report and Its Legacy* (Philadelphia: University of Pennsylvania Press, 2015).

16. Interview with Jose Yglesias, "Dr. King's March on Washington, Part II," *New York Times Magazine,* March 31, 1968. https://timesmachine.nytimes.com /timesmachine/1968/03/31/103473891.pdf

17. "There must be two Americas: one that sets the captive free, and one that takes a once-captive's new freedom away from him, and picks a quarrel with him with nothing to found it on; then kills him to get his land." Mark Twain, "To the Person Sitting in Darkness" (New York: Anti-Imperialist League of New York, 1901). http://xroads.virginia.edu/~drbr/sitting.html

18. King gave his "Other America" speech several times, notably on April 14, 1967 at Stanford University and on March 14, 1968 at Grosse Pointe High School. http://www.gphistorical.org/mlk/mlkspeech

19. Charles W. Mills, *Black Rights/White Wrongs: The Critique of Racial Liberalism* (New York: Oxford University Press, 2017), 206.

20. Dona Cooper Hamilton and Charles V. Hamilton, "The Dual Agenda of African American Organizations since the New Deal: Social Welfare Policies and Civil Rights," *Political Science Quarterly,* vol. 107, no. 3 (Autumn 1992).

21. President Lyndon B. Johnson, "To Fulfill These Rights," Commencement Address at Howard University, June 4, 1965. http://www.presidency.ucsb.edu /ws/?pid=27021

22. Martin Luther King Jr., Interview by Mr. Smith, 18 March 1966, Stanford King Institute Archives. https://kinginstitute.stanford.edu/encyclopedia /chicago-campaign

23. Hilliard Lawrence Lackey, *Marks, Martin and the Mule Train* (Marks, MS: Town Square Books, 1998).

24. "No amount of gold could provide an adequate compensation for the exploitation and humiliation of the Negro in America down through the centuries. Not all the wealth of this affluent society could meet the bill. Yet a price can be placed on unpaid wages. The ancient common law has always provided a remedy for the appropriation of the labor of one human being by another. This law should be made to apply for American Negroes. The payment should be in the form of a massive program by the government of special, compensatory measures which could be regarded as a settlement in accordance with the accepted practice of common law. Such measures would certainly be less expensive than any computation based on two centuries of unpaid wages and accumulated interest. I am proposing, therefore, that, just as we granted a GI Bill of Rights to war veterans, America launch a broad-based and gigantic Bill of Rights for the Disadvantaged, our veterans of the long siege of denial." Martin Luther King, Jr., *Why We Can't Wait* (Boston: Beacon Press, 1964), 99.

25. Darren Lenard Hutchinson, "Racial Exhaustion," 86 Wash. U. L. Rev. 917 (2009): 917-74.

26. Yglesias, "Dr. King's March on Washington, Part II."

27. Martin Luther King, Jr., "Non Violence and Social Change." Massey Lecture Series of the Canadian Broadcasting Corporation, December 1967. Printed in Martin Luther King, Jr., *The Trumpet of Conscience* (Boston: Beacon Press, 2010), 344.

28. "Alex Haley Interviews Martin Luther King, Jr.," *Playboy*, January 1965.

29. *Time*, May 31, 1968. In Gordon Mantler, "'The Press Did You In': The Poor People's Campaign and the Mass Media," *The Sixties: A Journal of History, Politics and Culture*, vol. 3, no. 1 (2010): 34.

30. Robert T. Chase, "Class Resurrection: The Poor People's Campaign of 1968 and Resurrection City," *Essays in History*, 40 (1998). http://salemwitchtrials.org/journals/EH/EH40/chase40.html

31. Gerald McKnight, *The Last Crusade: Martin Luther King, Jr., the FBI and the Poor People's Campaign* (Boulder: Westview Press, 1998).

32. The French Commune de Paris was a radical egalitarian insurrection by the city of Paris against the French government, which lasted from March 18 to May 28, 1871. In the wake of Prussia's victory over France, the people of Paris began organizing an alternative regime to the defeated government in the capital.

33. Daniel S. Lucks, *Selma to Saigon: The Civil Rights Movement and the Vietnam War* (Lexington: University Press of Kentucky, 2014).

34. Andrew E. Kersten and Clarence Lang, eds. *Reframing Randolph: Labor, Black Freedom, and the Legacies of A. Philip Randolph* (New York: New York University Press, 2015).

35. Kenneth O'Reilly, *Racial Matters: The FBI's Secret File on Black America, 1960-1972* (New York: Free Press, 1989).

36. McKnight, *Last Crusade*.

37. "Poverty: Balance on Resurrection City," *Time*, July 5, 1968.

38. Mantler, "The Press Did You In," 38.

39. Romano Renee and Raiford Leigh, eds., *The Civil Rights Movement in American Memory* (Athens: University of Georgia Press, 2006).

40. Robert W. Widell, Jr., *Birmingham and the Long Black Freedom Struggle* (London: Palgrave Macmillan, 2013).

41. Michael C. Dawson, *Blacks In and Out of the Left* (Cambridge MA: Harvard University Press, 2014).

42. Mary Frances Berry, *History Teaches Us to Resist: How Progressive Movements Have Succeeded in Challenging Times* (Boston: Beacon Press, 2018). As Berry demonstrates, resisting oppressive policies might not usher in immediate changes for society but so-called failures can actually reverberate and galvanize organizers in the long run. They can thus be seen as having *succeeded*, by laying the groundwork for further acts of resistance.

43. Clayborne Carson compellingly demonstrates that the politics of the mid to late 1960s were not so much a revolutionary departure but a continuation of King's radicalism. "Rethinking the Black American Political Thought in the Post-revolutionary era," in Brian Ward and Tony Badger, eds., *Making of Martin Luther King and the Civil Rights Movement* (New York: New York University Press, 1996), 115–31.

44. Jesse Jackson for instance, ran in the Democratic primaries in the early 1980s, hoping to build a "coalition of the rejected" and a "Rainbow coalition."

45. Martin Luther King, Jr., Speech at Staff Retreat: Penn Center, Frogmore, North Caroline, May 1967. In Lewis V. Baldwin *The Voice of Conscience: The Church in the Mind of Martin Luther King, Jr.* (New York: Oxford University Press, 2010), 100.

46. Amy Nathan Wright, "Civil Rights 'Unfinished Business': Poverty, Race, and the 1968 Poor People's Campaign," Ph.D. dissertation, University of Texas at Austin, 2007; Gordon K. Mantler, *Power to the Poor: Black-Brown Coalition and the Fight for Economic Justice, 1960–1974* (Chapel Hill: University of North Carolina Press, 2013).

47. See the testimonies in Wright, "Civil Rights 'Unfinished Business.'"

48. Bernard LaFayette, Thomas Jackson, and Mark Gonnerman, "Martin Luther King and Economic Justice: The Fortieth Anniversary Commemoration of Dr. King's 'The Other America' Speech at Stanford Aurora Forum at Stanford University," April 15, 2007. https://auroraforum.stanford.edu/ . . . /Aurora_Forum _Transcript

49. Jackson, *From Civil Rights to Human Rights*, 32.

50. Michael Eric Dyson, *I May Not Get there with You: The True Martin Luther King Jr.* (New York: Free Press, 2000).

51. Derrick P. Alridge, "The Limits of Master Narratives in History Textbooks: An Analysis of Representations of Martin Luther King, Jr.," *Teachers College Record*, vol. 108, no. 4 (April 2006): 662–86. https://www.civilrightsteaching. org/wp-content/uploads/2013/08/Alridge-Essay-on-King-and-textbooks.pdf

52. Jackson, *From Civil Rights to Human Rights*.

53. Martin Luther King, Jr., "The 'New Negro' of the South: Behind the Montgomery Story" (June 1956). In Clayborne Carson, Stewart Burns, Susan Carson, Peter Holloran, and Dana L. H. Powell, eds., *The Papers of Martin Luther King, Jr. Volume III: Birth of a New Age, December 1955-December 1956* (Berkeley: University of California Press, 1997), 286.

54. Jose Yglesias, "Dr. King's March on Washington," *New York Times Magazine*, March 31, 1968. In August Meir, John Bracey, Jr., and Elliot Rudwick, eds., *Black Protest in the Sixties* (New York: Markus Wiener Publishing, 1991), 277.

55. Douglas Sturm, "Martin Luther King, Jr., as Democratic Socialist," *Journal of Religious Ethics*, vol. 18, no. 2 (1990): 79–105.

56. R. E. Birt, *The Liberatory Thought of Martin Luther King Jr: Critical Essays on the Philosopher King* (Lanham, MD: Lexington Books, 2012), 165.

57. Carol A. Horton Caro, *Race and the Making of American Liberalism* (New York: Oxford University Press, 2005).

58. Michael C. Dawson, *Black Visions: The Roots of Contemporary African-American Political Ideologies* (New York: Oxford University Press, 2002); Nikhil Pal Singh, *Black Is a Country: Race and the Unfinished Struggle for Democracy* (Cambridge, MA: Harvard University Press, 2005).

59. Minkah Makalani, *In the Cause of Freedom: Radical Black Internationalism from Harlem to London, 1917–1939* (Chapel Hill: University of North Carolina Press, 2011), 31.

60. Jeff Woods, *Black Struggle, Red Scare: Segregation and Anti-Communism in the South, 1948–1968* (Baton Rouge: Louisiana State University Press, 2004).

61. Sturm, "Martin Luther King, Jr., as Democratic Socialist"; Adam Fairclough, "Was Martin Luther King a Marxist?" *History Workshop*, no. 15 (Spring 1983).

62. Spencer Resnick cogently defines social democracy as "a political and economic system that preserves the capitalist mode of production but seeks to redistribute wealth and regulate capitalism's worst abuses, employing a top down method of regulation and redistribution through the state." He distinguishes it from "democratic socialism," which "seeks to fundamentally alter power relationships, thus abolishing capitalism itself." Spencer Resnick, "From Social Democracy to Democratic Socialism: Martin Luther King, Jr. as a Radical Democrat and the Crisis of Democratic Revolution," *The Oak Door*, no. 1 (2010). http://pages.vassar.edu/theoakdoor/issue-3–2012/spencer-resnick/

63. Marxian thinkers do not identify with the communist political agenda endorsed by orthodox Marxists and instead have developed a critical approach to Marx's theory while being compelled by its main concepts. Other close concepts are "neo-Marxism," "post-Marxism," or "humanist Marxism."

64. In *Stride Toward Freedom,* King stressed that poor whites too were crippled by "scars of ignorance, deprivation and poverty" and pondered about their ability to join rank with poor blacks and thereby to abdicate their symbolic privilege. Jackson, *From Civil Rights to Human Rights,* 93.

65. Ibram X. Kendi, "Reclaiming MLK's Unspeakable Nightmare: The Progression of Racism in America," *Black Perspectives,* January 22, 2016.

66. Nell Irvin Painter, "How Donald Trump Made 'Working Class' White," *Princeton Alumni Weekly,* March 13, 2017.

PART I: THE LONG MARCH

1. See Philip S. Foner, *Organized Labor and the Black Worker, 1619–1981* (New York: International Publishers, 1982), Eric Arnesen, *Waterfront Workers of*

New Orleans: Race, Class, and Politics, 1863–1923 (New York: Oxford University Press, 1991), and Eric Arnesen, ed., *The Black Worker: Race, Labor, and Civil Rights since Emancipation* (Urbana: University of Illinois Press, 2007).

CHAPTER ONE. THE PATRIARCHS

1. Aldon D. Morris, *The Origins of the Civil Rights Movement: Black Communities Organizing for Change* (New York: Free Press, 1984).

2. Nikhil Pal Singh, *Black Is a Country: Race and the Unfinished Struggle for Democracy* (Cambridge, MA: Harvard University Press, 2005).

3. Nick Bromell, *The Time Is Always Now: Black Thought and the Transformation of U.S. Democracy* (New York: Oxford University Press, 2013).

4. Clayborne Carson, *The Autobiography of Martin Luther King, Jr.* (New York: Warner Books, 2001), 10.

5. Keith D. Miller, *Voice of Deliverance: The Language of Martin Luther King, Jr., and Its Sources* (Athens: University of Georgia Press, 1998), 5, 41–44.

6. Maurice Saint Pierre, "Martin Luther King as Social Intellectual: Trailblazer or Torchbearer?" in Robert E. Birt, *The Liberatory Thought of Martin Luther King Jr.: Critical Essays on the Philosopher King* (Lanham, MD: Lexington Books, 2012), 109–133.

7. David Howard-Pitney, "Wars, White America, and the Afro-American Jeremiad: Frederick Douglass and Martin Luther King, Jr.," *Journal of Negro History*, vol. 71, no. 1/4 (Winter–Autumn 1986): 23–37.

8. Frederick Douglass, "The Significance of Emancipation in the West Indies," August 3, 1857, in John W. Blassingame, ed., *The Frederick Douglass Papers Series One: Speeches, Debates and Interviews, vol. 3, 1855–1863* (New Haven: Yale University Press, 1985), 204.

9. Ellen Meiksins Wood, *The Origin of Capitalism* (New York: Monthly Review Press, 1999).

10. Frederick Douglass, "Property in Soil and Property in Man," November 18, 1848, in Philip S. Foner, ed., *The Life and Writings of Frederick Douglass*, vol. 5 (New York: International Publishers, 1975), 105.

11. Waldo E. Martin, *The Mind of Frederick Douglass* (Chapel Hill: University of North Carolina Press, 1984), 186.

12. Frederick Douglass, "The Labor Question," *The New National Era*, October 12, 1871, in Nicholas Buccola, *The Political Thought of Frederick Douglass: In Pursuit of American Liberty* (New York: New York University Press, 2012), 53.

13. Martin Luther King, Jr., "Beyond Vietnam: A Time to Break Silence." Sermon delivered at Riverside Church, New York City, April 4, 1967. http://www.americanrhetoric.com/speeches/mlkatimetobreaksilence.htm

14. Hans L. Trefousse, *Thaddeus Stevens: Nineteenth-Century Egalitarian* (Chapel Hill: University of North Carolina Press, 1997).

15. Buccola, *Political Thought of Frederick Douglass*.

16. Letter to *The Christian Recorder*, August 7, 1869. Quoted in Foner, *Life and Writings of Frederick Douglass*, 40.

17. *The National Anti-Slavery Standard*, May 29, 1869. Quoted in ibid.

18. Martin, *Mind of Frederick Douglass*, 186.

19. Martin Luther King, Jr., "Remaining Awake Through a Great Revolution," Sermon delivered at the National Cathedral, Washington, DC, March 31, 1968. https://kinginstitute.stanford.edu/king-papers/publications/knock-midnight -inspiration-great-sermons-reverend-martin-luther-king-jr-10

20. Karl Marx's early works were known by 1848 and Douglass had constant contacts with Germany through his friend Ottilie Assing. Besides, Joseph Wey-demeyer, friend to Marx and Friedrich Engels and forceful advocate of Marxism, lived in the United States from 1851 and 1866. Nonetheless, there is no evidence suggesting that Douglass, who took issue with utopian socialist movements' involvement in abolitionism, had access to Marx's books.

21. Manning Marable, "Marxism, Memory, and the Black Radical Tradition," *Souls: A Critical Journal of Black Politics, Culture, and Society*, vol. 13, no. 1 (2011).

22. Frederick Douglass, Address delivered before the National Convention of Colored Men, at Louisville, September 24, 1883. http://coloredconventions.org /items/show/554

23. Quoted in James Oakes, *The Radical and the Republican: Frederick Douglass, Abraham Lincoln, and the Triumph of Antislavery Politics* (New York: W. W. Norton, 2007), 254.

24. Frederick Douglass, *My Bondage and My Freedom*, ed. William L. Andrews (Chicago: University of Illinois Press, 1987), 188.

25. Martin Luther King, Jr., Remarks at the Convocation on Equal Justice Under Law of the NAACP Legal Defense Fund, Americana Hotel, Arlington, VA, May 28, 1964. The King Center, Atlanta.

26. Barbara J. Fields and Karen E. Fields. *Racecraft: The Soul of Inequality in American Life* (London and New York: Verso, 2012). "Racecraft" stands for the procedure and actions through which racism is transformed into race. The authors explain more extensively: "The term *race* stands for the conception of the doctrine that nature produced humankind in distinct groups, each defined by inborn traits that its members share and that differentiate them from the members of other distinct groups of the same kind but of unequal rank. . . . Fitting actual humans to any such grid inevitably calls forth the busy repertoire of strange maneuvering that is part of what we call *racecraft*. . . . *Racism* refers to the theory and practice of applying a social, civic, or legal double standard based on ancestry, and to the ideology surrounding such a double standard" (p. 16).

27. Richard Fraser, "The Negro Struggle and the Proletarian Revolution," in "In Memoriam: Richard S. Fraser," *Prometheus Research Series*, no. 3 (August 1990); see also *In Memoriam: Richard S. Fraser* (New York: Spartacist Publishing, 1990).

28. Justin Behrend, *Reconstructing Democracy: Grassroots Black Politics in the Deep South after the Civil War* (Athens: University of Georgia Press, 2015).

29. David Montgomery, *Beyond Equality: Labor and the Radical. Republicans, 1862–1872* (New York: Alfred A. Knopf, 1967).

30. Alex Gourevitch, *From Slavery to the Cooperative Commonwealth: Labor and Republican Liberty in the Nineteenth Century* (New York: Cambridge University Press, 2014).

31. Nikki M. Taylor, *America's First Black Socialist: The Radical Life of Peter H. Clark* (Lexington: University of Kentucky Press, 2013).

32. Jefferson Davis would explicitly draw this parallel in 1861: "In fact, the European Socialists, who, in wild radicalism . . . are the correspondents of the American abolitionists, maintain the same doctrine as to all property, that the abolitionists, do as to slave property. He who has property, they argue, is the robber of him who has not." Quoted in John Ashworth, *Slavery, Capitalism, and Politics in the Antebellum Republic*, vol. 1 (New York: Cambridge University Press, 1995), 205.

33. Singh, *Black Is a Country*, 213.

34. I borrow this term from Richard Fraser and Tom Boot, *Revolutionary Integration: A Marxist Analysis of African American Liberation* (Seattle: Red Letter Press, 2004).

35. Letter to Isaac Rubinov (1904). Quoted in Mark Van Wienen and Julie Kraft, "How the Socialism of W. E. B. Du Bois Still Matters: Black Socialism in 'The Quest of the Silver Fleece'—and Beyond," *African American Review*, vol. 41, no. 1 (2007): 67–68.

36. Ibid.

37. W. E. B. Du Bois, "Of our Spiritual Striving," *The Souls of Black Folk* (1903; New York: Penguin Random Books, 2003), 1-9.

38. Walton Hanes, Jr., and Robert C. Smith, *American Politics and the African American Quest for Universal Freedom* (New York: Pearson and Longman, 2006).

39. W. E. B. Du Bois, *Black Reconstruction in America: An Essay Toward a History of the Part Which Black Folk Played in the Attempt to Reconstruct Democracy in America, 1860–1880* (1935; New York: Routledge, 2013), 30.

40. W. E. B. Du Bois, "The Class Struggle," *The Crisis*, vol. 22 (August 1921): 151.

41. W. E. B. Du Bois, "Marxism and the Negro Problem," *The Crisis*, vol. 40 (May 1933): 364.

42. Ibid., 358.

43. Nell Irvin Painter, *The Narrative of Hosea Hudson: The Life and Times of a Black Radical* (Cambridge, MA: Harvard University Press, 1979); Andor Skotnes, *A New Deal for All? Race and Class Struggles in Depression-Era Baltimore* (Durham, NC: Duke University Press, 2012); Ruth Needleman, *Black Freedom Fighters in Steel: The Struggle for Democratic Unionism* (Ithaca: Cornell University Press, 2003).

44. Michael Goldfield, *The Color of Politics: Race and the Mainsprings of American Politics* (New York: New Press, 1997).

45. Joseph Gerteis, *Class and the Color Line: Interracial Class Coalition in the Knights of Labor and the Populist Movement* (Durham, NC: Duke University Press, 2007), 205.

46. Gourevitch, *From Slavery to the Cooperative Commonwealth.*

47. W. E. B. Du Bois, *John Brown: A Biography,* ed. John David Smith (New York: M. E. Sharpe, 1997), 83.

48. W. E. B. Du Bois, *Dusk of Dawn: An Essay Toward an Autobiography of a Race Concept* (1940; New York: Oxford University Press, 2014), 103.

49. Du Bois, *Black Reconstruction,* 567.

50. W. E. B. Du Bois: "Marxism and the Negro Problem," *The Crisis,* vol. 40, no. 5 (May 1933): 103.

51. Gerald Horne, *Black and Red: W. E. B. Du Bois and the Afro-American Response to the Cold War, 1944-1963* (Albany: State University of New York Press, 1986), 145.

52. Andrew J. Douglas, "W. E. B. Du Bois and the Critique of the Competitive Society," *Du Bois Review,* vol. 12, no. 1 (2015): 25– 40.

53. Du Bois, *Black Reconstruction,* 635.

54. Adolph Reed et al., *Renewing Black Intellectual History: The Ideological and Material Foundations of African American Thought* (Boulder: Paradigm, 2010), 258.

55. Michael O'Malley, "Specie and Species: Race and the Money Question in Nineteenth-century America," *American Historical Review,* vol. 99, no. 2 (1994): 369–95.

56. Edward E. Baptist, *The Half Has Never Been Told: Slavery and the Making of American Capitalism* (New York: Basic Books, 2014).

57. Martin Luther King, Jr., Address at the Conclusion of the Selma to Montgomery March. March 25, 1965. http://kingencyclopedia.stanford.edu/encyclopedia/documentsentry/doc_address_at_the_conclusion_of_selma_march.1.html

58. Du Bois, *Black Reconstruction,* 30.

59. Oliver C. Cox, *Caste, Class and Race* (New York: Modern Reader, 1948), 322.

60. Nikhil Pal Singh, *Black Is a Country,* 214.

61. Du Bois, "The Class Struggle," 151.

62. Reiland Rabaka, *Africana Critical Theory:Reconstructing the Black Radical Tradition, from W. E. B. Du Bois and C. L. R. James to Frantz Fanon and Amilcar Cabral* (Lanham, MD: Lexington Books, 2010), 49.

63. W. E. B. Du Bois, "Socialism and the Negro Problem," *The New Review: A Weekly Review of International Socialism*, 1 (February 1913).

64. W. E. B. Du Bois, "Marxism and the Negro Problem," *The Crisis*, May 1933. In Cary D. Wintz, *African American Political Thought, 1890–1930: Washington, Du Bois, Garvey and Randolph* (New York: Routledge, 2014), 151.

65. W. E. B. Du Bois, "Socialism and the Negro Problem" (1960). In Herbert Aptheker, ed., *Against Racism: Unpublished Essays, Papers, Addresses, 1887–1961* (Amherst: University of Massachusetts Press, 1985), 307.

66. "The Parting of the Ways," *World Today* 6 (April 1904): 521–23, in David Levering Lewis, *W. E. B. Du Bois: Biography of a Race, 1868–1919* (New York: Henry Holt, 1993), 329.

67. W. E. B. Du Bois, "Where Do We Go from Here?" Address delivered at the Rosenwald Economic Conference in Washington, DC, May 1933. In Andrew Paschal, ed., *W. E. B. Du Bois: A Reader* (New York: Macmillan, 1971), 156.

68. W. E. B. Du Bois, *Dusk of Dawn: An Essay Toward an Autobiography of a Race Concept*, ed. Henry Louis Gates, introduction by Kwame Anthony Appiah (1940; New York: Oxford University Press, 2014).

69. W. E. B. Du Bois, "Marxism and the Negro Problem," *The Crisis*, vol. 40, no. 5 (May 1933): 103.

70. W. E. B. Du Bois, "The Negro and Communism," *The Crisis*, vol. 38 (September 1931): 313–15.

71. Du Bois, "Where Do We Go from Here?" (1933), 156.

72. W. E. B. Du Bois, "The Talented Tenth Memorial Address," *Boulé Journal*, vol. 15, no. 1 (October 1948).

73. W. E. B. Du Bois, "Socialism and the American Negro," Speech at Madison Wisconsin Memorial Union, April 9, 1960. In Herbert Aptheker, ed., *Against Racism: Unpublished Essays, Papers, Addresses, 1887–1961* (Amherst: University of Massachusetts Press, 1985), 303–7.

74. Du Bois, "Where Do We Go from Here?" (1933).

75. Van Wienen and Kraft, "How the Socialism of W. E. B. Du Bois Still Matters," 80.

76. In Eric Foner and Manning Marable, eds., *Herbert Aptheker on Race and Democracy: A Reader* (Urbana: University of Illinois Press, 2010).

77. If, to the advocates of pure capitalism, the separation of the economy and the state should be absolute, the role of the latter being limited to the protection of individual rights, in a social democracy, individuals and corporations continue to own the capital and the means of production but government regulations and redistributions work toward constraining inequities.

78. Du Bois, "Socialism and the American Negro."

79. Martin Luther King, Jr., "Where Do We Go from Here?" Speech delivered at the 11th Annual SCLC Convention, Atlanta, August 16, 1967.

80. Du Bois, "Where Do We Go from Here?" (1933), 153–54.

81. Martin Luther King, Jr., *Where Do We Go from Here: Chaos or Community?* (Boston: Beacon Press, 2010), 186.

CHAPTER TWO. THE PROPHETS OF JUSTICE

1. Shawn Leigh Alexander, "The Afro-American Council and Its Challenge of Louisiana's Grandfather Clause," in Chris Green, Rachel Lee Rubin, and James Smethurst, eds., *Radicalism in the South since Reconstruction* (New York: Palgrave Macmillan, 2006), 13.

2. Eric Arnesen, ed., *The Black Worker: Race, Labor, and Civil Rights Since Emancipation* (Urbana: University of Illinois Press, 2007), 2.

3. George Lipsitz, *A Life in the Struggle: Ivory Perry and the Culture of Opposition* (Philadelphia: Temple University Press, 1988).

4. Steven A Reich, "The Great War, Black Workers, and the Rise and Fall of the NAACP in the South," in Arnesen, *The Black Worker*, 163.

5. Ira Kipnis, *The American Socialist Movement 1897–1912* (Chicago: Haymarket Books, 2005).

6. See William Jones, "'Nothing Special to Offer the Negro': Revisiting the 'Debsian View' of the Negro Question," *International Labor and Working-Class History*, vol. 74, no. 1 (September 2008): 212–24.

7. Eugene Debs, "The Negro and his Nemesis" (1904), in Charles H. Kerr, ed., *The International Socialist Review*, vol. 4, July 1903–June 1904 (Chicago: Charles Kerr, 1904), 393.

8. William Jones, "Something to Offer," *Jacobin Magazine*, August 2015.

9. Hubert Harrison, "Socialism and the Negro," *International Socialist Review* (1912); in *The Negro and the Nation* (New York: Cosmo-Advocate Publishing, 1917).

10. A. Philip Randolph, "The State of the Race," *The Messenger,* April 1923; in Cary D. Wintz, *African American Political Thought, 1890–1930: Washington, Du Bois, Garvey and Randolph* (New York: Routledge, 2015), 286.

11. Harrison, "Socialism and the Negro."

12. Sally M. Miller, "The Socialist Party and the Negro, 1901–20," *The Journal of Negro History*, vol. 56, no. 3 (July 1971), 228.

13. Jeffrey B. Perry, *Hubert Harrison: The Voice of Harlem Radicalism, 1883–1918* (New York: Columbia University Press, 2008), 123.

14. Sethard Fisher, "Marxist Prescriptions for Black American Equality," *Phylon*, vol. 45, no. 1 (1984): 52–66.

15. Harry Haywood, *Black Bolshevik: Autobiography of An American Communist* (Chicago: Liberator Press, 1978), 264.

16. Philip S. Foner and James S. Allen, eds., *American Communism and Black Americans: A Documentary History, 1919–1929* (Philadelphia: Temple University Press, 1987).

17. Claude Lightfoot, *Ghetto Rebellion to Black Liberation* (New York: International Publishers, 1968), 136.

18. In Cathy Bergin, "Unrest among the Negroes: The African Blood Brotherhood and the Politics of Resistance," *Race and Class Journal,* vol. 57, no. 3 (January–March 2016): 45–58.

19. Ibid.

20. Mark Solomon, *The Cry Was Unity: Communists and African Americans, 1917–1936* (Jackson: University Press of Mississippi, 1998), 47.

21. Leon Trotsky, *On Black Nationalism and Self Determination* (Atlanta: Pathfinder Press), 1994.

22. In Scott McLemee, ed., *C.L.R. James on the 'Negro Question,'"* (Jackson: University Press of Mississippi, 1996), 71.

23. Robin D.G. Kelley, *Freedom Dreams: The Black Radical Imagination* (Boston: Beacon Press, 2002).

24. Cathy Bergin, "Race/Class Politics: The Liberator, 1929–1934," *Race and Class Journal* (April 2006), 86–104.

25. In Nell Irvin Painter, *The Narrative of Hosea Hudson: His Life as a Negro Communist in the South* (Cambridge, MA: Harvard University Press, 1979), 102.

26. Robin D.G. Kelley, *Hammer and Hoe: Alabama Communists During the Great Depression* (Chapel Hill: University of North Carolina Press, 1990).

27. Allison McNeill, Richard C. Hanes, and Sharon M. Hanes, eds., "Minority Groups and the Great Depression," *Great Depression and the New Deal Reference Library,* vol. 1: Almanac (Detroit: UXL, 2003), 172–86.

28. Cass R. Sustein, *The Second Bill of Rights: FDR's Unfinished Revolution and Why We Need It More than Ever* (New York: Basic Books, 2004).

29. Abram Harris, "Future Plan and Program of the NAACP," September 1934. Quoted in Manfred Berg, "Black Civil Rights and Liberal Anticommunism: The NAACP in the Early Cold War," *Journal of American History,* vol. 94, no. 1 (June 2007): 78.

30. John C. Inscoe, *Georgia in Black and White: Explorations in Race Relations of a Southern State, 1865–1950* (Athens: University of Georgia Press, 1994).

31. Lindsey R. Swindall, *Paul Robeson: A Life of Activism and Art* (Lanham MD: Rowman & Littlefield, 2013), 92.

32. Quoted in Ben Keppel, *The Work of Democracy: Ralph Bunche, Kenneth B. Clark, Lorraine Hansberry, and the Cultural Politics of Race* (Cambridge, MA: Harvard University Press, 1995), 49.

33. Bill V. Mullen, *Popular Fronts: Chicago and African-American Cultural Politics, 1935–46* (Urbana: University of Illinois Press, 1999).

34. Touré F. Reed, *Not Alms But Opportunity: The Urban League and the Politics of Racial Uplift, 1910–1950* (Chapel Hill: University of North Carolina Press, 2008), 137.

35. Solomon, *The Cry Was Unity*.

36. Quoted in Manning Marable, "Marxism, Memory, and the Black Radical Tradition," *Souls: A Critical Journal of Black Politics, Culture, and Society*, vol. 13, no. 1 (2011).

37. Charles P. Henry, *Ralph Bunche: Model Negro or American Other* (New York: New York University Press, 1999), 49.

38. Jeff Henderson argues that Randolph purposely sought to challenge a notoriously racist institution. Jeff Henderson, "A. Philip Randolph and the Dilemmas of Socialism and Black Nationalism in the United States, 1917–1941," *Race and Class Journal*, 20 (October 1978): 143–60.

39. The Brotherhood finally became a full-fledged member of the AFL-CIO when they merged in 1955.

40. Rhonda Jones, "A. Philip Randolph, Early Pioneer," in *The Economic Civil Rights Movement: African Americans and the Struggle for Economic Power*, ed. Michael Ezra, pp. 9–21 (New York: Routledge, 2013).

41. Cornelius L. Bynum, *A. Philip Randolph and the Struggle for Civil Rights* (Urbana: University of Illinois Press, 2010), 157.

42. Glenda Elizabeth Gilmore, *Defying Dixie: The Radical Roots of Civil Rights, 1919–1950* (New York: W. W. Norton, 2008), 96.

43. Don West, a white communist and Congregational minister from Georgia, helped Horton to launch the Highlander Folk School in Tennessee. He would be very involved in the defense of Angelo Herndon. See James J. Lorence, *A Hard Journey: The Life of Don West* (Chicago: University of Illinois Press, 2007).

44. John M. Glen, *Highlander: No Ordinary School, 1932–1962* (Lexington: University Press of Kentucky, 1988).

45. George S. Schuyler, *Black No More* (New York: Dover Publications, 2011), 83.

46. Erik S. McDuffie, "The March of Young Southern Black Women: Esther Cooper Jackson, Black Left Feminism, and the Personal and Political Costs of Cold War Repression," in *Anticommunism and the African American Freedom Movement*, ed. Robbie Lieberman and Clarence Lang, pp. 81–115 (New York: Palgrave Macmillan, 2009).

47. "James Jackson: Fighter for Equality, Democracy, Peace and Socialism," December 7, 2001. http://www.cpusa.org/article/james-jackson-fighter-for-equality-democracy-peace-and-socialism/

48. In Esther Cooper Jackson and Constance Pohl, eds., *Freedomways Reader: Prophets in Their Own Country* (Boulder: Westview Press, 2000), xviii.

49. "Proclamation of Southern Negro Youth" (1941), in Alvin Hughes, "We Demand Our Rights: The Southern Negro Youth Congress, 1937–1949," *Phylon* (1960–), vol. 48, no. 1 (1987): 49.

50. "Norfolk Journal and Guide," February 15, 1937, in Hughes, "We Demand Our Rights," 41.

51. Kelley, *Hammer and Hoe*, 107.

CHAPTER THREE. THE CITY AND THE CHURCH

1. Editorial, "The Colored American," November 1901. In Lawrence E. Carter, ed., *Walking Integrity: Benjamin Elijah Mays, Mentor to Martin Luther King Jr.* (Macon, GA: Mercer University Press, 1998), 35.

2. David Fort Godshalk, *Veiled Visions: The 1906 Atlanta Race Riot and the Reshaping of American Race Relations* (Chapel Hill: University of North Carolina Press), 2005.

3. Stephen G. N. Tuck, *Beyond Atlanta: The Struggle for Racial Equality in Georgia, 1940–1980* (Athens: University of Georgia Press), 2001.

4. William A. Link, *Atlanta, Cradle of the New South: Race and Remembering in the Civil War's Aftermath* (Chapel Hill: University of North Carolina Press, 2013), 3.

5. Tera Hunter, *To 'Joy My Freedom: Southern Black Women's Lives and Labors after the Civil War* (Cambridge, MA: Harvard University Press, 1997).

6. Dayo F. Gore, *Radicalism at the Crossroads: African American Women Activists in the Cold War* (New York: New York University Press, 2010).

7. Robert Korstad, *Civil Rights Unionism: Tobacco Workers and the Struggle for Democracy in the Mid-Twentieth South* (Chapel Hill: University of North Carolina Press, 2003).

8. "Early Years," in Clayborne Carson, ed., *The Autobiography of Martin Luther King, Jr.* (New York: Grand Central Publishing, 2001), 1.

9. Louis Rudolph Harlan, *Booker T. Washington: The Wizard of Tuskegee, 1901–1915*, vol. 2 (New York: Oxford University Press, 1983), 2.

10. Robin D. G. Kelley "'We Are Not What We Seem': Rethinking Black Working-Class Opposition in the Jim Crow South," *Journal of American History*, vol. 80, no. 1 (June 1993): 75.

11. Karen Ferguson, *Black Politics in New Deal Atlanta* (Chapel Hill: University of North Carolina Press, 2002), 2.

12. Ibid., 4.

13. Robin D. G. Kelley, *Hammer and Hoe: Alabama Communists During the Great Depression* (Chapel Hill: University of North Carolina Press, 1990).

14. "Mother of Scottsboro Victim Denounces NAACP Leaders as Bunch of Liars, Fakers," *Daily Worker*, July 17, 1931, p. 1. In Lashawn Harris, "Running

with the Reds: African American Women and the Communist Party during the Great Depression," *Journal of African American History,* vol. 94, no. 1 (Winter 2009): 21.

15. Glenda Elizabeth Gilmore, *Defying Dixie: The Radical Roots of Civil Rights, 1919-1950,* (New York: W.W. Norton, 2008), 118.

16. James A. Miller, R*emembering Scottsboro: The Legacy of an Infamous Trial* (Princeton: Princeton University Press, 2009).

17. After the war, Patterson kept demanding international condemnation of the United States in regard to its treatment of African Americans. In 1951, he presented the "We Charge Genocide" petition to the United Nations in December 1951. The petition was presented simultaneously in Paris by Patterson and in NYC at the UN by Paul Robeson. Gerald Horne. *Black Revolutionary: William Patterson and the Globalization of the African American Freedom Struggle* (Champaign: University of Illinois Press, 2013), 46.

18. Barbara Jean Hope, "The Story of Hosea Hudson: Lessons of a 'Black Worker in the Deep South' Still Loom Large," *People's Weekly World,* February 4, 1995.

19. After the Second World War, the CIO unsuccessfully attempted to unionize southern workers in "Operation Dixie."

20. Harvey Klehr, *The Heyday of American Communism: The Depression Decade* (New York: Basic Books, 1984).

21. Michael Goldfield, *The Color of Politics: Race and the Mainsprings of American Politics* (New York: New Press, 1997), 185.

22. Franklin Folsom, *Impatient Armies of the Poor: The Story of Collective Action of the Unemployed, 1808-1942* (Niwot: University Press of Colorado, 1991).

23. Chad Alan Goldberg, "Contesting the Status of Relief Workers during the New Deal: The Workers Alliance of America and the Works Progress Administration, 1935-1941," *Social Science History,* vol. 29, no. 3 (Fall 2005): 338.

24. Mary Poole, *The Segregated Origins of Social Security: African Americans and the Welfare State* (Chapel Hill: University of North Carolina Press, 2006).

25. Douglas L. Fleming, "The New Deal in Atlanta: A Review of the Major Programs," *Atlanta Historical Journal,* vol. 30, no. 1 (Spring 1986).

26. Quoted in Gilmore, *Defying Dixie,* 106.

27. Angelo Herndon, *Let Me Live* (Ann Arbor: University of Michigan Press, 2007), 20.

28. In Gerald Horne, Bl*ack Liberation/Red Scare: Ben Davis and the Communist Party* (Newark: University of Delaware Press, 1994), 28.

29. James J. Lorence, *The Unemployed People's Movement: Leftists, Liberals, and Labor in Georgia, 1929-1941* (Athens: University of Georgia Press, 2009), 223.

30. Ferguson, *Black Politics,* 56.

31. Tomiko Brown-Nagin, *Courage to Dissent: Atlanta and the Long History of the Civil Rights Movement* (New York: Oxford University Press, 2011).

32. Ibid.

33. Glenn Feldman, ed., *Before Brown: Civil Rights and White Backlash in the Modern South* (Tuscaloosa: University of Alabama Press, 2004), 16.

34. See Kelley, "We Are Not What We Seem"; Eric Arnesen, ed., *The Black Worker: Race, Labor, and Civil Rights since Emancipation* (Urbana: University of Illinois Press, 2007).

35. Kelley, *Hammer and Hoe.*

36. Ibid., 107.

37. Cynthia A. Taylor, *Philip Randolph: The Religious Journey of an African American Labor Leader* (New York: New York University Press, 2006), 4.

38. J. Dorn, "The Social Gospel and Socialism: A Comparison of the Thought of Francis Greenwood Peabody, Washington Gladden, and Walter Rauschenbusch," *Church History*, vol. 62, no. 1 (1993): 82–100. http://corescholar.libraries.wright.edu/history/26

39. Martin Luther King, Jr., "Preaching Ministry," 14 September–24 November 1948, in Clayborne Carson, Susan Carson, Susan Englander, Troy Jackson, and Gerald L. Smith, eds. *The Papers of Martin Luther King, Jr. Volume VI: Advocate of the Social Gospel, September 1948–March 1963* (Berkeley: University of California Press, 2007), 123.

40. Gary Dorrien, *The New Abolition: W. E. B. Du Bois and the Black Social Gospel* (New Haven: Yale University Press, 2015), 2.

41. Martin Luther King, Jr., "My Pilgrimage to Nonviolence," September 1, 1958, in Clayborne Carson, Susan Carson, Adrienne Clay, Virginia Shadron, and Kieran Taylor, eds., *The Papers of Martin Luther King, Jr. Volume IV: Symbol of the Movement, January 1957–December 1958* (Berkeley: University of California Press, 2000), 474.

42. Walter Rauschenbush, *Christianizing the Social Order* (New York: Macmillan, 1913), 328.

43. Dan McKanan, "The Implicit Religion of Radicalism: Socialist Party Theology, 1900–1934," *Journal of the American Academy of Religion* vol. 78, no. 1 (September 2010): 752.

44. Norman Thomas, "The Christian and the Social Revolution," *The World Tomorrow* vol. 2 (1919): 292–94. In McKanan, "Implicit Religion of Radicalism," 768.

45. Raymond F. Gregory, *Norman Thomas: The Great Dissenter* (New York: Algora Publishing, 2008).

46. Charles Howard Hopkins, *The Rise of the Social Gospel in American Protestantism, 1865–1915* (New York: Ams Press, 1940), 244.

47. "The Bravest Man I Ever Met," *Pageant Magazine*, June 1965. In Cornel West, ed., *The Radical King* (Boston: Beacon Press, 2015), 225.

48. Gary Dorrien, *The New Abolition: W.E.B. Du Bois and the Black Social Gospel* (New Haven: Yale University Press, 2015), 4.

49. Robert H. Craig, *Religion and Radical Politics: An Alternative Christian Tradition in the United States* (Philadelphia: Temple University Press, 1992).

50. A.J. Muste, "Pacifism and Class War," *The World Tomorrow* (1928). In Leilah Danielson, *American Gandhi: A.J. Muste and the History of Radicalism in the Twentieth Century* (Philadelphia: University of Pennsylvania Press 2014), 103.

51. Danielson, *American Gandhi*.

52. Ibid. Emphasis by the author.

53. Dorrien claims that "Du Bois is central to almost everything that the Black social gospel became, and King is even more so" (Dorrien, *The New Abolition*, xi).

54. Philip S. Foner, ed. *Black Socialist Preacher: The Teachings of Reverend George Washington Woodbey and His Disciple, Reverend G.W. Slater, Jr.* (San Francisco: Synthesis Publications, 1983).

55. Walter Rauschenbusch, *Christianity and the Social Crisis* (1907; Eugene, OR: Wipf and Stock Publishers, 2003), 84.

56. Ibid., 138.

57. Dorrien, *The New Abolition*, 31.

58. Du Bois, "Postscript," *The Crisis 35* (1928): 203–4. In *The Negro Church: With an Introduction by Alton B. Pollard III* (Eugene, OR: Cascade Books, 2011), xxii.

59. Peter Goodwin Heltzel, *Resurrection City: A Theology of Improvisation* (Grand Rapids, MI: William B. Eerdmans, 2012), 17.

60. Dorrien, *The New Abolition*, 481.

61. Martin Luther King, Jr., "The True Mission of the Church," Sermon delivered at the Atlanta Missionary Baptist Association, 1940. In Carson Clayborne, Ralph E. Luker, and Penny A. Russell, eds. *The Papers of Martin Luther King, Jr. Volume I: Called to Serve, January 1929–June 1951* (Berkeley: University of California Press, 1992), 34.

62. Clayborne Carson. "Martin Luther King, Jr., and the African-American Social Gospel," in *African-American Christianity*, ed. Paul E. Johnson, pp. 159–177 (Berkeley: University of California Press, 1994).

CHAPTER FOUR. THE TORCHBEARER

1. Keith D. Miller, *Voice of Deliverance: The Language of Martin Luther King, Jr., and Its Sources* (Athens: University of Georgia Press, 1998), 105.

2. Harry Belafonte, *My Song: A Memoir* (New York: Knopf, 2011), 328.

3. David Garrow, *Bearing the Cross: Martin Luther King, Jr., and the Southern Christian Leadership Conference* (New York: William Morrow, 2004), 213–14.

4. Paul Le Blanc, "Martin Luther King: Christian Core, Socialist Bedrock," *Against The Current,* no. 96 (January/February 2002).

5. See Mary L. Dudziak, *Cold War Civil Rights: Race and the Image of American Democracy* (Princeton: Princeton University Press, 2000); Carl Lang, *Anti-communism and the African American Movement* (New York: Palgrave Macmillan, 2009); Eric Arnesen, ed., *The Black Worker: Race, Labor, and Civil Rights since Emancipation* (Urbana: University of Illinois Press, 2007). Also, Eric Arnesen, "The Final Conflict? On the Scholarship of Civil Rights, the Left and the Cold War," *American Communist History,* vol. 11, no. 1 (April 2012): 63–80.

6. Mary Helen Washington, *The Other Blacklist: The African American Literary and Cultural Left of the 1950s* (New York: Columbia University Press, 2014), 43.

7. Jeff Woods, *Black Struggle, Red Scare: Segregation and Anti-Communism in the South, 1948–1968* (Baton Rouge: Louisiana State University Press, 2004), 33.

8. Claudia Jones was deported in 1955 after years of harassment by the FBI. See Howard Brick and Christopher Phelps, *Radicals in America: The US Left since the Second World War* (Cambridge: Cambridge University Press, 2015) and James Zeigler, *Red Scare Racism and Cold War Black Radicalism* (Jackson: University Press of Mississippi, 2015).

9. In Esther Cooper Jackson and Constance Pohl, eds.,*Freedomways Reader: Prophets in Their Own Country* (Boulder: Westview Press, 2000), 36.

10. Washington, *The Other Blacklist.*

11. Alain Supiot, *The Spirit of Philadelphia. Social Justice against the Total Market* (New York: Verso, 2012).

12. Philadelphia has had its share of racism and violence. The year the delegates signed the declaration, Philadelphia was engulfed in the largest racially motivated strike of the Second World War era, illustrating the relevance of issues it raised. Forced by Randolph's activism, Roosevelt signed Executive Order 8802 on June 25, 1941 to prohibit racial discrimination within the national defense industry, but hundreds of Philadelphia Transit Company's white employees utterly refused integration. Their labor union advocated for the preservation of a segregated workplace. Racial tensions had been escalating for years as African American workers flooded to Philadelphia, attracted by abundant job openings. On August 1, 1944 white workers refused to operate their trolleys and shut down the city's transit system for a week. Because Philadelphia was one of the nation's key centers of defense-related manufacturing and also because he was forced to intervene by the progressive coalition of NAACP local organizers with the CIO-affiliated Transport Workers Union, Roosevelt sent in the army and ended the strike. Black workers regained their rights, and their victory was a significant milestone in the fight against discrimination and inequality. It was the concomitant grassroots pressure from socialist labor organizations and civil rights

leaders which compelled the federal government to side with the black workers. Such a major strike was a telling example of the fracturing of the working class on racial ground and the urgent need to work for class solidarity.

13. Robert C. Lieberman, *Shaping Race Policy: The United States in Comparative Perspective* Princeton: Princeton University Press, 2005).

14. W. E. B. Du Bois, "Socialism and the American Negro," in *Against Racism: Unpublished Essays, Papers, and Addresses, 1887–1961*, ed. Herbert Aptheker (Amherst: University of Massachusetts Press, 1985), 304.

15. Woods, *Black Struggle, Red Scare*, 16.

16. Lewis V. Baldwin, *The Voice of Conscience: The Church in the Mind of Martin Luther King, Jr.* (New York: Oxford University Press, 2010), 47.

17. Martin Luther King, Jr., *Strength to Love* (1958; Philadelphia: Fortress Press, 1981),90.

18. Martin Luther King, Jr. "To Coretta Scott," 18 July 1952. Atlanta GA. http://kingencyclopedia.stanford.edu/encyclopedia/documentsentry/to_coretta_scott/index.html

19. Clayborne Carson, ed., *The Autobiography of Martin Luther King, Jr.* (New York: Warner Books, 2001), 83.

20. "Examination Answers, History of Recent Philosophy." 26 May–5 June 1952, Boston MA, King Papers. https://kinginstitute.stanford.edu/king-papers/documents/examination-answers-history-recent-philosophy

21. Some scholars suggest that the young Marx was particularly appealing to American thinkers. Pierre Birnbaum, "Marxisme et marxologie aux États-Unis," *Revue française de science politique*, vol. 18, no. 6 (1968): 1262–73.

22. Herbert Marcuse, *Reason and Revolution* (New York: Oxford University Press, 1941). Another influential thinker in the United States, Erich Fromm, in his 1961 *Marx's Concept of Man* (New York: Frederick Ungar Publishing), insisted on presenting Marx as an anti-alienation philosopher, mainly concerned with the liberation of mankind. Inversely, Daniel Bell and Sidney Hook would dismiss his early writing to portray Marx as primarily an economist. Daniel Bell, "The Rediscovery of Alienation," *Journal of Philosophy* (November 1959), 935; Sidney Hook, "Marxism in the Western World," *Encounter* (1966), 11–15.

23. "My Pilgrimage to Nonviolence," September 1, 1958, New York. https://kinginstitute.stanford.edu/king-papers/documents/my-pilgrimage-nonviolence

24. "How Should a Christian View Communism?" in Martin Luther King, Jr., *Strength to Love* (Philadelphia: Fortress Press, 1981), 98.

25. Ibid., 105.

26. A. Fairclough, "Was Martin Luther King a Marxist?" *History Workshop*, no. 15 (Spring 1983): 120.

27. Ibid., 124.

28. Martin Luther King, Jr., *Where Do We Go from Here: Chaos or Community?* (1967; Boston: Beacon Press, 2010), 187.

29. Michael C. Dawson, *Behind the Mule: Race and Class in African-American Politics* (Princeton: Princeton University Press, 1994).

30. Pierre Bourdieu developed the notion of a "probable class" (a work in progress, a virtuality perpetually redefining itself) contrasting with the "mobilized class," the abstract ideal. Rather than an essentialized category, narrowly defined by its position regarding the means of production, "class" is to be understood as a mode of social relations, dependent on the historical context, in which some are exploited and self-conscious. Pierre Bourdieu, "Avenir de classe et causalité du probable," *Revue française de sociologie*, vol. 15, no. 1 (1974): 3–42.

31. Rick Fantasia, *Cultures of Solidarity: Consciousness, Action, and Contemporary American Workers* (Berkeley: University of California Press, 1988).

32. Martin Luther King, Jr., Speech at National Conference for a New Politics, August 31, 1967. https://www.marxists.org/ . . . /NEC%201967/60-national -conference

33. Jill Lepore, "How a New Yorker Article Launched the First Shot in the War Against Poverty," *Smithsonian Magazine*, September 2012.

34. Benjamin Mays, "Democratizing and Christianizing America in this Generation," *Journal of Negro Education*, vol. 14, no. 4 (Fall 1945): 530.

35. Nathan W. Schlueter,--fixed in .txt file *One Dream or Two? Justice in America and in the Thought of Martin Luther King, Jr.* (Lanham, MD: Lexington Books, 2003), 95.

36. Georges Davis, "God in History," *Crozer Quarterly*, 20 (January 1943). In Michael G. Long, *Against Us, But for Us: Martin Luther King, Jr., and the State* (Macon GA: Mercer University Press, 2002), 52.

37. Rustin as quoted in Paul Goodman, *Seeds of Liberation* (New York: Braziller, 1964), 323.

38. A. Philip Randolph, Address to the AFL-CIO, 1963. Quoted in Philip S. Foner, *Organized Labor and the Black Worker, 1619–1981* (New York: International Publishers, 1982), 79.

39. Dana Cooper Hamilton and Charles V. Hamilton, "The Dual Agenda of African American Organizations since the New Deal: Social Welfare Policies and Civil Rights," *Political Science Quarterly*, vol. 107, no. 3 (Autumn 1992).

40. Hearings Before the Subcommittee on Executive Reorganization of the Committee on Government Operations, United States Senate. Eighty-Ninth Congress, Second Session, December 14 and 15, 1966, Part 14 (Washington, DC: Government Printing Office, 1967), 2967–82.

41. L. L. Knowles and K. Prewitt, *Institutional Racism in America* (Englewood Cliffs: Prentice-Hall, 1969).

42. King, *Where Do We Go from Here*, 72.

43. Ibid., 115.

44. Eric Olin Wright, *Classes* (London: Verso, 1985).

45. Martin Luther King, Jr., Speech to the SCLC staff, November 14, 1966. In Michael Eric Dyson, *I May Not Get There with You: The True Martin Luther King Jr.* (New York: Free Press, 2000), 87.

46. Ibid., 213.

47. On Marx and slavery, see Jared Hickman, *Black Prometheus: Race and Radicalism in the Age of Atlantic Slavery* (New York: Oxford University Press, 2017).

48. Karen R. Miller, *Managing Inequality: Northern Racial Liberalism in Interwar Detroit* (New York: New York University Press, 2015), 4.

PART TWO. THE CAMPAIGN

1. Fernand Braudel, *La Méditerranée et le Monde méditerranéen à l'époque de Philippe II*, Préface (Colin, 1949).

2. See Amy Nathan Wright, "Civil Rights 'Unfinished Business': Poverty, Race, and the 1968 Poor People's Campaign" (Ph.D. dissertation, University of Texas at Austin, 2007); Gordon K. Mantler, *Power to the Poor: Black-Brown Coalition and the Fight for Economic Justice, 1960–1974* (Chapel Hill: University of North Carolina Press, 2013).

CHAPTER FIVE. THE PAUPER

1. Martin Luther King, Jr., "Negroes Are Not Moving Too Fast," *Saturday Evening Post* (November 7, 1964). In James Washington, *A Testament of Hope: The Essential Writing of Martin Luther King Jr.* (San Francisco: HarperCollins, 1991), 176–77.

2. Quoted in Catherine M. Paden, "Disentangling Race and Poverty: The Civil Rights Response to Antipoverty Policy," *The DuBois Review*, vol. 5, no. 2 (2008): 358.

3. William Jones, *The March on Washington: Jobs, Freedom, and the Forgotten History of Civil Rights* (New York: W. W. Norton, 2013).

4. Charles Euchner, *Nobody Turn Me Around: A People's History of the 1963 March on Washington* (Boston: Beacon Press, 2011).

5. Johnson was misled into thinking that as a Democrat, he had to be hawkish on foreign policy to establish his stature as commander in chief. His strategy proved illusory when conservatives regained ground in the 1966 midterms, blaming him for an ever-expanding and costly war. See Julian Zelizer, *The Fierce Urgency of Now: Lyndon Johnson, Congress, and the Battle for the Great Society* (New York: Penguin Press, 2015).

6. Young called for a decennial plan to improve poor schools, build housing, and provide healthcare to all Americans but with particular emphasis on Afri-

NOTES TO PAGES 103–104

can Americans. Preferential treatment in hiring would compensate for past discriminations, Young argued.

7. The August 1964 Atlantic City convention was meant to nominate the incumbent president, Lyndon Johnson, for a second term. The recent interracial effort of SNCC's Mississippi Freedom Summer, which brought white students and black sharecroppers together to claim voting rights for African Americans in a context of unleashed violence, drew the attention of the media to the convention. Willing to disrupt Jim Crow from within, the Mississippi Freedom Democratic Party (MFDP), a shadow but integrated local Democratic Party, joined the convention. Led by Aaron Henry and Fanny Lou Hammer (who gave a poignant and shocking account of the brutality she had endured as a grassroots militant, which applied to all disenfranchised blacks of the state who sought to register), the MFDP unsuccessfully demanded to replace the southern state's segregationist delegation. Johnson, fearful of alienating Southern white voters, only gave them lip service (see John C. Skipper, *Showdown at the 1964 Democratic Convention: Lyndon Johnson, Mississippi and Civil Rights*, New York: McFarland Publishing, 2012). Unwilling to accept being turned down, many black activists were resentful and more than ever concerned about the real implementation of the antidiscriminatory practices and civil rights agenda of the Johnson administration. Despite the passage of the Voting Rights Act in August 1965, the Atlantic City convention came off as a "democratic debacle" (Joshua Zeitz, "Democratic Debacle," *American Heritage*, vol. 55, no. 3, June/July 2004. https://www.ameri canheritage.com/content/democratic-debacle), hastening the call for "Black Power" that Stokely Carmichael would articulate two years later.

8. Full Employment Bill of 1945, S. 380, 79th Cong. (1945). Quoted in Murray Weidenbaum, "The Employment Act of 1946: A Half Century of Presidential Policymaking," *Presidential Studies Quarterly*, vol. 26, no. 3 (Summer 1996): 880–86.

9. On June 10, 1963, the National Urban League had called for a domestic "Marshall Plan for Negro citizens," pushing for special help for the ghetto dwellers. Whitney Young, its executive director since 1961, was a fierce advocate of economic reparation and so-called "preferential treatment" for blacks. Critics disparaged the plan as "reverse discrimination," but the Urban League argued that if Johnson could massively infuse federal money into Appalachia, he could just as well initiate a Marshall Plan for poor urban blacks. The Urban League's case, that African Americans could not "racially assimilate . . . if they are failed economically," was wholeheartedly supported by King but the preacher would expand its scope so as to be applicable to poor whites as well. See Sterling Tucker, "The Role of Civil Rights Organizations—A Marshall Plan Approach," *Boston College Law Review*, vol. 7, no. 3 (1966): 4–1. In 1962–1963, though his controversial (at the time) vision was publicized, King failed to build a consensus among civil rights leaders.

10. David Garrow, *Bearing the Cross: Martin Luther King, Jr., and the Southern Christian Leadership Conference* (New York: William Morrow, 2004), 312.

11. Robert A. Gorman, *Michael Harrington: Speaking American* (New York: Routledge, 1995), 53.

12. Paul Steckler, interview with Daniel Schorr, conducted by Blackside, December 5, 1988, for Washington University Libraries, Film and Media Archive, Henry Hampton Collection. http://digital.wustl.edu/e/eii/eiiweb/sch5427.0241 .145danielschorr.html.

13. Catherine M. Paden, *Civil Rights Advocacy on Behalf of the Poor* (Philadelphia: University of Pennsylvania Press, 2011).

14. Marisa Chappell, *The War on Welfare: Family, Poverty, and Politics in Modern America* (Philadelphia: University of Pennsylvania Press, 2011), 22.

15. Bayard Rustin, "From Protest to Politics: The Future of the Civil Rights Movement," *Commentary* (February 1, 1965). https://www.commentarymagazine .com/articles/from-protest-to-politics-the-future-of-the-civil-rights-movement/

16. Mathew Forstater, "From Civil Rights to Economic Security: Bayard Rustin and the African American Struggle for Full Employment, 1945–1978," *International Journal of Political Economy*, vol. 36, no. 3 (2007).

17. The first American "war on poverty" was waged in the 1930s when the New Deal enacted an unprecedented set of measures aimed at eradicating the cruel misery that had swept across the nation. The Great Depression had given a face to poverty, with New Deal photographers, social commentators, and moral educators capturing the courage, resilience, and tenacity of the dispossessed. But Roosevelt's war on poverty was badly crippled by its inability to address racism and segregation. The majority of African Americans were denied the benefits of most social welfare programs, including Aid to Dependent Children and the GI Bill. Not only did New Deal programs not challenge segregation but some scholars have argued that the policies enacted on behalf of the underprivileged actually contributed to the deep-rooted segregation system. In contrast, Johnson's antipoverty agenda was inextricably related to the black liberation movement, which initially wholeheartedly supported the war on poverty it had helped to set in motion.

18. Jill Quadagno, *The Color of Welfare: How Racism Undermined the War on Poverty* (New York: Oxford University Press, 1996).

19. Carl M. Brauer, "Kennedy, Johnson, and the War on Poverty," *Journal of American History*, vol. 69, no. 1 (June 1982): 98–119.

20. "To Fulfill These Rights," President Lyndon B. Johnson's Commencement Address at Howard University, June 4, 1965, Lyndon Baines Johnson Presidential Library.

21. *The Negro Family: The Case for National Action* (Washington, DC: Office of Policy Planning and Research, U.S. Department of Labor, 1965), 3. Quoted in Daniel Geary, *Beyond Civil Rights: The Moynihan Report and Its Legacy* (Philadelphia: University of Pennsylvania Press, 2015).

22. They were given little credit for their insights. Political scientist Daniel Patrick Moynihan, who not only wrote the speech but as assistant secretary of Labor would stand as the War on Poverty's main engineer, said: "At this time the American poor, black and white, were surprisingly inert. The Negro civil rights movement in the South was still just that: a movement in the South for civil rights. There was almost no economic content to the protest." See Patrick Moynihan, *Maximum Feasible Misunderstanding: Community Action in the War on Poverty* (New York: Free Press, 1969), 24-25.

23. Patrick Moynihan, "Poverty and Progress." *American Scholar* 33 (1964): 603.

24. In Nick Kotz, *Judgment Days: Lyndon Baines Johnson, Martin Luther King Jr., and the Laws That Changed America* (Boston: Houghton Mifflin, 2005), 253.

25. Paden, *Civil Rights Advocacy,* 102. See also Paden, "Disentangling Race and Poverty."

26. N. A. Naples, *Grassroots Warriors: Activist Mothering, Community Work, and the War on Poverty* (New York: Routledge, 1997); Ellen Reese, *Backlash Against Welfare Mothers: Past and Present* (Berkeley: University of California Press, 2005).

27. Annelise Orleck and Lisa Gayle Hazirjian, eds., *The War on Poverty: A New Grassroots History, 1964-1980* (Athens: University of Georgia Press, 2011).

28. W. S. Clayson. *Freedom Is Not Enough: The War on Poverty and the Civil Rights Movement in Texas* (Austin: University of Texas Press, 2010).

29. Sidney M. Milkis and J. M. Mileur, *The Great Society and the High Tide of Liberalism* (Amherst: University of Massachusetts Press, 2005).

30. Gavin Wright demonstrates, for instance, how the opening to black workers of the textile industry, "the most extreme case of segregation," was "a true accomplishment of the Civil Rights Act," Gavin Wright, *Sharing the Prize: The Economics of the Civil Rights Revolution in the American South* (Cambridge, MA: Harvard University Press, 2013), 105.

31. Nick Kotz and Mary Lynn Kotz, *A Passion for Equality: George A. Wiley and the Movement* (New York: W. W. Norton, 1977), 162.

32. The Mobilization for Youth program in New York is one the most significant in that regard. See Noel A. Cazenave, *Impossible Democracy: The Unlikely Success of the War on Poverty Community Action Programs.* (Albany: State University of New York Press, 2007).

33. Quadagno, *Color of Welfare,* 28.

34. Clayborne Carson, *The Student Voice, 1960-1965: Periodical of the Student Nonviolent Coordinating Committee* (Westport, CT: Meckler, 1990), 230.

35. Thomas F. Jackson, "The State, the Movement and the Urban Poor: The War on Poverty and Political Mobilization," in Michael B. Katz, ed., *The*

"Underclass" Debate: Views from History (Princeton: Princeton University Press, 1993), 432.

36. Ibid., 438.

37. Although he initiated the antipoverty effort and had been close to Keynesian economist John Kenneth Galbraith, President Kennedy dismissed public spending and direct intervention in the structure of the economy, relying rather on the maintenance of overall economic growth through tax cuts.

38. Karlyn Forner, *Why the Vote Wasn't Enough for Selma* (Durham, NC: Duke University Press, 2017). See also Timothy J. Minchin, *From Rights to Economics: The Ongoing Struggle for Black Equality in the U.S. South* (Gainesville: University Press of Florida, 2007).

39. Thomas J. Sugrue, *Sweet Land of Liberty: The Forgotten Struggle for Civil Rights in the North* (New York: Random House, 2008).

40. Orleck and Hazirjian, *War on Poverty*.

41. Michael Katz contends that the OEO received less than 10 percent of the budget necessary to be effective. In Michael B. Katz, *In the Shadow of the Poorhouse: A Social History of Welfare in America* (New York: Basic Books, 1986).

42. Allen J. Matusow, *The Unraveling of America: A History of Liberalism in the 1960s* (New York: Harper Torchbooks, 1986), 250.

43. Martin Luther King, Jr., *Where Do We Go from Here: Chaos or Community?* (Boston: Beacon Press, 2010), 86.

44. Oscar Lewis, "The Culture of Poverty," *Scientific American*, vol. 215, no. 4 (October 1966): 20. In Mitchell Duneier, *Ghetto: The Invention of a Place, the History of an Idea* (New York: Farrar, Straus & Giroux, 2016), 109.

45. Geary, *Beyond Civil Rights*, 31.

46. Ibid., 92.

47. Shatema Threadcraft and Brandon M. Terry, "Gender Trouble: Manhood, Inclusion, and Justice," in Tommie Shelby and Brandon M. Terry, eds., *To Shape a New World: Essays on the Political Philosophy of Martin Luther King, Jr.* (Cambridge, MA: Harvard University Press, 2018), 205–36.

48. Martin Luther King, Jr., "Family Planning—A Special and Urgent Concern," May 5, 1966. https://www.plannedparenthood.org/planned-parenthood-gulf-coast/mlk-acceptance-speech

49. Statement of Martin Luther King, Jr., October 23, 1967. http://www.thekingcenter.org/archive/document/mlk-statement-national-advisory-commission-civil-disorders

50. Franklin Frazier, *The Negro Family in the United States* (Chicago: University of Chicago Press, 1966), 362. In Geary, *Beyond Civil Rights*, 61.

51. Statement of Martin Luther King, Jr., October 14, 1966. In Thomas F. Jackson, *From Civil Rights to Human Rights: Martin Luther King, Jr., and the*

Struggle for Economic Justice (Philadelphia: University of Pennsylvania Press, 2007), 296.

52. Cornelius L. Bynum, *A. Philip Randolph and the Struggle for Civil Rights* (Urbana: University of Illinois Press, 2010).

53. Leon Keyserling was the main inspiration for the plan. An "integrative liberal," Keyserling advocated a form of progressivism which saw "alienation and exploitation as the twin challenge to the democratic order." Donald K. Pickens, *Leon H. Keyserling: A Progressive Economist* (New York: Lexington Books, 2009), 2.

54. A. Philip Randolph Institute, "Freedom Budget" (1966). www.prrac.org /pdf/FreedomBudget.pdf

55. Jackson, *From Civil Rights to Human Rights*, 258.

56. SNCC, "Position on the Freedom Budget," November 22, 1966. In Paden, "Disentangling Race and Poverty,", 71. See also M. Forstater, "The Freedom Budget at 45: Functional Finance and Full Employment," Levy Economics Institute, Working Paper no. 668 (May 3, 2011).

57. Simon Hall, *Peace and Freedom: The Civil Rights and Antiwar Movements in the 1960s* (Philadelphia: University of Pennsylvania Press, 2005).

58. Martin Luther King, Jr., "Along this Way: The Violence of Poverty," *New York Amsterdam News*, January 1, 1966. http://www.thekingcenter.org/archive /document/along-way-violence-poverty

59. Martin Luther King, Jr., "A Freedom Budget for All Americans; Budgeting Our Resources, 1966–1975, to Achieve Freedom from Want" (A. Philip Randolph Institute, 1966). https://archive.org/details/freedomBudgetForAllAmeri cahsBudgetingOurResources1966-1975

60. Jackson, *From Civil Rights to Human Rights*, 277. Point also made by Michael K. Honey, *Going Down Jericho Road: The Memphis Strike, Martin Luther King's Last Campaign* (New York: W. W. Norton, 2007), 234.

61. Clayborne Carson, Clayborne, ed., *The Autobiography of Martin Luther King, Jr.* (New York: Warner Books, 2001), 293.

62. Ibid., 300.

63. Hearings Before the Subcommittee on Executive Reorganization of the Committee on Government Operations, United States Senate, Eighty-Ninth Congress, Second Session, December 14 and 15, 1966, Part 14 (Washington, DC: Government Printing Office, 1967), 2967–82.

64. Tommie Shelby, "Prisons of the Forgotten: Ghettos and Economic Injustice," in Tommie Shelby and Brandon M. Terry, eds., *To Shape a New World: Essays on the Political Philosophy of Martin Luther King, Jr.* (Cambridge, MA: Harvard University Press, 2018), 195.

65. Carson, *Autobiography of Martin Luther King, Jr.*, 301.

66. Ralph David Abernathy, *And the Walls Came Tumbling Down: An Autobiography* (New York: Harper & Row, 1989), 413.

67. "Dr. King Carries Fight to Northern Slums," *Ebony*, April 1966, p. 96. In M. L. Finley et al., *The Chicago Freedom Movement: Martin Luther King Jr. and Civil Rights Activism in the North* (Lexington: University Press of Kentucky, 2015), 224.

68. David Halberstam, "The Second Coming of Martin Luther King," *Harper's*, August 1967, p. 42.

69. On the critical influence of the campaign during this period, see James R. Ralph, Jr., *Northern Protest: Martin Luther King, Jr., Chicago, and the Civil Rights Movement* (Cambridge MA: Harvard University Press, 1993).

70. In Finley, *Chicago Freedom Movement*, 71.

71. Stokely Carmichael and Charles V, Hamilton, *Black Power: The Politics of Liberation* (New York: Vintage Books, 1967), 36.

72. In Finley, *Chicago Freedom Movement*, 31.

73. Felicia A. Kornbluh, *The Battle for Welfare Rights: Politics and Poverty in Modern America* (Philadelphia: University of Pennsylvania Press, 2007).

74. Orleck and Hazirjian, *War on Poverty*, 2.

75. Jackson, "The State, the Movement and the Urban Poor," 429.

76. N. A. Naples, *Grassroots warriors: Activist Mothering, Community Work, and the War on Poverty* (New York: Routledge, 1997).

77. See Robert Hawkins, "Brotherhood Men and Singing Slackers: A. Philip Randolph's Rhetoric of Music and Manhood," in Andrew E. Kersten and Clarence Lang, eds. *Reframing Randolph: Labor, Black Freedom, and the Legacies of A. Philip Randolph,* pp. 101–29 (New York: New York University Press, 2015).

78. Until it was struck down by the Supreme Court in 1968, this regulation that applied in certain jurisdictions denied poor families welfare payments in the event that a man resided under the same roof with them.

79. Martin Luther King, Jr., Speech at Soldier Field Rally, July 10, 1966. In Jackson, *From Civil Rights to Human Rights,* 285.

80. In Gordon K. Mantler, *Power to the Poor: Black-Brown Coalition and the Fight for Economic Justice, 1960–1974* (Chapel Hill: University of North Carolina Press, 2013), 55.

81. Title of a 1964 SDS pamphlet edited by Tom Hayden.

82. Original draft of Port Huron statement available online at http://www .sds-1960s.org/PortHuronStatement-draft.htm

83. SDS 1963 statement available in online archives at http://www.sds-1960s .org/documents.htm

84. See Amy Sonnie and James Tracy, *Hillbilly Nationalists, Urban Race Rebels, and Black Power: Community Organizing in Radical Times* (Brooklyn: Melville House, 2011).

85. Jennifer Frost, *An Interracial Movement of the Poor": Community Organizing and the New Left* (New York: New York University Press, 2001).

86. Finley, *Chicago Freedom Movement,* 71.

87. Ibid.

88. Karen R. Miller, *Managing Inequality: Northern Racial Liberalism in Interwar Detroit* (New York: New York University Press, 2015).

89. King, *Where Do We Go from Here?* 146.

90. Rustin, "From Protest to Politics."

91. Jackson, *From Civil Rights to Human Rights,* 323.

92. Hearings Before the Subcommittee on Executive Reorganization of the Committee on Government Operations, United States Senate, Eighty-Ninth Congress, Second Session, December 14 and 15, 1966, Part 14 (Washington, DC: Government Printing Office, 1967), 2967–82.

93. James C. Harvey. *Black Civil Rights During the Johnson Administration* (Jackson: University Press of Mississippi, 1973).

94. Interview with John Conyers, *Pittsburgh Courier,* September 2, 1967, p. 12.

95. Full Opportunity Act available online at http://www.thekingcenter.org /archive/document/full-opportunity-act-summary.

96. Tom Talburt, "Dr. King Asks LBJ to do as Hero FDR did," Scripps Howard (January 15, 1968). Available in The King Center's digital archives online at http://www.thekingcenter.org/archive/document/scripps—howard—dr —king—asks—lbj—do—hero—fdr—did.

97. Simon Hall, *Peace and Freedom: The Civil Rights and Antiwar Movements in the 1960s* (Philadelphia: University of Pennsylvania Press, 2005).

98. Martin Luther King, Jr., "Beyond Vietnam," Speech at Riverside Church meeting, New York, April 4, 1967. http://mlk-kpp01.stanford.edu/index.php /encyclopedia/documentsentry/doc_beyond_vietnam

99. Martin Luther King, Jr., "Why I Am Opposed to the War in Vietnam," Sermon at Ebenezer Baptist Church, April 30, 1967. http://www.thekingcenter.org/ archive/document/mlk-sermon-why-i-am-opposed-war-vietnam

100. "The War on Poverty," PBS documentary, 1991.

101. Richard B. Freeman and Harry J. Holzer, *The Black Youth Employment Crisis* (Chicago: University of Chicago Press, 1986).

102. "Negro Unemployment Scored by AFL-CIO," *Chicago Defender,* May 18, 1963, p. 1. In Elizabeth Hinton, *From the War on Poverty to the War on Crime: The Making of Mass Incarceration in America* (Cambridge, MA: Harvard University Press, 2016), 28.

103. Robert W. Fairlie and William A. Sundstrom, "The Racial Unemployment Gap in Long-Run Perspective," *American Economic Review,* vol. 87, no. 2 (1997): 306–10.

104. Martin Luther King Jr., "Domestic Impact of the War," November 1967, National Labor Leadership Assembly for Peace. http://www.aavw.org/special_ features/speeches_speech_king03.html

105. According to a *Time* magazine poll, Americans were supportive of a massive plan to eradicate the ghetto. Gwen Bellisfield, "White Attitudes toward

Racial Integration and the Urban Riots of the 1960s," *Public Opinion Quarterly*, vol. 36, no. 4 (Winter 1972–1973): 579–84.

106. In Hinton, *From the War on Poverty to the War on Crime*, 100.

107. Official report available online at https://www.ncjrs.gov/pdffiles1/nij/42.pdf.

108. Martin Luther King, Jr., Statement on riots in Watts, Calif., August 17, 1965. In Carson, *Autobiography of Martin Luther King, Jr.*, 156.

109. Zelizer, *Fierce Urgency of Now*.

110. Julian E. Zelizer, "Is America Repeating the Mistakes of 1968?" *Atlantic Monthly*, July 8, 2016.

111. Jackson, *From Civil Rights to Human Rights*, 193.

112. Statement by Dr. Martin Luther King Jr., President, Southern Christian Leadership Conference, Atlanta, GA, December 4, 1967. http://www.crmvet.org/docs/6712_mlk_ppc-anc.pdf

113. *Look*, April 1968. In Robert T. Chase, "Class Resurrection: The Poor People's Campaign of 1968 and Resurrection City," *Essays in History*, vol. 40 (Charlottesville: University of Virginia, 1998). http://www.essaysinhistory.com/class-resurrection-the-poor-peoples-campaign-of-1968-and-resurrection-city/

114. Carson, *Autobiography of Martin Luther King, Jr.*, 347.

CHAPTER SIX. AN "AMERICAN COMMUNE"

1. In W. E. B. Du Bois, *The Souls of Black Folk* (1903; New York: Penguin Random House Books, 2003), 160.

2. David Garrow, *Bearing the Cross: Martin Luther King, Jr., and the Southern Christian Leadership Conference* (New York: William Morrow, 2004), 581–82.

3. Bernard Lafayette, "From Freedom Rides to Ferguson: Narratives of Nonviolence in the American Civil Rights Movement" (Emory University online course), Lesson 24, "The Poor People's Campaign." https://www.coursera.org/learn/nonviolence/lecture/hfHCc/the-poor-peoples-campaign.

4. Martin Luther King, Jr., Address delivered at Southern Christian Leadership Conference staff meeting, January 17, 1968, Atlanta. In Thomas F. Jackson, *From Civil Rights to Human Rights: Martin Luther King, Jr. and the Struggle for Economic Justice* (Philadelphia: University of Pennsylvania Press, 2007), 333.

5. Marian Wright Edelman, "Revisiting Marks, Mississippi," *Huffington Post*, March 25, 2011. According to Larry Tye, this trip was a turning point in the senator's life, transforming him into a truly progressive liberal. See Larry Tye, *Bobby Kennedy: The Making of a Liberal Icon* (New York: Random House, 2016).

6. See Steven W. Bender, *One Night in America: Robert Kennedy, César Chávez, and the Dream of Dignity* (Boulder: Paradigm, 2008) and Miriam

Pawel, *The Union of Their Dreams: Power, Hope, and Struggle in Cesar Chavez's Farm Worker Movement* (New York: Bloomsbury Press, 2010).

7. See Julia Cass, *"Held Captive": Child Poverty in America* (Washington, DC: Children's Defense Fund, 2010).

8. Enrico Beltramini, "Race, Capitalism, and Power: The Economic Thought of the Young Jesse Jackson," *Journal of Economic and Social Thought.* vol. 3, no. 3 (September 2016): 333–48.

9. Garrow, *Bearing the Cross,* 585.

10. "MLK's Dream of Economic Justice," April 5, 2013. http://billmoyers.com/episode/mlks-dream-of-economic-justice

11. Martin Luther King, Jr., Statement delivered at a press conference announcing the Poor People's Campaign, December 4, 1967. The King Center, Atlanta. http://www.thekingcenter.org/archive/document/mlk-public-statement-poor-peoples-campaign

12. Jimmy Collier, New York City organizer for the PPC, in M. L. Finley et al., *The Chicago Freedom Movement: Martin Luther King Jr. and Civil Rights Activism in the North* (Lexington: University Press of Kentucky, 2015), 73.

13. Martin Luther King, Jr., "The Crisis in America's Cities," August 15, 1967. http://www.thekingcenter.org/archive/document/crisis-americas-cities

14. Gerald McKnight, *The Last Crusade: Martin Luther King, Jr., the FBI and the Poor People's Campaign* (Boulder: Westview Press, 1998), 20.

15. Michael Eric Dyson, *I May Not Get There with You: The True Martin Luther King, Jr.* (New York: Free Press, 2000).

16. David Halberstam, "The Second Coming of Martin Luther King," *Harper's,* August 1967. In Clayborne Carson, David J. Garrow, and Bill Kovach, eds., *Reporting Civil Rights* (New York: Library of America, 2003), 564.

17. Ibid., 40.

18. Martin Luther King. Jr., Speech at a rally in Albany, GA, March 22, 1968. The King Center, Atlanta (680323-002).

19. *Look,* April 16, 1968.

20. Martin Luther King, Jr., Statement before the National Advisory Commission on Civil Disorders, October 23, 1967. http://faculty.washington.edu/qtaylor/documents_us/Kerner%20Report.htm

21. Michael C. Dawson, *Black Visions: The Roots of Contemporary African-American Political Ideologies* (New York: Oxford University Press, 2002).

22. Norman Thomas, "The Implicit Religion of Radicalism," *The World Tomorrow,* August 1920.

23. Bayard Rustin, "From Protest to Politics: The Future of the Civil Rights Movement," *Commentary,* February 1, 1965. https://www.commentarymagazine.com/articles/from-protest-to-politics-the-future-of-the-civil-rights-movement/

24. Martin Luther King, Jr., *Where Do We Go from Here: Chaos or Community?* (Boston: Beacon Press, 2010), 154.

25. "Poor People's Campaign Starts April 22 in Washington," *SCLC News,* March 4, 1968.

26. Guian McKee in Annelise Orleck and Lisa Gayle Hazirjian, eds., *The War on Poverty: A New Grassroots History, 1964–1980* (Athens: University of Georgia Press, 2011).

27. King, *Where Do We Go from Here,* 233.

28. Hollins interview, in Finley, *Chicago Freedom Movement,* 72.

29. Amy Nathan Wright, "Poor People's Campaign," in Gary L. Anderson and Kathryn G. Herr, eds., *Encyclopedia of Activism and Social Justice,* pp. 1140–42 (Thousand Oaks, CA: Sage, 2007).

30. Gordon K. Mantler, *Power to the Poor: Black-Brown Coalition and the Fight for Economic Justice, 1960–1974* (Chapel Hill: University of North Carolina Press, 2013), 100.

31. Amy Nathan Wright, "Civil Rights 'Unfinished Business': Poverty, Race, and the 1968 Poor People's Campaign" (Ph.D. dissertation, University of Texas at Austin, 2007), 184.

32. Martin Luther King, Jr., "The Trumpet of Conscience," in James Washington, *A Testament of Hope: The Essential Writing of Martin Luther King Jr.* (San Francisco: HarperCollins, 1991), 651.

33. Ibid.

34. Martin Luther King, Jr., *Stride Toward Freedom: The Montgomery Story* (1958; Boston: Beacon Press, 2010), 123. It is worth noting that Bayard Rustin and Stanley Levison, both influenced by socialist ideas, were instrumental in the drafting of the manuscript.

35. King, *Where Do We Go from Here,* 17.

36. Quoted in Jack Bloom, *Race, Class, and the Civil Rights Movement* (Bloomington: Indiana University Press, 1987), 212.

37. Martin Luther King, Jr., "Drum Major Instinct," Sermon, February 8, 1968. http://mlkkpp01.stanford.edu/index.php/encyclopedia/documentsentry/doc_the_drum_major_instinct/

38. Philip S. Foner, *U.S. Labor and the Vietnam War* (New York: International Publishers, 1989), 21.

39. Michael K. Honey, *All Labor Has Dignity* (Boston: Beacon Press, 2011), 107.

40. John M. Glen, *Highlander: No Ordinary School, 1932–1962* (Lexington: University Press of Kentucky, 1988), 211.

41. McKnight, *Last Crusade.*

42. Amy Sonnie and James Tracy, *Hillbilly Nationalists, Urban Race Rebels, and Black Power: Community Organizing in Radical Times* (Brooklyn: Melville House, 2011).

43. Peggy Terry, "Solidarity Day Speech at Lincoln Memorial," June 19, 1968, quoted in Sonnie and Tracy, *Hillbilly Nationalists,* 59.

44. William Clayson, "Mexican versus Negro Approaches to the War on Poverty: Black-Brown Competition and the Office of Economic Opportunity in Texas," in Brian Behnken, ed., *The Struggle in Black and Brown: African American and Mexican American Relations During the Civil Rights Era* (Lincoln: University of Nebraska Press, 2012), 125–48.

45. Neil Foley, *Quest for Equality: The Failed Promise of Black-Brown Solidarity* (Cambridge, MA: Harvard University Press, 2010) and Brian D. Behnken, *Fighting Their Own Battles: Mexican Americans, African Americans, and the Struggle for Civil Rights in Texas* (Chapel Hill: University of North Carolina Press, 2011).

46. The prominent conservative League of American Citizens (LULAC), founded in 1929, defended Hispanics citizenship within the frame of whiteness. See Behnken, *Fighting Their Own Battles*. But as Ian F. Haney López demonstrated in his study of the March 1968 high school walkouts which occurred in East Los Angeles, Mexican American and African American students joined with Chicano/a students to engage in nonviolent protest. The legal violence unleashed against them convinced Chicano activists that they were nonwhite. See Ian F. Haney López, *Racism on Trial: The Chicano Fight for Justice* (Cambridge, MA: Harvard University Press, 2003).

47. Lauren Araiza, *To March for Others: The Black Freedom Struggle and the United Farm Workers* (Philadelphia: University of Pennsylvania Press, 2014), 170.

48. Ibid., 185.

49. Mantler, *Power to the Poor*, 45–46.

50. King, *Where Do We Go from Here*, 149.

51. Bender, *One Night in America*, 157.

52. Jorge Mariscal, "Cesar and Martin, March '68," in Behnken, *Struggle in Black and Brown*, 148–79.

53. Ending the Mexican War, the Treaty of Guadalupe Hidalgo was signed in February 2, 1848, between the United States and Mexico. Half of Mexico's territory, about 500,000 square miles, passed to American sovereignty. The treaty drew the boundary between the United States and Mexico at the Rio Grande and Gila Rivers and supposedly guaranteed land and language rights to the people on the former Mexican lands. But the outright appropriation of their lands by American interests sparked the local population's outrage.

54. Tijerina merged with the Black Panthers Party, whose platform stated that "We believe that this racist government has robbed us, and now we are demanding the overdue debt of forty acres and two mules. Forty acres and two mules were promised 100 years ago as restitution for slave labor and mass murder of Black people. We will accept the payment in currency which will be distributed to our many communities." Black Panther Party, "The Ten-Point Program" (October 15, 1966).

55. José A. Cobas, Jorge Duany, and Joe R. Feagin, eds., *How the United States Racializes Latinos: White Hegemony and Its Consequences* (Boulder: Paradigm, 2009).

56. Gordon K. Mantler, "Black, Brown and Poor: Martin Luther King Jr., the Poor People's Campaign and its Legacy" (Ph.D. dissertation, Duke University, 2008), 246. https://edisciplinas.usp.br/pluginfile.php/1017575/mod_resource/content/1/D_Mantler_Gordon_Thesis_poor_peoples%20Project.pdf

57. "Statements of Demands for Rights of the Poor Presented to Agencies of the U.S. Government by the Poor People's Campaign and Its Committee of 100," April 29-30, 1968, SCLS-PPC Information Office, Washington, DC. http://www.crmvet.org/docs/6805_ppc_demands.pdf

58. See Daniel M. Cobb, *Native Activism in Cold War America: The Struggle for Sovereignty* (Lawrence: University Press of Kansas, 2008).

59. Carlos Muñoz, Jr., *Youth, Identity, Power: The Chicano Movement* (New York: Verso, 2007), 26.

60. Patricia Bell Blawis, *Tijerina and the Land Grants: Mexican Americans in Struggle for Their Heritage* (New York: International Publishers, 1971), 114.

61. Richard Delgado, *Explaining the Rise and Fall of African American Fortunes—Interest Convergence and Civil Rights Gains*, 37 Harv. C.R.-C.L. L. Rev. 369, 377, 382–85 (2002).

62. Blawis, *Tijerina and the Land Grants*, 111.

63. Gordon K. Mantler, "Grassroots Voices, Memory, and the Poor People's Campaign," American Radioworks. http://americanradioworks.publicradio.org/features/king/mantler.html (accessed April 4, 2009); Mantler, "Black, Brown and Poor," 59–60.

64. Tillie Walker, director of United Scholarship Service, interview by Kay Shannon, July 1968, Washington, DC. Quoted in Mantler, "Black, Brown and Poor," 229.

65. Frederick Douglass Opie, *Upsetting the Apple Cart: Black-Latino Coalitions in New York City from Protest to Public Office* (New York: Columbia University Press, 2014).

66. Philip S. Foner, *Women and the American Labor Movement: From World War I to the Present* (New York: Free Press, 1980), 436.

67. Sonia Song-Ha Lee, *Building a Latino Civil Rights Movement, and the Pursuit of Racial Justice in New York City* (Chapel Hill: University of North Carolina Press, 2014)

68. Gregory Rodriguez, *Mongrels, Bastards, Orphans, and Vagabonds: Mexican Immigration and the Future of Race in America* (New York: Vintage Press, 2007).

69. Martin Luther King, Jr., Public statement on the Poor People's Campaign, December 4, 1967. http://www.thekingcenter.org/archive/document/mlk-public-statement-poor-peoples-campaign

70. "Black and White Together," SCLC News, March 15, 1968. http://www.thekingcenter.org/archive/document/poor-peoples-campaign-news#

71. Ibid.

72. Felicia Kornbluh, *The Battle for Welfare Rights: Politics and Poverty in Modern America* (Philadelphia: University of Pennsylvania Press, 2007), 9.

73. As Felicia Kornbluh demonstrates, "the overwhelming majority of male trade unionists were allergic to collaboration with welfare mothers" (ibid., 168).

74. Annelise Orleck, *Storming Caesars Palace: How Black Mothers Fought Their Own War on Poverty* (Boston: Beacon Press. 2005), 110.

75. Ibid.

76. Frances Fox Piven and Richard Cloward, "The Weight of the Poor: A Strategy to End Poverty," *The Nation*, March 8, 2010.

77. Premilla Nadasen, *Welfare Warriors: The Welfare Rights Movement in the United States* (New York: Routledge, 2005), 146.

78. David Garrow, *Bearing the Cross: Martin Luther King, Jr., and the Southern Christian Leadership Conference* (New York: William Morrow, 2004), 434.

79. Mitchell Duneier. *The Ghetto: The Invention of a Place, the History of an Idea* (New York: Farrar, Straus, and Giroux, 2016), 105.

80. Thomas F. Jackson, *From Civil Rights to Human Rights: Martin Luther King, Jr. and the Struggle for Economic Justice* (Philadelphia: University of Pennsylvania Press, 2007), 285.

81. Martin Luther King, Jr., Speech to mass meeting, Edward, Mississippi, February 15, 1968. In Thomas F. Jackson, *From Civil Rights to Human Rights: Martin Luther King, Jr., and the Struggle for Economic Justice* (Philadelphia: University of Pennsylvania Press, 2007), 346.

82. Ibid.

83. Gwendolyn Mink and Rickie Solinger, eds., *Welfare: A Documentary History of U.S. Policy and Politics* (New York: New York University Press, 2003), 284.

84. Michael K Honey, *To the Promised Land: Martin Luther King and the Fight for Economic Justice* (New York, W. W. Norton, 2018), 165.

85. "Martin Luther King: Telegram to Pennsylvania's Welfare Rights Organization," March 25, 1968. http://www.thekingcenter.org/archive/document/telegram-mlk-pennsylvania-state-welfare-rights-organization

86. Brian D. Behnken, *The Struggle in Black and Brown: African American and Mexican American Relations During the Civil Rights Era* (Lincoln: University of Nebraska Press, 2011), 166.

87. The two versions of Lewis's speech are available online at http://billmoyers.com/content/two-versions-of-john-lewis-speech/

88. Chana Kai Lee, *For Freedom's Sake: The Life of Fannie Lou Hamer* (Urbana: University of Illinois Press, 1999), 125.

89. Emma J. Folwell, "The Legacy of the Child Development Group of Mississippi: White Opposition to Head Start in Mississippi, 1965–1972," *Journal of Mississippi History* vol. 76, no. 1 (2014): 43–68.

90. Jackson, *From Civil Rights to Human Rights*, 349.

91. Joseph Peniel, *Stokely, a Life* (New York: Basic Civitas Books, 2014), 238.

92. Ibid., 242.

93. King, *Where Do We Go from Here*, 50.

94. Quoted in Michael K. Honey, *Going Down Jericho Road: The Memphis Strike, Martin Luther King's Last Campaign* (New York: W. W. Norton, 2007), 186.

95. King, *Where Do We Go from Here*, 140.

96. Andrew Young, *An Easy Burden: The Civil Rights Movement and the Transformation of America* (New York: HarperCollins, 1996), 457.

97. Honey, *Going Down Jericho Road*, 3.

98. Ibid.

99. Robert Zieger, *For Jobs and Freedom: Race and Labor in America since 1865* (Lexington: University of Kentucky Press, 2007).

100. Martin Luther King, Jr., Speech delivered at the American Federation of State, County, and Municipal Employees mass meeting, Bishop Charles Mason Temple, Church of God in Christ, Memphis, Tennessee, March 18, 1968. In Cornel West, ed., *The Radical King* (Boston: Beacon Press, 2015), 245–53.

101. Michael K. Honey, ed., *All Labor Has Dignity* (Boston: Beacon Press, 2011), 172.

102. Ibid.

103. Ibid., 300.

104. Martin Luther King, Jr., Address at Poor People's Campaign Rally, Eutaw, Alabama, March 20, 1968. In Jackson, *From Civil Rights to Human Rights*, 347.

105. Honey, *All Labor Has Dignity*, 176.

106. Steve Estes, *I Am a Man! Race, Manhood, and the Civil Rights Movement* (Chapel Hill: University of North Carolina Press, 2005), 132.

107. Ibid., 140.

108. Laurie B. Green, "Race, Gender, and Labor in 1960s Memphis: 'I Am a Man' and the Meaning of Freedom," *Journal of Urban History* 30 (March 2004): 475.

109. Dyson, *I May Not Get There with You*.

110. Honey, *Going Down Jericho Road*, 395.

111. Illinois Representative John Conyers unsuccessfully called for an $80 billion "Marshall Plan," in ibid., 445.

112. In Charles Fager, *Uncertain Resurrection: The Poor People's Washington Campaign.* (Grand Rapids, MI: William B. Erdmans Publishing, 1969), 32. For the role of the FBI in the hoax, see McKnight, *Last Crusade.*

113. In Fager, *Uncertain Resurrection,* 40.

114. Rhonda Williams points out that many African American welfare mothers embraced Black Power politics and rhetoric. Rhonda Y. Williams, "Black Women, Urban Politics and Engendering Black Power," in Joseph Peniel, ed., *The Black Power Movement: Rethinking the Civil Rights-Black Power Era,* pp. 79–103 (New York: Routledge, 2006).

115. In Jackson, *From Civil Rights to Human Rights,* 344.

CHAPTER SEVEN. A COUNTER-WAR ON POVERTY

1. Charles Fager, *Uncertain Resurrection: The Poor People's Washington Campaign* (Grand Rapids, MI: William B. Erdmans Publishing, 1969), 24.

2. Martin Luther King, Jr., *Why We Can't Wait* (Boston: Beacon Press, 1964), 151.

3. Martin Luther King, Jr., "Non-violence: The Only Road to Freedom," May 4, 1966. Quoted in Willie Baptist, Shailly Barnes, and Chris Caruso, "The Right To Not Be Poor: The Growing Global Struggle for Economic Human Rights," *Kairos* (November 2012).

4. SCLC, "Poor People in America: Economic Fact Sheet for the Poor People's Campaign, January 1968," Organizational Records, The Southern Christian Leadership Conference Records, 1954–1970.

5. Literally "ledgers of complaints," they were lists of grievances drawn up by each of the three Estates in France between March and April 1789 and submitted to King Louis XVI. To some extent, they sparked the revolution.

6. Demands made by a Poor People's Campaign Appalachian group from Kentucky to Senator John Sherman, quoted in Robert T. Chase, "Class Resurrection: The Poor People's Campaign of 1968 and Resurrection City," *Essays in History,* vol. 40 (Charlottesville: University of Virginia, 1998). http://www.essaysinhistory.com/class-resurrection-the-poor-peoples-campaign-of-1968-and-resurrection-city/

7. David Garrow, *Bearing the Cross: Martin Luther King, Jr., and the Southern Christian Leadership Conference* (New York: William Morrow, 2004), 601.

8. Proposal, April 28, 1968, "Declaration," in Amy Nathan Wright, "Civil Rights 'Unfinished Business': Poverty, Race, and the 1968 Poor People's Campaign" (Ph.D. dissertation, University of Texas at Austin, 2007), 194.

9. See Richard Lentz, *Symbols, the News Magazines and Martin Luther King* (Baton Rouge: Louisiana State University Press, 1990); Gordon Mantler, "'The Press Did You In': The Poor People's Campaign and the Mass Media," *The Sixties: A Journal of History, Politics and Culture,* vol. 3, no. 1 (2010): 33–54.

10. Fager, *Uncertain Resurrection*, 32.

11. Carson Walker, "Slain Activist Had Roots in Civil Rights Movement." http://www.jfamr.org/raymlk.html

12. Amy Nathan Wright, "Civil Rights 'Unfinished Business,'" 202.

13. Gordon K. Mantler, *Power to the Poor: Black-Brown Coalition and the Fight for Economic Justice, 1960–1974* (Chapel Hill: University of North Carolina Press, 2013), 132.

14. Wright, "Civil Rights 'Unfinished Business,'" 209.

15. Statement of Demands of Rights for the Poor Presented to Agencies of the U.S. Government by the SCLC and its Committee of 100, April 29–30, May 1, 1968. "Poor People's Campaign Is Massive Lobby Effort," *Congressional Quarterly Almanac*, 24th ed. (1968), 15-773-15-778 (Washington, DC, 1969). http://library.cqpress.com/cqalmanac/cqal68-1282236.

16. Wright, "Civil Rights 'Unfinished Business,'" 249.

17. Martin Luther King, Jr., *Where Do We Go from Here: Chaos or Community?* (Boston: Beacon Press, 2010), 209.

18. Alyosha Goldstein, *Poverty in Common: The Politics of Community Action During the American Century* (Durham, NC: Duke University Press, 2012), 137.

19. Kathy Lohr, "Poor People's Campaign: A Dream Unfulfilled," National Public Radio, June 19, 2008.

20. Ben A. Franklin, "5,000 Open Poor People's Campaign in Washington," *New York Times*, May 13, 1968.

21. "The Scene at ZIP Code 20013," *Time*, May 24, 1968, p. 29.

22. "18 Marchers Arrested in Hill Protest," *Washington Post*, May 24, 1968.

23. "Marchers Besiege Court: Panes Broken, 3 Arrested in Hill Protest," *Washington Post*, May 30, 1968. Quoted in Joule Voelz, "Interpreting the Failure of the Poor People's Campaign," *Exposé Magazine* (2014). https://projects.iq.harvard.edu/expose/book/interpreting-failure-poor-people%E2%80%99s-campaign#_ftnref25.

24. Paul Steckler, Interview with Daniel Schorr, conducted by Blackside December 5, 1988, for Washington University Libraries, Film and Media Archive, Henry Hampton Collection.

25. *Eyes on the Prize II: America at the Racial Crossroads 1965–1985*, episode 7 (Henry Hampton; Blackside; Corporation for Public Broadcasting; PBS Video; Lotus Development Corp.

26. Jean White and Willard Clopton, Jr., "Hill Delegation Visits Resurrection City, Promises Hearings," *Washington Post*, June 6, 1968.

27. The 1968 act expanded on previous acts and prohibited discrimination concerning the sale, rental, and financing of housing based on race, religion, national origin, sex, and (as amended) handicap and family status. Title VIII of the act is also known as the Fair Housing Act (of 1968).

28. Predating New Deal programs, notably the WPA, Coxey proposed a Good Roads Bill to Congress in 1892. See Carlos Arnaldo Schwantes, *Coxey's Army: An American Odyssey* (Caldwell, ID: Caxton Press, 1985).

29. Donald Le Crone McMurray, *Coxey's Army: A Study of the Industrial Movement of 1894* (Seattle: University of Washington Press, 1968).

30. Coxey ran unsuccessfully as the People's Party (the Populist Party) candidate for Ohio governor in 1895 and 1897.

31. Wright, "Civil Rights 'Unfinished Business,'" 174.

32. Roland L. Freeman, *The Mule Train: A Journey of Hope Remembered* (Nashville: Rutledge Hill Press, 1998).

33. "Pilgrimage of the Poor," *New Republic*, May 11, 1968; quoted in Wright, "Civil Rights 'Unfinished Business,'" 289.

34. "A Threat of Anarchy in Nation's Capital," *U.S. News & World Report*, May 20, 1968, quoted in Wright, "Civil Rights 'Unfinished Business,'" 252.

35. In Fager, *Uncertain Resurrection*, 36. Charles Fager was the *Washington Post* reporter appointed to cover the campaign from its inception to its end.

36. Ralph Abernathy, *And the Walls Came Tumbling Down: An Autobiography* (New York: Harper and Row, 1989), 503–504.

37. John Wiebenson, "Planning and Using Resurrection City," *Journal of American Institute of Planners*, vol. 35, no. 6 (1969): 58–68.

38. Jill Freedman, *Old News: Resurrection City* (New York: Grossman Publishers, 1970), 31.

39. Walter E. Afield and Audrey B. Gibson, *Children of Resurrection City* (Washington, DC: Association for Childhood Education International, 1970), 14.

40. In Wright, "Civil Rights 'Unfinished Business,'" 365.

41. Afield and Gibson, *Children of Resurrection City.*

42. In Wright, "Civil Rights 'Unfinished Business,'" 416.

43. "Marchers Run into Problems," *Knoxville Journal*, May 4, 1968, p. 1.

44. Maurice Isserman, *The Other American: The Life of Michael Harrington* (New York: Perseus Books, 2001), 281.

45. Lily Gay Lampinen, "The Poor People's Campaign," *International Socialism* (1st series), no. 34 (Autumn 1968): 8–10. https://www.marxists.org/history/etol/newspape/isj/1968/no034/lampinen.htm

46. David Abernathy, Address to Solidarity Day march in support of the Poor People's Campaign, Washington, D.C., June 19, 1968. Quoted in Wright, "Civil Rights 'Unfinished Business,'"454.

47. The audio recording of her speech is available at http://pastdaily.com/2013/06/19/solidarity-day-coretta-scott-king-june-19–1968/

48. *The Worker,*" June 23, 1968, quoted in Mantler, "The Press Did You In," 45.

49. Lentz, *Symbols,* 332.

50. David A. Jewell and Paul Valentine, "Police, Poor Clash Outside Tent City; A Community Concerned by Growing Violence," *Washington Post,* June 21, 1968. Quoted in Florence Ridlon, *A Black Physician's Struggle for Civil Rights: Edward C. Mazique, M.D.* (Albuquerque: University of New Mexico Press, 2005), 263.

51. Ibid., 276.

52. Gerald McKnight, *The Last Crusade: Martin Luther King, Jr., the FBI and the Poor People's Campaign* (Boulder: Westview Press, 1998), 122.

53. Andrew Young, *An Easy Burden: The Civil Rights Movement and the Transformation of America* (New York: HarperCollins, 1996), 483.

54. Ibid., 481-82.

55. Michael Honey, *Going Down Jericho Road: The Memphis Strike, Martin Luther King's Last Campaign* (New York: W. W. Norton, 2007), 189.

56. Lampinen, "The Poor People's Campaign."

57. Tali Hatuka, "The Challenge of Distance in Designing Civil Protest: The Case of Resurrection City in the Washington Mall and the Occupy Movement in Zuccotti Park," *Planning Perspectives,* July 15, 2015. http://dx.doi.org/10.1080/0 2665433.2015.1058183

58. Gordon K. Mantler, *Power to the Poor: Black-Brown Coalition and the Fight for Economic Justice, 1960-1974* (Chapel Hill: University of North Carolina Press, 2013), 123.

59. Reies Tijerina, Interview by James Mosby, June 12, 1968. Quoted in Wright, "Civil Rights 'Unfinished Business,'" 392.

60. Rudy Gonzales, Interview by Mantler, *Power to the Poor,* 160.

61. Tom Kahn, "Why the Poor People's Campaign Failed," *Commentary,* September 1, 1968. https://www.commentarymagazine.com/articles/why-the -poor-peoples-campaign-failed/

62. Darren Lenard Hutchinson, *Racial Exhaustion,* 86 Wash. U. L. Rev. 917 (2009).

63. Kahn, "Why the Poor People's Campaign Failed."

64. Bayard Rustin, "The Anatomy of Frustration," in *Time on Two Crosses: The Collected Writings of Bayard Rustin,* ed. Devon W. Carbado and Donald Weise (San Francisco: Cleiss Press, 2003).

65. Sterling Tucker, "The Role of Civil Rights Organizations—A Marshall Plan Approach," *Boston College Law Review,* vol. 7, no. 3 (1966): 4-1.

66. In Kahn, "Why the Poor People's Campaign Failed."

67. Wright, "Civil Rights 'Unfinished Business,'" 449.

68. *Washington Post,* June 10, 1968. In Robert T. Chase, "Class Resurrection: The Poor People's Campaign of 1968 and Resurrection City," in *Essays in History,* vol. 40 (Charlottesville: University of Virginia, 1998), 256. http://www .essaysinhistory.com/archive/1998-issue/

69. Ben W. Gilbert, *Ten Blocks from the White House* (New York: Praeger, 1969), 202.

70. Fager, *Uncertain Resurrection*, 115.

71. Robert G. Kaiser, "Resurrection City Falls—With a Song," *Washington Post*, June 25, 1968.

72. Paul Steckler, Interview with Daniel Schorr, conducted by Blackside December 5, 1988, for Washington University Libraries, Film and Media Archive, Henry Hampton Collection. http://digital.wustl.edu/e/eii/eiiweb /sch5427.0241.145danielschorr.html

73. In "Gordon K. Mantler, "Black, Brown and Poor: Martin Luther King Jr., the Poor People's Campaign and its Legacy" (Ph.D. dissertation, Duke University, 2008), 358. As shown by Mantler, the Chicano movement framed its ongoing local struggles in terms of connecting issues of identity, poverty, and land rights. Rodolfo "Corky" Gonzalez and the group Crusade for Justice, which played a leading role in the campaign in Denver, emphasized cultural nationalism and community empowerment within the framework of race and class. In Philadelphia, the October 4th Organization attempted to convince the white working class to collaborate with black and brown communities in order to fight big business and police brutality. Jennifer Frost, *An Interracial Movement of the Poor: Community Organizing and the New Left* (New York: New York University Press, 2005).

74. Young, *An Easy Burden*, 488.

75. Amy Sonnie and James Tracy, *Hillbilly Nationalists, Urban Race Rebels, and Black Power: Community Organizing in Radical Times* (Brooklyn: Melville House, 2011).

76. Frost, *An Interracial Movement of the Poor.*

77. Fred Hampton, "Power Anywhere Where There's People," Speech delivered at Olivet Church, 1969. Available at http://www.historyisaweapon.com/defcon1 /fhamptonspeech.html

78. The idea of a "Rainbow Coalition" was revived by Chicago's first African American mayor, Harold Washington. In 1983, he appointed key figures of the original Rainbow to a "Rainbow Cabinet." Jesse Jackson nationalized the term in the 1980s when he appropriated it and its intersectional purpose.

79. Sonnie and Tracy, *Hillbilly Nationalists*, 67.

80. Casey Peters, "South State Chair of the Peace and Freedom Party of California, Peace and Freedom Party from 1967 to 1997," *Synthesis/Regeneration* 12 (Winter 1997). http://www.greens.org/s-r/12/12-05.html

81. Jakobi E. Williams, *From the Bullet to the Ballot: The Illinois Chapter of the Black Panther Party and Racial Coalition Politics in Chicago* (Chapel Hill: University of North Carolina Press, 2013), 125–66.

82. James Tracy, "The Original Rainbow Coalition: An Interview with Bobby Lee," January 3, 2007. https://jamestracybooks.org/2007/01/03/the-original -rainbow-coalition-an-interview-with-bobby-lee/#more-4

83. Sonnie and Tracy, *Hillbilly Nationalists*, 50.

84. Quoted in Michael McCanne, "The Panthers and the Patriots," Jacobin. com, posted May 19, 2017. https://www.jacobinmag.com/2017/05/black -panthers-young-patriots-fred-hampton

85. Ibid.

86. Ibid.

87. Franziska Meister, "Racism and Resistance: How the Black Panthers Challenged White Supremacy," Political Science Transcript, 23. www.transcript -verlag.de/978-3-8376-3857-8

88. Premilla Nadasen, *Welfare Warriors: The Welfare Rights Movement in the United States* (New York: Routledge, 2005), 213–14.

89. Felicia Kornbluh, *The Battle for Welfare Rights: Politics and Poverty in Modern America* (Philadelphia: University of Pennsylvania Press, 2007).

PART THREE. THE VISION

1. "King's Challenge to the Nation's Social Scientists," *Journal of Social Issues*, vol. 24, no. 1 (1968).

CHAPTER EIGHT. FACING STRUCTURAL INJUSTICE

1. Hearings Before the Subcommittee on Executive Reorganization of the Committee on Government Operations, United States Senate, Eighty-Ninth Congress, Second Session, December 14 and 15, 1966, Part 14 (Washington, DC: Government Printing Office, 1967), 2967–82.

2. William A. Darity, Jr., and Samuel L. Myers., with Emmett D. Carson and William Sabol, *The Black Underclass: Critical Essays on Race and Unwantedness* (New York: Garland Publishing, 1994).

3. Alice O'Connor, *Poverty Knowledge: Social Science, Social Policy, and the Poor in Twentieth-Century U.S. History* (Princeton: Princeton University Press, 2001).

4. Kenneth Clark, *Youth in the Ghetto: A Study of the Consequences of Powerlessness and a Blueprint for Change* (New York: Harlem Youth Opportunities Unlimited, 1964), 79–80.

5. Franklin E. Frazier, *The Negro Family in the United States* (1939; Chicago: University of Chicago Press, 1966).

6. Kenneth B. Clark, "The Present Dilemma of the Negro," Paper presented at the Annual Meeting of Southern Regional Council, Atlanta, November 2, 1967.

7. "Alex Haley's interview with Martin Luther King," *Playboy*, January 1965. https://www.thedailybeast.com/alex-haleys-1965-playboy-interview-with-rev -martin-luther-king-jr

8. Martin Luther King, Jr. *Where Do We Go from Here: Chaos or Community?* (Boston: Beacon Press, 2010), 169.

9. Martin Luther King, Jr., "The Role of the Behavioral Scientist in the Civil Rights Movement," Address at American Psychological Association Convention, September 1, 1967. Reprinted in "King's Challenge to the Nation's Social Scientists," *Journal of Social Issues*, vol. 24, no. 1 (1968).

10. Mitchell Duneier, *Ghetto: The Invention of a Place, The History of an Idea* (New York: Farrar, Straus and Giroux, 2016), 117.

11. King, *Where Do We Go from Here*, 198.

12. Robert Blauner, "Internal Colonialism and Ghetto Revolt," *Social Problems*, vol. 16, no. 4 (Spring 1969), 393-408.

13. Barbara Arneil, *Domestic Colonies: The Turn Inward to Colony* (London: Oxford University Press, 2017), 8.

14. James H. Cone, *Martin & Malcolm & America: A Dream or a Nightmare* (Maryknoll, NY: Orbis Books, 1991).

15. Martin Luther King, Jr., Address at the Chicago Freedom Festival, March 12, 1966. http://www.crmvet.org/docs/6603_sclc_mlk_cfm.pdf

16. See Kathryn Gines, "Martin Luther King Jr. and Frantz Fanon, Reflections on the Politics and Ethics of Violence and Non Violence," in Robert E. Birt, *The Liberatory Thought of Martin Luther King Jr: Critical Essays on the Philosopher King* (Lanham, MD: Lexington Books, 2012), 243-263.

17. "King's Challenge to the Nation's Social Scientists," *Journal of Social Issues*, vol. 24, no. 1 (1968).

18. Undated Black Panther Party pamphlet entitled "Defend the Ghetto." Quoted in Lisa Vario, "All Power to the People: The Influence and Legacy of the Black Panther Party, 1966—1980" (Masters' thesis, Youngstown State University, December 2007), 61. https://etd.ohiolink.edu/rws_etd/document/get/ . . . /inline.

19. Martin Luther King, Jr., Press Conference on Washington Campaign, Ebenezer Baptist Church, Atlanta, December 4, 1967.

20. Daniel Matlin, "Ghettos of the Mind: Kenneth B. Clark and the Psychology of the Urban Crisis" (chapter), *On the Corner: African American Intellectuals and the Urban Crisis* (Cambridge, MA: Harvard University Press, 2013), 36-123.

21. Kenneth B. Clark, "Beyond the Ghetto" (unpublished manuscript, August 6, 1979), 28-29. In Duneier, 133.

22. Martin Luther King, Jr., "Where Do We Go From Here?" Sermon delivered at the Eleventh Annual SCLC Convention, Atlanta, GA, August 16, 1967. In

James Washington, ed., *A Testament of Hope: The Essential Writing of Martin Luther King, Jr.* (New York: HarperCollins, 1991), 250.

23. King, "Where Do We Go From Here?" 87.

24. Martin Luther King, Jr., "Showdown for Nonviolence," *Look,* in Washington, *Testament of Hope,* 64–72.

25. King, "A Testament of Hope," *Playboy* interview, January 1969. In Washington, *Testament of Hope,* 325–26. http://www.playboy.com/articles/a-testament-of-hope-martin-luther-king-jr.

26. Douglass Massey and Nancy Denton, *American Apartheid: Segregation and the Making of the Underclass* (Cambridge, MA: Harvard University Press, 1998), 195. The assumption that the bill was intentionally doomed to fail is challenged, but not the fact of the disappointing outcome. See Jonathan Zasloff, "The Secret History of the Fair Housing Act (2016)," 53 *Harvard Journal on Legislation* 247 (2016); UCLA School of Law Research Paper No. 10–21. https://ssrn.com/abstract = 1661237.

27. See Matt Wray and Annalee Newitz, *White Trash: Race and Class in America* (New York: Routledge, 1997); Nancy Isenberg, *White Trash: The 400-Year Untold History of Class in America* (New York: Viking, 2016).

28. Robert Blauner, *Racial Oppression in America* (New York: Harper and Row, 1972), 28–29.

29. William Julius Wilson, *The Truly Disadvantaged: The Inner City, the Underclass, and Public Policy* (Chicago: The University of Chicago Press, 1987), 12. Wilson thus summed up his study: "I argued in *The Truly Disadvantaged* that the central problem of the underclass is joblessness, a problem that is rendered even more severe by an increasing social isolation in impoverished neighborhoods." William Julius Wilson, "When Work Disappears," *Political Science Quarterly,* 111 (1997): 567–95.

30. William Julius Wilson, "Social Theory and the Concept 'Underclass,'" In David Grusky and Ravi Kanbur, eds., *Poverty and Inequality* (Palo Alto: Stanford University Press, 2005), 103-16.

31. King, "A Testament of Hope," *Playboy* Interview, January 1969, in Washington, *Testament of Hope,* 325–26.

32. John F. Kain, *The Effect of the Ghetto on the Distribution and Level on non-White Unemployment in Urban Areas* (Santa Monica, CA; Rand Corporation, 1965). Later he would establish that, in 1963, half of the manufacturing jobs were located in the outskirts of the forty metropolitan areas he observed.

33. Wilson, *Truly Disadvantaged,* 126.

34. Ibid., 132.

35. Martin Luther King, Jr., "Showdown for Nonviolence," *Look,* April 16, 1968, in Washington, *Testament of Hope,* 64–72.

36. Quoted in Marcus Pohlmann, *Capitalism vs. Collectivism: 1945 to the Present: African American Political Thought* (New York: Routledge, 2003), 87–95.

37. Interview with William Julius Wilson by Henri Louis Gates, "The Two Nations of Black America," PBS documentary, May 6, 2008.

38. Martin Luther King, Jr., *The Trumpet of Conscience* (Boston: Beacon Press, 2010), 148.

39. King, "Where Do We Go From Here?" in Washington, *Testament of Hope*, 255.

40. Alex Haley's interview, *Playboy*, January 1965, in Washington, *Testament of Hope*, 340–78.

41. In his introductory chapter, "Racial Antagonism and the Expanding Ranks of the Have-Nots," Wilson writes: "As the new millennium dawns, the movement for racial equality needs a new political strategy. That strategy must appeal to America's broad multiracial population while addressing the many problems that afflict disadvantaged minorities and redressing the legacy of historic racism in America." In *Truly Disadvantaged*, 11–44. See also William Julius Wilson, *The Declining Significance of Race: Blacks and Changing American Institutions* (Chicago: The University of Chicago Press, 1980).

42. William Julius Wilson, *The Bridge Over the Racial Divide: Rising Inequality and Coalition Politics* (Berkeley: University of California Press, 1999).

43. King, *Where Do We Go from Here*, 106–107.

44. Ibid., 121.

45. "Bank of Sweden Opens Account," *Jet*, April 14, 1966.

46. Entitled *An American Dilemma: The Negro Problem and Modern Democracy*, the final report was a compendious two-volume, 1500-page scientific work which synthesized 20,000 pages of empirical evidence. E. Stina Lyon, "Researching Race Relations: Myrdal's American Dilemma from a Methodological Perspective," *Acta Sociologica*, vol. 47, no. 3 (September 2004): 203–17.

47. Myrdal inaugurated the concept of "cumulative causation" in the report, which he would apply in his later scholarship on development economics.

48. Colin Wayne Leach compellingly argues that this argument anticipated contemporary scholarship. "Democracy's Dilemma: Explaining Racial Inequality in Egalitarian Societies," *Sociological Forum*, vol. 17, no. 4 (December 2002): 681–96. As a telling example, one can read Karen E. Fields and Barbara J. Fields, *Racecraft: The Soul of Inequality in American Life* (New York: Verso, 2012).

49. Kenneth B. Clark, *Dark Ghetto: Dilemmas of Social Power* (New York: Harper and Row, 1965).

50. Gunnar Myrdal, in Nathan Glazer, "Liberalism and the Negro: A Round-Table Discussion," *Commentary*, March 1, 1964. https://www.commentarymaga zine.com/articles/liberalism-the-negro-a-round-table-discussion/

51. James Baldwin, in Glazer, "Liberalism and the Negro."

52. David W. Southern, *Gunnar Myrdal and Black-White Relations* (Baton Rouge: Louisiana State University Press, 1987), 220.

53. Ralph Ellison, "An American Dilemma: A Review," in Ellison, *Shadow and Act* (New York: Random House, 1964), 303-23.

54. See Jackson A. Walter, *Gunnar Myrdal and America's Conscience: Social Engineering and Racial Liberalism, 1938–1987* (Chapel Hill: University of North Carolina Press, 1990).

55. See Guglielmo Forges Davanzati, "Gunnar Myrdal on Labour Market Regulation and Economic Development," *Œconomia*. http://oeconomia.revues .org/573; DOI:10.4000/oeconomia.573.

56. Ibid., 49.

57. Actually, Sweden had not always been a nation devoted to equality and regulation. Myrdal recalled that he stood in opposition to the prevailing laissez-faire mainstream: "Like most economists of my generation in Sweden, I had different views on policy. To begin with, we were of an interventionist mind. We wanted, for instance, to plan public action in order to mitigate the widespread unemployment during the depression after the end of the First World War. We had, then, to refute our elders" (Gunnar Myrdal, *Objectivity in Social Research*, New York: Pantheon Books, 1969, p. 7).

58. Martin Luther King, Jr., Nobel Lecture at University of Oslo, December 11, 1964. https://www.nobelprize.org/nobel_prizes/peace/laureates/1964 /king-acceptance_en.html

59. Martin Luther King, Jr., Speech at Southern Methodist University, Dallas, March 17, 1966. https://www.smu.edu/News/2014/mlk-at-smu-transcript -17march1966

60. Gunnar Myrdal, *Beyond the Welfare State. Economic Planning in the Welfare States and its International Implications* (London: Methuen, 1958), 47.

61. Ibid., 28.

62. King, *Where Do We Go from Here*, 172.

63. Ibid.

64. Martin Luther King, Jr., Press conference of the Annual Meeting of Medical Committee for Human Rights, Chicago, March 25, 1966.

65. Baldwin, in Glazer, "Liberalism and the Negro," 46.

66. Hearings Before the Subcommittee on Executive Reorganization of the Committee on Government Operations, United States Senate, Eighty-Ninth Congress, Second Session, December 14 and 15, 1966, Part 14 (Washington, DC: Government Printing Office, 1967), 2967–82.

67. Michael Ezra, ed., *The Economic Civil Rights Movement, African Americans and the Struggle for Economic Power* (New York: Routledge, 2013).

68. The Poor People's Campaign," SCLC pamphlet. http://anna.lib.us m. edu/~spcol/crda/adams/vga044_3.jpg 7 (accessed September 4, 2005). In Amy Nathan Wright, "Civil Rights 'Unfinished Business': Poverty, Race, and the 1968 Poor People's Campaign" (Ph.D. dissertation, University of Texas at Austin, 2007), 239.

69. Carole Shammas, "A New Look at Long-Term Trends in Wealth Inequality in the United States, *American Historical Review,* vol. 98, no. 2 (April 1993): 412–31.

70. John Kenneth Galbraith, *The Affluent Society* (New York: Houghton Mifflin, 1998), 79.

71. Ibid., 154.

72. King, Speech at Southern Methodist University, Dallas, March 17, 1966.

73. King, *Where Do We Go from Here,* 119.

74. Martin Luther King, Jr., "Remaining Awake Through a Great Revolution," Commencement Address at Oberlin College, June 1965. https://kinginstitute .stanford.edu/king-papers/publications/ knock-midnight-inspiration-great-sermons-reverend-martin-luther-king-jr-10

75. Martin Luther King, Jr., "If the Negro Wins, Labor Wins," Address at AFL-CIO Fourth Constitutional Convention, Miami Beach, December 11, 1961. In Michael K. Honey, ed., *All Labor Has Dignity* (Boston: Beacon Press, 2011), 39.

76. Martin Luther King, Jr., Press Conference announcing the Poor People's Campaign, Atlanta, December 4, 1967.

77. Martin Luther King, Jr., "The Other America," Speech at Stanford University, April 14, 1967. KQED TV Archive by Stanford University, aired April 14,1967. Transcript available: "Martin Luther King and Economic Justice: The Fortieth Anniversary Commemoration of Dr. King's 'The Other America' Speech at Aurora Forum at Stanford University," April 15, 2007. http://www.crmvet.org /docs/otheram.htm

78. Hearings Before the Subcommittee on Executive Reorganization of the Committee on Government Operations, United States Senate, Eighty-Ninth Congress, Second Session, December 14 and 15, 1966, Part 14 (Washington, DC: Government Printing Office, 1967), 2967–82.

79. Gavin Wright, *Sharing the Prize: The Economics of the Civil Rights Revolution in the South* (Cambridge, MA: Harvard University Press, 2013).

80. Michael K. Brown, "Divergent Fates: The Foundations of Durable Racial Inequality, 1940–2013" (unpublished paper, Demos and Rockefeller Foundation, 2013).

81. James Smith and Finis R. Welch, "Black Economic Progress after Myrdal," *Journal of Economic Literature,* vol. 27, no. 2 (June 1989): 519–64.

82. The Stanford Center on Poverty and Inequality has made outstanding contributions to our understanding of the mechanics of inequality. Among many studies, the scholarship of Harvard economist Raj Chetty on the determinants of social mobility points to the role of space and segregation in the opportunity to experience upward mobility. https://inequality.stanford.edu/about/people /raj-chetty.

83. Michael B. Katz, *The Undeserving Poor: America's Enduring Confrontation with Poverty* (New York: Oxford University Press, 2013), 114.

84. King, *Where Do We Go from Here*, 14.

85. Today, Harvard professor William Julius Wilson, Duke economics and public policy professor William Darity, Jr., and New School economist Darrick Hamilton as well as Ronald B. Mincy, Manning Marable, the National Urban League, Jarvis Tyner, and the Black Radical Congress all advocate for a program by which the federal government would guarantee employment, with benefits and a living wage, to every American willing and able to work. It is sometimes called the "job guarantee" or the "employer of last resort."

86. Nina Banks, "The Black Worker, Economic Justice and the Speeches of Sadie T. M. Alexander," *Review of Social Economy*, vol. 66, no. 2 (June 2008).

87. William E. Forbath, "Constitutional Welfare Rights: A History, Critique and Reconstruction," 69 Fordham L. Rev. 1821 (2001), 1861. http://ir.lawnet .fordham.edu/flr/vol69/iss5/12

88. Tommie Shelby and Brandon M. Terry, eds., *To Shape a New World: Essays on the Political Philosophy of Martin Luther King, Jr.* (Cambridge, MA: Harvard University Press, 2018), 234.

89. University of Chicago libertarian economist Milton Friedman introduced the idea in his 1962 essay, *Capitalism and Freedom*.

90. Felicia Kornbluh, "Is Work the Only Thing that Pays? The Guaranteed Income and Other Alternative Anti-Poverty Policies in Historical Perspective," *Policies in Historical Perspective*, 4 Nw. J. L. & Soc. Pol'y 61 (2009). http://scholarly commons.law.northwestern.edu/njlsp/vol4/iss1/4.

91. Nixon's Family Assistance Plan (FAP) was expected to expand the federal welfare budget, adding about $2.5 billion to provide low-income citizens with a minimum income. Replacing the AFDC, FAP was infused with conservative undertones with regard to family and also required work obligations. Nixon's disparaging comments on welfare recipients and the plan's ambiguities alienated liberals and welfare rights activists. Eventually, Congress rejected FAP twice, in 1970 and 1972.

92. Lawrie Balfour, "Living in the Red: Time, Debt and Justice," in Shelby and Terry, *To Shape a New World*, 236-39.

93. Martin Luther King, Jr., "The Three Evils of Society," Address delivered at the National Conference on New Politics, August 31, 1967. https://fr.scribd.com /doc/134362247/Martin-Luther-King-Jr-The-Three-Evils-of-Society-1967

94. Ibid.

95. Telegram to Lyndon Johnson, July 25, 1967. http://americanradioworks .publicradio.org/features/king/telegram-7-25-67.html

96. "Freedom Budget" (A. Philip Randolph Institute, 1966).

97. Bayard Rustin, "The Influence of the Left and Right in the Civil Rights Movement," Paper prepared for the Negro Leadership Conference, January 30-31, 1965. In Bayard Rustin, *Down the Line: The Collected Writings of Bayard Rustin* (Chicago: Quadrangle Books, 1971), 130.

98. King, *Where Do We Go from Here*, 222.

99. Ibid., 173.

100. Carole Pateman, *Democracy, Feminism, Welfare* (New York: Routledge, 2011), 165.

101. Alice Kressler-Harris, "In Pursuit of Economic Citizenship," *Social Politics: International Studies in Gender, State and Society*, vol. 10, no. 2 (Summer 2003): 169.

102. King, *Where Do We Go from Here*, 209.

103. Ibid., 210.

104. Ibid, 174.

105. Ibid, 150.

106. Ibid.

107. Frank I. Michelman, "The Supreme Court 1968 Term-Foreword: On Protecting the Poor Through the Fourteenth Amendment," 83 Harv. L. Rev. 7 (1969).

108. Robert Goodman, *After the Planners* (New York: Simon and Schuster, 1971), 32.

109. "A Statement by Economists on Guaranteed Income and Supplement," May 27, 1968. In Jyotsna Sreenivasan, ed., *Poverty and the Government in America: A Historical Encyclopedia*, vol. 1 (Santa Barbara, CA: ABC-CLIO, 2009), 269.

110. Working-class Americans of recent immigrant descent as well as non-Wasp intellectuals couched the debate over racial equality in terms of unworthiness, ungratefulness, and accountability; see Matthew Frye Jacobson, *Roots Too: White Ethnic Revival in Post-Civil War America* (Cambridge, MA: Harvard University Press).

111. Daniel Geary, *Beyond Civil Rights: The Moynihan Report and Its Legacy* (Philadelphia: University of Pennsylvania Press, 2015), 172–206.

112. Stephen Hess, *The Professor and the President: Daniel Patrick Moynihan in the Nixon White House* (Washington, DC: Brookings Institution Press, 2015). http://www.jstor.org/stable/10.7864/j.ctt7zsvxq

113. Peter Passell and Leonard Ross, "Daniel Moynihan and President-elect Nixon: How Charity Didn't Begin at Home," *New York Times Book Review*, January 14, 1973.

114. In January 1970, Patrick Moynihan sent a memorandum to President Nixon advising a stance of "benign neglect." Arguing that racial equality had almost been achieved by the Johnson administration, and that the remaining black progress was self-perpetuating, he provoked once again a firestorm of controversy.

115. Dean J. Kotlowski, *Nixon's Civil Rights: Politics, Principles, and Policy* (Cambridge, MA: Harvard University Press, 2001).

116. B. Drummond Ayres, Jr., "New Jobs Law Is Urged as Humphrey Honor," *New York Times*, January 15, 1978.

117. Ginsburg, H. L. "Historical Amnesia: The Humphrey-Hawkins Act, Full Employment and Employment as a Right," 39 Rev. Black Polit. Econ. (2012): 121. doi:10.1007/s12114–011–9121–3.

118. Ayres, "New Jobs Law."

119. In Marisa Chappell, *The War on Welfare, Family, Poverty and Politics in America* (Philadelphia: University of Pennsylvania Press, 2011), 125.

120. Ayres, "New Jobs Law."

121. In 1978, Representative John Conyers, Jr., Democrat of Michigan, strongly endorsed the bill: "This is the most important bill I've ever worked on since I've been in Congress." In 2013, while running for reelection, he defended the reintroduction of the bill: "It is my hope that with the reintroduction of my bill, the Humphrey-Hawkins Full Employment and Training Act, Congress will begin to seriously examine the idea that the federal government can, and must, play a major role in putting Americans back to work." http://www.johnconyers.com/hr-1000 -humphrey-hawkins-full-employment-and-training-act#.WWjWe5VK3X4

122. Wilson, *The Bridge over the Racial Divide*.

CHAPTER NINE. A "RIGHT NOT TO STARVE"

1. Sidney M. Milkis and Jerome M. Mileur, *The New Deal and the Triumph of Liberalism* (Amherst: University of Massachusetts Press, 2002). See also Sidney M. Milkis and J. M. Mileur, *The Great Society and the High Tide of Liberalism* (Amherst: University of Massachusetts Press, 2005).

2. Franklin Delano Roosevelt, "State of the Union Message to Congress," January 11, 1944. http://www.presidency.ucsb.edu/ws/?pid = 16518.

3. Ibid.

4. Ira Katznelson, "Limiting Liberalism: The Southern Veto in Congress, 1933–1950," *Political Science Quarterly*, vol. 108, no. 2 (Summer 1993): 283–306.

5. Roosevelt's second term was not only crippled by the economic recession but also by political setbacks: the appropriations for the Works Progress Administration were gutted, other New Deal innovations were dropped or rendered ineffective, and the National Resources Planning Board, a presidential agency created in 1939 to overview social policies, succumbed to opposition.

6. Full Employment Bill of 1945, S. 380, 79th Cong. (1945), quoted in Stephen Kemp Bailey, *Congress Makes a Law: The Story behind the Employment Act of 1946* (New York: Columbia University Press, 1950), 243.

7. Alan Brinkley, *The End of Reform: New Deal Liberalism in Recession and War* (New York: Knopf, 1995).

8. Robert C. Lieberman, *Shaping Race Policy: The United States in Comparative Perspective* (Princeton: Princeton University Press, 2005).

9. Steve Fraser and Gary Gerstle, *The Rise and Fall of the New Deal Order, 1930–1980* (Princeton: Princeton University Press, 1989).

10. Adolph Reed, Jr., "Race and the New Deal Coalition," *The Nation,* March 20, 2008.

11. On King's human rights perspectives, see Thomas F. Jackson, "'Bread of Freedom': Martin Luther King, Jr. and Human Rights," *OAH Magazine of History,* vol. 22, Issue 2 (April 2008): 14–16. https://doi.org/10.1093/maghis/22.2.14

12. Cynthia Soohoo, Catherine Albisa, and Martha F. Davis, *Bringing Human Rights Home: A History of Human Rights in the United States* (Philadelphia: University of Pennsylvania Press, 2009).

13. See Brinkley, *End of Reform.*

14. Martin Luther King, Jr., *The Trumpet of Conscience,* quoted in Cornell West, ed., *The Radical King* (Boston: Beacon Press, 2015), 149.

15. Irving Louis Horowitz, "Louis Hartz and the Liberal Tradition: From Consensus to Crack-Up," *Modern Age,* vol. 47, no. 3 (Summer 2005).

16. Louis Hartz, *The Liberal Tradition in America: An Interpretation of American Political Thought Since the Revolution* (New York: Houghton Mifflin Harcourt, 1955).

17. Roger Smith, "Beyond Tocqueville, Myrdal and Hartz: The Multiple Traditions in America," *American Political Science Review,* vol. 87, no. 3 (September 1993): 549–66; Brian Abel-Smith, "The Beveridge Report: Its Origins and Outcomes," *International Social Security Review,* vol. 45, no. 1–2 (January 1992): 5–16.

18. Cass Sustein, *The Second Bill of Rights: FDR's Unfinished Revolution and Why We Need It More Than Ever* (New York: Basic Books, 2004).

19. Smith, "Beyond Tocqueville"; Karen Orren and Stephen Skowronek, *The Search for American Political Development* (New York: Cambridge University Press, 2004), 56–72.

20. The article reads: "(1) Everyone has the right to work, to free choice of employment, to just and favourable conditions of work and to protection against unemployment. (2) Everyone, without any discrimination, has the right to equal pay for equal work. (3) Everyone who works has the right to just and favourable remuneration ensuring for himself and his family an existence worthy of human dignity, and supplemented, if necessary, by other means of social protection. (4) Everyone has the right to form and to join trade unions for the protection of his interests." http://www.un.org/en/universal-declaration-human-rights/

21. T. H. Marshall, *Citizenship and Social Class, and Other Essays* (Cambridge: Cambridge University Press, 1950), 29.

22. Ibid., 220.

23. Joshua Cohen and Joel Rogers, *On Democracy: Toward a Transformation of American Society* (Middlesex: Penguin, 1983).

24. Carole Pateman, *Democracy, Feminism, Welfare* (New York: Routledge 2011), 155.

25. Martin Luther King, Jr., "Address at the Illinois State Convention of the American Federation of Labor and Congress of Industrial Organizations," July 10, 1965. In Michael K. Honey, *All Labor Has Dignity* (Boston: Beacon Press, 2011), 178.

26. Michael G. Long, *Against Us, but for Us: Martin Luther King, Jr. and the State* (Macon, GA: Mercer University Press, 2002), 52.

27. King, *Trumpet of Conscience*, in West, *Radical King*, 149.

28. Since the 2008 elections, Democratic candidates have defended universal social rights, most notably free healthcare.

29. Judith N. Shklar, "American Citizenship: The Quest for Inclusion," The Tanner Lectures on Human Values Delivered at University of Utah. May 1 and 2, 1989, 387. https://tannerlectures.utah.edu/_documents/a-to-z/s/shklar90.pdf

30. Ibid., 438.

31. Ibid.

32. William Julius Wilson, *The Truly Disadvantaged: The Inner City, the Underclass, and Public Policy* (Chicago: The University of Chicago Press, 1987), 159–63.

33. John Rawls, *A Theory of Justice* (Cambridge, MA: Harvard University Press, 1971), 137.

34. H. L. A. Hart, "Rawls on Liberty and Its Priority," *Essays in Jurisprudence and Philosophy* (November 1983), 220-76.

35. Ibid., 302.

36. Ibid., 307.

37. Ibid., 545.

38. Ibid., 440.

39. Simon Birnbaum, *Basic Income Reconsidered: Social Justice, Liberalism, and the Demands of Equality* (New York: Palgrave Macmillan, 2012).

40. Shelby Tommie, "Race and Ethnicity, Race and Social Justice: Rawlsian Considerations," 72 Fordham L. Rev. 1697 (2004), 1712.

41. William E. Forbath, "Constitutional Welfare Rights: A History, Critique and Reconstruction," 69 Fordham L. Rev. 1821 (2001). http://ir.lawnet.fordham.edu/flr/vol69/iss5/12

42. Chris Armstrong, *Rethinking Equality: The Challenge of Equal Citizenship* (Manchester: Manchester University Press, 2006), 23.

43. Rawls, *Theory of Justice*, 96, 99

44. J. Rawls, *Political Liberalism* (New York: Columbia University Press, 1996), 157.

45. Forbath, "Constitutional Welfare Rights." See also Frank I. Michelman, "The Supreme Court 1968 Term-Foreword: On Protecting the Poor Through the Fourteenth Amendment," 83 Harv. L. Rev. 7 (1969).

46. Robert Michael Franklin, "In Pursuit of a Just Society: Martin Luther King, Jr., and John Rawls," *The Journal of Religious Ethics*, vol. 18, no. 2 (Fall 1990): 57–77.

47. Ibid.

48. Shin-Heang Lee, "The Concept of Justice in the Political Thought of Martin Luther King, Jr.," *Journal of East and West Studies*, vol. 13, no. 2 (1984): 43–64.

49. Rawls actually hinted at race in three instances: the status of race as a feature of the veil of ignorance; racial minorities, the least advantaged, and the difference principle; and the role of arguments posited by antebellum abolitionist dissidents and Martin Luther King Jr. in favor of racial equality in Rawls's reformulation of his notion of public reason. He considered the religious arguments of antebellum abolitionists against slavery and by Martin Luther King Jr. against racial segregation to be compatible with the "inclusive view" of public reason.

50. Ai-Thu Dang, "Eyes Wide Shut: John Rawls's Silence on Racial Justice," *Documents de travail du Centre d' Economie de la Sorbonne*, no. 30 (2015).

51. Charles W. Mills, "Rawls on Race/Race in Rawls," *The Southern Journal of Philosophy*, vol. 48 (2009): 161.

52. Charles W. Mills, *Black Rights/White Wrongs: The Critique of Racial Liberalism* (New York: Oxford University Press, 2017).

53. G. A. Cohen, *Rescuing Justice and Equality* (Cambridge, MA: Harvard University Press, 2008); Thomas McCarthy, "Political Philosophy and Racial Injustice: From Normative to Critical Theory," in S. Benhabib and N. Fraser, eds., *Pragmatism, Critique, Judgment* (Cambridge, MA: MIT Press, 2004), 149–70; Seana Valentine Shiffrin, "Race, Labor, and the Fair Equality of Opportunity Principle," 72 Fordham L. Rev. 5 (2004): 1643–75.

54. Tommie Shelby, *Dark Ghettos: Injustice, Dissent, and Reform* (Cambridge, MA: Harvard University Press, 2016), 171.

55. Martin Luther King, Jr., *Why We Can't Wait* (Boston: Beacon Press, 1964), 137.

56. Timothy Waligore, "Rawls, Race, and a Historicized Difference Principle," Paper presented at "John Rawls: Past, Present, and Future" Conference at Yale University, November 30, 2012 (mimeo).

57. Brandon Terry, "Critical Race Theory and the Tasks of Political Philosophy: On Rawls and *The Racial Contract*" (mimeo, Harvard University, 2015).

58. John Rawls, *Justice as Fairness*, ed. Erin Kelly (Cambridge, MA: Harvard University Press, 2001), 64–65.

59. Quoted in Thomas Nagel, "John Rawls and Affirmative Action," *The Journal of Blacks in Higher Education*, no. 39 (Spring 2003): 82–84.

60. Nicholas Brommel, *The Time Is Always Now: Black Thought and the Transformation of US Democracy* (Oxford: Oxford University Press, 2013), 158.

61. Anita Haya Patterson, *From Emerson to King: Democracy, Race, and the Politics of Protest* (New York: Oxford University Press, 1997), 176.

62. Michael C. Dawson, *Black Visions: The Roots of Contemporary African-American Political Ideologies* (New York: Oxford University Press, 2002), 33.

63. In Nikhil Pal Singh, *Black Is a Country: Race and the Unfinished Struggle for Democracy* (Cambridge, MA: Harvard University Press, 2005), 162.

64. In Charles P. Henry, *Ralph Bunche: Model Negro or American Other?* (New York: New York University Press, 1999), 299.

65. In David F. Ericson and Louisa Bertch Green, eds., *The Liberal Tradition in American Politics; Reassessing the Legacy of American Liberalism* (New York: Routledge, 2013), 111.

66. Antoine L. Joseph, *The Dynamics of Racial Progress: Economic Inequality and Race Relations since Reconstruction* (New York: Routledge, 2005), 164.

67. Alice O'Connor, *Poverty Knowledge: Social Science, Social Policy, and the Poor in Twentieth-Century U.S. History* (Princeton: Princeton University Press, 2001), 102–7.

68. Lani Guinier, "From Racial Liberalism to Racial Literacy: Brown V. Board of Education and the Interest-Divergence Dilemma," *Journal of American History*, vol. 91, no. 1 (June 2004): 92–118. https://doi.org/10.2307/3659616

69. Ibid.

70. Nathan W. Schlueter, *One Dream or Two? Justice in America and in the Thought of Martin Luther King, Jr.* (Lanham, MD: Lexington Books, 2003).

71. Mary L. Dudziak, *Cold War Civil Rights: Race and the Image of American Democracy.* (Princeton: Princeton University Press, 2000).

72. Robbie Lieberman and Clarence Lang, eds., *Anticommunism and the African American Freedom Movement* (New York: Palgrave Macmillan, 2009); Eric Arnesen, "The Traditions of African-American Anti-Communism," *Twentieth Century Communism*, vol. 6, no. 6 (March 2014): 124–48.

73. Martin Luther King, Jr., "The Last Steep Ascent," *The Nation*, March 14, 1966. https://www.thenation.com/article/last-steep-ascent/

74. Gary Gerstle, "Race and the Myth of the Liberal Consensus," *Journal of American History*, vol. 82, no. 2 (September 1995): 579–86.

75. Martin Luther King, Jr., *Where Do We Go from Here: Chaos or Community?* (Boston: Beacon Press, 2010), 98.

76. Martin Luther King, Jr., Letter to A. Hawkins, March 16, 1966. http://www.thekingcenter.org/archive/document/letter-augustus-f-hawkins-mlk

77. Martin Luther King, Jr., "Stride Toward Freedom," in Washington, *Testament of Hope*, 117.

78. Press release of U.S. Representative John Conyers, Jr. asking support of the "Full Opportunity Act," October 1, 1967, Martin Luther King Archives. http://www.thekingcenter.org/archive/document/news-release-congressman-john-conyers-jr#

79. Quoted in H. B. Shaffer, *Negro Power Struggle,* Editorial Research Reports, vol. 1 (Washington, DC: Congressional Quarterly Press, 1968). http://library.cqpress.com/cqresearcher/document.php?id = cqresrre1968022108

80. Carol A. Horton, *Race and the Making of American Liberalism* (New York: Oxford University Press, 2005), 11.

81. See for instance, Joseph E. Lowndes, *From the New Deal to the New Right: Race and the Southern Origins of Modern Conservatism* (New Haven: Yale University Press, 2008); Michael J. Klarman, "How Brown Changed Race Relations: The Backlash Thesis," *Journal of American History,* vol. 81, no. 1 (June 1994): 81–118; George Lewis, *Massive Resistance: The White Response to the Civil Rights Movement* (London: Hodder Arnold, 2006), 24.

82. King, *Trumpet of Conscience,* in West, *Radical King,* 5–10.

83. Martin Luther King, Jr., "A Testament of Hope," *Playboy* interview, January 1969, in James Washington, ed., *A Testament of Hope: The Essential Writing of Martin Luther King Jr.* (San Francisco: HarperCollins, 1991), 316. http://www.playboy.com/articles/a-testament-of-hope-martin-luther-king-jr.

84. Thomas J. Sugrue, "Crabgrass-Roots Politics: Race, Rights, and the Reaction against Liberalism in the Urban North, 1940–1964," *Journal of American History,* vol. 82, no. 2 (September 1995): 551–78.

85. Tom Khan, "Why the Poor People's Campaign Failed," *Commentary* (September 1968).

86. Falguni A. Sheth and George Yancy, "How Liberalism and Racism Are Wed," *New York Times,* February 27, 2015.

CONCLUSION

1. Amy Nathan Wright, "Civil Rights 'Unfinished Business': Poverty, Race, and the 1968 Poor People's Campaign" (Ph.D. dissertation, University of Texas at Austin, 2007), 434-38.

2. Martin Luther King, Jr., Speech at the District 5 Union, Monticello, New York, September 8, 1962. In Michael Honey, *All Labor Has Dignity* (Boston: Beacon Press, 2011), 43.

3. Joseph E. Stiglitz, "How Dr. King Shaped My Work in Economics," *New York Times,* August 27, 2013.

4. Joseph Peniel, "Heroic Period of the Civil Rights Movement 1954-1965," in Manning Marable and Elizabeth Kai Hinton, eds., *The New Black History: Revisiting the Second Reconstruction* (New York: Palgrave Macmillan, 2011), 158.

5. Brandon Terry, "Critical Race Theory and the Tasks of Political Philosophy: On Rawls and *The Racial Contract*" (mimeo, Harvard University, 2015).

6. Michael Eric Dyson, *April 4, 1968: Martin Luther King, Jr.'s Death and How It Changed America* (New York: Civitas Books, 2008).

7. In the early 1970s, Corky Gonzales created the Chicano Youth Liberation Conference and La Raza Unida in Texas. See Gordon K. Mantler, *Power to the Poor: Black-Brown Coalition and the Fight for Economic Justice, 1960–1974* (Chapel Hill: University of North Carolina Press, 2013).

8. Richard Rorty, *Achieving Our Country: Leftist Thought in Twentieth-Century America* (Cambridge, MA: Harvard University Press, 1998).

9. For an invigorating critique of the identity politics thesis, see Robin D. G. Kelley, "Identity Politics and Class Struggle," *New Politics,* vol. 6, no. 2 (new series), whole no. 22 (Winter 1997).

10. Jose Yglesias, "Dr. King's March on Washington, Part II," *New York Times Magazine,* March 31, 1968. https://timesmachine.nytimes.com/timesmac hine/1968/03/331/103473891.pdf

11. Andrew Hartman, *A War for the Soul of America: A History of the Culture Wars* (Chicago: The University of Chicago Press, 2015), 59.

12. Linda Nicholson, "Identity After Identity Politics," 33 Wash. U. J. L. & Pol'y 43 (2010). http://openscholarship.wustl.edu/law_journal_law_policy/vol33/iss1/

13. Rodolpho Gonzales, *Hispanic Civil Rights Series: Message to Aztlan* (Houston: Arte Publico Press, 2001), 34.

14. Jesse Jackson, "Resurrection City, the Dream, the Accomplishments," *Ebony,* October 1968.

15. Nancy Fraser, "Social Justice in the Age of Identity Politics: Redistribution, Recognition, and Participation," The Tanner Lectures on Human Values, Delivered at Stanford University, April 30–May 2, 1996, p. 20.

16. Charles Taylor, *Multiculturalism and "The Politics of Recognition"* (Princeton: Princeton University Press, 1992), 39.

17. As early as 1963, King explicitly defended a form of reparation for slavery: "No amount of gold could provide an adequate compensation for the exploitation and humiliation of the Negro in America down through the centuries. Not all the wealth of this affluent society could meet the bill. Yet a price can be placed on unpaid wages. The ancient common law has always provided a remedy for the appropriation of the labor of one human being by another. This law should be made to apply for American Negroes. The payment should be in the form of a massive program by the government of special, compensatory measures which could be regarded as a settlement in accordance with the accepted practice of common law. Such measures would certainly be less expensive than any computation based on two centuries of unpaid wages and accumulated interest. I am proposing, therefore, that, just as we granted a GI Bill of Rights to war veterans, America launch a broad-based and gigantic Bill of Rights for the Disadvantaged, our veterans of the long siege of denial." Martin Luther King, Jr., *Why We Can't Wait* (Boston: Beacon Press, 1964), 163.

18. For a compelling analysis of King's rhetoric of the debt, see Lawrie Balfour, "Living 'in the Red': Time, Debt and Justice," in Tommie Shelby and

Brandon M. Terry, eds., *To Shape a New World: Essays on the Political Philosophy of Martin Luther King, Jr.* (Cambridge, MA: Harvard University Press, 2018), 236-52.

19. Lani Guinier and Torres Gerald, *The Miner's Canary: Enlisting Race, Resisting Power, and Transforming Democracy* (Cambridge, MA: Harvard University Press, 2002).

20. William Barber, "We Must Have A New Poor People's Campaign and Moral Revival," Black Press USA, September 11, 2017. http://www.blackpress usa.com/we-must-have-a-new-poor-peoples-campaign-and-moral-revival

Bibliography

Abel-Smith, Brian. "The Beveridge Report: Its Origins and Outcomes." *International Social Security Review*, vol. 45, no. 1–2 (January 1992): 5–16.

Abernathy, Ralph David. *And the Walls Came Tumbling Down: An Autobiography*. New York: Harper and Row, 1989.

Afield, Walter E., and Audrey B. Gibson. *Children of Resurrection City*. Washington, DC: Association for Childhood Education International, 1970.

Allen, Anita L. "Race, Face, and Rawls." 72 Fordham L. Rev. 1677 (2004): 402.

Anderson, Gary L., and Kathryn G. Herr, eds. *Encyclopedia of Activism and Social Justice*. Thousand Oaks, CA: Sage, 2007.

Aptheker, Herbert, ed. *Against Racism: Unpublished Essays, Papers, and Addresses, 1887–1961 (Correspondence of W.E.B. Du Bois)*. Amherst: University of Massachusetts Press, 1985.

Arneil, Barbara. *Domestic Colonies: The Turn Inward to Colony*. London: Oxford University Press, 2017.

Arnesen, Eric. *Waterfront Workers of New Orleans: Race, Class, and Politics, 1863–1923*. New York: Oxford University Press, 1991.

———, ed. *The Black Worker: Race, Labor, and Civil Rights since Emancipation*. Urbana: University of Illinois Press, 2007.

Araiza, Lauren. *To March for Others: The Black Freedom Struggle and the United Farm Workers*. Philadelphia: University of Pennsylvania Press, 2014.

Ashmore, Susan Youngblood. *Carry It On: The War on Poverty and the Civil Rights Movement in Alabama, 1964–1972*. Athens: University of Georgia Press, 2008.

Ashworth, John. *Slavery, Capitalism, and Politics in the Antebellum Republic*. Vol. 1: *Commerce and Compromise, 1820–1859*. Cambridge, MA: Cambridge University Press, 1995.

Ayres, B. Drummond, Jr. "New Jobs Law Is Urged as Humphrey Honor." *New York Times*, January 15, 1978.

Bailey, Stephen Kemp. *Congress Makes a Law: The Story behind the Employment Act of 1946*. New York: Columbia University Press, 1950.

Baldwin, Lewis. *The Voice of Conscience: The Church in the Mind of Martin Luther King, Jr*. New York: Oxford University Press, 2010.

Banks, Nina. "The Black Worker, Economic Justice and the Speeches of Sadie T. M. Alexander." *Review of Social Economy*, vol. 66, no. 2 (June 2008).

Baptist, Edward E. *The Half Has Never Been Told: Slavery and the Making of American Capitalism*. New York: Basic Books, 2014.

Barber, William J., II. *The Third Reconstruction. How a Moral Movement Is Overcoming the Politics of Division and Fear*. Boston: Beacon Press, 2017.

Behnken, Brian D. *Fighting Their Own Battles: Mexican Americans, African Americans, and the Struggle for Civil Rights in Texas*. Chapel Hill: University of North Carolina Press, 2011.

———, ed. *The Struggle in Black and Brown: African American and Mexican American Relations During the Civil Rights Era*. Lincoln, University of Nebraska Press, 2012.

Behrend, Justin. *Reconstructing Democracy: Grassroots Black Politics in the Deep South after the Civil War*. Athens: University of Georgia Press, 2015.

Belafonte, Harry. *My Song: A Memoir*. New York: Knopf, 2011.

Bellisfield, Gwen. "White Attitudes Toward Racial Integration and the Urban Riots of the 1960's." *Public Opinion Quarterly*, vol. 36, no. 4 (Winter 1972–73): 579–84.

Bender, Steven W. *One Night in America: Robert Kennedy, César Chávez, and the Dream of Dignity*. Boulder: Paradigm Publishers, 2008.

Berg, Manfred. "Black Civil Rights and Liberal Anticommunism: The NAACP in the Early Cold War." *Journal of American History*, vol. 94, no. 1 (June 2007): 75–96.

Bergin, Cathy. "Race/Class Politics: *The Liberator*, 1929–1934." *Race and Class Journal* (April 2006): 86–104.

———. "Unrest among the Negroes: The African Blood Brotherhood and the Politics of Resistance." *Race and Class Journal*, vol. 57, no. 3 (January–March 2016): 45–58.

Bernstein, Shana. *Bridges of Reform: Interracial Civil Rights Activism in Twentieth-Century Los Angeles*. New York: Oxford University Press, 2011.

Berry, Mary Frances. *History Teaches Us to Resist: How Progressive Movements Have Succeeded in Challenging Times.* Boston: Beacon Press, 2018.

Biles, Roger. *The South and the New Deal.* Lexington: University Press of Kentucky, 1994.

Birnbaum, Simon. *Basic Income Reconsidered: Social Justice, Liberalism, and the Demands of Equality.* New York: Palgrave Macmillan, 2012.

Birt, Robert E. *The Liberatory Thought of Martin Luther King Jr.: Critical Essays on the Philosopher King.* Lanham, MD: Lexington Books, 2012.

Blauner, Robert. "Internal Colonialism and Ghetto Revolt." *Social Problems,* vol. 16, no. 4 (Spring 1969): 393–408.

———. *Racial Oppression in America.* New York: Harper and Row, 1972.

Blawis, Patricia Bell. *Tijerina and the Land Grants: Mexican Americans in Struggle for their Heritage.* New York: International Publishers, 1971.

Bloom, Jack. *Race, Class, and the Civil Rights Movement.* Bloomington: Indiana University Press, 1987.

Bogues, Anthony. *Black Heretics, Black Prophets: Radical Political Intellectuals.* New York: Routledge, 2003.

Borgwardt, Elizabeth. *A New Deal for the World: America's Vision for Human Rights.* Cambridge, MA: Harvard University Press, 2005.

Boyce, Davies Carole. *Left of Karl Marx: The Political Life of Black Communist Claudia Jones.* Durham, NC: Duke University Press, 2007.

Breitman, George, ed. *Leon Trotsky on Black Nationalism.* New York: Pathfinders Press, 1978.

Brick, Howard, and Christopher Phelps. *Radicals in America: The US Left since the Second World War.* Cambridge: Cambridge University Press, 2015.

Brilliant, Mark. *The Color of America Has Changed: How Racial Diversity Shaped Civil Rights Reform in California, 1941–1978.* New York: Oxford University Press, 2010.

Brinkley, Alan. *The End of Reform: New Deal Liberalism in Recession and War.* New York: Knopf, 1995.

Brommel, Nicholas. *The Time Is Always Now: Black Thought and the Transformation of US Democracy.* Oxford: Oxford University Press, 2013.

Brown, Michael K. *Race, Money, and the American Welfare State.* Ithaca: Cornell University Press, 1999.

Brown-Nagin, Tomiko. *Courage to Dissent: Atlanta and the Long History of the Civil Rights Movement.* New York: Oxford University Press, 2011.

Buccola, Nicholas. *The Political Thought of Frederick Douglass: In Pursuit of American Liberty.* New York: New York University Press, 2012.

Bush, Roderick D. *We Are Not What We Seem: Black Nationalism and Class Struggle in the American Century.* New York: New York University Press, 2000.

Bynum, Cornelius L. *A. Philip Randolph and the Struggle for Civil Rights.* Urbana: University of Illinois Press, 2010.

Carbado, Devon W., and Donald Weise, eds. *Time on Two Crosses: The Collected Writings of Bayard Rustin.* San Francisco: Cleiss Press, 2003.

Carmichael, Stokely, and Charles V. Hamilton. *Black Power: The Politics of Liberation.* New York: Vintage Books, 1967.

Carson, Clayborne. "Martin Luther King, Jr., and the African-American Social Gospel." In *African-American Christianity*, edited by Paul E. Johnson, pp. 159–177. Berkeley: University of California Press, 1994.

———, ed. *The Student Voice, 1960–1965: Periodical of the Student Nonviolent Coordinating Committee.* Westport, CN: Meckler Publishers, 1990.

———, ed. *The Autobiography of Martin Luther King, Jr.* New York: Grand Central Publishing, 2001.

Carson, Clayborne, Ralph E. Luker, and Penny A. Russell, eds. *The Papers of Martin Luther King, Jr. Volume I: Called to Serve, January 1929–June 1951.* Berkeley: University of California Press, 1992.

Carson, Clayborne, Ralph E. Luker, Penny A. Russell, and Peter Holloran, eds., *The Papers of Martin Luther King, Jr. Volume II: Rediscovering Precious Values, July 1951–November 1955.* Berkeley: University of California Press, 1994.

Carson, Clayborne, Stewart Burns, Susan Carson, Peter Holloran, and Dana L. H. Powell, eds. *The Papers of Martin Luther King, Jr. Volume III: Birth of a New Age, December 1955–December 1956.* Berkeley: University of California Press, 1997.

Carson, Clayborne, Susan Carson, Adrienne Clay, Virginia Shadron, and Kieran Taylor, eds. *The Papers of Martin Luther King, Jr. Volume IV: Symbol of the Movement, January 1957–December 1958.* Berkeley: University of California Press, 2000.

Carson, Clayborne, Tenisha Hart Armstrong, Susan Carson, Adrienne Clay, and Kieran Taylor, eds. *The Papers of Martin Luther King, Jr. Volume V: Threshold of a New Decade, January 1959–December 1960.* Berkeley: University of California Press, 2005.

Carson, Clayborne, Susan Carson, Susan Englander, Troy Jackson, and Gerald L. Smith, eds. *The Papers of Martin Luther King, Jr. Volume VI: Advocate of the Social Gospel, September 1948–March 1963.* Berkeley: University of California Press, 2007.

Carson, Clayborne, and Tenisha Hart Armstrong, eds. *The Papers of Martin Luther King, Jr. Volume VII: To Save The Soul of America, January 1961–August 1962.* Berkeley: University of California Press, 2014.

Carter, Lawrence E., ed. *Walking Integrity: Benjamin Elijah Mays, Mentor to Martin Luther King Jr.* Macon, GA: Mercer University Press, 1998.

Cass, Julia. *"Held Captive": Child Poverty in America*. Washington, DC: Children's Defense Fund, 2010.

Cazenave, Noel A. *Impossible Democracy: The Unlikely Success of the War on Poverty Community Action Programs*. Albany: State University of New York Press, 2007.

Chakrabarty, Bidyut. *Confluence of Thought: Mahatma Gandhi and Martin Luther King Jr.* Oxford: Oxford University Press, 2013.

Chappell, Marisa. *The War on Welfare, Family, Poverty and Politics in America*. Philadelphia: Penn University Press, 2011.

Chase, Robert T. "Class Resurrection: The Poor People's Campaign of 1968 and Resurrection City," in *Essays in History*, vol. 40. Charlottesville: University of Virginia, 1998.

Clark, Kenneth B. *Dark Ghetto: Dilemmas of Social Power*. New York: Harper and Row, 1965.

———. *Youth in the Ghetto: A Study of the Consequences of Powerlessness and a Blueprint for Change*. New York: Harlem Youth Opportunities Unlimited, 1964.

Clayson, William S. *Freedom Is Not Enough: The War on Poverty and the Civil Rights Movement in Texas*. Austin: University of Texas Press, 2010.

Cloward, Richard A., and Frances Fox Piven. *Poor People's Movements: Why They Succeed, How They Fail*. New York: Vintage Books, 1979.

Cobas, José A, Jorge Duany, and Joe R. Feagin, eds. *How the United States Racializes Latinos: White Hegemony and Its Consequence*s. Boulder: Paradigm, 2009.

Cobb, Daniel M. *Native Activism in Cold War America: The Struggle for Sovereignty*. Lawrence: University Press of Kansas, 2008.

Cohen, G.A. *Rescuing Justice and Equality*. Cambridge, MA: Harvard University Press, 2008.

Cone, James H. *Martin & Malcolm & America: A Dream or a Nightmare*. Maryknoll, NY: Orbis Books, 1991.

Cowie, Jefferson. *Stayin' Alive: The 1970s and the Last Days of the Working Class*. New York: New Press, 2010.

Cox, Oliver C. *Capitalism as a System*. New York: Monthly Review Press, 1964.

———. *Caste, Class and Race*. New York: Modern Reader, 1948.

Craig, Robert H. *Religion and Radical Politics: An Alternative Christian Tradition in the United States*. Philadelphia: Temple University Press, 1992.

Danielson, Leilah. *American Gandhi: A.J. Muste and the History of Radicalism in the Twentieth Century*. Philadelphia: University of Pennsylvania Press, 2014.

Darity, William, Jr. "Who Loses from Unemployment." *Journal of Economic Issues*, vol. 33, no. 2 (June 1999).

Darity, William A., Jr., and Samuel L. Myers, Jr., with Emmett D. Carson and William Sabol. *The Black Underclass: Critical Essays on Race and Unwantedness*. New York: Garland Publishing, 1994.

Dawson, Michael C. Behind the Mule: Race and Class in African-American Politics. Princeton: Princeton University Press, 1994.

———. *Black Visions: The Roots of Contemporary African-American Political Ideologies*. New York: Oxford University Press, 2002.

———. Blacks In and Out of the Left. Cambridge, MA: Harvard University Press, 2014.

Debs, Eugene V. "The Negro in the Class Struggle." *International Socialist Review* (November 1903). Reprinted in Eugene V. Debs, *Writings and Speeches of Eugene V. Debs*, pp. 63–66. New York: Hermitage Press, 1948.

Denning, Michael. *The Cultural Front: The Laboring of American Culture in the Twentieth Century*. London: Verso, 1996.

Dorrien, Gary. *The New Abolition: W. E. B. Du Bois and the Black Social Gospel*. New Haven: Yale University Press, 2015.

Douglas, Andrew J. "W. E. B. Du Bois and the Critique of the Competitive Society." *Du Bois Review*, vol. 12, no. 1 (2015): 25–40.

Douglass, Frederick. *My Bondage and My Freedom*, ed. William L. Andrews. Chicago: University of Illinois Press, 1987.

Du Bois, W. E. B. *Black Reconstruction in America: An Essay Toward a History of the Part Which Black Folk Played in the Attempt to Reconstruct Democracy in America, 1860–1880* (1935). New York: Routledge, 2013.

———. *Dusk of Dawn: An Essay Toward an Autobiography of a Race Concept* (1940), ed. Henry Louis Gates, introduction by Kwame Anthony Appiah. New York: Oxford University Press, 2014.

———. *The Negro Church: With an Introduction by Alton B. Pollard III*. Eugene, OR: Cascade Books, 2011.

———. *The Souls of Black Folk* (1903). New York: Penguin Random Books, 2003.

Du Bois, W. E. B., and John David Smith, eds. *John Brown: A Biography*. New York: M. E. Sharpe, 1997.

Dudziak, Mary L. *Cold War Civil Rights: Race and the Image of American Democracy*. Princeton: Princeton University Press, 2000.

Duneier, Mitchell. *Ghetto: The Invention of a Place, The History of an Idea*. New York: Farrar, Strauss and Giroud, 2016.

Dyson, Lowell K. *Red Harvest: The Communist Party and American Farmers*. Lincoln: University of Nebraska Press, 1982.

Dyson, Michael Eric. *April 4, 1968: Martin Luther King, Jr.'s Death and How It Changed America*. New York: Civitas Books, 2008.

———. *I May Not Get There with You: The True Martin Luther King Jr.* New York: Free Press, 2000.

Egerton, John. *Speak Now Against the Day: The Generation Before the Civil Rights Movement in the South*. New York: Alfred A. Knopf, 1994.

Engler, Mark, and Paul Engler. *This Is an Uprising: How Nonviolent Revolt Is Shaping the Twenty-First Century*. New York: Nation Books, 2016.

Ericson, David F., and Louisa Bertch Green, eds. *The Liberal Tradition in American Politics; Reassessing the Legacy of American Liberalism*. New York: Routledge, 2013.

Estes, Steve. *I Am a Man! Race, Manhood, and the Civil Rights Movement*. Chapel Hill: University of North Carolina Press, 2005.

Euchner, Charles. *Nobody Turn Me Around: A People's History of the 1963 March on Washington*. Boston: Beacon Press, 2011.

Ezra, Michael, ed. *The Economic Civil Rights Movement, African Americans and the Struggle for Economic Power*. New York: Routledge, 2013.

Fabre, Genevieve, and Robert O'Meally, eds. *History and Memory in African-American Culture*. New York: Oxford University Press, 1994.

Fager, Charles. *Uncertain Resurrection: The Poor People's Washington Campaign*. Grand Rapids, MI: William B. Erdmans Publishing, 1969.

Fantasia, Rick. *Cultures of Solidarity: Consciousness, Action, and Contemporary American Workers*. Berkeley: University of California Press, 1988.

Feldman, Glenn, ed. *Before Brown: Civil Rights and White Backlash in the Modern South*. Tuscaloosa: University of Alabama Press, 2004.

Ferguson, Karen. *Black Politics in New Deal Atlanta*. Chapel Hill: University of North Carolina Press, 2002.

Fields, Barbara J. "Ideology and Race in American History," in *Region, Race, and Reconstruction: Essays in Honor of C. Vann Woodward*, ed. J. Morgan Kousser and James M. McPherson, pp. 143–177. New York: Oxford University Press, 1982.

Fields, Barbara J., and Karen E. Fields. *Racecraft: The Soul of Inequality in American Life*. New York: Verso, 2012.

Finley, Mary Lou, Bernard LaFayette, Jr., James R. Ralph, Jr., and Pam Smith. *The Chicago Freedom Movement: Martin Luther King Jr. and Civil Rights Activism in the North*. Lexington: University Press of Kentucky, 2015.

Fisher, Sethard. "Marxist Prescriptions for Black American Equality." *Phylon*, vol. 45, no. 1 (1984): 52–66.

Foley, Neil. *Quest for Equality: The Failed Promise of Black-Brown Solidarity*. Cambridge, MA: Harvard University Press, 2010.

Folsom, Franklin. *Impatient Armies of the Poor: The Story of Collective Action of the Unemployed, 1808–1942*. Niwot: University Press of Colorado, 1991.

Folwell, Emma J. "The Legacy of the Child Development Group of Mississippi: White Opposition to Head Start in Mississippi, 1965–1972." *Journal of Mississippi History*, vol. 76, no. 1 (2014): 43–68.

Foner, Eric, and Manning Marable. *Herbert Aptheker on Race and Democracy: A Reader*. Urbana: University of Illinois Press, 2010.

Foner, Philip S. *American Socialism and Black Americans: From the Age of Jackson to World War II*. Westport, CN: Greenwood Press, 1977.

———. *Organized Labor and the Black Worker, 1619–1981*. New York: International Publishers, 1982.

———. *U.S. Labor and the Vietnam War*. New York: International Publishers, 1989.

———. *Women and the American Labor Movement: From World War I to the Present*. New York: Free Press, 1980.

———, ed. *Black Socialist Preacher: The Teachings of Reverend George Washington Woodbey and His Disciple, Reverend G.W. Slater, Jr.* San Francisco: Synthesis Publications, 1983.

———, ed. *The Life and Writings of Frederick Douglass*. New York: International Publishers, 1975.

Foner, Philip S., and James S. Allen, eds. *American Communism and Black Americans: A Documentary History, 1919–1929*. Philadelphia: Temple University Press, 1987.

Foner, Philip S., Ronald Lewis, and Robert Cvornyek, eds. *The Black Worker since the AFL-CIO Merger, 1955–1980*. Philadelphia: Temple University Press, 1984.

Forbath, William E. "Constitutional Welfare Rights: A History, Critique and Reconstruction." 69 Fordham L. Rev. 1821 (2001). http://ir.lawnet.fordham.edu/flr/vol69/iss5/12

Forstater, Mathew. "The Freedom Budget at 45: Functional Finance and Full Employment." Levy Economics Institute, Working Paper No. 668 (May 3, 2011).

———. "From Civil Rights to Economic Security: Bayard Rustin and the African American Struggle for Full Employment, 1945–1978." *International Journal of Political Economy*, vol. 36, no. 3 (2007).

———. "Full Employment and Economic Flexibility." *Economic and Labour Relations Review*, vol. 11 (1999).

Frank, Gerold. *An American Death: The True Story of the Assassination of Dr. Martin Luther King, Jr., and the Greatest Manhunt of Our Time*. New York: Doubleday, 1972.

Franklin, Robert Michael. "In Pursuit of a Just Society: Martin Luther King, Jr., and John Rawls." *Journal of Religious Ethics*, vol. 18, no. 2 (Fall 1990): 57–77.

Fraser, Nancy. "Social Justice in the Age of Identity Politics: Redistribution, Recognition, and Participation." The Tanner Lectures on Human Values, Delivered at Stanford University, April 30–May 2, 1996.

Fraser, Richard, and Tom Boot. *Revolutionary Integration: A Marxist Analysis of African American Liberation*. Seattle: Red Letter Press, 2004.

Fraser, Steve, and Gary Gerstle. *The Rise and Fall of the New Deal Order, 1930–1980*. Princeton: Princeton University Press, 1989.

Frazier, Franklin E. *Black Bourgeoisie* (1957). New York: Free Press, 1997.

———. *The Negro Family in the United States.* Chicago: The University of Chicago, 1966.

Freedman, Jill. *Old News: Resurrection City.* New York: Grossman Publishers, 1970.

Freeman, Roland L. *The Mule Train: A Journey of Hope Remembered.* Nashville, TN: Rutledge Hill Press, 1998.

Frost, Jennifer. *An Interracial Movement of the Poor: Community Organizing and the New Left.* New York: New York University Press, 2001.

Gaines, Kevin K. *Uplifting the Race: Black Leadership, Politics, and Culture in the Twentieth Century.* Chapel Hill: University of North Carolina Press, 1996.

Galbraith, John Kenneth. *The Affluent Society,* New York: Houghton Mifflin, 1998.

Gans, Herbert. *The War Against the Poor: The Underclass and Antipoverty Policy.* New York: Basic Books, 1995.

Garrow, David. *Bearing the Cross: Martin Luther King, Jr., and the Southern Christian Leadership Conference.* New York: William Morrow, 2004.

Geary, Daniel. *Beyond Civil Rights: The Moynihan Report and Its Legacy.* Philadelphia: University of Pennsylvania Press, 2015.

Gerstle, Gary. "Race and the Myth of the Liberal Consensus." *Journal of American History,* vol. 82, no. 2 (September 1995): 579–86.

Gerteis, Joseph. *Class and the Color Line: Interracial Class Coalition in the Knights of Labor and the Populist Movement.* Durham, NC: Duke University Press, 2007.

Gilbert, Ben W. *Ten Blocks from the White House.* New York: Praeger, 1969.

Gilmore, Glenda Elizabeth. *Defying Dixie: The Radical Roots of Civil Rights, 1919–1950.* New York: W.W. Norton, 2008.

Ginsburg, H. L. "Historical Amnesia: The Humphrey-Hawkins Act, Full Employment and Employment as a Right." *The Review of Black Political Economy,* vol. 39 (2012): 121. doi:10.1007/s12114–011–9121–3.

Ginsburg, Helen. *Full Employment and Public Policy: The United States and Sweden.* Lexington, MA: Lexington Books, 1983.

Gitlin, Todd, and Nanci Hollander. *Uptown: Poor Whites in Chicago.* New York: Harper and Row, 1970.

Glassman, James K. "Trouble in the Poor People's Campaign." *Harvard Crimson,* May 21, 1968.

Glen, John M. *Highlander: No Ordinary School, 1932–1962.* Lexington: University Press of Kentucky, 1988.

Godshalk, David Fort. *Veiled Visions: The 1906 Atlanta Race Riot and the Reshaping of American Race Relations.* Chapel Hill: University of North Carolina Press, 2005.

Goebel, Thomas. "The Political Economy of American Populism from Jackson to the New Deal." *Studies in American Political Development,* vol. 11, Issue 1 (Spring 1997): 109–48.

Goldberg, Chad Alan. "Contesting the Status of Relief Workers during the New Deal: The Workers Alliance of America and the Works Progress Administration, 1935–1941." *Social Science History,* vol. 29, no. 3 (Fall 2005): 337–71.

Goldfield, Michael. *The Color of Politics: Race and the Mainsprings of American Politics.* New York: New Press, 1997.

Goldstein, Alyosha. *Poverty in Common: The Politics of Community Action During the American Century.* Durham, NC: Duke University Press, 2012.

Goluboff, Risa L. *The Lost Promise of Civil Rights.* Cambridge, MA: Harvard University Press, 2007.

Gonzales, Rodolpho. *Hispanic Civil Rights Series: Message to Aztlan.* Houston: Arte Publico Press, 2001.

Goodman, Paul. *Seeds of Liberation.* New York: Braziller, 1964.

Goodwin, Heltzel Peter. *Resurrection City: A Theology of Improvisation.* Grand Rapids, MI: Wm. B. Eerdmans, 2012.

Goodwyn, Lawrence. *Democratic Promise: The Populist Movement in America,* New York: Oxford University Press, 1976.

———. "Rethinking 'Populism': Paradoxes of Historiography and Democracy." *Telos* (June 20, 1991): 37–56.

Gore, Dayo F. *Radicalism at the Crossroads: African American Women Activists in the Cold War.* New York: New York University Press, 2010.

Gorman, Robert A. *Michael Harrington: Speaking American.* New York: Routledge, 1995.

Gourevitch, Alex. *From Slavery to the Cooperative Commonwealth: Labor and Republican Liberty in the Nineteenth Century.* New York: Cambridge University Press, 2014.

Green, Chris, Rachel Lee Rubin, and James Smethurst, eds. *Radicalism in the South since Reconstruction.* New York: Palgrave Macmillan, 2006.

Green, Laurie B. "Race, Gender, and Labor in 1960s Memphis: 'I Am a Man' and the Meaning of Freedom." *Journal of Urban History* 30 (March 2004): 475.

Gregory, Raymond F. *Norman Thomas: The Great Dissenter* New York: Algora Publishing, 2008.

Griffiths, Frederick T. "Ralph Ellison, Richard Wright, and the Case of Angelo Herndon." *African American Review* 35 (Winter 2001): 615–36.

Grusky, David, and Ravi Kanbur, eds. *Poverty and Inequality.* Palo Alto: Stanford University Press, 2005.

Guinier, Lani. "From Racial Liberalism to Racial Literacy: *Brown v. Board of Education* and the Interest-Divergence Dilemma." *Journal of American History,* vol. 91, no. 1 (2004).

Guinier, Lani, and Torres Gerald. *The Miner's Canary: Enlisting Race, Resisting Power, and Transforming Democracy*. Cambridge, MA: Harvard University Press, 2002.

Haines, Herbert H. *Black Radicals and the Civil Rights Mainstream, 1954–1970*. Knoxville: University of Tennessee Press, 1988.

Halberstam, David. "The Second Coming of Martin Luther King." *Harper's*, August 1967.

Hall, Simon. *Peace and Freedom: The Civil Rights and Antiwar Movements in the 1960s*. Philadelphia: University of Pennsylvania Press, 2005.

Hamilton, Dona Cooper, and Charles V. Hamilton. "The Dual Agenda of African American Organizations since the New Deal: Social Welfare Policies and Civil Rights." *Political Science Quarterly,* vol. 107, no. 3 (Autumn 1992).

Haney López, Ian F. *Racism on Trial: The Chicano Fight for Justice*. Cambridge, MA: Harvard University Press, 2003.

Hanes, Walton, Jr., and Robert C. Smith. *American Politics and the African American Quest for Universal Freedom*. New York: Pearson and Longman, 2006.

Harlan, Louis Rudolph. *Booker T. Washington: The Wizard of Tuskegee, 1901–1915, Vol. 2*. New York: Oxford University Press, 1983.

Hartman, Andrew. *A War for the Soul of America: A History of the Culture Wars*. Chicago: The University of Chicago Press, 2015.

Harris, Lashawn. "Running with the Reds: African American Women and the Communist Party during the Great Depression." *Journal of African American History,* vol. 94, no. 1 (Winter 2009): 21.

Hartz, Louis. *The Liberal Tradition in America: An Interpretation of American Political Thought Since the Revolution*. New York: Houghton Mifflin Harcourt, 1955.

Harvey, James C. *Black Civil Rights During the Johnson Administration*. Jackson: University Press of Mississippi, 1973.

Harvey, Philip. *Securing the Right to Employment: Social Welfare Policy and the Unemployed in the United States*. Princeton: Princeton University Press, 1989.

Haywood, Harry. *Black Bolshevik: Autobiography of An American Communist*. Chicago: Liberator Press, 1978.

Henderson, Jeff. "A. Philip Randolph and the Dilemmas of Socialism and Black Nationalism in the United States, 1917–1941." *Race and Class Journal,* 20 (1978): 143–60.

Henry, Charles P. *Ralph Bunche: Model Negro or American Other*. New York: New York University Press, 1999.

Herndon, Angelo. *Let Me Live*. Ann Arbor: University of Michigan Press, 2007.

Hess, Stephen. *The Professor and the President: Daniel Patrick Moynihan in the Nixon White House.* Washington, DC: Brookings Institution Press, 2015. http://www.jstor.org/stable/10.7864/j.ctt7zsvxq

Hickman, Jared. *Black Prometheus: Race and Radicalism in the Age of Atlantic Slavery.* New York: Oxford University Press, 2017.

Hinton, Elizabeth. *From the War on Poverty to the War on Crime: The Making of Mass Incarceration in America.* Cambridge, MA: Harvard University Press, 2016.

Honey, Michael K. *Going Down Jericho Road: The Memphis Strike, Martin Luther King's Last Campaign.* New York: W. W. Norton, 2007.

———. *To the Promised Land: Martin Luther King and the Fight for Economic Justice.* New York: W. W. Norton, 2018.

———, ed. *All Labor Has Dignity.* Boston: Beacon Press, 2011.

Horne, Gerald. *Black Liberation/Red Scare: Ben Davis and the Communist Party.* Newark: University of Delaware Press, 1994.

———. *Black and Red: W. E. B. Du Bois and the Afro-American Response to the Cold War, 1944–1963.* Albany: State University of New York Press, 1986.

———. *Black Revolutionary: William Patterson and the Globalization of the African American Freedom Struggle.* Champaign: University of Illinois Press, 2013.

———. *Communist Front? The Civil Rights Congress, 1946–1956.* Rutherford, NJ: Fairleigh Dickinson University Press, 1987.

Horton, Carol A. *Race and the Making of American Liberalism.* New York: Oxford University Press, 2005.

Hopkins, Charles Howard. *The Rise of the Social Gospel in American Protestantism, 1865–1915.* New Haven: Yale University Press, 1940.

Hughes, Alvin. "We Demand Our Rights: The Southern Negro Youth Congress, 1937–1949." *Phylon* (1960–), vol. 48, no. 1 (1987): 38–50.

Hunter, Tera. *To 'Joy My Freedom: Southern Black Women's Lives and Labors after the Civil War.* Cambridge, MA: Harvard University Press, 1997.

Hutchinson, Darren Lenard. "Racial Exhaustion." 86 Wash. U. L. Rev. 917 (2009): 917–74.

Inscoe, John C. *Georgia in Black and White: Explorations in Race Relations of a Southern State, 1865–1950.* Athens: University of Georgia Press, 1994.

Isenberg, Nancy. *White Trash: The 400-Year Untold History of Class in America.* New York: Viking, 2016.

Isserman, Maurice. *The Other American: The Life of Michael Harrington.* New York: Perseus Books, 2001.

Jackson, Esther Cooper, and Constance Pohl, eds. *Freedomways Reader: Prophets in Their Own Country.* Boulder: Westview Press, 2000.

Jackson, Thomas F. "'Bread of Freedom': Martin Luther King, Jr. and Human Rights." *OAH Magazine of History*, vol. 22, Issue 2 (April 2008): 14–16. https://doi.org/10.1093/maghis/22.2.14

———. *From Civil Rights to Human Rights: Martin Luther King, Jr., and the Struggle for Economic Justice*. Philadelphia: University of Pennsylvania Press, 2007.

———. "The State, the Movement and the Urban Poor: The War on Poverty and Political Mobilization," in Michael B. Katz, ed., *The "Underclass" Debate: Views from History*, pp. 403-438. Princeton: Princeton University Press, 1993.

Jackson, Walter A. *Gunnar Myrdal and America's Conscience: Social Engineering and Racial Liberalism, 1938–1987*. Chapel Hill: University of North Carolina Press, 1990.

Johnson, Terrence L. *Tragic Soul-Life: W.E.B. Du Bois and the Moral Crisis Facing American Democracy*. New York: Oxford University Press, 2012.

Jones, William P. *The March on Washington: Jobs, Freedom, and the Forgotten History of Civil Rights*. New York: W.W. Norton, 2013.

———. "'Nothing Special to Offer the Negro': Revisiting the 'Debsian View' of the Negro Question." *International Labor and Working-Class History*, vol. 74, no. 1 (September 2008): 212–24.

Joseph, Antoine L. *The Dynamics of Racial Progress: Economic Inequality and Race Relations since Reconstruction*. New York: Routledge, 2005.

Kai Lee, Chana. *For Freedom's Sake: The Life of Fannie Lou Hamer*. Women in American History Series. Urbana: University of Illinois Press, 1999.

Katz, Michael B. *In the Shadow of the Poorhouse: A Social History of Welfare in America*. New York: Basic Books, 1986.

———. *The Undeserving Poor: America's Enduring Confrontation with Poverty*. New York: Oxford University Press, 2013.

———, ed. *The "Underclass" Debate: Views from History*. Princeton: Princeton University Press, 1993.

Katznelson, Ira. "Limiting Liberalism: The Southern Veto in Congress, 1933–1950." *Political Science Quarterly*, vol. 108, no. 2 (Summer 1993): 283–306.

Kelley, Robin D.G. *Freedom Dreams: The Black Radical Imagination*. Boson: Beacon Press, 2002.

———. *Hammer and Hoe: Alabama Communists during the Great Depression*. Chapel Hill: University of North Carolina Press, 1990.

———. "Identity Politics and Class Struggle." *New Politics*, vol. 6, no. 2 (new series), whole no. 22, Winter 1997.

———. "'We Are Not What We Seem': Rethinking Black Working-Class Opposition in the Jim Crow South." *Journal of American History*, vol. 80, no. 1 (June 1993): 75.

Kendi, Ibram X. "Reclaiming MLK's Unspeakable Nightmare: The Progression of Racism in America." *Black Perspectives,* January 22, 2016.

Keppel, Ben. *The Work of Democracy: Ralph Bunche, Kenneth B. Clark, Lorraine Hansberry, and the Cultural Politics of Race.* Cambridge, MA: Harvard University Press, 1995.

Kersten, Andrew E., and Clarence Lang, eds. *Reframing Randolph: Labor, Black Freedom, and the Legacies of A. Philip Randolph.* New York: New York University Press, 2015.

Kipnis, Ira. *The American Socialist Movement 1897–1912.* Chicago: Haymarket Books, 2005.

King, Martin Luther, Jr. "A Freedom Budget for all Americans; Budgeting Our Resources, 1966–1975, to Achieve Freedom from Want." Philip Randolph Institute, 1966. https://archive.org/details/freedomBudgetForAllAmericans-BudgetingOurResources19 66–1975

———. "The Other America," Speech given at Stanford University, April 14, 1967 and at the Grosse Pointe High School, March 14, 1968. http://www.crmvet.org/docs/otheram.htm

———. *Pilgrimage to Nonviolence: On Gandhi's Legacy.* Boston: Beacon Press, 2012.

———. *Strength to Love.* Philadelphia: Fortress Press. 1981.

———. *The Trumpet of Conscience.* Boston: Beacon Press, 2010.

———. *Where Do We Go from Here: Chaos or Community?* Boston: Beacon Press, 2010.

———. *Why We Can't Wait.* Boston: Beacon Press, 1964.

Klarman, Michael J. "How Brown Changed Race Relations: The Backlash Thesis." *Journal of American History,* vol. 81, no. 1 (June 1994): 81–118.

Klehr, Harvey. *The Heyday of American Communism: The Depression Decade.* New York: Basic Books, 1984.

Knowles, L. L., and K. Prewitt. *Institutional Racism in America.* Englewood Cliffs: Prentice-Hall, 1969.

Kornbluh, Felicia. *The Battle for Welfare Rights: Politics and Poverty in Modern America.* Philadelphia: University of Pennsylvania Press, 2007.

Korstad, Robert. *Civil Rights Unionism: Tobacco Workers and the Struggle for Democracy in the Mid-Twentieth South.* Chapel Hill: University of North Carolina Press, 2003.

Kotlowski, Dean J. *Nixon's Civil Rights: Politics, Principles, and Policy.* Cambridge, MA: Harvard University Press, 2001.

Kotz, Nick. *Judgment Days: Lyndon Baines Johnson, Martin Luther King Jr., and the Laws That Changed America.* Boston: Houghton Mifflin, 2005.

Kotz, Nick, and Mary Lynn Kotz. *A Passion for Equality: George A. Wiley and the Movement.* New York: W. W. Norton, 1977.

Lackey, Hilliard Lawrence. *Marks, Martin, and the Mule Train.* Marks, MS: Town Square Books, 1998.

Lampinen, Lily Gay. "The Poor People's Campaign." *International Socialism* (1st series), no. 34 (Autumn 1968): 8–10. https://www.marxists.org/history/etol/newspape/isj/1968/no034/lampinen.htm

Lang, Carl. *Anticommunism and the African American Movement.* New York: Palgrave Macmillan, 2009.

Le Blanc, Paul, and Michael D. Yates. *A Freedom Budget for All Americans: Recapturing the Promise of the Civil Rights Movement in the Struggle for Economic Justice Today.* New York: Monthly Review Press, 2013.

Lee Shin-heang. "The Concept of Justice in the Political Thought of Martin Luther King, Jr." *Journal of East and West Studies,* vol. 13, no. 2 (1984): 43–64.

Lentz, Richard. *Symbols, the News Magazines, and Martin Luther King.* Baton Rouge: Louisiana State University Press, 1990.

Lepore, Jill. "How a New Yorker Article Launched the First Shot in the War Against Poverty." *Smithsonian Magazine,* September 2012.

Lewis, Andrew B. *The Shadows of Youth.* New York: Hill and Wang, 2009.

Lewis, Earl. *In Their Own Interests: Race, Class, and Power in Twentieth-Century Norfolk, Virginia.* Berkeley: University of California Press, 1991.

Lewis, George. *Massive Resistance: The White Response to the Civil Rights Movement.* London: Hodder Arnold, 2006.

———. *The White South and the Red Menace: Segregationists, Anticommunists, and Massive Resistance, 1945–1965.* Gainesville: University Press of Florida, 2004.

Lewis, David Levering. *W. E. B. Du Bois: Biography of a Race, 1868–1919.* New York: Henry Holt, 1993.

Lieberman, Robbie, and Clarence Lang, eds. *Anticommunism and the African American Freedom Movement.* New York: Palgrave Macmillan, 2009.

Lieberman, Robert C. *Shaping Race Policy: The United States in Comparative Perspective.* Princeton: Princeton University Press, 2005.

Link, William A. *Atlanta, Cradle of the New South: Race and Remembering in the Civil War's Aftermath.* Chapel Hill: University of North Carolina Press, 2013.

Lipsitz, George. *A Life in the Struggle: Ivory Perry and the Culture of Opposition.* Philadelphia: Temple University Press, 1988.

Long, Michael G. *Against Us, but For Us: Martin Luther King, Jr. and the State.* Macon, GA: Mercer University Press, 2002.

Lorence, James J. *A Hard Journey: The Life of Don West.* Chicago: University of Illinois Press, 2007.

———. *The Unemployed People's Movement: Leftists, Liberals, and Labor in Georgia, 1929–1941.* Athens: University of Georgia Press, 2009.

Lucks, Daniel S. *Selma to Saigon: The Civil Rights Movement and the Vietnam War*. Lexington: University Press of Kentucky 2014.

Lyon, E. Stina. "Researching Race Relations: Myrdal's American Dilemma from a Methodological Perspective." *Acta Sociologica*, vol. 47, no. 3 (September 2004): 203–17.

Makalani, Minkah. *In the Cause of Freedom: Radical Black Internationalism from Harlem to London, 1917–1939*. Chapel Hill: University of North Carolina Press, 2011.

Mantler, Gordon K. "Black, Brown and Poor: Martin Luther King Jr., the Poor People's Campaign and its Legacy." Ph.D. dissertation, Duke University, 2008. https://edisciplinas.usp.br/pluginfile.php/1017575/mod_resource/content/1/D_Mantler_Gordon_Thesis_poor_peoples%20Project.pdf

———. *Power to the Poor: Black-Brown Coalition and the Fight for Economic Justice, 1960–1974*. Chapel Hill: University of North Carolina Press, 2013.

———. "'The Press Did You In': The Poor People's Campaign and the Mass Media." *The Sixties: A Journal of History, Politics and Culture*, vol. 3, no. 1 (2010): 33–54.

Marable, Manning. "Marxism, Memory, and the Black Radical Tradition." *Souls: A Critical Journal of Black Politics, Culture, and Society* (Special Issue: Black Critiques of Capital: Radicalism, Resistance, and Visions of Social Justice), vol. 13, no. 1 (2011).

Marable, Manning, and Elizabeth Kai Hinton, eds. *The New Black History: Revisiting the Second Reconstruction*. New York: Palgrave, 2011.

Mariscal, George. *Brown-Eyed Children of the Sun: Lessons from the Chicano Movement, 1965–1975*. Albuquerque: University of New Mexico Press, 2005.

Mark, Solomon. *The Cry Was Unity: Communists and African Americans, 1917–1936*. Jackson: University Press of Mississippi, 1998.

Marshall, T. H. *Class, Citizenship and Social Development*. New York: Doubleday, 1964.

Marshall, T. S. *Citizenship and Social Class and Other Essays*. Cambridge: Cambridge University Press, 1950.

Martin, Waldo E. *The Mind of Frederick Douglass*. Chapel Hill: University of North Carolina Press, 1984.

Maxwell, William J. *Old Negro, New Left: African-American Writing and Communism Between the Wars*. New York: Columbia University Press, 1999.

Mays, Benjamin. "Democratizing and Christianizing America in This Generation." *Journal of Negro Education*, vol. 14, no. 4 (Fall 1945).

McCarthy, Thomas. "Political Philosophy and Racial Injustice: From Normative to Critical Theory," in S. Benhabib S and N. Fraser, eds., *Pragmatism, Critique, Judgment*, pp. 149–170. Cambridge, MA: MIT Press, 2004.

McDuffie, Erik S. *Sojourning for Freedom: Black Women, American Communism, and the Making of Black Left Feminism.* Durham, NC: Duke University Press, 2011.

McKanan, Dan. "The Implicit Religion of Radicalism: Socialist Party Theology,
1900–1934." *Journal of the American Academy of Religion,* vol. 78, no. 3
(September 2010): 750–89.

———. *Prophetic Encounters: Religion and the American Radical Tradition.*
Boston: Beacon Press, 2011.

McKnight, Gerald. *The Last Crusade: Martin Luther King, Jr., the FBI and the
Poor People's Campaign.* Boulder: Westview Press, 1998.

McLemee, Scott, ed., *C. L. R. James on the 'Negro Question.'* Jackson: University
Press of Mississippi, 1996.

McMurray, Donald Le Crone. *Coxey's Army: A Study of the Industrial Movement of 1894.* Seattle: University of Washington Press. 1968.

McNeill, Allison, Richard C. Hanes, and Sharon M. Hanes, eds. "Minority
Groups and the Great Depression," in *Great Depression and the New Deal
Reference Library,* vol. 1: Almanac, pp. 172–186. Detroit: UXL, 2003.

Michelman, Frank I. "The Supreme Court 1968 Term-Foreword: On
Protecting the Poor Through the Fourteenth Amendment." 83 Harv. L. Rev.
7 (1969).

Mieder, Wolfgang. *Making a Way Out of No Way—Martin Luther King's
Sermonic Proverbial Rhetoric.* New York: Peter Lang, 2010.

Milkis, Sidney M., and Jerome M. Mileur. *The New Deal and the Triumph of
Liberalism.* Amherst: University of Massachusetts Press, 2002.

———. *The Great Society and the High Tide of Liberalism.* Amherst: University
of Massachusetts Press, 2005.

Miller, James A. *Remembering Scottsboro: The Legacy of an Infamous Trial.*
Princeton: Princeton University Press, 2009.

Miller, Karen R. *Managing Inequality: Northern Racial Liberalism in Interwar
Detroit.* New York: New York University Press, 2015.

Miller, Keith D. *Voice of Deliverance: The Language of Martin Luther King, Jr.,
and Its Sources.* Athens: University of Georgia Press, 1998.

Miller, Sally M. "The Socialist Party and the Negro, 1901–20." *Journal of Negro
History,* vol. 56, no. 3 (July 1971).

Mills, Charles W. *Black Rights/White Wrongs: The Critique of Racial Liberalism.* New York: Oxford University Press, 2017.

———. "Contract of Breach: Repairing the Racial Contract," in *Contract and
Domination,* ed. Carole Pateman and Charles Mills, pp. 106–133. Malden,
MA: Polity Press, 2007.

———. "Race and the Social Contract Tradition." *Social Identities,* vol. 6 (2000).

———. "Rawls on Race/Race in Rawls." *Southern Journal of Philosophy,* vol. 47
(2009).

Minchin, Timothy J. *From Rights to Economics: The Ongoing Struggle for Black Equality in the U.S. South.* Gainesville: University Press of Florida, 2007.

Mink, Gwendolyn, and Rickie Solinger, eds. *Welfare: A Documentary History of U.S. Policy and Politics.* New York: New York University Press, 2003.

Minsky, H. P. "The Role of Employment Policy," in *Poverty in America,* ed. M. S. Gordon. San Francisco: Chandler, 1965.

Montgomery, David. *Beyond Equality: Labor and the Radical Republicans, 1862–1872.* New York: Alfred A. Knopf, 1967.

Morris, Aldon D. *The Origins of the Civil Rights Movement: Black Communities Organizing for Change.* New York: Free Press, 1984.

Mullen, Bill V. *Popular Fronts: Chicago and African-American Cultural Politics, 1935–46.* Urbana: University of Illinois Press, 1999.

Muñoz, Carlos, Jr. *Youth, Identity, Power: The Chicano Movement.* New York: Verso, 2007.

Myers-Lipton, Scott J. *Ending Extreme Inequality: An Economic Bill of Rights Approach to Eliminate Poverty.* Boulder: Paradigm, 2015.

———. *Social Solutions to Poverty: America's Struggle to Build a Just Society.* Boulder: Paradigm, 2006.

Myrdal, Gunnar. *Beyond the Welfare State. Economic Planning in the Welfare States and its International Implications.* London: Methuen, 1958.

Nadasen, Premilla. *Welfare Warriors: The Welfare Rights Movement in the United States.* New York: Routledge. 2005.

Nagel, Thomas. "John Rawls and Affirmative Action." *Journal of Blacks in Higher Education,* no. 39 (Spring 2003): 82–84.

Naison, Mark. *Communists in Harlem During the Great Depression* (1983). Chicago: University of Illinois Press, 2005.

Naples, N. A. *Grassroots Warriors: Activist Mothering, Community Work, and the War on Poverty.* New York: Routledge, 1997.

Needleman, Ruth. *Black Freedom Fighters in Steel: The Struggle for Democratic Unionism.* Ithaca: Cornell University Press, 2003.

Nicholson, Linda. "Identity After Identity Politics." 33 Washington U. Journal of Law and Policy, 43 (2010). http://openscholarship.wustl.edu/law_journal_law_policy/vol33/iss1/4

Oakes, James. *The Radical and the Republican: Frederick Douglass, Abraham Lincoln, and the Triumph of Antislavery Politics.* New York: W. W. Norton, 2007.

O'Connor, Alice. *Poverty Knowledge: Social Science, Social Policy, and the Poor in Twentieth-Century U.S. History.* Princeton: Princeton University Press, 2001.

O'Malley, Michael. "Specie and Species: Race and the Money Question in Nineteenth-century America." *American Historical Review,* vol. 99, no. 2 (1994): 369–95.

O'Reilly, Kenneth. *Racial Matters: The FBI's Secret File on Black America, 1960–1972.* New York: Free Press, 1989.

Opie, Frederick Douglass. *Upsetting the Apple Cart: Black-Latino Coalitions in New York City from Protest to Public Office.* New York: Columbia University Press, 2014.

Orleck, Annelise. *Storming Caesars Palace: How Black Mothers Fought Their Own War on Poverty.* Boston: Beacon Press. 2005.

Orleck, Annelise, and Lisa Gayle Hazirjian. *The War on Poverty: A New Grassroots History, 1964–1980.* Athens: University of Georgia Press, 2011.

Paden, Catherine M. *Civil Rights Advocacy on Behalf of the Poor.* Philadelphia: University of Pennsylvania Press, 2011.

———. "Disentangling Race and Poverty: The Civil Rights Response to Anti-Poverty Policy." *The DuBois Review,* vol. 5, no. 2 (2008): 339–68.

Painter, Nell Irvin. "How Donald Trump Made 'Working Class' White." *Princeton Alumni Weekly,* March 13, 2017.

———. *The Narrative of Hosea Hudson: His life as a Negro Communist in the South.* Cambridge, MA: Harvard University Press, 1979.

Paschal, Andrew, ed. *W. E. B. Du Bois: A Reader.* New York: Macmillan, 1971.

Passell, Peter, and Leonard Ross. "Daniel Moynihan and President-elect Nixon: How Charity Didn't Begin at Home." *New York Times Book Review,* January 14, 1973.

Pateman, Carole. *Democracy, Feminism, Welfare.* New York: Routledge, 2011.

Pateman, Carole, and Charles Mills. *Contract and Domination.* Malden, MA: Polity Press, 2007.

Patterson, Anita Haya. *From Emerson to King: Democracy, Race, and the Politics of Protest.* New York: Oxford University Press, 1997.

Pawel, Miriam. *The Union of Their Dreams: Power, Hope, and Struggle in Cesar Chavez's Farm Worker Movement.* New York: Bloomsbury Press, 2010.

Pickens, Donald K. *Leon H. Keyserling: A Progressive Economist.* New York: Lexington Books, 2009.

Piven, Frances Fox. *Lessons for our Struggle.* New York: Haymarket Books, 2012.

Piven, Frances Fox, and Richard A. Cloward. *Poor Peoples Movements: Why They Succeed, How They Fail.* New York: Pantheon Books, 1977.

———. *Regulating the Poor: The Functions of Public Welfare.* New York: Vintage Books, 1971.

Pohlmann, Marcus. *Capitalism vs. Collectivism: 1945 to the Present: African American Political Thought.* New York: Routledge, 2003.

Poole, Mary. *The Segregated Origins of Social Security: African Americans and the Welfare State.* Chapel Hill: University of North Carolina Press, 2006.

Prout, Jerry. *Coxey's Crusade for Jobs: Unemployment in the Gilded Age.* DeKalb: Northern Illinois University Press, 2016.

Quadagno, Jill. *The Color of Welfare: How Racism Undermined the War on Poverty.* New York: Oxford University Press, 1996.

Rabaka, Reiland. *Africana Critical Theory: Reconstructing the Black Radical Tradition, from W. E. B. Du Bois and C. L. R. James to Frantz Fanon and Amilcar Cabral.* Lanham, MD: Lexington Books, 2010.

Ralph, James R., Jr. *Northern Protest: Martin Luther King Jr., Chicago, and the Civil Rights Movement.* Cambridge, MA: Harvard University Press, 1993.

Rauschenbusch, Walter. *Christianity and the Social Crisis* (1907). Eugene, OR: Wipf and Stock Publishers, 2003.

———. *Christianizing the Social Order.* New York: Macmillan, 1913.

Rawls, John. *Justice as Fairness,* ed. Erin Kelly. Cambridge, MA: Harvard University Press, 2001.

———. *Political Liberalism.* New York: Columbia University Press, 1996.

———. *Theory of Justice.* Cambridge, MA: Harvard University Press, 1971.

Reed, Adolph, Jr. "Race and the New Deal Coalition." *The Nation,* March 20, 2008.

———. *W. E. B. Du Bois and American Political Thought: Fabianism and the Color Line.* New York: Oxford University Press, 1997.

———, et al. *Renewing Black Intellectual History: The Ideological and Material Foundations of African American Thought.* Boulder: Paradigm, 2010.

Reed, Touré F. *Not Alms But Opportunity: The Urban League and the Politics of Racial Uplift, 1910–1950.* Chapel Hill: University of North Carolina Press, 2008.

Reese, Ellen. *Backlash Against Welfare Mothers: Past and Present.* Berkeley: University of California Press, 2005.

Reisch, Michael, and Janice Andrews. *The Road Not Taken: A History of Radical Social Work in the United States.* New York: Routledge, 2002.

Ridlon, Florence. *A Black Physician's Struggle for Civil Rights: Edward C. Mazique, M.D.* Albuquerque: University of New Mexico Press, 2005.

Robinson, Cedric. *Black Marxism: The Making of the Black Radical Tradition* (1983). Chapel Hill: University of North Carolina Press, 2000.

Rodriguez, Gregory. *Mongrels, Bastards, Orphans, and Vagabonds: Mexican Immigration and the Future of Race in America.* New York: Vintage Press, 2007.

Romano, Renee, and Raiford Leigh, eds. *The Civil Rights Movement in American Memory.* Athens: University of Georgia Press, 2006.

Ross, Jack. *The Socialist Party of America: A Complete History.* Lincoln, NE: Potomac Books, 2015.

Rustin, Bayard. *Down the Line: The Collected Writings of Bayard Rustin.* Chicago: Quadrangle Books, 1971.

————. "From Protest to Politics: The Future of the Civil Rights Movement." *Commentary*, February 1, 1965. https://www.commentarymagazine.com/ articles/from-protest-to-politics-the-future-of-the-civil-rights-movement/

Schlueter, Nathan W. *One Dream or Two? Justice in America and in the Thought of Martin Luther King, Jr.* Lanham, MD: Lexington Books, 2003.

Schuyler, George S. *Black No More.* New York: Dover Publications, 2011.

Schwantes, Carlos Arnaldo. *Coxey's Army: An American Odyssey.* Caldwell, ID: Caxton Press, 1985.

Shammas, Carole. "A New Look at Long-Term Trends in Wealth Inequality in the United States." *American Historical Review*, vol. 98, no. 2 (April 1993): 412–31.

Shelby, Tommie. *Dark Ghettos: Injustice, Dissent, and Reform.* Cambridge, MA: Harvard University Press, 2016.

————. "Race and Ethnicity, Race and Social Justice: Rawlsian Considerations." 72 Fordham L. Rev. 1697 (2004).

————. "Race and Social Justice: Rawlsian Considerations." 72 Fordham L. Rev. 1698 (2004): 1697–1714.

Shelby, Tommie, and Brandon M. Terry, eds. *To Shape a New World: Essays on the Political Philosophy of Martin Luther King, Jr.* Cambridge, MA: Harvard University Press, 2018.

Sheth, Falguni A., and George Yancy. "How Liberalism and Racism Are Wed." *New York Times*, February 27, 2015.

Shiffrin, Seana Valentine. "Race, Labor, and the Fair Equality of Opportunity Principle." 72 Fordham L. Rev. 1643–1675 (2004).

Shklar, Judith N. "American Citizenship: The Quest for Inclusion." The Tanner Lectures on Human Values (1989). Cambridge, MA: Harvard University Press, 1991. https://tannerlectures.utah.edu/_documents/a-to-z/s/shklar90. pdf

Singh, Nikhil Pal, *Black Is a Country: Race and the Unfinished Struggle for Democracy.* Cambridge, MA: Harvard University Press, 2005.

Sivanandan, Ambalavaner. *Communities of Resistance: Writings on Black Struggles for Socialism.* London: Verso, 1990.

Skipper, John C. *Showdown at the 1964 Democratic Convention: Lyndon Johnson, Mississippi and Civil Rights.* New York: McFarland Publishing, 2012.

Skotnes, Andor. *A New Deal for All?: Race and Class Struggles in Depression-Era Baltimore.* Durham, NC: Duke University Press, 2012.

Smallwood, James. *Reform, Red Scare, and Ruin: Virginia Durr, Prophet of the New South.* Xlibris, 2008.

Smethurst, James Edward. *The New Red Negro: The Literary Left and African American Poetry, 1930–1946.* New York: Oxford University Press, 1999.

Smith, Roger. "Beyond Tocqueville, Myrdal and Hartz: The Multiple Traditions in America." *American Political Science Review,* vol. 87, no. 3 (September 1993): 549–66.

Solomon, Mark. *The Cry Was Unity: Communists and African Americans, 1917–1936.* Jackson: University Press of Mississippi, 1998.

Sonnie, Amy, and James Tracy. *Hillbilly Nationalists, Urban Race Rebels, and Black Power: Community Organizing in Radical Times.* Brooklyn: Melville House, 2011.

Soohoo, Cynthia, Catherine Albisa, and Martha F. Davis. *Bringing Human Rights Home: A History of Human Rights in the United States.* Philadelphia: University of Pennsylvania Press, 2009.

Southern, David W. *Gunnar Myrdal and Black-White Relations.* Baton Rouge: Louisiana State University Press, 1987.

Stiglitz, Joseph E. "How Dr. King Shaped My Work in Economics." *New York Times,* August 27, 2013.

Sturm, Douglas. "Martin Luther King, Jr., as Democratic Socialist." *Journal of Religious Ethics,* vol. 18, no. 2 (1990): 79–105.

Sugrue, Thomas J. "Crabgrass-Roots Politics: Race, Rights, and the Reaction against Liberalism in the Urban North, 1940–1964." *Journal of American History,* vol. 82, no. 2 (September 1995): 551–78.

———. *The Origins of the Urban Crisis: Race and Inequality in Postwar Detroit.* Princeton: Princeton University Press, 1996.

———. *Sweet Land of Liberty; The Forgotten Struggle for Civil Rights in the North.* New York: Random House. 2008.

Sustein, Cass R. *The Second Bill of Rights: FDR's Unfinished Revolution and Why We Need It More than Ever.* New York: Basic Books, 2004.

Supiot, Alain. *The Spirit of Philadelphia. Social Justice against the Total Market.* New York: Verso, 2012.

Swindall, Lindsey R. *Paul Robeson: A Life of Activism and Art.* Lanham, MD: Rowman and Littlefield, 2013.

Tabb, William K. *The Political Economy of the Black Ghetto* New York: W. W. Norton, 1970.

Taylor, Charles. *Multiculturalism and "The Politics of Recognition."* Princeton: Princeton University Press, 1992.

Taylor, Cynthia *A. Philip Randolph: The Religious Journey of an African American Labor Leader.* New York: New York University Press, 2006.

Taylor, Nikki M. *America's First Black Socialist: The Radical Life of Peter H. Clark.* Lexington: University of Kentucky Press, 2013.

Trotsky. Leon. *On Black Nationalism and Self Determination.* Atlanta: Pathfinder Press, 1994.

Tuck, Stephen G. N. *Beyond Atlanta: The Struggle for Racial Equality in Georgia, 1940–1980.* Athens: University of Georgia Press, 2001.

Tucker, Sterling. "The Role of Civil Rights Organizations—A Marshall Plan Approach." *Boston College Law Review*, vol. 7, no. 3 (1966): 4–1.

Tye, Larry. *Bobby Kennedy: The Making of a Liberal Icon*. New York: Random House, 2016.

Urquhart, Brian. *Ralph Bunche: An American Life*. New York: W.W. Norton, 1993.

Van Wienen, Mark, and Julie Kraft. "How the Socialism of W.E.B. Du Bois Still Matters: Black Socialism in 'the Quest of the Silver Fleece'—and Beyond." *African American Review* vol. 41, no. 1 (2007): 67-85.

Vario, Lisa. "'All Power to the People': The Influence and Legacy of the Black Panther Party, 1966—1980." Master's thesis, Youngstown State University, 2007. https://etd.ohiolink.edu/rws_etd/document/get/ . . . /inline

Viscount, Nelson H., Jr. *Sharecropping, Ghetto, Slum: A History of Impoverished Blacks in Twentieth-Century America*. Xlibris, 2015.

Waligore, Timothy. "Rawls, Race, and a Historicized Difference Principle." Paper presented at "John Rawls: Past, Present, and Future" Conference at Yale University, November 30, 2012. Mimeo.

Walton, Hanes, Jr., and Robert C. Smith. *American Politics and the African American Quest for Universal Freedom*. New York: Pearson and Longman, 2006.

Ward, Brian, and Tony Badger, eds. *Making of Martin Luther King and the Civil Rights Movement*. New York: New York University Press, 1996.

Washington, James, ed. *A Testament of Hope: The Essential Writing of Martin Luther King Jr*. San Francisco: HarperCollins, 1991.

Washington, Mary Helen. *The Other Blacklist: The African American Literary and Cultural Left of the 1950s*. New York: Columbia University Press, 2014.

Wayne, Colin. "Democracy's Dilemma: Explaining Racial Inequality in Egalitarian Societies." *Sociological Forum*, vol. 17, no. 4 (December 2002): 681–96.

Weidenbaum, Murray. "The Employment Act of 1946: A Half Century of Presidential Policymaking." *Presidential Studies Quarterly*, vol. 26, no. 3 (Summer 1996): 880–86.

Widell, Robert W., Jr. *Birmingham and the Long Black Freedom Struggle*. New York: Palgrave Macmillan, 2013.

West, Cornell, ed. *The Radical King*. Boston: Beacon Press, 2015.

Wheeler, John H. "Civil Rights Groups—Their Impact Upon the War on Poverty." 31 *Law and Contemporary Problems* 152–158 (Winter 1966).

White, Deborah Gray. *Too Heavy a Load: Black Women in Defense of Themselves, 1894-1994*. New York: W.W. Norton, 1999.

Widell, Robert W. Jr., *Birmingham and the Long Black Freedom Struggle*, London: Palgrave Macmillan, 2013.

Williams, Jakobi E. *From the Bullet to the Ballot: The Illinois Chapter of the Black Panther Party and Racial Coalition Politics in Chicago*. Chapel Hill: University of North Carolina Press, 2013.

Wilson, William Julius. *The Bridge over the Racial Divide: Rising Inequality and Coalition Politics*. Berkeley: University of California Press, 1999.

———. *The Declining Significance of Race: Blacks and Changing American Institutions*. Chicago: The University of Chicago Press, 1980.

———. *The Truly Disadvantaged: The Inner City, the Underclass, and Public Policy*. Chicago: The University of Chicago Press, 1987.

Wintz, Cary D. *African American Political Thought, 1890–1930: Washington, Du Bois, Garvey and Randolph*. New York: Routledge, 2015.

Wood, Ellen Meiksins. *The Origin of Capitalism*. New York: Monthly Review Press, 1999.

Woods, Jeff. *Black Struggle, Red Scare: Segregation and Anti-Communism in the South, 1948–1968*. Baton Rouge: Louisiana State University Press, 2004.

Wray, L. R., and Forstater, M. "Full Employment and Economic Justice," in *The Institutionalist Tradition in Labor Economics,* ed. D. Champlin and J. Knoedler. Armonk, NY: M. E. Sharpe, 2004.

Wray, Matt, and Annalee Newitz. *White Trash: Race and Class in America*. New York: Routledge, 1997.

Wright, Amy Nathan. "Civil Rights 'Unfinished Business': Poverty, Race, and the 1968 Poor People's Campaign." Ph.D. dissertation, University of Texas at Austin, 2007.

Wright, Edelman Marian. "Revisiting Marks, Mississippi." *Huffington Post,* March 25, 2011.

Wright, Eric Olin. *Classes*. London: Verso, 1985.

Wright, Gavin. *Sharing the Prize: The Economics of the Civil Rights Revolution in the South*. Cambridge, MA: Harvard University Press, 2013.

Yglesias, Jose. "Dr. King's March on Washington, Part II." *New York Times Magazine,* March 31, 1968. https://timesmachine.nytimes.com/timesmachine/1968/03/331/103473891.pdf

Young, Andrew. *An Easy Burden: The Civil Rights Movement and the Transformation of America*. New York: HarperCollins, 1996.

Zamir, Shamoon. *Dark Voices, W. E. B. Du Bois and American Thought, 1888–1903*. Chicago: The University of Chicago Press, 1995.

Zeigler, James. *Red Scare Racism and Cold War Black Radicalism*. Jackson: University Press of Mississippi, 2015.

Zelizer, Julian E. *The Fierce Urgency of Now: Lyndon Johnson, Congress, and the Battle for the Great Society*. New York: Penguin Press, 2015.

———. "Is America Repeating the Mistakes of 1968?" *Atlantic Monthly,* July 8, 2016.

Zieger, Robert. *For Jobs and Freedom: Race and Labor in America since 1865*. Lexington: University of Kentucky Press, 2007.

Index